Sabaor Abu Avira

# The Tear of Isis

Freemasonry Under Its Veil

www.dolphinmarketingpress.com

All rights reserved. This book was published by
Dolphin Marketing Press Ltd 9016144 England and Wales.
All moral rights of Sabaor Abu Avira to be identified as the
author of this work has been asserted in accordance with
the Copyright, Designs, and Patents Act of 1988. No part
of this publication may be reproduced, stored, in a retrieval
system, or transmitted in any form or by any means
(electronic, mechanical, photocopying, recording, video, and
audio or otherwise) without the prior and formal permission
of the copyright owner.

**The Tear of Isis**

Freemasonry Under Its Veil

**Copyright © 2021 Sabaor Abu Avira**

**ISBN 978-619-90465-4-8**

Published by Danaya International LTD
Printed by Alliance Print LTD
Sofia, 2021

**Translated from Bulgarian**

*Original title:* **Сълзата на Изида**
*Original subtitle:* **Забуленото масонство**
*Name of the author*
*in the original language:* **Сабаор Абу Авира**

First Bulgarian edition:
ISBN 978-954-9464-18-4

Published by Ni Plus Publishing House and Peak Advertising Agency
Sofia, 2017

Sabaor Abu Avira

# The Tear of Isis

## Freemasonry Under Its Veil

Sofia
2021

*You owe more than gold to him who serves you.
Give him of your heart or serve him.*
**Khalīl Jubrān**


**This book is what it IS
thanks to the creative commitment
of Brother Liubomir Petrov.**

*Sabaor Abu Avira*


**Authors of the pictures/ engravings:**

On the front cover – Sabaor Abu Avira
Figure 2 – Sabaor Abu Avira
Figure 3 – Mural painting in *St. John Ba Harim Church* (Ein Karem, Jerusalem)
Figure 4 – From Paracelsus's book *Archidoxes Magicae*
Figure 5 – From Paracelsus's book *Archidoxes Magicae*
Figure 7 – From Paracelsus's book *Archidoxes Magicae*
Figure 9 – Lucas van Leyden
Figure 10 – Alexander Slade
Figure 19 – Engraving by Gerard Hoet from a Bible edition of 1728
Figure 20 – Rider – *Waite Card Set*
Figure 26 – John Melius
Figure 28 – Sabaor Abu Avira
Figure 38 – Éliphas Lévi
Figure 45 – Michael Maier, *Atalanta Fugiens*
Figure 46 – Éliphas Lévi
Figure 48 – Gustave Doré
Figure 53 – William Blake

# CONTENTS

I. ATRIUM .......................................................................... 9

II. NARTHEX ...................................................................... 11

  1. **The Core Essence of Freemasonry** ........................... 12
     Faith ............................................................................ 15
     The Doctrine of Symbols .......................................... 18
     Etymology of the Name ............................................ 28
     Operative and Speculative Masonry ........................ 29
     The Origin of Freemasonry ...................................... 31

III. UPPER ROOM ............................................................. 34

  2. **Woman and Freemasonry** ....................................... 34
     The Garden of Eden .................................................. 38
     Ramsay and the Bacchanalia .................................... 44
     The Vedic Tradition .................................................. 49
     In a Kabalistic Key .................................................... 51
     Women in Freemasonry ........................................... 52
     The Prohibition ......................................................... 53
     The Goal ..................................................................... 55
     The Force ................................................................... 57

IV. CATECHUMEN ............................................................ 59

  3. **The Sacred Initiation** ............................................... 59
     The Formal Initiation ................................................ 61
     The Master Teacher ................................................... 66
     The Truth ................................................................... 67

  4. **The Astral Plane** ....................................................... 71
     Spirit, Soul and Body ................................................ 75
     The Astrosome .......................................................... 76
     Astral Clichés ............................................................ 77
     Magic Chain .............................................................. 78
     Egregor ...................................................................... 84

V. NAOS .............................................................................. 86

  5. **Magic and Freemasonry** .......................................... 86
     The Magic Implementation Formula ...................... 88
     Pentagrammatica Libertas ........................................ 88
     Reality and Evil ......................................................... 96

Oneness ........................................................................................ 99
The Fall and Divisiveness .......................................................... 101
The Ego ...................................................................................... 102

**6. Christ and Golgotha** .............................................................. 106
The Path ..................................................................................... 110
The Spiritual Discipleship ......................................................... 112

**7. The Soul – a Temple of Wisdom** .......................................... 116
Freedom of Choice .................................................................... 119
The Breath ................................................................................. 122

**8. The Secret Kiss of the Master** .............................................. 125
Kundalini ................................................................................... 126
Twice-Born ................................................................................ 127
Image and Likeness ................................................................... 130

**9. The Arcanorum System** ........................................................ 133
Ad Fontes ................................................................................... 133
Core Essence .............................................................................. 134
The First Arcanum .................................................................... 136
The Arcana Algorithm .............................................................. 138

**10. The Posture of the Magus** ................................................... 140
Binary – Ternary – Quaternary ................................................ 140
The Path of the Arcana ............................................................. 143
The Fool ..................................................................................... 145

**11. Kabala** .................................................................................... 149
Core Essence .............................................................................. 149
Linguistic Clarifications ........................................................... 151
Origin ......................................................................................... 152
Fundamental Terms and Clarifications ................................... 153
The Sfarotic Tree in Its Traditional Form ............................... 154
More Keys .................................................................................. 164
The "Ladder of Jacob" ............................................................... 166

**12. The Lord's Prayer ("Our Father")** ....................................... 170
"Our Father" and the "Ladder of Jacob" .................................. 179
Karma ......................................................................................... 188
The Eye of a Needle .................................................................. 191
Rebirth ....................................................................................... 193
Death .......................................................................................... 196
Kabala, Rosicrucianism and Martinism ................................... 200

### 13. The Spiritual Centre .................................................................. 203
The Wise Men ........................................................................................ 204
Melkitsedek – the King of Justice ...................................................... 206
The Heavenly River .............................................................................. 209

### 14. Alchemy ............................................................................................. 211
The Holy Grail ....................................................................................... 215

### 15. The Chief Cornerstone ................................................................... 219
The Cornerstone .................................................................................... 219
Eben ha-Shetiyah .................................................................................. 223
The Psalm ............................................................................................... 228

### 16. Undressed and Dressed Stone ....................................................... 230
The Undressed Stone ........................................................................... 230
The Dressed Stone ................................................................................ 231
The Undressed Stone and the Apprentice ....................................... 235
Fragments of Masonic Minutes ......................................................... 242
René Guénon .......................................................................................... 246
Keystone .................................................................................................. 250
Legend of the Stone ............................................................................. 251

### 17. The Temple of Solomon ................................................................. 253
Sources .................................................................................................... 253
The Tabernacle ...................................................................................... 257
The Testament of Solomon ................................................................. 260
The Master's Degree ............................................................................ 263
The Meaning of "Rejected" ................................................................. 266
The Kabalistic Interpretation ............................................................. 269

### 18. Head of the Corner .......................................................................... 274
The Kabalistic Key ................................................................................ 274
"My God, My God, Why Have You Forsaken Me?" ...................... 277
Our Version ............................................................................................ 278
The Philosophers' Stone ...................................................................... 285
The Chief Cornerstone ........................................................................ 290

### 19. "Masonic Regularity of the Temple" ............................................ 294
The Temple ............................................................................................. 294
The Pillars in front of the Temple ..................................................... 295
About Left and Right, Masculine and Feminine ............................ 297
The Kabalistic Tree and the Pillars in front of the Temple ........... 300
Movement inside the Temple ............................................................. 302

- Masonic Regularity of the Temple ....... 307
- Squaring the Circle ....... 309
- Mer-Ka-Ba ....... 311
- The All-Seeing Eye ....... 313

## VI. APSE ....... 317

### 20. The Devil ....... 317
- The Sin ....... 317
- Satan ....... 319
- Shatan ....... 320
- Lucifer ....... 323
- Nahash ....... 327
- Nahash – Shatan – Mashiach ....... 333
- The Three Wise Men ....... 344
- The Devil ....... 345

### 21. The "Lost Word" ....... 347
- The Legend of the Temple ....... 347
- The Masonic Secret ....... 347
- The Master's Word ....... 353
- The Masonic Tradition ....... 356

## VII. THE HOLY OF HOLIES ....... 359

### 22. The Name of God ....... 359
- The Secret Name ....... 359
- Shem Ha-Meforash ....... 364
- The Divine Speech ....... 366
- The Old Bulgarian Alphabets ....... 372

## VIII. THRONE ....... 379
- The Great Architect of the Universe ....... 379

## IX. AMBON ....... 383

Homily
- O human, wake up, wake up from your deep sleep! ....... 383
- Epiklesis ....... 385

## X. ESCHATON ....... 387
- Finis Coronat Opus ....... 387

# I
# ATRIUM

**The only reason for us being here is to go back Home again!**

The soul is my beloved.
She has accepted me into her innermost womb, giving me life in this world.
She has sacrificed herself for me so that she can carry me inside herself,
Keeping watch over my vulnerability.
She has tenderly embraced me, nurturing me with her love,
Like a mother nurturing her unborn child.
So she, the soul, my beloved,
Shall keep and guard me in her arms along all her earthly path –
Me, her grown-up baby, her beloved one,
Against the hardships and temptations of life.
And she, again, through the birth pains of her own death,
Shall take me back into the Heavenly Realms,
Endowing me with eternal existence.
My beloved loves me, and I love her.
Sometimes she is wayward and capricious;
Sometimes she is tender and loving; and sometimes – cruel.
Her flesh is temptation,
Her flesh is thirst for beauty and Truth.
Get to know her, and her body will be a gift of God for you,
Taking you into the Gardens of Eden
That are giving out the sweet perfume of flowers.
Her burning passion burns to ashes my rotten trunk with its fire;
However, from these ashes, the shoots of a young sapling sprout,
And this sapling will give sweet fruit.
Pick up this delicate peach from the Gardens of Love
And drink its sweet nectar with your parched lips!

I love you, my soul, just the way you are – imperfect;
However, you – the imperfect one, have sacrificed yourself
For the sake of my perfection.
Where is your kindred soul whom you have parted with,
For the sake of me – your beloved?
Who knows where she is wandering right now,
And whether she is beloved of her beloved one?
I know, I know: You are grieving for this kindred soul so much;
And I know that you will find this soul,
And that you will both return into your Home
Together, in each other's arms.
As for me, the perfect one, I shall be grieving for you – the imperfect one,
And yet – my beloved forever.

Sabaor Abu Avira

# II
# NARTHEX

*Vita via est[1]*

> *There are only two mistakes one can make along the Path towards the Truth: not going all the way to the very end, and not starting at all.*
>
> **The Buddha**

This book initiates into deep esoteric Secrets and Truths, which are not the exclusive property only of the Masonic tradition, and yet, they are embedded in its symbolism. There will definitely be some readers who will not find these Truths in the written here, rejecting them just as the builders "rejected" the stone which became "the head of the corner". Others might see already well-known Truths, passing them by, as if they were pecks of sand in the dunes. There will also be still others who will not recognize the Truth, just as they would not recognize a diamond yet unpolished. To those ones, we shall say that the Truth is always in front of us; however, in order to become aware of the Truth, we have to be ready for It. The Truth is inconspicuous, unattractive, in most cases even corny and boring – and yet, IT IS the way IT IS. The Truth is the point in the centre of the circle – and all who are therein use one and the same expressions about the Truth. There are no author's rights on the Truth which speaks through the Spirit. Whoever would like to present the Truth in their own way, in order to sound originally, adding to what is said the characteristic traits of exceptionality and uniqueness, will drift away from the Truth and distort It. That is why this book does not reveal any shocking or mind-blowing secrets – unless the reader recognizes them as such. Its word is the language of the central point, not the periphery, where the Truth is being polished in order to be pleasing.

This book carries such energy which has the purpose to open up the consciousness so that the Truth may be known. This book is for the pathless so that they may find the Path; it is also for those who have a Path so that they may get to its end; it is for those who have already reached there – so that they may understand that, actually, there is no end, and therefore they themselves have to become the very Path; as for those who already have become that Path, this book is only a Path. In the Initiatic traditions, this walking along the Spiritual Path is called simply *The Path*. In the Masonic tradition, this Path is called *Building the Edifice*. The core essence of Freemasonry is contained in this process of *Building the Edifice*.

---

1  From Latin: "Life is a journey", or "Life is a path" – *AN*.

# 1
# The Core Essence of Freemasonry

> *Sacred and profane are two modes of being in the world.*
>
> **Mircea Eliade**

There are two meanings defining the nature of Freemasonry. One of them is the *profane*[2] meaning, which characterizes it as viewed from its aspects related to etymology, moral and ethics, social and everyday life, and religion; the other one is the *sacral* meaning. We shall dwell on the first one only essentially, because it is the aspect that is most written about and discussed; moreover, the purpose of this book is the second one, in the person of the so-called *Esoteric Freemasonry*.

Let us begin from the etymology of the very word – *mason*, or also *free-mason*. It is well-known that *mason* is traditionally translated as *stone-builder*, especially *free stone-builder*, noting that, since Middle Ages, it does not designate any building craft. Even though, in its literal meaning (as for the hidden sense, we shall dwell on it further) this word is being associated with the words *builder* and *building* as a process, there should be a predominating comprehension that, still, it refers to a certain intellectual and spiritual process of building.

Regarding the moral and ethical aspect, we shall mention the only requirement in the contemporary male Masonry for the seeker of Light, that he should be a "free-born" man "of good report" in society. His social, property, educational and religious status, as well as his living style and conditions, are of no significance.

In *General Head III* of *The Constitutions of the Free-Masons* (1734) by J. Anderson, it is written: "The Persons admitted Members of a Lodge must be good and true Men, free-born, and of mature and discreet Age, no Bond-men, no Women, no immoral or scandalous Men, but of good Report."

Here we shall quote also a definition of *Freemasonry*, formulated by a genius making all Freemasons proud that he belongs to their Brotherhood – Goethe: "What is Freemasonry? It is kindness at home, honesty in business, courtesy in society, fairness at work, compassion for the miserable, resistance against injustice, help for the weak, loyalty to the Code, oblivion against all

---

2 From Latin: *profanus*, composed of two parts: *pro* – "outside of", "in front of"; and *fanum* – "temple", "sanctuary" – *AN*.

lies, complacency for the happy, devotion for humankind, humility and tolerance towards your fellow, and Love – in front of God."

Regarding the religious aspect, we cannot but note also the existence of the common misunderstanding that any man with a good reputation can become a Freemason, even if being an atheist. Well, the fundamental stone in Freemasonry is faith and trust in the Great Architect of the Universe, is that not right? Some might say, "That is Nature!" Yes, but Nature represents God... Others might claim, "This is the Universal Intelligence, the Universal Idea!" Yes; and yet, that is God again... Still others might announce, "That is the Universal World-Wide Energy!" Well, that is God again, is that not?... And all these definitions can surely fit into the notion of *Great Architect of the Universe*, cannot they? Well, is not that God, after all? Actually, what is the difference between a believer and a non-believer; what does the former believe in, and what does the latter not believe in? A believer considers Creation to be a conscious process of cause and effect; while a non-believer does not believe that there is any logic in the Edifice of Existence, considering everything to be a play of random chance... And yet, as Albert Einstein says, *"God does not play dice with the Universe!"* Atheists also believe in God, only in some God of Accidental Chance. Then, how will they possibly swear by and act for the sake of the Great Architect of the Universe?!

In *General Head I* of Anderson's *Constitution,* we read the following: "A Mason is obliged, by his Tenure, to obey the moral Law; and if he rightly understands the Art, he will never be a stupid Atheist, nor an irreligious Libertine."

Albert Mackey, a Freemason possessing great authority, states clearly and unequivocally, in the above sense: "*T*he Speculative Mason is supposed to be engaged in the construction of a Spiritual Temple... He lays its foundation in a firm belief and an unshaken confidence in the Wisdom, Power, and Goodness of God. This is his first step. Unless his trust is in God, and in Him only, he can advance no further..."

Once again, we are facing the main question: "Is there a God – Creator of Everything?" Humans have always asked themselves what has been there before birth, what the meaning of life is, what happens after death... Each one of us has, at least once, pondered on whether we have come from the nothing, getting back there again, and whether our existence in this time interval is so accidental and transient. Is it possible that we are simply a product of someone's sexual desire and reproductive or egocentric procreative instinct? Are humans really only a consequence of the play of random chance, and does their existence actually serve only for the survival and improvement of their species towards perfection?

The hyper-rational and conceptual thinking of atheists leads them to the conclusion that those who have faith in God have begun to believe in something unproved and improvable, in something absurd. However, if we think deeper, they have started believing in something else that is also improvable and much more absurd: the randomness of life and of the Edifice of Existence. The human perceptive empiricism reveals that everything emerges as a consequence of a certain cause, which, on its turn, is dictated by a certain chain of logic. Our apperception reveals to us that nothing conceives or creates itself by itself before our eyes accidentally, just like that, for no reason and without any purpose – *De (ex) nihilo nihil.*[3] On the contrary: things in this world happen in result of someone's action, someone's creative activity – and, in this sense, the conviction that there is logic in the Creation is much more rational and feasible. To sustain this, we shall give the following example: the Creation, in which a universal principle is laid down – a centre and its circular emanation. On this principle, all the universes, nebulae and solar systems are organized, as well as the cells of the living organisms, and also the even smaller building unit – the atom, and so on... We cannot accept that the existence of this universal principle is not the outcome of some kind of entelechy, but of situative accidental chance. Therefore, contrary to the commonly accepted view, the concept that God does not exist is irrational and unconditioned by experience. If everything has its reasonable cause, then one Primary Cause ought to exist. God is the Non-Caused Reasonable Cause of the manifested worlds – which, however, is generated by the Attitude that is Love; therefore, it is said that "God has created the world through Love." The cause leading to the emergence of our world is the very Attitude of God Himself.

---

3  From Latin: "Out of nothing, nothing (comes)" – Lucretius – *AN.*

# Faith

> *Faith begins whererereason ends.*
> **Kierkegaard**
>
> *Our faith stops where true knowledge begins.*
> **Éliphas Lévi**

We think that the above statement of Lévi tastes like Truth because faith resides in the conditions of the "Concealed God" – for, if you get to know Him, then you do not need to believe: then you will have already anchored your trust in Him.

Faith in God is not numinous; it represents evolved knowledge. Faith is being build up through becoming aware of our Divine Nature and through constantly anchored trust in the Creator; it is the result of a persistent and conscious study of the Spiritual Laws, making them part of our life. This can be expressed by what Siddhartha Gautama Buddha has said: "Take the knowledge, make it part of your experience – and then it will become part of your faith." Becoming conscious of our Divine Nature builds in us a compassionate view regarding the world and the humankind. Thus, the active pole of Faith is this awareness of the Divine Nature of humans, while the passive pole is Hope. The higher form of Faith is the anchored Trust, which is a property only of the true believers who have come to know God. An Ancient Egyptian saying reads: "The strength belongs to those who are firm in their anchored trust." That firm Trust puts one in the position of a faithful son; and this position is manifested only in dialogic mode because it interacts with God's Intelligence and is generated in the conditions of the "Visible God". If we see an object, then is it necessary for us to believe in its existence? Well, we see it, after all... Likewise, if we "see" God and if we "know" a particle of His Core Essence, then we will not believe, we will not nurture hope, but rather we shall have firm Trust in Him. Faith is not a product of ignorance, of superstition, of fear or of mere hope. Faith is an attainment of the enlightened mind; and yet, it is neither to be acquired nor conquered: it is granted from High Above whenever we are ready to carry it, stand up for it, and sacrifice ourselves for it.

Now we can already proceed with the esoteric sense which defines the fundamental essence of Freemasonry. In his book *La Franc-Maçonnerie (Freemasonry)*, Jean Palou defines Freemasonry as one of the main esoteric forms of Christian tradition.

First of all, let us examine the meaning of the term *esoteric*. It was introduced in the 6th century BC by Pythagoras – a great magus, teacher, poet, musician, and mathematician – and it literally means *belonging to the inner circle,* opposite to *exoteric*[4] – *belonging to the outer circle.* Here we will have to just point out – for those who have been shocked by the word *magus* – that, in its essential aspect, this word means *capable, skillful, knowing.* If we ought to trace back its etymology more precisely, it derives from the ancient Eastern words *mog,* Мegh, Мagh, meaning "priest", "wise", "excellent", reaching our times through the Greek word μάγος ("magician"), which, however, does not reflect the true core essence of the term *magus.*

Originally, all sciences and arts were *esoteric,* being accessed only by the Priests and Initiates, i.e. by the Magi. The outline of the inner circle was the boundary of knowledge, while the Spiritual Masters and the Magi had the task to guard it, because the humankind was not ready for it. This was actually the esoteric secret itself. In the contemporary society of information, the "secrets" (i.e. the pieces of knowledge) are accessible to everyone: they are already within the outer circle, having become *exoteric* ones. Now the boundaries of the inner circle are marked by the "Law of Lack of Understanding". Nowadays the so-called "Masonic Secrets" can be read in any book or in the Internet space. Then, why Freemasons – some might ask – keep on using secret words, signs and symbols, identifying their particular Degree, given that any profane may come to know them? The answer is: It is because profanes are outside the Temple, so the Law of Lack of Understanding acts upon them. Unfortunately, this law acts upon the very Freemasons as well, because the profanation in Freemasonry has doomed esoterism to profound oblivion.

We think that, in our society, some became Freemasons because they wished so and because they strived towards it, while others became such because they were invited. Therefore, we have categorized Freemasons into *Seekers* and *Invited,* which originally predetermines their attitude and relation to Freemasonry. The Brothers who are Seekers keep on seeking even after they become Masters. The Invited also remain such; however, unlike the former ones, they are characterized by this constant in a negative sense – therefore, we can note, to our regret, that they represent a great majority. Unfortunately, the situation was the same also 140 years ago, as we can see

---

4 Exoteric – deriving from the Greek *éxō:* "outside", "external", and hence *exōterikós,* which has reached the contemporary languages through its Latin form *exotericu(m).* It relates to a philosophical or religious doctrine meant to be widely spread even among profanes – *AN.*

from a Masonic Minutes text of 1875 by John Edwin, in which he quotes some thoughts from an article by Albert Mackey, entitled *Reading Masons and Masons Who Do Not Read*, where the following is written:

"I suppose there are more Masons who are ignorant of all the principles of Freemasonry than there are men of any other class who are chargeable with the like ignorance of their own profession...

... Nothing is more common than to encounter Freemasons who are in utter darkness as to everything that relates to Freemasonry... They have no comprehension of the esoteric meaning of its symbols or its ceremonies...

... The great body of Masons may be divided into three classes.

The first consists of those who made their application for initiation not from a desire for knowledge, but from some accidental motive, not always honorable. Such men have been led to seek reception either because it was likely, in their opinion, to facilitate their business operations, or to advance their political prospects, or in some other way to personally benefit them...

... There is a second class consisting of men who are the moral and Masonic antipodes of the first. These make their application for admission, being prompted, as the ritual requires, "by a favorable opinion conceived of the Institution, and a desire of knowledge."...

... This third class consists of Masons who joined the Society with unobjectionable motives, and with, perhaps the best intentions. But they have failed to carry these intentions into effect.

They have made a grievous mistake. They have supposed that initiation was all that was requisite to make them Masons, and that any further study was entirely unnecessary. Hence, they never read a Masonic book."

How familiar this sounds to us, due to the disappointing fact that the above words are still valid nowadays! In spite of all, though, we think that the existence of Freemasonry is nevertheless a serious attainment of humankind. Here is the place to start revealing the hidden symbolism of the word *Freemasonry* that has given the name of the whole Initiatic society, through the commonly accepted more popular term *Masonry*. However, before that, it is necessary to explain the reason why the secret meaning of these symbols and also their core essence and their origin must be known, having in mind that we shall dwell on the most important of them further on. Now we will only mention that *the point in the centre of a circle* – a two-dimensional image of a *sphere* – is a Divine symbol possessing implementation power of authority. This is the first of all the possible geometric forms in the Universe. The sphere represents Trinity: the central point is the Father; the circumference (the sphere) is the Son, and the equal distance between the central point and the circumference is the Spirit. This figure is the archetype of the Initiatic esoteric circle – a Master and all the disciples. For this reason, Freemasonry has survived over the centuries – because it is based on archetypes. Its original archetype is in the mind of the Great Architect of the Universe, and this archetype is manifested in the first hierarchic structure: a point in the centre of a circle. Masonry had the following archetypal setup: one head craftsman of the whole Lodge, with the mission of a Teacher (*Master*), who was the central point; whereas the circle consisted of apprentices and fellow crafts (journeymen), or generally said – disciples. This is the reason why the Compass represents itself an archetypal symbol in Freemasonry, expressing the archetypal form – a circle with its centre. This is the esoteric knowledge of symbols without which the compass remains just an ordinary instrument. Unfortunately, even today, we can join the following affirmation from the beginning of the 20th century, stated by a Mason respected by us – an esoterist, a writer, one of the greatest explorers of symbolism – René Guénon[5]: "Nowadays, the majority of Freemasons do not understand the true meaning of their own symbols, as well as most Christians do not understand theirs." That is why we will try to present, in an essential form, our view on the Doctrine of Symbols.

## The Doctrine of Symbols

*Information is not knowledge.*
**Albert Einstein**

The Path of the Mason is accompanied by achievements and impediments, and leads to transformation of personality and raising the consciousness towards Wisdom and Truth. The beginning of this Path represents listening and reflexion, which can only be implemented while keeping silent,

---

5  René Guénon (1886 – 1951) – a French esoterist and writer who renounced his university studies in Mathematics to enroll at Papus's *École des Sciences Hermétiques (School of Hermetic Sciences)*. In 1907, he became a Freemason. Later, he adopted Islam, taking the name of 'Abd al-Wāḥid Yaḥyā. His numerous works are dedicated to Mysticism, Sufism, and Hinduism – *AN*.

because only within the depths of speechlessness can we achieve the occult[6] piece of Wisdom adopted as a motto by Freemasonry: *"Know thyself"*. If we get to know ourselves, we shall get to know also the Supreme Force. A human is a miniature copy, image and likeness of the personalized Supreme Core Essence – God; and, as such, each human represents a composite symbol with a vast *eidos*[7], in which, meditatively and purposefully, we must begin to penetrate in order to get to know it. Thus, getting to know ourselves, we get to know God. This symbolic thinking will give us the opportunity to harmoniously build the true picture of the World; however, to this end, we should know everything – or almost everything – about symbols.

Symbols are condensed, compressed *eidoses* of things – so that the vast, infinite volume of their information may fit into our finite intellect, which is a likeness of the Supreme Intelligence, only reduced many times – and, for that reason, all the knowledge needs to be fit within it somehow. In the *First Book of Moses* in the *Old Testament, Genesis (KJV)*, it is said: "And God said, "Let there be Light!" – and there was Light." Further, in the *Holy Gospel of St. John (KJV)*, it is also said, "In the beginning was the Word"[8].

Following the word order of the first verse, it can be seen that, before there was Light, God "said". In this way, the systematic interpretation leads to the strictly formal conclusion that "In the beginning was the Word". If we continue along the same line of reasoning, the Beginning is before the Word – and the Beginning is identical with God. Thus, God is the *Beginning* and the *End, All* and *Nothing,* in one word: the *Whole;* whereas the Word and the Light are His embodiment, His manifested forms. The *Logos* is the tangible, formative expression of the Non-Manifested, Concealed God. God's Language is a language of symbols – because, we could hardly imagine God as a sheer chatterbox. Thus, the Word of the Supreme Core Essence resembles

---

6 *Occult* – a term deriving from the Latin word *occŭltu(m),* meaning "concealed", "secret", both in the literal sense and regarding the humans and the penetration into the "knowledge of what is concealed" through the studying of a deeper Reality which cannot be grasped through the pure reason and through material means. Synonyms: *mysterious, impenetrable, unknowable, inexplicable, enigmatic, obscure.* The Latin verb is *occulĕre* – "to conceal", "to cover up", "to hide", "to keep silent about" – *AN.*

7 *Eidos* – from Ancient Greek: εἶδος – "look", "appearance", "image": a term from the philosophy and literature of Antiquity, which was later expanded and modified to the extent of a multilayer category, initially denoting the visible, and subsequently – also everything invisible and unknowable. In the Middle Ages, the *eidos* was updated as an archetypal basis of things as a prototype in God's thinking – *AN.*

8 *Genesis* 1:3. Most of the verses from the *Old Testament* and the *New Testament* quoted in this book are taken from the *King James Version (KJV)* or the *New King James Version (NKJV)* of the Bible – *AN.*

a computer language, through which the huge bulk of information is reduced to small quantities that can fit within the capacity of the human mind, and through which we must learn to operate. These quantities are the very symbols; however, they differ from the computer language because they contain spiritual information, already constituting knowledge, in the meaning of what is said by Einstein. In this way, the mind operates not through logical quantities but through *spiritual* ones, which is why the mind acquires a tendency towards infinite expansion, enhancing the speed and productivity of its own functioning.

Symbols differ in context and meaning; and the ability to comprehend and embrace them completely, in all their interconnections, leads to voluminosity of the mind. The power of symbols is determined by the amount of dynamic force and energy inside them, which form their implementation power of authority. This power may be *primordial*, invested still during the very Creation, or *secondary*, i.e. acquired during the consecration by people. The most common and simplified definition we can give of the term *implementation power of authority* (or *implementation power*, for the sake of brevity) is *productive willpower*. In the context of the human being, this is the faculty to materialize one's thoughts, ideas and desires on the physical plane. We can define the term *symbol* also from a general theoretical point of view as "designated information about a certain reality". This definition is liable to differentiation, vertically and horizontally. However, the fundamental subdivision works according to the understanding of a certain symbol on the *exoteric* and the *esoteric* plane. On the exoteric plane, a symbol is the designated information through which society – or part of it – differentiates a given reality; whereas, on the esoteric plane, it expresses a certain spiritual reality.

Now we ought to explicate also the term *archetype of a symbol*. This is an idea existing on the spiritual plane which is in continuous connection with the symbol. Thus, all objective, primordial symbols are archetypal, because, within the Intelligence of the Supreme Force, there exist both an idea and a providential design of them; this idea and this design endue them with a Divine Core Essence. Perhaps an emblematic example of this is the Compass, the archetype of which is the central point within a circle. The archetype is the idea, the primary basis which is contained in the symbol, and which represents its core essence. The Masonic symbol of the Compass has a Divine Core Essence because the Primordial Principle of Creation is laid down in it: a centre and a circular emanation; this Principle is the foundation of the first created form – a circle (a sphere) with a central point. It is no coincidence that we called this example "emblematic". The Masonic society consists of builders – and their appliances and instruments are the magic attributes of the process of *Building the Edifice*. In the symbolism of Freemasonry, the Compass – by means of which a circle with a central point is drawn – is much more emblematic than the figure itself[9].

**Figure 1**

Setting aside the notion of good and evil, the most important quality of a symbol is its possession of implementation power of authority – dynamic force and energy. This implementation power, concentrated upon a symbol, can be either human or archetypal. In the first case, it contains the willpower and energy of a person or group of people; whereas, in the second one, it was generated still at the moment of Creation. When the human and the archetypal implementation power unite, then a Higher implementation power of the symbol is attained.

Every single thing possesses two types of energy: primordial, potential energy; and kinetic energy, capable of reviving. This capacity of anything to become alive is called by the Egyptians *consecration*. Later, this tradition is passed on to Judaism, and from there – to Christianity. Consecration is the act of exerting influence by the human willpower upon a given object, during which a two-way process takes place: the willpower impregnates the object with energy, which endues it with new dimensions of quality, at the same time liberating its own potential energy resources.

Only inside the speechlessness of being silent, within the depth of mind, and in meditative contemplation, can a given symbol be consecrated. In this way, we create this symbol within ourselves, activating its implementation power, attracting the Supreme Force and setting it into motion. The role of

---

9 Here we have in mind the figure representing a circle with a central point with two parallel lines symbolizing the two Johns in the Bible, which is not so popular – *AN*.

*magic* art, particularly the Masonic one, is to establish a bond between the embodied symbols and their Heavenly prototypes – the archetypes. The vivifying of symbols through their permanent presence in the mind maintains constant contact with the Spiritual World, leading to the gift of the so-called *direct knowledge*. This represents establishing a contact between the human mind and the archetype of Wisdom. The penetrating insight is one of the great fruits in building the Temple of Wisdom, where the Truth performs the sacred rites. When reasoning, contemplating, meditating, understanding, becoming aware of the symbols, they acquire the power of living *eidoses*. However, we should discern between *understanding, becoming aware* and the processes of *enlightenment*. Understanding is a faculty of the logical mind, compared in the esoteric teachings to an axe through which we cut out windows in the walls so that light may come in. Symbolic thinking leads us to understanding, after which, in permanent meditation, we become aware – so that, in the end, we reach enlightenment. Through symbols, we understand the logic of matters, and we realize that the conceptual mind has built barriers for the light which can only shine through if we make cracks in these barriers.

The art of thinking by symbols and the usage of the symbolic language were led to perfection in Egyptian Theology. In a text about *Neter*[10], it is said: „His Ba descends from Heaven upon his earthly image. His majesty spreads out over his Sekhem. The reverential Heart is Sekhem's Mother." The *Sekhem*[11] of the symbol means the vivifying of a given image or sign and connecting it with the archetype.

The Masonic sign, taken alone, means nothing else but the belonging to the Brotherhood, to a certain Lodge, also giving information about the Degree or position there, indication of the type of the Rite, etc. However, this sign is powerless unless its Sekhem is attracted. The knowledge of the symbol is the key to it; meditating upon the symbol vivifies it; and, by means of the penetrating insight, we acquire its implementation power.

We have chosen to dwell on Ancient Egypt and its symbolism because it is fundamental regarding knowledge and comprehension of symbols, just as the Egyptian civilization has laid down the foundations of the Western

---

10  The singular of the word *Neteru*, literally meaning "The Gods". *Neter* means also "Force", in the abstract sense of this word – *AN*.

11  The root of the word means „that which uplifts things". In its interpretations, *Sekhem* has the meanings of *living force, image of the force, symbol of the force, Divine Energy, Kundalini, individual willpower*. It is related to the Goddess Lioness *Sekhmet*, guardian and defender of this energy, as well as the star known as *Sirius*. Sekhem is depicted as a falcon dashing down upon the temple, being a symbol of uniting the earthly image with the Heavenly Archetype – *AN*.

civilization. It is no secret also that the Masonic Art is associated with the Art of Pharaohs, or the so-called *Royal Art,* the core essence of which is Sacred Magic. Therefore, if the Worshipful Master opens the Sacred Book and lays on the Square and the Compass without having penetrated into their core essence and without being able to attract their Sekhem, then his actions are not symbolic but rather stagy. Unless the images of the symbols get "engraved" upon the participants in the Rite, and unless the Sekhem descends upon their Ba[12], then we are witnessing just an ordinary staged show. The right symbolic thinking is embedded in the foundation of comprehension of the correlation between the Sublime Worlds and our world, with everything happening in it.

It would be good to know that symbols can be joined and arranged into a symbolic picture. This order of arrangement is very important: it expresses the significance and the hierarchic sequence of each symbol, as well as their interrelations. Unless all the symbols of the Masonic carpet are successively activated, it remains just a carpet and nothing more. Its elucidation during the Rite represents not only an interpretation of the symbols but mostly their integration within the Brothers. On the one hand, the carpet, as a symbolic picture, is a specific Arcanum; however, on the other hand, is resembles the glyph of the Kabalistic Tree, because it is an attempt to fit the whole philosophy of Microcosm and Macrocosm into a single image. Therefore, it represents itself a compilation between the Arcana and the Sefirotic Tree, the presentation of which is forthcoming.

Now we are going to give a short example of what the hierarchical order of symbols on the Masonic carpet of the Apprentice Degree represents, without being thoroughly comprehensive, because its *eidos* is too vast. On the carpet, there is a presentation of the plan of *Solomon's Temple,* known also as the *Temple of Bread* (*Beit Lehem* in Hebrew), or the *Temple of Wisdom,* representing itself a symbol of the Soul. In view of the order of symbols that we visualize, the very Temple represents the *monad,* the geometrical image of which is the *point,* whereas the numeric expression – the *number 1.*

The *monad* is the synthesis, the beginning, the initial principle, which, through its own differentiation, unfolds in a creative way. Following this order of symbols, we should proceed with the *dyad,* illustrated by the two pillars standing in front of the Temple: *Jahin* and *Voaz (Boaz)* (*3 Kings* 7:21), illustrating the two poles of antagonism, between which the profane wander

---

12 According to the Egyptian esoteric tradition, Ba represents one's *personality, individuality, soul,* and *memory.* Each human, as an individual, is Ba, by means of one's own physical and psychological properties. Ba is not part of the personality but the very personality itself. Ba is the astral body, being depicted as a bird with a human head. The dead fly away, in the form of birds, towards a new life in the hereafter, the realm beyond – *AN.*

and waver before entering the Temple. These two pillars are symbolically connected with the left and the right pillar of the Kabalistic Tree, representing the two unbalanced polarized forces, the feminine and the masculine. In this configuration, the Temple itself is the middle pillar, representing the dynamic balance of these forces that forms the symmetry of the Tree, known as "Masonic Regularity of the Temple", which we shall dwell on later. Going further into the *eidos* of the latter symbol, we will plunge into the boundless ocean of Kabala, realizing that this *"Masonic Regularity of the Temple"* is actually the process of building the energy model of the Kabalistic Tree, by means of which we are able to synthesize the *"Philosophers' Stone"*, attaining the *"Harmony of the Spheres"* of Pythagoras. From everything explained so far, the explicit conclusion follows that, in the basis of Masonic esoterism, there stands the ancient science called *Kabala*. Without studying it, Freemasonry is *Qlifotic* – that is, like a nutshell without a nut: a form without its archetypal filling, which leads to the lack of implementation power and to the distortion of primordial ideas. We cannot fail to mention also the mosaic flooring with its black-and-white checkerboard pattern, also symbol of the number 2 and of the binary nature of the illusionary world. The black and the white colour in humans symbolize the mortal and the Immortal, the body and the Spirit; and as far as the latter are "two birds, inseparably merged into one", which are mentioned in the *Upanishads,* this reminds also of another symbol – that of the two-headed eagle, figuring in some of the higher Freemason Degrees. We can give a parallel example also by the Egyptian esoteric tradition, in which Isis is the *One Who Reveals* the Secrets to the Initiates, whereas Nephthys, being the concealed aspect of her sister, is the *One Who Conceals* the Secrets from the profane. She is a symbol of the deep sub-consciousness which only rarely appears in the focus of the human consciousness. Nephthys is the spouse of the god of chaos, Set – which shows that the sub-consciousness contains unmastered and unconscious impulses, provoking a great part of our emotions and acts. This means that, in order to be controlled, first of all, they have to be brought to one's awareness in the light of the conscious, and after that – subdued to one's willpower. These examples once again bring testimony to the universality of the language of symbols.

We shall move on to the triangular pediment of the Temple, symbolizing the Law of the Ternary, as well as the ideal triangular form in the Spiritual World, and the number 3 as its expression. God and the human being symbolize the Unity of Creation. However, in Unity, the Law of Trinity acts; it manifests itself everywhere, including in the Masonic symbolism: the interior of the Temple is divided into three parts, being the expressions of the three planes of the Edifice of Existence; the admittance to the Temple is granted by three distinct knocks; the steps at entering it are three; the journeys while seeking the Light are also three; three bigger and three smaller lights illuminate the Temple; three are the main Degrees; one of the names of Freemasons is "Three Point Brothers", etc. The triangle is the perfect geometrical form of the Non-Manifested, whereas the number 3 is Sacred and is present in all Divine Pantheons. Much has been written about its vast *eidos;* and our aim is not to penetrate into it, so that is why we stop at this point. However, we cannot miss to point out that the Holy Trigrammaton also consists of three hieroglyphs: *Yod, He* and *Vau:* יהו. However, in order for this Triunity to manifest Itself, a fourth element, a fourth hieroglyph is needed – and thus, the Tetragrammaton is formed, the Great Name of God: *YHVH:* יהוה.[13] The second *He* (ה) symbolizes the transition from one world into another, representing a specific *Yod* (י) in embryo. In this way, the idea of the quaternary, or the four-sided figure, is formed.

Thus we arrive at the explanation of the very carpet, which represents a quadrangle symbolizing the plan of Solomon's Temple – and, being such, figuratively and literally, it represents its foundation. In the Kabalistic science, the number 4 is the symbol of the quadrangle, which is the most stable form in the material world, and therefore, the foundations of the buildings are quadrangular in principle. The number 4 represents a perfect triunity of the manifested forces, being traditionally a symbol of the physical world. In this way, the unit of 1 is being completely accomplished through the fruitfulness of the triad (3), forming a 4 together with it. Actually, the 4 is all that is manifested, in which the creative Will of God acts, so this 4 originates from the Spirit, everything containing the 4, the quaternary in itself.

We proceed to the number 5 – the symbol of the pentagram represented in Freemasonry through the image of the blazing star; however, we shall dwell on its meaning in detail further on.

The number 6 follows, symbolized by Solomon's Star[14], which is present in Freemasonry both literally and by means of the Square and the Compass, placed in their specific configuration, which forwards us to the Hermetic Law of Analogy.

---

13 *YHVH* is pronounced as *Yod-He-Vav-He* and represents the Name of the Hebrew God that must not be pronounced; and that is why the substitute Names *Jehovah, Yahveh* and *Adonai* are used – *AN*.

14 Known also as *Solomon's Seal*, the *Star of David*, or the *Shield of David*. However, "the author's right" on this symbol does not belong to Jewish people, because it is archetypal, representing the Heaven and the Earth, the masculine and the feminine principle – *AN*.

The seven steps of the staircase leading to the Temple are, on their part, an expression of the vast *eidos* of the number 7. In Solomon's *Book of Proverbs, 9:1 (NKJV)*, it is said, "Wisdom has built Her house; She has hewn out Her seven pillars". Seven pillars, hewn by Wisdom – these are the seven supports upon which the victory and the firm establishment of Wisdom within the human soul are built. These are the first seven hieroglyphs of the Hebrew alphabet; these are the seven steps leading to the Temple. This symbolism is present also in the triangular pediment, which, upon the square base, configures a triangle over a quadrangle, thus (3+4=7) resulting in the number 7. Here, we are obliged to specify that the seven steps and the triangular pediment are introduced by Freemasonry, being rather symbols of which there is no evidence in the descriptions of Solomon's Temple.

As it is well-known, three Brothers "make up" a Lodge, five "form" it, and seven "make it complete" – and that is why at least seven Masters are needed so that a *"complete"* Rite of full value may be performed. Why seven precisely? Some might say that this is the minimum of the positions in the Lodge. And yet, why seven, we shall ask again? This is hardly an accidental number. Unfortunately, numerology in Freemasonry is also long-forgotten. We find a confirmation of this statement of ours in the Constitution of the *United Grand Lodge of Bulgaria (UGLB),* adopted by the *Grand Lodge of Ancient Free and Accepted Masons of Germany (GL AFAM),* where we can read the following: "When Masonry was still in its dawning, the bond with the Teaching of the value and the magic of numbers was still alive. Today, we have already lost it." The *eidos* of the number 7 is vast; but let us begin penetrating into it. Hermes, in his epoch, had already enunciated the Law of Sevenfoldness of Creation. Seven are also the couples of the Souls born by the Spirit Monad. The time periods in our life are seven, consisting of seven years each. Virgin Mary, when she first started walking as an infant, made seven steps towards her mother; whereas Enoch is the seventh descendant of Adam. Seven are the rainbow colours, and the Sun is represented with seven rays in the esoteric tradition. The Temple of Solomon, according to the Bible, was built in seven years. The Degrees of the so-called *Operative Masonry* were seven. Around the Kaaba in Mecca, seven ritual rounds are made, the first three being performed at a faster pace, while the other four – at a slower one. The seven-pointed star seems to be not so much included in the Masonic symbolism. This star consists of seven points, harmoniously interconnected and united in one circle. Three of the points, however, are above the other four, forming a triangle over a quadrangle, inscribed into the perfect form of the circle – a combination of a ternary, together with a quaternary, resting upon a sphere. In this way, again, the result is the number 7 – the number of victory. Victory, in its deep essence, is the triumph of the Spirit, represented by the number 3, over the form, symbolized by the number 4, thus enunciating the following Law: *Spiritus dominat formam.*[15] This is the first heading of the Seventh Arcanum of Sacred Magic, the septenary being its pentacle. The seven Masters of the craft are the points of support for the harmony in any Lodge where the Spirit of the Great Architect of the Universe reigns.

We shall stop here, because we only give examples of symbolic thinking, in which, if all the contexts of the symbols are known, a complete picture is attained, leading to voluminosity and implementation power of the mind – and, above all, to Truthfulness.

Besides the sequence of activation of the symbols, we should consider also the circumstance that each symbol possesses a vast *eidos*. For example, the rectangle, as a foundation of the Temple, contains in itself the *eidos* of the quaternary, the core essence of which is the Law of the Fruit. The Temple of Solomon is perhaps rather a symbol than a building that has actually existed. It is a Temple of Wisdom; and Wisdom, on its turn, is the Temple of our Soul. The *eidos* of the Soul is enormous; so what can we possibly say about that of Wisdom? Thus, the symbol expands from one *eidos* into another. A typical example of this are the Kabalistic Tree and its Sefirot, with each Sefira containing it itself another Tree, with still another Tree in each of its Sefirot, and so on, without end.

The whole information is contained in a latent state within the symbols, awaiting for the knowledge, in the form of Light, to summon them to life. From the knowledge and the desire, the thought is born, being transformed through the symbols into *"Unuttered Word"*, which is, in its core essence, the Divine Word. A process of thorough knowledge of symbols is necessary; hence, through meditation, we ought to acquire awareness of them so that we attain penetrating insight, which will transform them into living *eidoses* filled with Sekhem. Thus, we will obtain the implementation power to embody the Masonic ideas in life. Freemasonry, however, is an Initiatic Brotherhood, with Initiation being its Chief Cornerstone. The Initiation into the Masonic symbols through their Sekhem is able to lead to the desired transformation and implementation power. This tradition, of Initiation given by a Master to a disciple (by a Master craftsman to an apprentice and a fellow craft), has been lost somewhere across the centuries and should be brought to life again.

Now we can already proceed to the origin of the word *Freemason*.

---

15  From Latin: "The Spirit dominates over the form" – *AN*.

## Etymology of the Name

> *Stat Roma pristina nomine,*
> *nomina nuda tenemus.*[16]
>
> **Bernard de Cluny**

Much has been written on this topic, both by Freemasons and by researchers of Freemasonry. Therefore, taking the risk to repeat something, we shall draw only some essential conclusions.

The French word *franc* is equivalent to the English word *free*, meaning *at liberty* or *liberated;* therefore, *Freemason* (*Franc-maçon* in French) is usually interpreted as *free stonemason (free stone-builder)*. When given its interpretation, temporally and socially, it acquires the meaning of *free from taxes* and *moving freely*. In view of the profession of a builder, however, *freestone* stands for a type of *soft stone*. In this sense, *Freemason* would be more appropriately interpreted as *stone-builder of freestone*. Among the builders themselves, there was a division into two groups, according to their qualification: *freestone mason* – sculpturing and possessing practical and esoteric knowledge of the usage of the compass, the square, and the ruler; and *rough mason* – the one who hews, cuts and carves the stone: stone-hewer in the literal sense of this word. Thus, by the term *freemason*, the ones possessing perfect abilities were denoted, comprising the higher class of the guild. However, any Initiatic community would hardly use a name showing only and solely the position of its members in the guild or in society, unless with the aim of hiding its esoteric meaning.

The most appropriate symbol of the Soul within the building guild is the soft stone embodying the basic material with which builders work for the construction of the Temple of Spirit. Freemasons were a specific elite consisting of Operative Builders who used to liberate the Spirit of the soft stone, forming it according to the idea it contained. Thus, they brought also their own Spirit out of the prison of matter, becoming themselves free. Having this in mind, the name *Freemason* should be interpreted in the symbolic, deeply esoteric key rather than in its literal sense; therefore, the same is valid for the definition *franc (free)*, adopting in this way the meaning of *esoteric* (mason). One of the prominent Masons of the 18th century, Ramsay, declares in the same context: "The word Freemason must therefore not be taken in a literal, gross and material sense, as if our founders had been simple workers in stone."

Another Masonic author, George Steinmetz, in the middle of the 20th century, however, had another opinion, expressed in his book *The Lost Word*,

---
[16] From Latin: "The Ancient Rome only remains through its name, naked names are all that we hold" – *AN*.

*Its Hidden Meaning:* "The generally accepted theory is that our present Lodges are the outgrowth of the Operative Lodges, or Guilds, of the Middle Ages. There is no inclination to question the fact that our modern Lodges, AS ORGANIZATIONS, owe their origin to these Operative Lodges, but what of the esoteric teaching? Are we to believe that these craftsmen of the medieval guilds, most of whom were actually illiterate, conceived an entire philosophy such as Freemasonry, and then, with consummate cunning, concealed it beneath a complicated system of symbolism and allegory? The obvious answer to the question is that they did not." Further on, he continues: "There is ample reason to suspect that modern Freemasonry was profoundly influenced by, if not actually the outgrowth of, Rosicrucianism and Bacon's Secret Society." After that, he includes also a quote from the encyclopaedia of his patron Manly P. Hall: "Its symbolism is undoubtedly permeated with Bacon's two great ideals: universal education and universal democracy."

The "modern" Freemasonry which Steinmetz refers to is also called *Speculative* – and, in general, it adopts the designation *Freemasonry*. In this respect, it is necessary to elucidate the meaning of the term *Speculative*.

## Operative and Speculative Masonry

*One who works with his hands is a labourer.*
*One who works with his hands and his head is a craftsman.*
*One who works with his hands, his head and his heart is an artist.*
**Saint Francis of Assisi**

Most often, the contemporary, or, as it is also called, "Modern" Masonry is qualified as *Speculative* because the Masons of present times do not practise the craft, unlike the Ancient Masonry, which was *Operative*. This division is hardly the most appropriate, because, a sign of equality is incorrectly placed between *operative* and *practical*, in the meaning of "the process of constructing buildings". The etymology of the word *operative*, on the esoteric plane, is connected rather to *action* in principle, because Ancient Masons not only had the knowledge of Initiation but also performed a sequence of certain actions in order to receive it, thus implementing their spiritual power of authority. The most important consequence of an Initiation, in its operative aspect, is the attaining of implementation power. Therefore, the term *operative* is a symbol, meaning *development* of the human being towards attaining Spiritual Initiation and implementation power. The Ancient Masonry, called *Operative*, should be Speculative even in its literal sense, because the building craft includes labour through the mental ability to speculate, to reason. In this way, the correct terminology, in our opinion, should be *Ancient* Masons, because they are active builders; and *Accepted* ones, which actually are not in the builders' guild, so this formal criterion should not be valid on the esoteric plane. In the 17<sup>th</sup> century, the first admission of a non-operative Mason was registered on July 3<sup>rd</sup> 1634 in England. In France, on the other hand, there was a clear distinction between the Operative Craftsmen Guild *(Compagnonnage[17])* and the Speculative Freemasonry *(Franc-maçonnerie)*. Thus, esoterism in Freemasonry begins to slowly vanish, so it is quite justified that, at a certain point, it is already called simply *Masonry,* because the "franc" quality is already missing, especially after 1717, the birthdate of the so-called *Modern Masonry.* The latter radically differs from the Ancient Masonry, the main purpose of which consisted in the Initiations for building the physical temple that is the embodiment of the inner one. Modern Masonry strongly proclaims the ideas of equality and fraternity – however, without the might of Spiritual Initiation, they become illusionary. This type of Masonry turns into a political and socio-economical one, and is therefore too conjunctural, reaching as far as the recommendation to avoid the definition "Royal Art" regarding Masonry because of having a "royalist" twang. The most extreme view, however, is the one announcing that Masonry is the first hearth of atheism, and that it is therefore most natural for it to deal, above all, in the spirit of humanism, with charity and with the cultural and social development of humankind.

In 1877, the Grand Orient of France decides to abolish the obligation for its members to believe in the existence of God and in the immortality of the Soul, as well as the requirement for its Lodges to work "for the Glory of the Great Architect of the Universe". The decision to admit atheists was not approved by all, so it led, in 1894, to a schism in French Freemasonry, and the believers in God founded the Grand Lodge of France.

Therefore, maybe it is also quite natural that, in one of the first books about Bulgarian and Worldwide Masonry, *Синовете на вдовицата (The Sons of the Widow),* written in 1992 – that is, during the "awakening" of Freemasonry in Bulgaria – its author, Ivan Bogdanov, says the following: "The background of Freemasonry, too often represented as being an organic part of it so that a greater authority can be attributed to it, includes the origination and the activity of a series of organizations in the past, with religious and philosophical purpose, whose aim was to penetrate into the innermost secrets of Creation. To this category, the following should be assigned: the Egyptian and the Eleusinian Mysteries, the Hetaireia in Athens, the Societies of the Templars, of

---

[17] The word *compagnonnage,* deriving from the Middle-Age Latin form *companion/ companionem,* is composed of *cum* – "together with", and *panis* – "bread", the literal translation being "someone sharing someone's bread with another one" – *AN.*

the Rosicrucians, and of the Illuminati." Then the author continues: "Now by virtue of the cultural and historical continuity, now due to considerations of expediency, in the historical monuments and in the Rites of Freemasonry, quite a few characteristic features of its predecessors are included, thus suggesting to some of its ardent adepts to maintain that Masonry has been existing almost since the time of the first inhabitant of the Earth – Adam." According to Bogdanov, "Freemasonry appears on the stage of history together with bourgeoisie, in the beginning as its avant-garde, and later as its armour. Only to the naively thinking ones, Freemasonry is as old as the world, predestined to exist as long as the human society exists. Freemasonry develops on the social basis of bourgeoisie – so where the latter loses ground, Freemasonry ceases to exist."

It is obvious that this view is not only profane but also historically untrue, in view of the cathedrals built during the Middle Ages – an attainment of Operative Masonry. Esoterism in Freemasonry, however, is not irretrievably lost, as there remain Initiatic currents, followers of the Ancient Mysteries, of Hermetism, of Alchemy, of the Arcana Knowledge, of Kabala, of Rosicrucianism, and of esoterism in general. Two pronounced representatives are the evidence of this. Oswald Wirth wrote in 1936: "It is necessary for Freemasonry to remain Initiatic, and hence its duty to preserve everything that relates to Initiation. It is an indisputable landmark." The writer Mason René Guénon, on his part, reproaches Freemasonry that it has forgotten the fundamental principles of Initiation, and he has made it his object to remind these principles to Freemasonry; whereas, the already quoted Steinmetz writes the following: "No acknowledged Masonic authority advances the claim that Masonry is a CONTINUATION of the Mysteries, although many are agreed that the Mysteries must be that "mutual source" of the teaching and philosophy of both Rosicrucianism and Freemasonry".

## The Origin of Freemasonry

*Tradition does not mean to look after the ash, but to keep the flame alive.*

***Jean Jaurès***

We, however, and most surely, all our readers as well, know about many people of authority claiming that Freemasonry is a continuation of the Mysteries, tracing back its roots as far as Adam.

In the London newspaper *The Post Boy* of December 26th – 28th, 1723, an "exposure" of Freemasonry was published, containing a catechism of 42 couples of questions (Q.) and answers (A.):

> *"Q.: Where was the first Lodge kept?*
> *A.: In the City of Enoch.*
> *Q.: Who was the Master Mason?*
> *A.: Cain.*
> *Q.: Who was his Warden?*
> *A.: Seth."*

Some people even express the opinion that God was the first Freemason. We would not say that this is as absurd as it seems at first reading, having in mind that the Great Architect of the Universe is the God of all Masons. Even beyond the Masonic context, is not God the Creator (i.e. the Builder) of the World? Of course, these statements are speculative in view of the huge *eidos* and application of the word *builder,* which can be used for all forms of activity, both in the symbolical and the literal sense, since the beginning of the world. Perhaps precisely the building craft was one of the first joint human activities, together with the hunting of big animals and agriculture. We agree with Steinmetz that the Mysteries were the *"mutual source"* of the teaching of Freemasonry, adding that they were the source also of all Initiatic communities, regardless of their name. Such a source happen to be all esoteric teachings, one of the successors of which is the Masonic science, also called *Royal Art* – a direct reference to Ancient Egypt and its tradition, where, in the Pantheon of Memphis, the Supreme God *Ptah*[18], called *Master Architect,* was the God of builders.

Without going into detail, we shall also mention, in confirmation of what has been said, such emblematic symbols as the Pharaoh's *apron* and the *All-Seeing Eye,* replacing the pyramidion at the summit of the pyramid, an indication towards the "Concealed God". In this line of thoughts, we will also make a parallel between the image of the triangular apron of the Pharaoh with a square base (the number 3 squared), a reference to the number 9 and the Masonic "3 times 3". As for the number 9, sacred both to the Egyptians and the Masons who are worshipers of the Sun, we will dwell on it later.

There are also statements that Rosicrucianism is the cradle of Freemasonry. Such a theory is developed, for example, by Harvey Spencer Lewis[19], according to whom the Order of Rosicrucians was created during the time of Pharaoh Thutmose III, reaching its apogee at the time of Ehnaton, so after his

---

18  Ptah is considered to be the Demiurge in the Egyptian Pantheon, existing before everything else. Ptah conceives the world first in His thoughts, bringing it to accomplishment afterwards through the magic of His Word. He is considered also to be the patron of craftsmen, stone-hewers, architects, and arts. In the *Book of the Dead,* Ptah is described as "Great Worker in metals, Master Architect, Creator and Framer of everything in the Universe" – *AN.*
19  Harvey Spencer Lewis was initiated in France in 1909, and is one of the founders of the Rosicrucian Order in the United States – *AN.*

death, the teaching was spread, the *builders (masons)* of the Temple of Solomon being among its successors.

There is much to say on this topic, and yet, much can be also speculated with a variety of analogies and references as there are no undisputable written sources. From a historical point of view, however, we can say that after the tragic death of Jacques de Molay, the Templar Spirit has never ceased to exist thanks to the Brethren of the Order who have survived throughout the whole Europe. Their esoteric knowledge has been handed down over the centuries and can be found also in Freemasonry; however, we do not venture to comment whether Freemasonry is their source or merely their successor.

The majestic cathedrals built throughout Catholic Europe are a striking example of how the Masons have encoded in them the proportions and forms of sacred geometry originating from Ancient Egypt, and perhaps even from deeper Antiquity, thus making a transition from the clumpy cubic Romanesque style to the exquisite elevation of the Gothic one. This transition was sudden and not based on any figurative prehistory or experience. The construction of the cathedrals was due to a revolutionary discovery, namely, the use of huge stone beams – counterforts. Thus, the Romanesque arch was replaced by the stylishly elongated Gothic one, whereas the Romanesque round window – by the rosette. Freemasons embodied in the Gothic architecture sacral forms such as the *solar cross,* also known as the *hermetic cross,* the *pentagon,* the *hexagon* and the *octagon*. They also used the proportions of sacred geometry to come closer to the perfect characteristics set by the Great Architect of the Universe. Undoubtedly, they possessed exclusive knowledge – we may even say, Divine Knowledge – for building these amazing cathedrals, representing themselves a construction challenge even today. We will not outline the path and the continuity of this knowledge so that we do not enter the vast territory of speculation; and yet, we shall declare with conviction that Ancient Masonry used to grant Initiation into the secrets of building the physical temple as the embodiment of the spiritual one. That was accomplished through the Master who had mastered the Mysteries of the process of *Building the Edifice* and was himself the central point in the circle. The inner circle of humankind, however, has always been composed of men and women. As a confirmation of this, we will mention that, according to Initiates, the Spiritual Masters of the Earth come from Sirius – **"The Tear of Isis"**. The exceptional significance of this star, whose symbol is the Mother Goddess, to the spiritual development of humans, obliges us to dwell on the archetypal feminine essence and the role of woman as Her physical incarnation, mainly in the context of Freemasonry.

# III
# UPPER ROOM

## 2
## Woman and Freemasonry

*Procul, profani!*[20]

Nowadays, the essential requirement for a Seeker, in order to be admitted into the Orthodox Masonic Brotherhood, as we have already said, is to be "a free-born man of good report in society". This requirement has been, for several centuries, an unequivocal indication that a woman cannot be admitted into this Brotherhood.

According to Hebrew Kabala, a candidate for its mastering must be a man, at least 40 years old, married, with children, and thoroughly proficient in the *Torah*. It is obvious that, according to both the Kabalistic tradition and the not so distant Masonic one, secrets can only be passed on to men by men. We are drawing this parallel because Kabala is the fundamental esoteric foundation of Freemasonry. However, as is well known, there have long existed mixed and even entirely feminine Masonic Lodges. They all claim not only to have maintained the continuity of tradition, but also that they go on updating, modernizing and enriching it. The masculine Blue Freemasonry, however, considers that it alone carries the characteristics of Masonic Orthodoxy, which is why it claims to be the main one. This raises the question of whether this Freemasonry is the veritable, authentic repository of tradition, or it represents a mouldy retrograde form that really needs to be reformed. We have explained that the secret is already outside the circle of Freemasonry and is protected only by the Law of Lack of Understanding. Anyone may have access to the so-called "Masonic" secrets, symbols and rites, and formally practice them. How do these practices differ from those in Masonry which claims to be orthodox? Does not the Law of Lack of Understanding also work in it, and what kind of authenticity are we talking about – the continuity of the form or the authenticity of the Initiatic tradition? In Kabala, if a certain form is not filled with its adequate content, it is called *qlifa*, meaning *a shell, a husk*, as well as *a harlot*. Is Orthodox Masonry a shell, or is it a harlot giving herself to anyone who happens to want her? The answer to this question can be found through the universal criterion of the fruit (the result) formulated

---

20  From Latin: "Keep far away, you profane ones!" (Vergil) – *AN*.

by Jesus. Is the fruit of Freemasonry rotten, or is it a garden giving sweet and juicy fruits that quench the thirst and appease the hunger? Every Brother Mason, if plunging into the depths of his own heart, in which, somewhere at the bottom, conscience resides, can already answer this question himself. We shall say: If the conclusion is that the fruits are rotten, it means that only the authenticity of the form is not enough to have the necessary transformation and implementation power of authority. Otherwise, all Brethren who have sunk deep into the form of Freemasonry should at one point turn into radically different entities who are incapable of recognizing their own selves in the past, and who are called *Initiates* in the esoteric tradition. As for whether it is so, again, each one of the Brotherhood can come to his own answer by himself. Our answer is that the Initiatic custom of passing on the power of the Masonic symbols from a Master to a disciple (from a Master craftsman to an apprentice and a fellow craft) has been interrupted at some point during the centuries. Thus, these symbols have turned into *qlifot,* into shells, into empty vessels, which there is no one to fill up with anything. The Fire of Initiation has died away, and now Initiation has turned into an ordinary formal ritual of *"Raising to a Degree",* as the very Freemasons call it. In this sense, we will quote again George Steinmetz and his book *The Lost Word, Its Hidden Meaning:* "The Secret Doctrine in Freemasonry cannot be too strongly stressed. Firstly, because there are those, in the Order, who in their lack of knowledge claim that it does not exist; secondly, because the seeking Mason can gain no further light than is shed by the ritual itself, until he starts his quest for the REAL SECRETS of the hidden Mysteries of Freemasonry – and they are found WITHIN THE SECRET DOCTRINE!"

Should we move to Bulgarian Freemasonry, however, the question arises as to which Brother, having adequately and correctly walked the way of the Masonic Initiation Degrees, before the revival of Freemasonry in Bulgaria, has brought the Torch of Knowledge and of the formal Masonic tradition. Let us suppose there is such a Brother – and yet, is he given the opportunity to hand down this tradition so that it leaves an imprint and guides the movement? Does his personality fit into the content of those who are called *Initiates* in the esoteric tradition of the Mysteries? However, if there is no such Brother, then in what do the Freemasons in Bulgaria differ from any group of humans who would obtain the Masonic Rites – which is not difficult at all! – and start practising them. Both, without any experience and without any true Initiation, possess something written that claims to be an authentic Masonic Rite, and exercise in it.

Some Masons will sharply object that the first ones are regular while the others are not. Still, have those who call themselves *Regular* Masons attained true Spiritual Light, or merely a formality has been implemented? If the veritable Light has faded away at some point during the centuries, then the inner sense of the requirements for regularity and acceptance represents again just a formality. Is it not right that all people of both genders who call themselves *Freemasons* have received Light formally, their Lodges have also been installed, and they have been given the rules and the rites to work with? However, we shall stop here, because Freemasonry in Bulgaria is not our main topic. Therefore, the following questions arise: At this moment, is the Masonry claiming for authenticity winning or losing by professing the idea of totally male membership? And does it really carry the imprint of Masonic Orthodoxy and the continuity of tradition? Does the lack of female presence in contemporary Freemasonry represent a strict observance of an imposed tradition, or is it a reminiscence of the neglect towards women over the millennia, or is it merely the result of ordinary sexism? We will not be surprised if the attitude towards the feminine core essence is dominated by the sexist approach that can be described as *essentialistic*. *Essentialism* is a view according to which any core essence results in a certain unchanging set of qualities and properties. According to this view, individual humans are considered and evaluated in compliance with the general characteristics of the gender group to which each individual belongs, and not according to the individual's own abilities. As a result, the individual is categorized into one of the two gender categories: male or female. However, the main part of such sexism is directed against the female gender – a fact that has its own religious, and hence domestic, socio-economic, and political roots. The vulgarized aspect of what has been said so far represents a viewpoint considering women only as sexual objects – and many Masonic Brothers, unfortunately, take this as a well-grounded reason for women not to be present in the Brotherhood – something very similar to the sailor phrase *"Woman on board!"*

There exists also an esoteric antifeminist argument according to which Freemasonry is a solar rite, so women should not participate in it. We will note, however, that since the throne of Solomon was situated in the west, not in the east, therefore the movement in the Temple was a lunar one. Such was also the movement in the temple of the Lodges of Ancient Masonry, which invalidates the above argument.

The secondary and auxiliary role of women is assumed to be laid down ever since the way she was created in the abode of Eden, from Adam's rib. It can be declared with certainty that, since then, she has been neglected and considered to be only a sexual object and a womb for giving birth; but nevertheless, her core essence has been firmly rooted in the whole Creation. She is Goddess and Woman – mother, virgin and harlot, love and hatred, innocence and temptation, saint and sinner. With the image of the Goddess, men entered deadly battles, while women were burned on the stake as witches. Her nature is numinous, evoking the thirst for getting to know her.

Eve is the Primary Mother because the feminine principle is the receiving one, the one bearing children. At first, in the pantheon of the various nations, the Mother Goddess was the Supreme One precisely because of the symbol of fertility. However, the active masculine principle has gradually pushed the Goddess aside, to the point where, in patriarchal monotheism, She does not exist at all.

Perhaps the most universal essence of the feminine aspect of the Force is the one that, for Christians, symbolizes the Mother of God – the Virgin Mary, who, however, does not have the status of a Goddess. Mary, the mother of Jesus, is presented as an ordinary woman, but at the same time she is the *Virgin*, not because she is a virgin in the profane sense but because her soul is pure and immaculate. Two women were closest to Jesus: *Mary* and *Mary Magdalene* – the virgin and the harlot; two diametrically opposite entities, contained in the name *Woman*. One of them gives birth to Jesus, whereas the other one washes His feet with her tears and wipes them with her hair.[21] Which one of them is more worthy to bear the name *Woman?* The Immaculate Conception is opposed to the indiscriminate sexual indulgence. The organized and receiving force, focused on a purpose, is able to give birth to God's Son, whereas the unbalanced and scattered force ruins the body and devastates the soul. One and the same force, leading to different results depending on its structuring and ways of use! On a deeper plane, the Virgin embodies the idea of That Which gives birth to Everything but preserves Its virginity. Her creativity does not involve Her in the world of Her creatures but She remains behind as the foundation of manifestation, as the root substance from which matter arises.

There exists, however, also a third woman identified in the Gospels only as *Mary of Bethany*. Only she and John the Baptist carry out the two most important rituals upon Jesus: *anointing* and *baptizing*.[22] Anointing represents a pagan custom in which a chosen man is anointed by a priestess on the head, legs and genitals, after which a sexual ritual is performed, known as the *sacred marriage*, through which the chosen one is assigned a precisely determined mission. This is the anointing of the *sacred king*, in which the priestess merges sexually with him before his sacrificial death. Three days later, he comes back to life through resurrection, and nature is revived again.

---

21 *Holy Gospel of Luke* 7:37; 38 – *AN*.
22 There were still other women who also anointed Jesus, and yet, anointing in Bethany has the characteristics of a ritual – *AN*.

Anointing was carried out with different oils and was part of the crowning ceremony, thus turning the chosen one into king. This shows the utmost importance of this act, which, in the case of Jesus, is entirely spiritual and which actually transforms Him into Christ.

Orthodox Christianity has created a dogmatic image of woman which does not express her true core essence. The bold outlines of this image are that woman was created out of the man's rib to be his helper, which determines her secondary role and importance. Also, the woman is a conduit of sin, for the Serpent seduces her, and therefore she must be more punished than the man. The incorrect understanding of the scene of the original sin debases and defiles the great magic of fruitfulness and birth, casting the brand of vice permanently upon the feminine nature in the person of Eve. It is necessary to know the deep esoteric spiritual traditions so that delusion cannot strike root inside us.

**Figure 2**

## The Garden of Eden

*The heart of humans is their own Heaven or Hell.*

**Jean-Jacques Rousseau**

The traditional view that Moses is the author of the *Torah* is questioned and thoroughly analysed still in the 17th century due to the inconsistencies in the biblical text. In the end of the 19th century, it is assumed that there are four major sources, combined in their current form, that have become known as the *Jahwist (J)*, the *Elohist (E)*, the *Deuteronomist (D)*, and the *Priestly Writer (P)*. Many scientists have dealt with this question – however, the one who formulates the final hypothesis and the chronological sequence of *JEDP* is the German biblical scholar and orientalist Julius Wellhausen, presenting the history of the development of religion in Israel. The hypothesis developed by him expresses the opinion that the *Torah* has its origins in various independent parallel sources and narratives that have been subsequently edited by the so-called *redactors*, acquiring their current form.

According to this hypothesis about the Creation in the Bible, there are two separate narratives that have been connected with each other by the above mentioned "redactors". The oldest is called the *Jahwist*, and the newest – the *Elohist*, with which the *First Book of Moses – Genesis*, begins. Adam, according to the *Elohist* narrative, is an androgynous being: "He created them male and female. And on the same day He made them, He blessed them and called them 'humans'." (*Genesis* 5:2, *ERV*). The human being was created in the image of God, which is an indication also towards the androgyny of God Himself, Who in this part of the Bible is called *Elohim* – a word with a feminine root and a masculine ending. The androgynous Adam, from a Kabalistic point of view, is the Adam of *Bria*. The first differentiation is, in its essence, the separation of Adam and Eve of *Yetzira* from Adam of *Bria;* however, with the separation of the feminine essence from Adam, the beginning of the falling out of from the Perfect Wholeness is laid. Yahveh-Elohim "caused a deep sleep to fall on Adam" (*Genesis* 2:21, *NKJV*), meaning that He brought him into a level of consciousness known as *Katnut*, limiting him within the Lower Face of Formation, hence outside the world of Creation, where he is androgynous. At this level, the feminine essence of Adam was already separated into an individual form under the name of *Eve*, and they were both returned into the state of *Gadlut* in the Upper Face of *Yetzira*. Adam's Fall is a transition from the androgynous completeness of *Bria* into the one of the soul, and after that – into a corporal binary dividedness. The corporal sexual differentiation, however, is the result of a deeper process of the psyche towards alienation and separation of the human consciousness from the unified identity of the Divine World. At first, Adam and Eve did not feel ashamed in each other's presence because they had not become aware of themselves as two separate beings. There was no element of separation yet in their world – until the Serpent appeared. When they got ashamed, they became aware of the separation in their soul as a fact, which was inevitably bound to be projected into the sexual differentiation of their material bodies, and this is symbolically represented by the expulsion from Eden into the world of *Assia*. *Adam* is a common noun in the masculine gender extracted from the word *Adama*, which means *Earth*. This is not the name of the First Human and the First Man differentiated from this Human but rather a denomination of his essence: an earthly being destined to live on the Earth (and here we do not mean the planet Earth). In the Aramaic language, one of the words meaning *blood* is the word *dama* which, like the Old Hebrew word *dam*, is also used in the meaning of *juice, wine, sap*, or *essence*. The word derives from the same root as the word *Adam*, or the being through which the blood, the vital forces, the juice and the essence of the Divine can pass. Adam appears on the last Sixth Day of Creation and is therefore the crown of the Creator, but as an androgyne. Eve is created at a later stage of evolution, so feminists would say that she should be more perfect. However, she is separated from Adam of *Yetzira*, which means that they both originate from one and the same World and therefore occupy the corresponding positions of equal worth of the active and the passive pillar in the Kabalistic Tree of *Yetzira*. The core essence, however, is complete only in its archetypal androgynous wholeness: the image and likeness of God.

The question of why the Serpent starts a conversation with the woman, not the man, is as old as the dawn of time. The Bible does not offer answers. Christian dogmatists, however, respond that this is so because they are identical, the female nature and that of the Serpent, defined as "the most cunning": "The Serpent was more cunning than any beast of the field which the Lord God had made." (*Genesis* 3:1, *NKJV*)

The Serpent is initially in a "zooerectus" status; and, according to Moses' *Sefer*, it is the first being to initiate communication. Contrary to dogmatists, it can be assumed that the Serpent, as the wisest creature in the biblical narrative, would naturally wish to communicate with the closest ones. Eve is tempted through the promise to attain the Wisdom of Gods, and it means that, inside her, the aspiration is laid down for knowledge and for self-improvement towards perfection. The Holy Scripture does not give any answer to the question formulated above, but such an answer can be obtained from Kabala – namely, that the Serpent is an illustration of the human vital (animal) soul – *Nephesh*, and it is natural for the Serpent to communicate with the closest to it, and yet, higher part – *Ruah*, whose symbol is Eve.

From what has been explained so far, it becomes clear that we can point out arguments, regarding to both man and woman, determining the superiority and importance of the one over the other. This, however, leads to meaningless antagonism and confrontation. Gender antagonism comes from the lack of understanding that they are manifestations of a single united entity, of one whole called *Human* – image and likeness of God. It is also important to mention the existence of authors who claim that the first androgyne was divided into Adam and Lilith, and after the latter rebelled because she did not want to use the only sexual position permitted to her, *Venus observa*, she was expelled from (or she left by herself) the abode of Eden, and then Eve was created. Some Judaic sources and rabbinic texts known as *Midrash* also relate about the first woman of Adam – Lilith, who was created in the same way as Adam. These non-canonical versions are in correlation with the canonical understanding of the phrase *"He created them male and female"*, where the pronoun *them* is an indication of two separate entities; otherwise the phrase should be "He created *this being* male and female". In this context, we would say that it is not known what the exact phrase used in the *Sefer* is, so it is necessary to reflect upon the creation of the Human Being as an essential entity – image and likeness of its Creator. If we literally assume that Eve is a derivative of Adam, then she is a part of his core essence, but, as we have already explained – a part of his *Yetzira* nature. This is confirmed by the used word *tsela*, which, besides *bone, rib*, means also *part of something, part of the whole*.

Esoteric science is explicit that Adam, Eve and the Serpent are not separate physical entities but, respectively, the mind (the Spirit, or the masculine principle), the desire (the emotions, or the Soul) and the instinct drive (the body) – all the three forming the triune Human. The instinct drive (the Serpent) influenced the desire (Eve), which, on its turn, provoked the mind (Adam), and this resulted in the sinking into matter. Thus the Spirit and the Soul came to be dominated by the instinct drive of the body, and therefore this order has to be reversed by the rectifying of the Soul, which is the mediator between the Spirit and the body, and therefore the Soul is the key to restoring the hierarchic equilibrium. The rectifying of the Soul will transform the energies of the body, and subdue the ego, thus restoring the hierarchic order. In this way, the body will obey the pure (rectified) Soul, and they will both be governed by the Spirit (the only Ruler of the Kingdom) – hence, the important role of woman as the individualized feminine aspect of the Human Being, with a view to rectifying and regaining the original nature of the latter.

At the dawn of humankind, the only religious image is that of the Goddess, symbolizing motherhood and the nurturing might of the mother giving food to the world. The most constant cosmic symbol of the Goddess is the snake, and therefore it is often depicted as a snake-headed woman. Goddesses in Antiquity are represented with a vessel in their hands which has an important symbolic meaning because it contains the Eternal Waters. In India, this vessel is a symbol of the sacrum, containing the Living Water – *Kundalini*, the Inner Mother. The feminine core essence is the intuitive principle – the Wisdom governing the right hemisphere of the brain, and providing an opportunity for connection with the transcendent Truth. The female world was dominated by the action of the left half of the human body, which is subordinate to Wisdom, respectively to the right hemisphere. However, the masculine principle gradually begins to prevail, so intuition is displaced by logic, and the world becomes a masculine world of right-half activity ruled by the left hemisphere of the brain. This leads to Orthodox Judaism, where God is strictly patriarchal, and in it, there is no place for the feminine essence. This concept escalates in Catholicism, the theological pillar of which is Saint Augustine of Hippo, with his doctrine of the original sin. This sin is at the expense of women because Eve stands at the root of it, dooming humankind to depravity and suffering. In fact, this debasing of the attitude towards woman to the degree of hatred begins still with Paul the Apostle. However, it has no roots in the original Christianity – because, when the Apostles ask Christ whether a man may send his wife away, He replies, "So then, they are no longer two but one flesh. Therefore, what God has joined together, let not man separate!" (*Matthew 19:6, NKJV*) Christ hardly meant the marriage union blessed by the Church, or the so-called "marriage in the Church", otherwise He Himself would set an example for such a marriage. The answer can be found in the teaching of Christian Spiritualism about dual souls. According to it, initially, all created souls entered life as dual, and complementing each other, formed a spiritual energy unit. The feminine and the masculine principle were interconnected in a harmonious whole that was gradually working on self-perfection. Such initially contiguous double souls were called *dual souls* or *soul mates*. Some of them, as a result of egoism, changed their personal frequency, their etheric bodies became denser, and they began to "fall", moving away from the Centre of the Primordial Light. Thus they turned into differentiated male and female entities. Walking along the Spiritual Path, at one point everyone will meet their own "You", from which their egoistic "I" has separated. According to the Law of Duality, man and woman are parts of one whole, each with equal worth and significance, just as the poles of a magnet. It was namely this law which Jesus meant in His mysterious statement, according to which souls were created as two individualities with different polarity, set in one common tone that distinguished them from all other creatures. As a result of their separation and the different "falling", they moved away from each other but remained connected, by means of a force field, in a relationship that cannot be interrupted in any way. This is the Marriage contracted in Heaven, the formal analogue of which should be the earthly one. In its essence, this refers to *Hieros Gamos* – the inner Holy Marriage between *Anima* and *Animus*[23], ac-

---

23 *Anima* – the conscious masculine and the unconscious feminine core essence of the Soul; *Animus* – the conscious feminine and the unconscious masculine core essence of the Soul – *AN*.

cording to Jung's terminology. In the Gnosis, the main prayer of Christianity, *The Lord's Prayer ("Our Father")*, is different from the canonic one. In the *Gospel of Perfect Life* in the New Testament Apocrypha, Jesus Christ tells the Apostles, "This is what you ought to pray for: Our Father-Mother Who are above us and within us, hallowed be Your Name!"

Early Christians worshipped Jesus as an incarnation of *Hohma*. Wisdom (Sofia) is a hypostasis of the feminine nature before the Creation. Holy Wisdom is even before Eternity, Primordial, existing even before all visible forms, says Solomon. The feminine principle in the image of Wisdom manifests itself as the unifying principle preceding any division and separation. The merging into one of this Primordial Wisdom and God-Father is a symbol of the union of the masculine and the feminine principle, the elevation of the sub-consciousness to the light of consciousness, the marriage between darkness and light. From the Mystic Wedding of the Sun and the Moon, the "whole and complete Human" is born. *Hohma* (Wisdom) unites the opposites and the dismembered consciousness into the monolithic "I Am". The collective image of "I am" is the new feminine kingdom named *Shamayim Malkuta*, the *Kingdom of God* which Jesus talks about: the inner liberation of Kundalini that will accomplish the Self.

After all that has been said so far, which is a drop in the ocean of the feminine core essence, let us go back to the initial topic: woman's absence in Orthodox Freemasonry. If the archetypal Human, the image and likeness of God, is an androgyne, whereas the present-day human is differentiated regarding polarity, then the evolutionary development of humans must lead to the recovery of this likeness and to their transforming into what in psychology is called *Gestalt* (Wholeness, Integrity) so that they combine equally the masculine and the feminine core essence within themselves. According to the Eastern traditions, everything is caused to be generated in the Causal World, and therein resides our causal body, which is not divided into sexes. According to Kabala, that World is called *Bria*, and therein, the primordial androgynous Adam is created as a perfect, complete Human. That is why, in accordance with the Karmic Law, sometimes we are reborn as a man, and sometimes – as a woman. This circumstance once again eloquently shows the absurdity and stupidity of any antagonistic opposition of the two sexes regarding their significance. All esoteric Initiatic societies, Freemasonry being one of them, possess knowledge and spiritual practices leading to the retrieval of the Primordial Nature, from which we can in no way separate its feminine core essence. The question arises as to how this essence can be unfolded in a purely masculine environment and society. History shows that societies based on sex distinction and denial, and applying full differentiation of the opposite sex, generate deviations, some of which we would call "pathological". In any case, there is clear evidence of one-sidedness of development and also dominance of qualities characteristic of the gender comprising this society. Hence, it is necessary to conclude that the complete and harmonious Human Being is the one in whom both the masculine and the feminine core essence (Animus and Anima) are equally developed, just as God "created them male and female; and on the same day He made them, He blessed them and called them 'humans'." (*Genesis* 5:2, *ERV*)

Freemasonry is an Initiatic esoteric society, possessing the Royal Art, so hardly the processes in it are due to any accidental external circumstances. It has survived so far as a specific form because it is archetypal, and therefore it develops according to the plan of the Great Architect of the Universe. Do this feminine core essence, and also the very woman, as its embodiment, have their place in this plan?

Freemasons in the past were hostile to the initiation of women and their admission into the Masonic society, and this was mostly in the name of tradition. However, the following question arises: By whom and since when has this tradition been established? According to Oswald Wirth, a Mason who is an authority in this field, "Nowadays, we appreciate better the heritage of thinkers who have left us a profound symbolism, and we understand that it is absurd to offer any woman an Initiation program aimed at development of the masculine: she can be initiated only into the Mysteries of Femininity."

## Ramsay and the Bacchanalia

*The witches ceased to exist
when we stopped burning them.*

**Voltaire**

In his famous *Oration,* the Chevalier Ramsay says: "Yes, sirs, the famous festivals of Ceres at Eleusis, of Isis in Egypt, of Minerva at Athens, or Urania amongst the Phoenicians, of Diana in Scythia were connected with ours. In those places, Mysteries were celebrated which concealed may vestiges of the ancient religion of Noah and the Patriarchs. They concluded with no banquets and libations when neither that intemperance nor excess were known into which the heathen gradually fell. The source of these infamies was the admission to the nocturnal assemblies of persons of both sexes in contravention of the primitive usages. It is in order to prevent similar abuses that women are excluded from our Order. We are not so unjust as to regard the fair sex as incapable of keeping a secret. But their presence might insensibly corrupt the purity of our maxims and manners." Further, the oration goes on, reaching the following conclusion: "Our Order, therefore, must not be considered a revival of the Bacchanals, but as an Order founded in remote antiquity, renewed in the Holy Land by our ancestors in order to recall the memory of the most sublime Truths amidst the pleasures of society."

Ramsay uses the word *Mysteries,* which means that he has in mind the Ancient Mysteries, and they were, first and foremost, chthonic[24], built on the basis of the feminine element, as they were dedicated to cyclicity, fertility, birth, and death.

Since the ancient *festivals,* dedicated, generally speaking, to the Goddess, were part of the Masonic tradition, the logical question arises: Why woman, who should be part of the core essence of the Goddess, and also a transmitter of Her energies, has to be ignored? The explicit answer in the quoted text: "in order to prevent similar abuses…" (i.e. intemperance and excess), can be considered as profane, at the least. On the one hand, it turns out that Initiates in Freemasonry are weak-willed men who easily give in to their primal passions and sexual drive, while the initiated women are allotted the biblical role of temptresses. However, if it is a matter of men and women who are true Initiates, then the above arguments are actually groundless. On the other hand, there is a clear lack of understanding of the actual meaning of the Bacchanalia, which in Ramsay's *Oration* are obviously burdened with the negative connotation of sexual looseness, opposing them to the morality of "our Order". In this context, an obvious connection is made with the so-called *orgies,* which, in their popular interpretation, are also given a wrong content. *Orgy* comes from the Greek word οργια and means *sacred sacrificial ritual* in the early Ancient Greek and Roman Mysteries dedicated to Dionysus-Bacchus. This ritual ought to lead to mystical ecstasy in the form of a *"sacred orgasm"*. It is quite natural that modern thinking associates the word *orgasm* only and solely with the culmination of the sexual act. However, if we refer to its etymology deriving from the Latin word *orgasio* (1st person singular of the verb *orgasire*) – *to swell, to burst,* then orgasm is by definition an experience of incredibly strong excitement. As a consequence of this excitement, the ego is annihilated and an impersonal inward state arises, immanent to *prima materia,* and therefore having the characteristics of transcendence. The sexual act through which this state can be achieved unconsciously is a natural gift to humans. When they become aware of it,

---

24  *Chthonic* – relating to the earth (from Ancient Greek: *khthōn* – "earth", "soil"; *khthōnios* – "subterranean") – *AN.*

however, in this way, they can practice and act purposefully, which is embedded in many esoteric traditions such as Tantrism, Kama Sutra, etc., which we could unite under the general formulation of *sexual magic*. *Orgasm*, however, in view of the contextual meaning of this word, can also be obtained through other practices of the Mysteries in order to reach Divine ecstasy and transcendence of consciousness. In this connection, we should also dwell on the origin and significance of the Bacchanalia.

The root of the lexeme is *"bacch"* and obviously relates to *Bacchus* – the god of fertility, wine, vine-growing, and rejoicing, whose priestesses are the Bacchantes. *Bacchus* is the Latin name of the Greek god *Dionysus*, who was identified with the local god of fertility *Liber*. In his honour, the Romans celebrated the feast of wine and joy, called *Bacchanalia*, which later obviously adopted the Modern Greek vocalization "Vacchanalia". Initially, the Bacchanalia represented itself Mystery leading to entrancement, in which only the priestesses and the women undergoing Initiation took part, but further on it degenerated into a profane, nation-wide feast in which people got drunk and had fun.

If we go on searching for more gods with the same symbolism, then we will get to Sabazios, whose primal propagation is into the region of Phrygia, from where he penetrates Thrace and is honoured as Zagreus, then in Hellas as Dionysus; and, through the Roman legions – to the Western provinces of the Roman Empire, being transformed into Bacchus. That is why Bacchantes in the Dionysian Mysteries called themselves *"Sabs"* (i.e. "Sabazians"), as well as *"Maenads"*, the latter being a reference to Orphism. Maenads are depicted as half-naked women with insane look in the eyes, following Dionysus and uttering piercing screams. It is no coincidence that *Maenads* means *"being in a frenzy"*, *"raging"*, because, to the profane, those who have fallen into ecstasy look exactly like that. According to the legend, they ripped apart Orpheus to punish him for his contempt for them. Ovid narrates in *Metamorphoses*, Book 11, how "the Thracian Maenads got furious for being neglected by Orpheus on account of young men with feminine traits." According to another version, the reason for their fury was Orpheus's refusal to acknowledge the cult to Dionysus, as well as his fervour for the cult to Apollo. The common between these characters, however, is their relation to the Underworld and, above all, to the snake as a symbol.

The primeval image of the Mother Goddess represents reptilian zoomorphism, showing the chthonic nature of the birth-giving principle. Therefore, according to Thracian Orphism, the Great Mother Goddess gives birth to Her chthonic son, called *Zagreus* – "horned snake". The chthonic force is being fertilized by another of its kind, merging with the Divine Principle in the image of the Dragon – a symbol of the masculine core essence. Having adopted the image of a dragon, Zeus merged with Persephone, who had the image of a "horned monster". Sabazios, on his part, is initially identified with the stone, and, as it is with Zagreus, the snake is an inseparable attribute or image of Sabazios – hence, he can also be called a "chthonic" god, so, in this respect, he dominates both dead matter and living matter, and can therefore be dismembered and joined together again. According to legends, he and the other gods bearing his essential characteristics are dismembered or torn apart in pieces. Thus, Sabazios is dismembered into three parts; Dionysus-Zagreus-Liber was torn into seven parts (head, limbs, phallus and torso) by the Titans; the Maenads ripped Orpheus to pieces at the banks of the Hebros river, and his head floated along the river, still singing, and then rested right up at the island of Lesbos. According to the ancient authors, the god of the Sun, Apollo, is consubstantial with the god Liber, who, on his part, is equivalent to the already mentioned gods.

The chthonic nature of these gods, however, does not contradict their solar essence, because the two principles form the completeness of the whole Cosmos.

There is no doubt that the dismemberment, along with the reassembling after that, is a principle symbol corresponding to the Masonic formula "Gather what is scattered", according to which the task of the Masters consists in gathering and distributing the Light. If we go back to the one of the most ancient traditions, the Vedic tradition, we will see that, according to it, there are two independent principles – *Prakriti* and *Purusha*, which can be attributed to the concept of the cause-and-effect relation. It is assumed that all cause-and-effect chains originate from a common Primary Cause that has generated Nature and its development. The ancient sages called it *Prakriti*, "The First Woman". However, she, by herself, without any inseminating spiritual impulse, is not active. That is why in the cosmological picture of everything existing, one more fundamental principle is used: *Purusha*. In a metaphorical sense, Purusha is the masculine principle and has a multiple connotation. Purusha's multiple nature is a consequence of an ancient Vedic notion of Creation, according to which Purusha is the First Human and the first seed. To create the Cosmos, the Gods offer Purusha as a sacrifice, dismembering him, and from the separate pieces, as from seeds, Earth and Heaven, air and wind, humans and everything else is generated.

Obviously, all of this relates to the symbolic description of the transition from unity to multitude, without which there could be no manifestation at all.

Hence, now we can already understand the idea of "gathering what is scattered", or the retrieving of Purusha as he was "up to the beginning", that is, in a non-manifested state, this being nothing else but a return to the original Unity. This Purusha, as René Guénon says, is also *Vishvakarman* – that is, the Great Architect of the Universe; and, in His capacity of being such, He Himself makes a sacrifice, being at the same time the sacrifice Himself. In accordance with the rule which reads that Initiation represents both death and resurrection, those undergoing Initiation are actually sacrificing themselves. This immediately brings us back to the Masonic symbolism of the Master's Degree, in which the one who is being initiated actually identifies himself with the very sacrificial offering. It can be said that it is all about one and the same cosmogony process in different traditional forms of sacrificial offering: self-sacrifice or murder. Thus, also in Hebrew Kabala, through the disintegration of Adam Kadmon, the Universe was created, along with all the beings in it. In this way, the latter are as if particles of his body, so their "reintegration" into a unified whole emerges as a recovery of the very Adam Kadmon – the Universal Human. As far as the "Master" Degree virtually represents the level of the "small mysteries", in this case we are talking about the reintegration of the Initiate's consciousness.

Let us go back, however, to the myth about Zagreus, the son of Zeus and Persephone, whose name, translated from Greek, means "Son of Heaven and Earth". This definition cannot but bring us back to another ancient mythology related to the Primordial times of the God Osiris, who is also a "Son of Heaven and Earth", and is also torn apart, but in fourteen pieces. The number of the parts of the torn Gods cannot but draw our attention to the symbolism of the numbers 3–7–14, which obviously relates to the theogony and cosmogony connected with these Gods. Here, however, is not the place to make any arithmetical or semantic analysis of these numbers, but we cannot overlook the fact that only the phallus of Osiris was not found, and therefore Isis had to conceive by means of magic. This fragment of the legend carries emblematic symbolism and marks the idea of the insemination of matter by the Spirit. No less emblematic is also the preservation of the heart of the ripped Zagreus by Minerva (Athens). Although no bridge can be cast in time between the two myths, it is possible to see their ideological connection, namely, the indivisibility and immortality of the Divine Monad, in this case symbolized by the heart that makes the connection with it. That is why spiritual traditions speak of "knowledge of the heart". In Freemasonry, this is illustrated by the socalled "loss of illusion in the middle room", leading to the transference of the centre of knowledge from the brain to the heart. This brings about direct communication with the Source of Light, an echo of the "Lost Word".

## The Vedic Tradition

> *Tradition does not mean*
> *that the living are dead*
> *but that the dead are alive.*
> **Gilbert Keith Chesterton**[25]

In the Vedic tradition, the Sun is always in the centre of the Universe, whereas every state of being – around the circumference. At any point on the circumference, the Axis of the World goes out as both a radius of the circle and a beam of the Sun. There is also a Sun's ray, the extension of which is not susceptible to any geometric image. This is the *"Seventh Ray"* that crosses the Sun to penetrate into the Worlds above the Sun that are considered as an area of Immortality. Its extension beyond the bounds of the Sun cannot be presented in any way, which adds to it an arcane character. The transition beyond into the "Other Side of the Sun" which is the *"Last Death"*, as well as a transition to Immortality, is possible only on a purely spiritual plane. By means of this "Seventh Ray", the heart of each individual being is connected directly with the Sun. It is through it, namely, that this relationship is established as permanent and immutable. To the one facing the centre of one's own being, this "Seventh Ray" coincides with the Axis of the World. Precisely about such beings, it is said that "to them, the Sun rises in the Zenith and sets in the Nadir". It can also be said that this "Seventh Ray" is the only true fixed axis for anyone who identifies with it. The "Seventh Ray" is the Path through which the whole Creation, passing through the cycle of manifestation, returns to the Non-Manifested, and unites with the Primordial, from where it, nevertheless, even in its very manifestation, has never separated itself except in illusionary ways.

The heart, as a symbol of the immortal Soul and of life, is embedded in the mission of some women opposite to the Bacchantes – the *Vestals*. Vesta (analogous to the Greek goddess Hestia) was the ancient Roman goddess of the fire-hearth, the fire of which is the heart of each home – the central point, symbol of the life-giving aspect of the goddess. This fire ought to never be extinguished and is always a source of inspiration and renewal. In Kabala, this *Fire* is *Shekinah*, the eternal feminine presence of God; *Shakti* or *Kundalini* for the Indians; and *Hestia* for the Hellenes. In Ancient Rome, the priestesses of Vesta, the Vestal Virgins, not only maintained actual fire, which was the symbolic centre of the Roman Empire, but also the inner Fire, which is the vital Spirit (Breath). The Vestals were the ones that reflected the Light of the Sacred.

---

25  An English writer, poet, dramatist, philosopher, and literary critic (1874 – 1936) – *AN*.

The heart, as something inner and deep, can be associated with Persephone, who, according to the Orphic version of the legend, is the Queen of the Underworld and mother of Dionysus. The name *Persephone* means "the One to be afraid of". Before that, however, she was *Kore,* the virgin daughter of *Demeter* (the Roman *Ceres*). In the Eleusinian Mysteries, Dionysus is described as the miraculous child of Demeter. The Divine Child descends into the Underworld, but then he is sacrificed (ripped apart by the Maenads) to grow again as an intoxicating vine. Dionysus is the god of religious ecstasy. He rises from the dead, personified as wine, which is an indication of resurrection through ecstasy. Christ is also God's Child, being a God, Twice-Born and sacrificed on the cross, Who also descends into the Underworld to save the souls kept locked up there. The successful descending into the Underworld, which can be seen in the mythological images of *Inanna, Ishtar, Kore-Persephone,* is inherent to the feminine archetype. The process of Initiation through pain, anguish, darkness, death, and resurrection is definitely embedded in the feminine Mystery traditions, and is clearly part of the chthonic path of "Snake Wisdom". It becomes clear also from mythology that this path is not very suitable for the masculine core essence of humans. We know that missions in the Underworld of such demigods and heroes as Orpheus and Theseus have finished unsuccessfully. Only Dionysus descended into the Underworld and saved his mother, but he was said to be "raised by women and as a woman". Hermes was able to freely descend and go out of the domains of Hades, and yet, he is attributed some androgynous qualities. Christ is claimed to have successfully accomplished His mission in Hell; however, His Initiation Path is also the feminine one – that of the "Snake Wisdom". It is no coincidence that the words *mashiach* ("saviour") and *nahash* ("snake") have one and the same Gematria. Therefore, the chthonic Initiation (on the microcosmic plane – the descent into the sub-consciousness), even though done by men, is a typically feminine path under the authority of the egregor of the Goddess. Orpheus descended into the kingdom of Hades to save Eurydice, but failed, and then ignored all other women, so therefore they ripped him apart. Thus, according to some authors, Orpheus established homosexuality among the Thracians. On the profane plane, things may seem so – however, on the esoteric plane, they are established otherwise. *Orpheus* means „One who heals through Light", deriving from the Phoenician words *aur* ("light") and *rophae* ("healing"). Naturally, in view of the legend, this Light is transmitted through the sounds of the harp through vibration. Since it is mostly a matter of healing on the subtle levels, therefore the legend is an indication that Orpheus (the equilibrated astral light named *"or"*) has to descend and lead the soul (Eurydice) out of the darkness of materiality; however, in order to succeed *("eureka"),* he should not be split into two (the syllable *"di")* and be dependent on her. In the legend, this is indicated by the prohibition given to Orpheus: he was not supposed to turn back and face Eurydice if he wanted to succeed. According to the esoteric interpretation of this legend, Orpheus gets split between the feminine and the masculine path of Initiation, between the Mysteries of Dionysus and those of Apollo. Initially, he turns to the Feminine Mysteries (he does not observe the prohibition), but after the failure, he obviously chooses the Masculine Path, symbolically shown by the lost interest towards women. After all, was Ramsay, in his statement, willing to say that Freemasonry had made its choice just the way Orpheus did? It is unlikely so – because, otherwise, the fate of Orpheus awaits it, as well as of everyone who ignores the feminine principle.

We do not intend to discuss further the question about the Mysteries envisioned by Ramsay in the context of Freemasonry; however, we cannot but point out that, in his *Oration,* he mentions nothing of the Judaic esoteric tradition, having in mind that he says that Masonry can be traced back as far as Abraham.

## In a Kabalistic Key

Since Judaism is the cradle of Western European civilization, whereas Kabala – of Western esoteric science, including Freemasonry, we shall direct our glance towards them again.

*Jehovah,* or *Yahveh,* the Hebrew patriarchal God, is a lunar God with a feminine core essence; and, in the Tree of Life, it is God's Name of the Sefira *Bina,* which is at the top of the "feminine" pillar and is called the "Dark Sterile Mother". The Sefira *Malkut* (The Kingdom) is the "Bright Fertile Mother". *(See Fig. 14 on page 154.)* This corresponds to the dual essence of the Egyptian lunar Goddess Isis (positive aspect) and her negative aspect Nephthys, respectively Aphrodite and Ceres in Ancient Greek symbolism. God reveals Himself to Moses through the burning blackberry bush. In the Hebrew tradition, the latter symbolizes *Asherah* – the Heavenly Queen. The cult to Asherah was introduced by the great king and magus Solomon, known still in Ancient Hellas as the cult to *Astarte.* The roots of this cult are in Canaan (the Promised Land of Abraham), where they honoured *Ashureth (Ashtoreth),* analogous to *Ishtar* – the chief goddess of Babylon, called *Inanna* in Sumer. The inner sanctuary of Solomon's Temple *(The Holy of Holies)* was considered to be the womb of Ashureth and was situated facing the west, where the Sun sets, because, in this sanctuary, a lunar religion was being professed. Therefore, the wording stating that the Masonic Temple is a copy of Solomon's Temple cannot be considered accurate. Its true positioning is along the axis *east* (entrance) – *west* (altar), unlike that of the modern Masonic temples, which is along the axis *west* (entrance) – *east* (altar). Nevertheless, we will dwell on this in more detail when we examine the "Masonic Regularity of the Temple".

In the sexual imagery pervading Solomon's visions in the *Song of Songs*, the relationship between God and His people can be recognized as a relationship of love. The people of Israel are the "bride", and God is the "beloved" who allows to be found. Christianity has inherited this interpretation but has replaced the Hebrew people with the Church. The esoteric meaning, however, is the relationship between our Soul, having a feminine core essence, and God. In Kabala, the Holy Spirit also has a feminine essence, while Shekinah is God's deputy on the material plane. Sufis, the mystics of Islam, used to address the strictly patriarchal Muslim God with "Loved Lady", "Beloved Lady". These examples show that the feminine core essence of God cannot in any way be erased from the consciousness, and has always been present even in the most patriarchal religions. The biblical Elohim, creating the visible world, is actually a Divine Syzygy.

## Women in Freemasonry

*Cherchez la femme!*

In Freemasonry, containing in itself the rituality and part of the mythology of the Initiatic Mysteries, the feminine component should occupy an important place, including through women's physical presence as well. Then how and why was the feminine core essence, at one point, ignored by such an ancient Initiatic esoteric society, which Freemasonry is?

In the London newspaper *The Post Boy,* we find an explicit answer to the question tormenting us:

*Q.: What's the Reason Women are not admitted into your Society?*
A.: Because they can't keep a Secret.

It is so simply, clearly and precisely defined, and yet, we are still looking for the answer in some deep esoteric waters. Regarding the keeping of secrets, Freemason Benjamin Franklin[26] has a slightly different understanding: "Three can keep a secret, if two of them are dead." We wonder: Is this <u>conclusion not</u> actually the result of experience gained in the Brotherhood?

26 A Freemason, politician, publisher, diplomat, one of the "Founding Fathers of the United States", depicted on the $ 100 banknote. It is interesting to note that he and Alexander Hamilton, who is on the $ 10 banknote, were the only ones who were not US presidents – *AN.*

If, nevertheless, there are any Freemasons who believe that the reasons are those mentioned by Ramsay and Wirth, and, even more, that they are justified, then the masculine Freemasonry in the Age of Aquarius is doomed. It is interesting to note that even in the "male and gloomy" Middle Ages, women were not ignored but were admitted to various craft guilds. Many literary sources describe the participation of women in the construction process of cathedrals, which means they were part of Masonic Lodges. Following the historical development of women's participation in Freemasonry, the emergence at the end of the 17$^{th}$ and early 18$^{th}$ century should be mentioned of the so-called *Lodges of Adoption*, which represent themselves feminine Masonic Lodges deriving from a certain masculine Lodge. Modern mixed Freemasonry *(Co-Freemasonry)* arises in the middle of the 18$^{th}$ century and spreads rapidly throughout Europe. In the 20$^{th}$ century, a large number of Co-Masonic Lodges begin to be founded in the United States. In Bulgaria on June 13$^{th}$, 1926, the first Co-Masonic Lodge named *Bogomil* is founded in Sofia but does not last long. After 1934, mixed Lodges are set up, which, together with the masculine ones, exist until 1942, when they are dissolved under the National Defense Law. After 1991, the revival of Freemasonry in Bulgaria begins, including Co-Masonry; and in 2009, the first entirely feminine Lodge is established.

## The Prohibition

*The world would be imperfect
without the presence of woman.*

**Thomas Aquinas**

The explicit prohibition of the admission of women into Freemasonry is indicated in Anderson's Constitution of 1723, which states that "the Persons admitted Members of a Lodge must be... no Bondmen, no Women..."

We do not venture to comment whether this is the first written rule, as we can hardly study all the facts and knowledge on the subject. It is an unquestionable fact, however, that, since 1717 (which is the time when Modern Orthodox Freemasonry is considered to date back to), the basic law of Orthodox Freemasonry being the so-called *Anderson's Constitution,* by virtue of the latter, it is entirely masculine. From what has been reviewed so far, it cannot be concluded explicitly that this circumstance is a result of a steady and strict (i.e. Orthodox) following of the Masonic tradition. Rather, it can be said that it is the result of the particularities of the conservative English society of that time, and, above all, of the fact that James Anderson was a Scottish pastor, so his understanding of a religious community followed the model of the Church, which did not allow women as its ministers.

According to Robert Ambelain[27], Anderson has never received any ritual initiation, has never been a regularly elected Worshipful Master of a Lodge, and therefore, he initiated profanes out of the rule. He was just Chaplain in the Lodge, performing only the rites related to church ceremonies. His main transgression, according to Ambelain, however, was that he distorted the ancient rules of Operative Masonry. If this is so, then we are questioning ourselves: According to what logic, someone who was not initiated into Freemasonry has written its Constitution?

In *York Manuscript No.4* dated 1693, belonging to the *Grand Lodge of York*, it is narrated how, when an apprentice is being admitted, "The one of the elders takeing the Booke / and that *hee* or *shee* that is to be made Mason / shall lay their hands thereon / and the charge shall bee given".

Here is what Neville Cryer has written in *Masonic Times* – New York, in May, 1995, regarding the above quote: "Now I have to tell you that my predecessors in Masonic Research in England have all tried to pretend that the *"shee"* is merely a misprint for *"they"*. I now am the Chairman of the Heritage Committee of York. I know these documents; I've examined them, and I'm telling you, they say *"she"*, without any question."

In view of this explicit and unambiguous statement, we cannot fail to accept this manuscript as authentic and credible – and it represents certain evidence that the landmark of Anderson's Constitution of admitting only men is actually not in the tradition of Freemasonry. Another confirmation of this is the first documented case of a woman, regularly initiated into Freemasonry, called *The Lady Freemason*. On her memorial tablet in the town of Cork, Ireland, it is written:

"The Honourable
ELIZABETH ALDWORTH...
Initiated into Masonry in
Lodge No. 44, at Doneraile Court
In this County, A.D. 1712"

In the archive records of the *Corpus Christi Guild* of 1408, it is noted that an apprentice had to swear to obey "the Master, or Dame, or any other Freemason." Here, not the Master's wife is meant, as it is confirmed by another record of 1683 of *Mary's Chapel Lodge* in Edinburgh, in which a woman is

---

27  Robert Ambelain – a French esoterist and occultist, writer, historian, author of more than 40 works; Great Master of the *Grand Lodge of France of the Ancient and Primitive Rite of Memphis-Misraïm – AN*.

noted occupying the position of *Dame* or *Mistress* in the Masonic sense. She was the widow of a Freemason but she had equal rights with the other Operative Masons, and she was involved in the same ceremonies.

In conclusion, we will give some examples of women Freemasons before Anderson's Constitution.

In 1663, the widow *Margaret Wild* was a member of the *London Company of Masons* – a position she inherited from her late husband.

*The Masons' Court Book* records the names of two widows in 1696, who were admitted members of the *London Company of Masons*.

In 1713–1714, *Mary Bannister,* daughter of a barber from *Barking,* was apprenticed to a Mason for a term of 7 years, with the fee of 5 shillings duly paid to the *London Company of Masons.*

The following question arises: Is ignoring women from Freemasonry a deviation from the archetype essence of Freemasonry, or is it part of the providential design of the Great Architect of the Universe? We hope that it has already become clear that the Brotherhood is not entirely in the tradition and orthodoxy. Can this then be the result of the plan of the Great Architect of the Universe, Who is a hypostasis of the Hebrew *El Shadai Hai,* the Lord of *Yesod,* the Moon's Sefira, which is naturally a feminine archetype? *(See Fig. 14 on p. 154.)* We believe that the answer is negative, because only humans are given the sacred right to choose whether to move away or closer to the Primordial Light. The choice is up to the Brotherhood whether to be an Initiatic society in the authentic Masonic tradition, or a chain of men's clubs pretending to be part of the élite.

## The Goal

*Maybe the target nowadays is not to discover what we are but to refuse what we are. We have to imagine and to build up what we could become.*

**Michel Foucault**[28]

We cannot say for sure whether the current choice of masculine Masonry is determined by the Great Architect of the Universe; however, we do know that His Providence is that the human once again becomes the Primordial Adam Kadmon – the archetype of the complete human being, whose core es-

---

28  A French philosopher, sociologist, and historian (1926–1984) – *AN.*

sence is androgynous. For this purpose, whether or not the existence of an entirely masculine Freemasonry is within the plan of the Great Architect of the Universe, the Masonic Brothers have to develop inside themselves the feminine principle and core essence. A Master is that Initiate who combines and has equally mastered both one's masculine and feminine core essence, along with their inherent qualities and skills. If we presume that in the Brotherhood all are men (with already accomplished masculine core essence), then how can the feminine principle be developed in an entirely masculine society? We will give an example with a *battery* in which the plus and the minus are in one body, not in separate ones, so we cannot say that one of the two poles is more significant than the other. If there are both men and women in a Lodge, which is a large astral battery, then the *minus* will be the women, whereas the *plus* will be the men. The need for masculine and feminine energy is satisfied by bodily polarized humans who, as they strive to be the one pole or the other, will differentiate and develop themselves more and more unilaterally. As we have learned, Wirth and Ramsay consider this to be the right algorithm – namely, that women keep developing femininity in themselves, while men keep developing their masculinity. In this way, however, they will not achieve likeness to the androgynous qualities of God. That is why, when only men comprise a Lodge, they have to establish the *minus* pole within themselves, which means developing the feminine principle, their own feminine core essence, the feminine energies, and that is the way for them to become complete and consubstantial with the Great Architect of the Universe. Naturally, things will not happen by themselves simply because there is a Brotherhood. In the first place, Brothers ought to have the knowledge about all of this, accept this knowledge, making it part of themselves. Then, aspiration and willpower to accomplish it are necessary, by gaining insight into the Rites and by making sense of them in this key. It is no coincidence that the symbols of the Sun and the Moon are present in the east of the temple.

The modern world is still a masculine world, situated entirely on the surface of consciousness, having forgotten and suppressed its sub-consciousness, whereas the ancient world was mainly feminine and subconscious. When the two worlds unite and lead to the equal functioning of the opposites, the super-consciousness is formed. This is the goal of Initiates: to synchronize the function of the left and the right hemisphere of the brain, thus succeeding in developing and mastering intuition and logic to one and the same extent.

## The Force

*If you wish to possess and master the force,
then do not let the force possess you!*

*Éliphas Lévi*

Perhaps, as an authoritative illustration of the meaning of what has been said so far, there is still another image of a woman in the Gospel, namely that of Salome and her mother Herodias. Salome's dance of the *seven veils* was the reason why King Herod promised her with an oath, in the presence of the guests at his birthday feast, to give her whatsoever she would desire. As it is known, Salome asked for the head of John the Baptist on a platter[29]. It was, however, the wish of her mother, Herodias, who obviously knew the tantric secret rediscovered by present-day psychiatrists, that the sexually excited ones are hyper-suggestible. Besides, she had obviously mastered one of the most powerful weapons – the astral magnetism. Through the dance of temptation, she uses her daughter's body as a conductor of this magnetism in order to accomplish her intention. Hence, it becomes clear that Herodias and Salome are hypostases of the astral force. Herodias symbolizes its *"Od"* nature, whereas Salome is a symbol of its magical impact – *"Ob"*.[30] The head of John the Precursor is cut off as a consequence of their sexual magic. This is how the karmic knot is undone between Elijah the Prophet and the wife of King Ahab – Jezebel, as the already reborn John and Herodias. They are symbols of the enlightened mind and the instinctive soul, each wishing to win over the conceptual mind (Herod), who is the king of the illusive human order. The chthonic, magical, negative, astral force possessing feminine characteristics is rejected by John, but he is therefore destroyed by it. Herod is enchanted by Salome's astral fluids and falls under her power. On a deeper esoteric plane, Salome's dance of the seven veils symbolizes the *seven chakras*, activated by the awakened *Kundalini* force, rising from the "magician's hat" (*Conus medullaris*).

In this case, however, it is governed by the coagulating negative astral force, and therefore it acts in an involuntary way upon the lower, animal levels in the human being, and especially upon the sexual centre. Thus, through the animal magnetism, the sexual energy is activated through which the mind (Herod) can be manipulated, especially if intoxicated by the wine. John's fate is an illustration of what happens when this energy is being resisted. An

---
29  It is no coincidence that this symbol is embedded in the traditions of the Templars and the Rosicrucians, while in Freemasonry, a reference to the severed head of John is the sign of the apprentice – *AN*.
30  *Od* – the positive astral pole; *Ob* – the negative astral pole – *AN*.

example of how we should treat this force is given to us by Jesus Christ, who draws to Himself Mary Magdalene, called by the profane a "sinner", in order to transform her and incorporate her into the Deed. In the New Testament, she is described as a harlot with her freely falling red hair, which is clearly a reference to *Kundalini*. As for the word *harlot*, it is one of the meanings of the Hebrew word *qlifa*, and its literal translation is *a shell*. If we analyze these concepts in their interconnection, it can be concluded that they are an indication towards a force that, if not mastered, becomes destructive. Herod obeys this force; John, Orpheus, and all the gods who were ripped apart act with resistance against it, so it destroys them. Christ attracts it, transforms it and structures it, giving it an evolutionary direction, and it becomes a faithful helper to Him. We witness three different approaches and methods regarding one and the same essence that lead to different outcomes.

The Force is one – it is neither good nor bad. However, the Force has a feminine nature, so what is important is the attitude towards it, and also how it will be utilized and for what purpose. If we are despotic, it will obey us, but it will hate us and will use every weakness that we have in order to hurt us exactly where we are vulnerable. We ought to always be hard, heartless, uncompromising and always alert in order to master it in this manner. However, if we treat this force as we treat a beloved woman, it will love us, be faithful to us, and fulfil every will of ours just like a diligent wife. Get to know the Force and make it your beloved woman! It depends on you whether it will hate or love you, whether it will use every opportunity to cheat on you, or will obey you as one obeys a beloved master who is the undisputed favourite and authority. First of all, though, one should observe the maxim formulated by Éliphas Lévi: "If you wish to possess and master a certain force, you must never let this force possess you!"

Therefore, the Masonic Brothers have to unite with the Force into a Sacred Marriage Union, to master and guide it with Wisdom, and then it will be their faithful and beloved wife forever. Only in this way, together with the Force, the authenticity and orthodoxy of the Masonic Initiatic tradition will be restored, and the Brotherhood will be reunited with its archetype!

By ignoring women, Modern Freemasonry moves away from its authentic tradition, especially since the two Grand Lodges of England decided to introduce also a third Degree: *Master Mason;* for *"raising"* to this Degree, it is necessary to meet certain formal criteria. Thus, a Master turns out to be a functional position, not an Initiatic Degree. In this way, he becomes first among equals, and many "central points in the circle" appear, in the person of the other Masters, so the archetypal characteristic of the form is lost, hence its original inner sense – the *Sacred Initiation*.

# IV
# CATECHUMEN

## 3
## The Sacred Initiation

*Si sapis, sis apis*[31]

The other fundamental characteristic of Freemasonry, after its archetypal nature, is that it is an Initiatic society. The Initiatic institution, as a whole, is of "superhuman" origin because Sacred Initiation is given from Above, from the Sublime Spiritual Hierarchical Planes, after vast esoteric experience and knowledge have been accumulated through which profound changes in the soul and body have occurred. Sacred Initiation represents identification with the order of the Universe and the Truth. That is why, in the "Ancient" Masonry, Initiation was carried out by the Master, who was, however, the equivalent of a Teacher – a Spiritual Master Teacher. At that time there still did not exist the functional Degree of the Master but only that of the apprentice and the fellow craft (journeyman). The Master in the Lodge was only one, so only he could give Initiation into the various Degrees, which made him unique. Unfortunately, this tradition, as Guénon also says, has been lost in Modern Freemasonry, and now the Sacred Initiation has turned into an "official", "formal" initiation, culminating in the Master's Degree, which is the last one. Jean Palou, however, has a different opinion on that. In his book, *La Franc-Maçonnerie (Freemasonry)*, he writes: "We should in no case consider the Worshipful Master of the Lodge, even in the best period of Operative Masonry, and even more so nowadays, to be a *Teacher* in the meaning of a *Guru* or *Sheikh*, i.e. of a *Spiritual Guide*. Freemasonry does not give its members any personal Spiritual Guide, because the Initiatic deeds are based on the collective work of all the Brothers forming the Lodge." In this sense and context, Palou explains that, "... the hewing of the rough stone is actually done by the individual, who is yet connected with and integrated into the aggregate community of Initiates. The Masonic work towards spiritual fulfilment can only be a collective deed."

We will take the liberty not to agree with this statement, so explicit by nature. Mostly in Operative Masonry, which we have named the *"Ancient"* Masonry, a Master is required to pass on his experience and knowledge to the fellow craft, for otherwise the latter cannot obtain them. In this narrow sense, there is no way that a Master does not represent himself a teacher, and even more so – a personal one. Since Palou speaks also of "Initiatic deeds", and of

---

31  From Latin: "If you are wise, then be a bee!" – *AN*.

"spiritual fulfilment", it means that he considers Freemasonry to be a spiritual Initiatic society, so his standpoint is also in view of these characteristics. That is exactly why, with even greater power, a Master represents himself a Spiritual Teacher and Guide – as he manages the physical process of construction, the same way he generates and observes also the spiritual process of *Building the Edifice,* taking care of it. To explain this conviction of ours, we should clarify the inner sense and significance of Initiation. It consists of two parts: initiation given by an Initiate (*formal* initiation) and Sacred Initiation *from Above* – from the Sublime Spiritual Planes. The Sacred Initiation does not always coincide with the formal initiation, and there is no mandatory sequence. The Sacred Initiation is analogous to the Fire Baptism carried out by Spiritual Beings, unlike the Water Baptism which is a human act and corresponds to the formal initiation. The Sacred Initiation also has Degrees, leading to Perfection. Perfection itself represents Harmony, whereas Harmony is Truth because everything harmonious is real, for God's Providence shines through it. You need Wisdom in order to find God's Providential Design in everything. This Wisdom, however, has to be integrated through action that represents the moral and ethical aspect of expanded consciousness. From this expansion, as a kind of psychological process, an energy process begins. This energy expansion allows our vibrations to coincide, at a certain moment, with those of the Sublime Spiritual Planes. That is how our union and identification with the true, Divine nature of matters begins. An emanation of this expansion is the propagation through the co-creation of the fruit. Whenever we give off some "fruit", we expand upon those who "eat" this "fruit". This is one of the implementation aspects of Sacred Initiation: the principle of the fruit – of the good fruit.

Many authors, writing about *Initiation,* actually mean *Sacred Initiation.* Similarly, when speaking of the Soul, the Spirit is also included in most cases. Literature abounds in terms like *Initiation* and *Initiates,* but usually there is no clear distinction between the various contexts of these terms. Naturally, we do not mean any *avidya* but rather some principle distinction. The Sacred Initiation always has a *"Heavenly"* origin, no matter whether it will take place directly or through an intermediary. The Sacred Initiation is a sign that you are accepted by a certain level of the Divine Hierarchy, and it is never "performed": it simply happens. Whenever a given person, in his or her evolution, reaches a certain physical, psychological, and spiritual level of development, they may receive a Sacred Initiation. The Master, already having undergone the same experience, is a witness to this Initiation. He has assisted by guiding the disciple along the path of spiritual transformation; and yet, the very act of Sacred Initiation takes place independently of him. What does the initiation performed by the Master represent by itself, and what is its role? This question cannot be answered unambiguously. In any case, this is an *external ritual* having a deep spiritual meaning and content. We believe that it may *precede, coincide with,* or *follow* the very Sacred Initiation. The Sacred Initiation is a state of Spirit, not a ritual – unlike the formal initiation. The Sacred Initiation is a fruit: it is the factual manifestation of the personality in the environment.

The Sacred Initiation may have happened already, and then, the outer initiation is simply a formal act celebrating this event with a proper solemn ceremony containing information about the Sacred Initiation itself. Can the formal initiation precede the Sacred Initiation, and what is its inner meaning? We believe that such an initiation is a kind of *"intercession"* done by the Master, with the purpose to promote a Sacred Initiation. If a hierarchical transformation occurs in the initiated one on all three planes, then the Sacred Initiation has taken place during the formal one. This, however, can happen also after a certain number of days, usually twelve, which means that the "intercession" has been accepted. In case that nothing happens, it means that you are not approved by the Heavenly Hierarchy, that your offering is not accepted because the formal initiation represents a sacrificial offering, while the Sacred Initiation represents accepting the sacrifice offered. Therefore, the terms *formal initiation* and *Sacred Initiation* exist separately.

**Figure 3**

## The Formal Initiation

*Initiation is a sacred birth.*
**Apuleius**

What does the formal initiation represent, nevertheless, what is its core essence, and can there be a subsequent initiation if there is no Sacred Initiation?

In order to answer these questions, we must first clarify the role of the person performing the formal initiation. For this purpose, we will refer to the New Testament, which contains a description of a scene of a mass official initiation carried out by John, who baptized with water everyone who wished for it. This ritual was still unknown to the Jews; it is a reminiscence of the secret esoteric schools of Ancient Egypt in which the Pharaohs were subjected to ritual baptism as a symbol of the royal renewal corresponding to the daily immersion of the Sun into the sea. Many people belonging to various classes of society are described receiving baptism from John, which was a form of initiation. Does it mean that everyone received a Sacred Initiation? Not likely. However, this is certainly what Jesus of Nazareth received. If we accept the doctrine of the Church stating that Jesus Christ is the only Son of God conceived by the Holy Spirit, the following question arises: Why was it necessary for Jesus to undergo formal initiation? This was clearly needed as an act of testimony by an Initiate, a Master Teacher, that this was the Son of God – the Messiah. The opposite would mean that John the Baptist had to be more perfect than the Son of God, for it is written: "And without doubt, the lesser is blessed by the greater." (*Epistle of St. Apostle Paul to the Hebrews* 7:7, *NIV*). Among the *Mandaeans*[32], John the Baptist was known as the Supreme King of Light, defender of good against evil.

However, observed from an esoteric point of view, this event gives us information that John, as an Initiate and Master Teacher, initiated Jesus, who, during the formal initiation, received a Sacred Initiation from the highest hierarchical level and was transformed into God's Son – a certain Degree of Initiation. The expression *Son of God* was used regarding the adopted Son of God – the *Bar Alaha*[33], and not regarding the only such Son. Jesus is an example of how each human could consciously accomplish oneself as the "adopted child" of the Transcendent Logos. Being *Alaha's child,* in the way Jesus mentions it in the Seventh Beatitude (*Holy Gospel of Matthew* 5:9, *KJV*), literally means to be a "Peacemaker" – a Builder of Worlds. The exact Aramaic correspondence of "they shall be called the children of God" is "they will be the bond with the Oneness". Therefore, everyone who has received a Sacred Initiation, like Jesus, is a Son of God, but this must be testified by an irrefutable authority before it becomes an obvious fact.

In any case, in relation to Jesus, John represents this authority: an Initiate, a Teacher who registers and confirms this event. If we assume that he was the transmitter of God's Grace for Jesus, then he did so with the help of the "shadow and petrified neck"[34], because the focus of the event is on Jesus, not on himself.

---

32  Followers of John the Baptist, with a certain tribe in their basic core known as *Mandaeans,* inhabiting present-day Iran and Iraq, whose roots were in Egypt, where they were called *Sabaeans,* according to the *Quran.* The Mandaeans despised Jesus and called him "the false Messiah", "the distorter of all cults" – *AN.*
33  From Aramaic: "Son of God" – *AN.*
34  This is a parable narrating how a saint was endowed by the Gods with the gift of healing. In order not to become too proud of himself, he asked them to make him able to heal by means of his shadow, and also to petrify his neck so that he does not turn back – *AN.*

The formal initiation is a testimony witnessing that we have removed a certain part of the masks of personality, because Truth and falseness cannot live under the same roof. Liberation from these masks leads to illumination and awareness of the present personality – our true face. Identifying the personality with the true "I" represents the main testimony of the formal initiation. Their separateness has led to the Fall of humans and their possibility of becoming the Devil, forging from their freedom the chains that have transformed them into *"fallen angels"*. Ever since ancient times, fire has been the symbol of Sacred Initiation. John the Baptist knew that he was performing a formal initiation, not a Sacred one, for he says, "I indeed baptize you with water unto repentance; but He Who is coming after me… will baptize you with the Holy Spirit and Fire." (*Matthew* 3:11, *NKJV*) The formal initiation is intended for the astral body, and it washes the soul, waters it, and gives life-creating impetus to its inner forces. Fire burns everything that differs from the Truth, and therefore the Initiator turns into a pure transmitter of the Divine Fire, which burns to ashes the old personality of the one undergoing the initiation, in order for the new personality to be born, which is consubstantial with the true "I".

As is well known, John is the patron of Blue Masonry, which means that his essence is connected with the formal initiation leading to the Sacred Initiation – and therefore, it is called *Blue,* because John used to baptize with water, which is generally depicted in blue. It is no coincidence that the Grand Masonic Lodge of England was founded on the feast day of John the Baptist – June 24th, 1717. It is no coincidence as well that the sign of the apprentice symbolizes the severed head of the Baptist, and the Templars are said to have bowed before this head. Some believe that the decapitation of John was a ritual murder in order to preserve and use his head possessing *magic power.* As a confirmation of this, we will point out the following Templar saying: "Whoever owns the head of John the Baptist rules the world." When Jesus became known as a healer and miracle worker, King Herod exclaimed, scared: "This is John the Baptist; he is risen from the dead, and therefore these powers are at work in him" (*Holy Gospel of Matthew* 14:2, *NJKV*). If any Christian reader is troubled by word *magic,* anathematized by the Church, we will point out that the resurrection of Lazarus by Jesus was considered by Judaists to be some sort of *trading with demons.* After this event, they united around the idea of the elimination of Jesus.

When initiating a personality who has reached a high degree of conductivity regarding the Heavenly Fire, the formal initiation may coincide with the Sacred Initiation, as it happened with Jesus. We believe that such cases are very rare. If the Sacred Initiation takes place before the formal one, then the latter only confirms this fact; whereas, if it happens after the formal initiation, then this formal initiation is a proposition for entering the Divine. In the latter case, the Sacred Initiation may not take place, and then you remain only a "nominated" one. This, however, is not anything minor at all, because, if some analogy with cinema is applied, then the Oscar nominees are the best of the rest. It means that the one who is subject to formal initiation has stepped on the Path or has already walked a certain distance along it. Thus, one initiation follows another, in order to reach, at some moment, the Sacred Initiation, being transformed from a "summoned one" into a "chosen one". However, one ought to know and observe the old Initiatic rule: "Before the Initiation, you chop wood and carry water; after the Initiation – you carry water and chop wood", which can be deciphered also in the Alchemical phrase *Labore et constantia*[35].

Following this line of thoughts, we will state that Jesus also performed formal initiations, not Sacred ones. By analyzing the Holy Gospels, we find out that Jesus has bequeathed to us several types of Initiation: *Peter's Initiation* – by laying a hand upon the person's head; *John's Initiation,* ignoring the ties of blood – *"Woman, behold your son!",* says Jesus on the cross to His mother, pointing at John (*John 19:26, NKJV*); *Paul's Initiation* – by getting blind and a subsequent burst of one's spiritual ability to see; *Lazarus's Initiation,* representing itself a symbolic death and a new birth, which is practiced also in the Third Degree Rite of Freemasonry.

The Fifth Arcanum of Sacred Magic (we will dwell on the Arcana and the Arcanum Knowledge later on) is the Arcanum of Sacred Initiation. This is what the initiating hand of the Hierophant testifies as a sign of the Sacred Initiation. The five fingers of the hand are symbolized by the pentagram, which represents itself the emblem of the personality undergone a Sacred Initiation. The pentagram is an illustration of the *human being*[36] in principle, therefore in Kabala it is a sign of the Microcosm and is called *Microprosopos,* or *The Small Face,* or also *The Lesser Countenance.* In the above context, however, it is a symbol of the wholeness and unity of the human who has become an Initiate. The human personality is longing for a Sacred Initiation, since the aspiration towards wholeness is laid down inside it – and this is the longing for returning into its Primordial Core Essence, which is symbolically contained in the expression *"returning home".*

There are two basic types of pentagrams: the upright one and the reverse one, as well as two subtypes: the left-sided one and the right-sided one (ac-

---

35  From Latin: "Through labour and constancy" – *AN.*
36  The number 5 in Sacred Mathematics is considered to be the number of the human being – *AN.*

cording to the direction of their way of drawing). The upright one is with its apex upwards, and is the symbol of the human being having received the Sacred Initiation. The reverse one is with its apex pointing downwards, depicted with a goat's head, and is the antithesis of the perfect human. It is the sign of the beast inside humans because the reverse human is actually the Devil. Thus, the two pentagrams can be called *Christ's Pentagram* and *Pentagram of the Antichrist,* the main characteristic of the latter being the affirmation of the subjective will of the ego at all costs. In this sense, we can say that the ego is the Devil within the human being. The upright pentagram with the hieroglyph of fire *Shin* at the apex is called the *Pentagram of Fire* and symbolizes the *Mashiach* – the *Saviour.* Or, if the hieroglyphs of the Holy Tetragrammaton are placed at the other four rays, the name of Jesus is formed – *Yeshua* (יהשוה, *Yod-He-Shin-Vav-He*). That is why this pentagram is also the sign of the Incarnate Word. The Sacred Initiation comes with a great sacrifice, and therefore the most fundamental trial of the one who has embarked on the Path is to humble one's ego when facing the Truth. The sacred pentagram is a receptacle of magic power, a symbol of the illuminated mind, of the manifested willpower and implementation power of authority. That is why those walking along the Path, at a certain point, have to produce for themselves a positive, active pentagram to serve them as a guiding star, the analogue of which in Freemasonry is the Blazing Star.

According to Egyptian esoterism (which is embedded in the basis of Hermetism, Occultism and all subsequent Western esoteric teachings, including Freemasonry), the Sacred Initiation unlocks a series of transformations in the psyche that awaken the latent spiritual powers in humans. In the tradition of the Egyptian Mysteries, the very process of this transformation is called *Kheprer,* and through it, one invokes the powers of *Khepri,* the god of reincarnations, symbolized by the Holy Scarab. As a result of these metamorphoses, the bond between *(k)hat* – the physical body, *(k)haibit*[37] – the etheric body, and *ka* – the astral body, is softened, allowing the subtle bodies to be separated more easily. This is how the new personality is born, symbolized by the *Benu* bird, whose name derives from the root *Ben. Ben-Ben* is how the pyramidal summit stone is called, and it means *to give birth, to regenerate, to fertilize,* being associ-

---

37 *(K)haibit* – the person's shadow, able to separate itself from the body and travel at will, although it must stay close to its own *Ba*, with which it is closely connected. The *Khaibit* can take part in funeral and ceremonial offerings together with the *Ka* and *Ba*. The shadow of the soul is considered as a spiritual core essence, liberating itself from the bodily limitations after death, but this can also take place during one's life by means of spiritual techniques – *AN*.

ated with *Sah*[38] – the *Body of Glory,* analogous to *Keter* in Kabala. In this way, the Initiate unlocks all spiritual powers and becomes consubstantial with God. Thus, the Sacred Initiation leads to the acquisition of the "Osiris-Consciousness", to the transubstantiation of the form, and to the connection with the Spiritual Principles, the *Neters* – the *Generators of Life*.

This, however, can happen mostly through the active participation of a *Spiritual Master Teacher.*

## The Master Teacher

> *Never go searching for a Master Teacher! He will appear at your door the moment you are ready. Even starting to seek, how can you possibly look for him? How will you recognize him? If you have attained the ability of recognizing your Master Teacher, then there is nothing more to add to yourself.*
>
> **Ancient Egyptian papyrus**

Teachers teach what their own teachers have taught them. Initiates know and therefore do not speak; for words would distort the Truth, the taste of which they have felt – that Truth which they have experienced, not "learned". A Spiritual Master Teacher is a Perfect Initiate, having finally liberated himself from the vainglory and foppery of the ego, being only a pure transmitter of God's Grace. Such Beings are Initiates whose mission is to awaken the ones "fallen asleep", to "heal the blind" so that they begin to see, stepping onto the Path; whereas, to the sighted ones, they give Light so that they walk confidently along this Path. The main task of a Master Teacher is not to train the seekers in the literal sense, but to unlock the dormant Knowledge in them, which, along this Path, ought to turn into Learning and Awareness, and finally – into Life. An esoteric wise saying reads: "A bad teacher presents the Truth; a good one teaches others how to find the Truth" – and, according to a Chinese proverb, "The teacher opens the door but you have to enter by yourself".

Still, how do we recognize a Master Teacher? By the only measure of Truth that Jesus has left us in the words: "You will know them by their fruits." (*Matthew* 7:16, *NKJV*) If someone tells you, "I am your Master Teacher", think seriously upon it, and apply the criterion regarding the fruit. If your joint

---

38  *Sah (Sahu)* is the Immortal Body, the Incorruptible Soul, resembling, by its form, the physical body, and most often described as a Spirit Body, having all the mental and spiritual abilities of the living body. It is that part which is able to continue existing in Heaven after the successful passing through the Judgment of Osiris – *AN*.

work is not fruitful or if its fruit is rotten, then this is not the Master Teacher. It does not mean, however, that you should not do anything at all, waiting for the Teacher to appear and give you everything, without you making any effort, including the very Enlightenment. You ought to prepare for the Master Teacher. Unfortunately, you are not always given such a Teacher. Then the teacher that is not incarnated appears – the very suffering. The greatest art, however, is to share the pains, the troubles and the hardships of your neighbours, your close ones, whenever you are not in such a position as theirs.

In Freemasonry, a Spiritual Master Teacher is the Master performing the Initiatic Rites and "testimonies" of the mystical act of Sacred Initiation. He cannot give you all the knowledge; rather, his task is to help you remember. Knowledge is within you as a sort of cryptomnesia: you only have to take it out of the abyss of oblivion, and surmount the Law of Lack of Understanding with the help of the Master.

The Degrees of Modern Freemasonry are, unfortunately, granting neither a Sacred Initiation nor a formal one: they represent a merely administrative "raising" to hierarchical Degrees. Formally, the Mason "raised" to a Master's Degree receives the potential opportunity to perform a certain function in the Lodge; however, it does not necessarily mean a certain Degree of formal initiation, nor, even less, of a Sacred Initiation. This is because the very Master performing the ceremony has been "raised" in this way. This "Master" is not a Spiritual Master Teacher but only has a functional position, and therefore has not the power to carry out the initiation. Thus, the "raised" Mason remains merely one of the "profane in the Temple".

From what has been said so far, the following question arises: What is the Truth about Freemasonry, what kind of society is it, after all?

## The Truth

*There are three truths: my truth, your truth, and The Truth.*

**Chinese Proverb**

The Truth is the ideal of knowledge, which consists in the correct reflection of objective reality, verified by the criterion of practice. The attitude towards practice, representing itself the resultant judgment, seems to add, to a great degree, subjectivity to this criterion; so, in order to avoid such subjectivity, we shall point out three objective criteria for Truthfulness for every Initiatic society: immutability, tradition and a certain measure of the fruit. In view of these, there are three characteristics showing its non-transience: mastery of Eternal Truths; presence of continuity of tradition; spiritual results as a measure of Truthfulness. In Freemasonry, we can say that the first criterion is present in principle, because its underlying Truths are non-transitory. With respect to the second criterion, we hope that the Fire of esoteric Wisdom is still preserved in some Masonic Lodges. The last criterion, which we have already mentioned in another context, has been established since most ancient times and was formulated by Jesus: "You will know them by their fruits." The judgment regarding the "fruits" of Freemasonry is left to the readers.

According to the Hebrew tradition, the Truth is God's Word, perceived through speech. This conception is contained in one of the most quoted psalms in Kabalistic literature, in which it is said, "The origin of Your Word is the Truth, and all the judgments of Your Righteousness are for eternity." (*Psalms* 119:160, *Aramaic Bible in Plain English*).

Human beings, however, do not speak truths because they are not ready to face the Truth. How can any truth be said in a world dominated by the untruth? If you tell someone that they are ugly, fat and stupid, they will hate you, is that not right? In most cases, this can be addressed to someone out of hatred; and yet, must only hatred be a generator of truth? If you say any truth out of love, then you will also be hated because you will not be understood properly. All of this, however, relates to human truth, which is illusory, and it is being adjudged according to the imperfect human laws, unlike the Divine Truth, which is being judged according to God's Laws. What Jesus has said is to be understood in this sense, namely: Let us not *judge* so that we are not judged as well, for we ought to *adjudge* according to human laws, not *judge* according to God's Laws.

God's Truth is Absolute, and therefore it is denoted by one word only: *Truth*. Secret, Sacrament, Sacred Initiation – thirst, path, breath… This is the veil concealing the Truth; but, at the same time, it represents all the three keys for unveiling the Truth. The Secret is the thirst for the Truth; the Sacrament is the path towards the Truth; and the Sacred Initiation is the breath of Truth that has penetrated us. By analogy with the Masonic Degrees, this means that the Master "breathes the Truth". That is why this Degree represents the Crown of the Initiatic hierarchy, for there is nothing greater than the Truth. Our Spirit is a particle of God's Spirit, inspired into us with the Divine Breath, and it is the taste of the Truth. This is the taste through which we understand whether the fruit is rotten or not.

Between a Spiritual Society, a Spiritual School, and a Masonic Lodge, a sign of equality can be put. A Masonic Lodge is a Spiritual School of Sacred Initiation. It is not some organizational structure, it is not the Brothers, it is not the Masonic Minutes, and it is not even a way of living. It is a constructive exchange of energies in which a *brotherhood chain* is formed, which is the very foundation of the Lodge. We are aware what the stoutness of the brotherhood chain is, and yet, we will keep silent, absorbed in deep thought.

The Masonic Lodge has two states of being: a *Heavenly* one – the archetype of the Lodge, as a prototype of the Masonic teaching, materializing itself into particular people and deeds that represent the second state of being – the *physical* one. Freemasonry is a teaching which, at a certain point and place, dresses itself in flesh. The Lodge representing its form is an esoteric circle, in the basis of which is the Arcana knowledge, the Kabalistic science, and the esoteric tradition as a whole, each of them being an inseparable, integral part of Freemasonry.

It is claimed that one of the mottos of esoteric schools is *Caritas et Reversibilitas;* and, according to some people, it means *Identifying and Renewal.* However, we have not found such a meaning in Latin. The word *Caritas* means *loving kindness, love.* It comes from the adjective *Carus,* which means *dear, beloved.* In Christian theology, it represents one of the three Virtues, along with faith and hope. Etymologically, *Carus* derives from the Greek χάρις (pronounced "karis"), meaning *Grace.* In *The Divinatory Tarot* by Papus, one of the titles of the Twelfth Arcanum is *Caritas,* and that of the Fourteenth Arcanum is the French word *Réversibilité*. In the lectures of Gregory Mebes, delivered between 1911 and 1912, the word *Reversibilitas* is used, which we did not find in Latin. According to the explorers of esoterism, these lectures are based on Papus, who initiated Mebes into Martinism, with the aim of spreading his teachings and theories in Russia. We may assume that the original word should be the French *Réversibilité*, meaning *reversibility, regeneration,* which Mebes or his disciple turns into *Reversibilitas,* perhaps to resemble the Latin *Caritas.* Therefore, we think that the original quotation was or should be entirely in French and read the following: *Charité et Réversibilité,* meaning *Grace and Regeneration.* This phrase, in our opinion, has the power and nature of an Initiatic formula, even if it is not applied specifically in this form. Its core essence is implemented in every Initiatic society, including in the Masonic one, no matter whether it is used consciously and purposefully, or not. The word *Réversibilité*[39] is equivalent to *"Risen from the dead through Resurrection".* An Initiate is a resurrected, new human with a regenerated mind and soul, as any Master in Freemasonry should definitely be. The task of a Masonic Lodge, in the practical sense, is to welcome the human souls, transform them and heal them so that they themselves become

---

39  The word *réversibilité* literally means *returning, going back* (into a previous form and state) – or, in the given context: *to return, to restore, to revive, to regenerate* oneself in one's previous living state – *AN*.

after that a cure for the *"sick"* society. That is why *Paracelsus* has also said: "Heal yourself – and hundreds around you will also be healed." Naturally, this applies, above all, to the soul; for what is the point of curing the body of an unenlightened person? It is the same as washing a pig, which will immediately wallow into the mud again. Unless the pig nature of a human changes, this human will always wallow in the mud. The difference between a human and a pig is that the Primordial Core Essence of humans is Divine, so they are able to recognize it and follow it.

*Charité* means receiving the Grace of Masonic symbols. However, the achievement of this depends on how much we have self-identified with them. As we have already said, you cannot walk along the Path unless you have become the very Path. Self-identifying with Masonic symbols and bringing them to life within Brothers leads to the resurrection of Master Hiram in each Initiate. All these processes are guided by the Worshipful Master, who ultimately represents himself the Master Teacher guiding the process of *Building the Edifice,* the essence of which can be defined as *"Grace and Regeneration"*.

We are bound to agree with Jean Palou that the work on both the physical and the spiritual process of *Building the Edifice* is a joint work; on the other hand, however, we have to declare that it is determined and marked mostly by the *ha-harak*[40] of the Master.

What has been said so far, according to the criteria mentioned, refers generally to Masonry; and yet, whether it is valid nowadays or not, we leave that again to the reader's judgment. Whatever this judgment might be, however, our advice is that the whole of Modern Masonry should not, in any case, identify itself with it. In confirmation, we will quote Arthur Edward Waite, a Freemason and member of the *Golden Dawn Order:* "It has been recognized throughout that there is a Higher Mind of Masonry, that a wider meaning attaches to its chief allegory than that which appears on the surface, and that the essential greatness of certain degrees and rites has been realized by few only of the multitudes who know them at first hand."

Regardless of how distorted Freemasonry is, this Higher Mind is present in it, and therefore it is archetypal, so for that reason, it has preserved its Sacral nature. Freemasonry exists even to this day because it is under the influence of a powerful Ancient Egregor. However, to explain the essence and meaning of this concept, we need to clarify other basic esoteric concepts and categories.

---

40 The "power of the hammer" – *AN*.

# 4
# The Astral Plane

*Stars are holes in the sky through which the Light of the Infinite shines.*

***Confucius***

According to the esoteric tradition, there exist three worlds: a spiritual, an astral and a physical one. The representative of the first one is the Spirit; the energy (the force) – of the second one; and the physical world – of the third one. The second world penetrates into the other two, serving as a mediator between them. The source of energy is the Spirit; it is through energy that the Spirit manifests itself into matter, setting it in motion – *Mens agitat molem*[41]. Matter can be manifested in four states: *solids, liquids, gases,* and *plasma*. These are the *four elements* known in Antiquity: *earth, water, air* and *fire,* and therefore in Freemasonry they are part of the trials of the seeker. Apart from them, the Ancients knew still subtler matter, which they called *ether,* whereas the Hindus called it *akasha*. This fifth element represents the astral plane, which is also matter, but of a more spiritual nature. The astral plane has got its name from the Latin word *astrum – star,* because the astral matter, in its density, is analogous to the radiance of stars. Beyond the astral plane, according to the ancient teachings, there are still more types of matter depending on the degree of its closeness to the Spiritual Principle. This statement of the mystics is confirmed nowadays also by the latest scientific discoveries. Russian physicist Gennady Ivanovich Shipov, with his fundamental theory of physical vacuum, has scientifically discovered three new states of matter: the physical vacuum, the primary torsion fields, and the Absolute Nothing from which All is born. The physical vacuum is the ether of which the Ancients speak. Here, however, some clarity ought to be introduced. Scientists are already discussing ether as matter subtler than plasma; however, in the esoteric tradition, when referring to *ether,* we mean the astral ether, which is the lowest part of the astral plane, the one that structures and vivifies the physical matter. The astral ether is actually the filling of the world, connecting all the bodies and systems. The astral matter, being *etheric matter,* has an atomic structure, and just like matter, it vibrates and moves, because vibration is being transmitted from atom to atom.

The astral dimension is subdivided into *lower* and *higher,* corresponding, in the Christian religion, to *Purgatory* and *Hell,* on the one hand, and to

---

41  From Latin: "The Spirit moves the matter" (Vergil) – *AN*.

*Heaven*, on the other. Naturally, when talking about the Western religious and esoteric tradition, we should inevitably search for its roots in Ancient Egypt and Judea. The content of the term *astral plane* perhaps fits most precisely into the Egyptian *Duat* – an *intermediate place* where the souls of the dead move to. The sovereign there is the resurrected God Osiris, the members of his body reassembled, however, with a missing seminal organ, devoured, according to a legend, by three species of Nile fish, whereas, according to another – by one fish, called *medjed:* elephant fish. The impotence of this God is an indication that, in the World he rules, no physical materialization can be accomplished. This is not a particular place but a state of being through which one moves from the manifested world into the non-manifested ones, and vice versa; still, it should be associated with the sphere of the psyche and mostly with its unconscious part. Duat is depicted as the circular Asar (Aser/Asir) – Osiris, among the waters of the Heavenly Goddess Nut, as an autonomous area isolated for her subconscious. The disincarnated souls ought to go through this state of being in order to move into the spiritual worlds of God Re. This path is difficult, filled with trials and leading to purification and inner transformation, because that is the only way to move into the spiritual realms. For that purpose, an experienced guide is needed, and such guide is Anubis, the Master of the Holy Land – the necropolises, which, in the esoteric aspect, are symbols of the discerning mind. Therefore Duat is a proto-image rather of the Purgatory in the Christian religion than of Hell, where the souls reside forever, without any option to rectify themselves.

We have to point out that Anubis is also a god of mummification, and therefore Duat is associated also with the embalming (anointing) room, where the mummies stay for 70 days – the time needed for transformation and re-creation: the prototype of the Christian Eucharist. After that, the mummy receives the energy of the 12 Star Gods, guided by Horus. Embalming is a process related not so much to death, as is traditionally considered, but rather to life and to the idea that Immortality can be achieved still during the earthly life. This is one of the greatest secrets of the Egyptian esoteric tradition, laid in the basis of the rituals related to death and to the process of being "Twice-Born", or "Born Anew". Let us recall such emblematic expressions as "Twice-Born", "Resurrected from the dead", as well as the scene of the resurrected Lazarus, wrapped in a funeral white canvas like a mummy. The symbolism of the Master's Degree Rite is also in this sense.

We are obliged to mention that there is still another word indicating the place where the dead reside, namely *Amenti*. It was no coincidence that we said "the place" because, unlike Duat, *Amenti* means "hidden place" and also "west", being identified with the horizon where the Sun sets. According to Ancient Egyptians, the souls go westward after their death, following the Sun downwards to the Underworld. At the gates of Amenti, there is a gate-keeper standing who engulfs the souls with his open mouth – a symbol of the Earth absorbing the flesh. The term *Amenti* was personified as a beautiful goddess, the Mistress of the West, engulfing the Sun in the evening and giving birth to it in the morning. We can assume that, unlike Duat, this place is underground; however, again, we can identify it neither with the hopeless *Hell*, nor with the Greek *Hades*, nor with the Hebrew *Sheol*, where the souls are doomed to eternal stagnation.

Here we go back to the astral plane again, which, as we have seen, can be called "the analogue of Duat". In it, energies circulate, obeying the action of the centrifugal and the centripetal force, as a result of the fight between which, the balanced circular motion is obtained. The positive rays of the astral plane are symbolized by the Sun and the red colour, and in Ancient Hebrew they are called *aod*, whereas the negative rays are symbolized by the Moon and the blue colour, and are called *aob*. The *aod* and *aob* in equilibrium are called *aor*, which means *astral light*. At the basis of *aod* is the power of expansion, of life (its symbol is the dove), while at the basis of *aob*, the force of shrinking and death is contained (its symbol is the raven). A pair of snakes – *aob* and *aod* – are coiled around the sceptre of Hermes, which the Magi are able to balance and synthesize into astral light – *aor*. In the context of what has been said so far, the well-known Hermetic Law of Analogy: *Quod est inferius est sicut quod est superius, et quod est superius est sicut quod est inferius: ad perpetranda miracula rei unius,* is to be formulated as follows: "Whatever is below – *aob*, is similar to that which is above – *aod;* and whatever is above is similar to that which is below so that the miracles of oneness – *aor* – be performed." On the esoteric plane, it means that the astral light *aor*, called by Hermes Trismegistus *"telesma"* (the force of magnetism), is synthesized by the interaction and equilibration of the two astral poles: the *positive* one – *aod*, and the *negative* one – *aob* (in Ancient Hebrew, it also means "magic"). According to Hermes, "Telesma is the most powerful of all forces because it overcomes every subtle thing and penetrates everything that is gross".

Even still in the books of Moses, the astral plane is mentioned in the scene of the Original Sin, the Fall of our ancestors. The Serpent who seduced Eve is called by Moses *nahash*. The words in the texts of Moses's *Sefer*, especially in the *First Book of Moses – Genesis,* have threefold meaning: literal, symbolic and esoteric (hieroglyphic). In the ordinary sense, *nahash* means *serpent;* in the symbolic one, it means *instinct, sensuality, egoism;* and, in the esoteric (hieroglyphic) one – the *astral plane.*

On the exoteric plane, the Ancient Hebrew word *nahash* is formed by the three consonants *N-H-Sh (Nun-Het-Shin),* which, on the mental plane, have the meaning of *comprehending, penetrating into things.* If we enter the deep esoteric waters, however, we have to point out that the Ancient Hebrew word *nahash* contains the root *ash* and gives the idea of a circular movement. In the Egyptian pictogram writing system, this root was depicted as a serpent biting its tail. We must clarify that Moses wrote the *Pentateuch* using this writing system, since it is known that he was an Egyptian disciple and used the priestly wisdom and knowledge that could only be conveyed by being written through such a writing system. This is actually the hieroglyphic, or concealed, meaning of the Old Testament, which has been lost over the centuries, remaining as knowledge preserved only for Initiates.

In Ancient Egypt, the astral world was called "Heavenly Fire". The root *ash* in the word *nahash* means *fire,* as well as *movement* generated by external forces. It consists of the Hebrew hieroglyphs *Alef* and *Shin,* and in the language of symbols, this can be translated as "fire which has emanated and detached itself from the Spirit". In this way, the word *nahash* assumes the meaning of "fire (ether) that is in a circular motion initiated from the outside". This is an indication that it is passive by nature, receiving its energy from the Spirit, and represents extremely thin matter known in the esoteric tradition under the term *astral world,* which functions as a mediator between subtle and gross matter. *Nahash* (i.e. the Dragon, the Serpent, the astral world) draws the Spirit into matter. It is the life of nature seeking to enchain the Spirit to matter; it is the instinct dragging humans into the depths of feelings. It is likened to the evil principle, symbolized by the Devil (the instinct) acting through Eve (the passionate desire) upon Adam (the mind). Here, however, we must make the important clarification that the above said illustrates only the negative pole of the astral plane – *aob,* the manifestations of which are considered to be sin and evil from the moral and ethical point of view. They are associated with the soul, which, with its energy body (the so-called *astrosome*) inhabits the astral world. That is why people usually talk about the sinful souls and bodies, and their rectification, rather than about the Spirit, which, by definition, is incompatible with sinfulness.

## Spirit, Soul and Body

> *O you, falsely reasoning one!*
> *Forsake the thought*
> *that your "I" is made of this bundle*
> *of skin, bones, fat and filth!*
> *Know that your true Core Essence –*
> *this is the all-pervading, immutable Atman;*
> *and, in this, attain Supreme Peace!*
>
> ***Shri Shankaracharya ("Vivekachudamani")***

Regardless of some differences, all esoteric teachings ultimately bring everything to the *Law of Trinity,* and in harmony with this law, humans have a triune core essence: Spirit, soul and body. Usually, the concepts of *Spirit* and *soul* are mixed, this being contributed by the *Christian Council of Constantinople* in 869, during which the "holy fathers" leave to humans only their "sinful" soul, which can only be "saved" through the Church.

The Spirit of a human ought to be viewed not as an impersonal principle but as an individual, self-conscious core essence – a particle of God's Core Essence. The Spirit is the leading, driving, "motor" principle, the cause of things; and in the esoteric sense, it corresponds to the *"causal"* body. The Christian concept of the soul corresponds to the astral body, respectively the astral world, and is the connecting link between the Spirit and the body. The soul is not as incorporeal as the Spirit, nor as material as the body.

After death, some souls believe they are still alive, because inside them, there is some residual energy from the material world, and they continue to strive towards this world. However, this striving to stay here is also due to the thousands of attachments, to the feelings, emotions and thoughts at the time of death. A certain amount of time must have passed for the soul to realize and accept the fact of death. It is only then that the souls are ready to move on to their appointed dimension. Even if they go to the "higher" astral (the so-called *Paradise*), then, if wishing to grow up in their development, they must once again return into the physical world, which has been created as an experimental field, a testing ground for their trials and improvement towards perfection. That is why there is no justice in this world: because we need to learn what injustice is actually. Therefore, in our world we face hatred, jealousy, egoism, cruelty, and all possible negative feelings and actions, because only here can we experience them. They are embedded in the lessons we have come to learn, without which we cannot go on along the Spiritual Path. Astral beings can only go into the Spiritual World through the material one. To accomplish this, they have to reach awareness and freedom from any attachment to their own thoughts and feelings. This can hardly be done within the astral reality, which is subjective and governed by emotions and thoughts. In the physical world, it is much easier for an objective event to detach us from the mental processes or from certain emotions, so therefore God has created our world for our spiritual development towards perfection.

We go back again to the topic of the astral plane, the analogue of which inside humans is known under the exoteric term *soul*. Astral bodies called *astrosomes* are formed around its negative pole.

## The Astrosome

> *The way the Spirit is united with the body cannot be understood by humans; and yet, precisely that union represents itself the human being.*
>
> **Saint Augustine of Hippo**

The *astrosome* is the energy essence of the soul, possessing our feelings, passions and emotions. Before it, however, the closest to the physical body is the etheric body, the bearer of the vital and regenerating forces of life, which manages and maintains the functions of the organism, working independently of the willpower. The etheric and the astral body have the form of the physical one and can be consciously detached from the latter; and, if made denser, they can even be seen. The vibrations of the Spirit are transmitted through the astrosome to the physical body. The human Spirit first creates its astrosome, which, on its turn, creates its physical body, shaping it in the form given to it by the Spirit. During sleep (unconsciously), the astral body detaches itself from the physical one to "charge" itself in the astral world, holding on to a thin fluid thread that is broken only at death. This detachment may, however, be accomplished in a controlled manner. It is precisely such a process that takes place during the formal initiation; however, we will not dwell on it. There is also a deeper esoteric view that Judas had to kiss Jesus in order to find out whether this was His physical body, not His etheric-astral projection. In the same way, it is believed that it was the "Etheric Christ" Who practically delivered the famous "Sermon on the Mountain".

The movement of the Spirit generates the thought, which, in turn, is being imprinted into the astral plane, owing to its plasticity as an *astroidea*. Through the definite nature of the thought and the power of the will, the *astroidea* is being implemented into matter. The world is mental, as Hermes Trismegistus says. Every thought is being imprinted on the astral plane, so the existence of this imprint depends on the clarity and power of this thought, and therefore the astral world is filled with billions of *astroideas*. The astral plane, as we have noted, is *bipolar*, so there are two types of phenomena in it: *positive* and *negative*. The former have active nature and act dominantly upon the latter, which function as the passive one. By virtue of this, active thoughts seek to dominate over passive ones. Thoughts obey this Astral Law; however, since they are generated by the Spirit, they also obey the Law of Affinity, according to which *"Likeness attracts likeness"*. That is why positive thoughts attract their likeness and repel negative ones. Thinking upon Masonic ideas and symbols, we attract their power that not only transforms and enlightens us, but also embraces us in an energy cocoon protecting us from negative energies and influences.

## Astral Clichés

The imprints in the astral world caused by human actions and by other phenomena on Earth constitute astral imprints called *astral clichés*. Therefore, each event on Earth, regardless of its origin, is being imprinted on the astral plane. Astral clichés are also formed to determine future events, since the principle of each action and event is that it first emerges as an idea in the spiritual world, then is formed in the astral world, being after that implemented in the physical world. Thoughts, desires and images are imprinted and dwell in the astral world with exceptional force. Astral images are generated owing to the willpower and imagination of humans, drawing strength from their faith. When people are getting together in groups, connected with one idea and united by the willpower of one person, a *magic chain* is formed. All members of the chain ought to be with a "negative" charge except for their Master (Teacher), who has to be "positive". This means that the participants in the magic chain have to accept unconditionally the will of the Master. In this way, an *astro-psychic battery* is formed, and the Master can direct its astral currents for the implementation of a certain idea. Each collective *astroidea* is stronger than the *astroidea* of each individual human, unless this individual is an Initiate. Based on this principle, a *magic chain* is formed.

# Magic Chain

> *First focus, and then*
> *direct the astral force.*
> **Heinrich Khunrath**

Some people maintain that the idea of the magic chain was already formulated by Jesus in the following canonical text: "For where two or three are gathered together in My name, I am there in the midst of them." (*Holy Gospel of Matthew* 18:20, *NKJV*) However, we believe that this idea is most precisely and literally illustrated in the apocryphal *Gospel of Thomas,* where Jesus says, "Where there are three gods, they are gods; where there are two or one, I am with him". The above said undoubtedly refers to the power of triunity, which, by definition, has Divine dimensions – and, accordingly, *implementation force and power of authority.* The magic chain is, in its essence, a process of energy synchronization, i.e. of equalizing the waves and vibrations of its participants. This happens when they are united by one unified goal, focused on one and the same idea or symbol, when they perform one and the same spiritual practice, when they are present in one and the same place, experiencing similar feelings and states. The leader and initiator of a veritable magic chain can only be someone who, without any reserve, believes and lives in accordance with the central idea; and, in a Masonic Lodge, this someone is its Master. According to this idea, corresponding magic chains are formed with a view to its implementation. The white chains, bearers of light, whose ideas were created by Mystics, Magi and Initiates, have many times managed to change the countenance of the Earth. The Templar magic chain, for example, has given rise to several spiritual orders and movements. As for the Rosicrucian magic chain, the cultural and scientific Renaissance stemmed from it; whereas, some of the results of the Masonic chain are the French Revolution and the founding of the USA. The Templar chain has formed a strong army, gaining exceptional financial might; it has established the most modern and comprehensive banking system and has built its own units and temples in many places and countries. How has the Templar chain acquired such might on the physical plane, on the energy plane and on the spiritual plane? Around what idea have the Templars been united? According to the official history of the Order, the goal was to guard the hundreds of pilgrims on the road from Europe to the Holy Land, the task being entrusted to nine knights, which seems rather unserious. Rather, it probably refers to the symbolism of the number 9. Actually, we believe that the Templars have discovered the spiritual treasures of the First Jerusalem Church. This is, in our view, the central idea around which the Templar magic chain has arisen, whose purpose was to protect these teachings from destruction, and preserve them for future times when humankind would be ready for them. It is clear that the Templars possessed knowledge and confessed ideas that were contrary to the official doctrine of the Christian Church. It is no coincidence that the first Christian mystics used the symbol of the fish, not the symbol of the cross of the Crucifixion, because, to them, the latter was a tool for torturing their Master. For the same reasons, the Templars used to wear on their cloaks not a Christian cross but a Hermetic one.

All societies which are united by inner discipline and unified willpower constitute magic chains without even suspecting that. Therefore, the Initiatic tradition and the deep esoteric Wisdom aim, first and foremost, at destroying the bond of the individuals seeking Sacred Initiation with the paradigms established by the unconscious, vehement collective energy activity in which they are involved without being aware of it.

From the texts of the Qumran Gospels, it becomes clear that the community of the Essenes actually constituted a magic chain. For this reason, we believe that Jesus has also built and practiced such a chain together with His disciples. There are records indicating that Orpheus practised the same as well.[42]

There exist, figuratively speaking, "black", "white", and "grey" magic chains. *"Grey"* chains are formed when humans synchronize mutually not in the name of some constructive idea but for the sake of something that nourishes their egocentricity – thus, their souls become a suitable object for all sorts of manipulations and interventions. This can be prevented or corrected through various astral and spiritual practices. In the core of the *"black"* magic chains, there stand destructive ideas meant to be purposefully implemented. These chains can be broken down by "luminous", or "light" magic chains, at least as powerful as the other ones. The *"white"* chains are formed around "luminous" ideas, some of which, as we have said, have changed the world.

Two are the basic principles in any magic chain: a *personal* one and a *non-personal* one. A personal magic chain is usually aimed at attracting human souls in order to multiply someone's personal energy. This does not mean that it cannot have high spiritual goals as well. It can also be non-personal, but then a spiritual element is inevitably present. Through magic chains, humans can be "caught", and it is of great importance who the "hunter" or "fisher" is! Jesus says, "Follow Me, and I will make you fishers of people!" So at once they left their nets and followed Him" (*Holy Gospel of Matthew* 4:19 – 20, *ISV*).

---

[42] This chain was called *Samothracian Magic Chain*. According to Pythagoreans, it was established on the island of Samothrace by the disciples of Orpheus – *AN*.

The fundamental rule for the process of building and functioning of a magic chain, which exists also in Freemasonry, is the following: "First gather together – and then spread!" Another such rule is contained in the words of Jesus, which we have already quoted, where not only the idea, but also the operative formula of the magic chain is present. It reads that, in order to obtain the magic effect, it is necessary to have at least two interacting, polarized energies: a positive and a negative one. This principle of the presence of polar opposites in the chain is a rule, which, however, becomes invalid when there is a transcendent state of the participants in the chain in order to achieve spiritual purposes. This is the case with Orthodox Masonry as a whole. This principle does not apply also to the so-called *"mental magic chain"*, based on mystical spiritual teachings.

The magic chain is a hyperphysical phenomenon, the result of which is manifested on the physical plane. The leader of the chain focuses on himself the synchronized collective willpower of the participants, and closes it upon a fulcrum: an image, a symbol – in general, something material, existing on the physical plane.

A mere idea is not enough. There has to be also a physical centre. Therefore, the main type of magic chain is the closed one, represented symbolically by a circle with a point in its centre. As we have already mentioned, the *circle with a point in its centre* is the archetypal form of Freemasonry and, in particular, of any Lodge, hence it represents a large magic chain, with the Grand Master, or the Worshipful Master of the Lodge, in its centre. However, they are hardly aware of this. It is no coincidence that the Masonic Rites contain the ancient formula used also by Jesus: "Breaking the chain of hands, the chain of hearts remains joined forever". It is definitely all about a constant, not a temporary, magic chain, which in Freemasonry is called a *"brotherly chain"*, but it cannot be said that Brothers are clearly aware of the deep esoteric mechanism of its action.

Depending on the different planes on which it manifests itself, the magic chain can be *astral* or *mental*. The astral one is the foundation of the magic action upon which the mental chain is built further. In the astral magic chain, an incantation is implemented, whereas, in the mental one, a prayer is performed, and therefore it is also called a *theurgic magic chain*. The participants in a magic chain have to be in a passive state, accepting the will of the Magus without demur. A theurgic chain is created on the spiritual plane and is a form of a higher moral magic influence upon a group of people. The theurgic effect of the magic chain is the Brotherhood effect. The participants in this chain, if fully committed (i.e. open) and full of faith, can be bestowed with mystical healing. Jesus used to heal with the formula "El Fatah" ("Be open to God!"), and also "According to your faith let it be to you!" (*Matthew* 9:29, *NKJV*)

The power of influence of the Magus upon the participants depends on whether he possesses any theurgic authority – which, most of all, is being given by God. Through his famous curse pronounced at the stake, Jacques de Molay activated a magic chain in a theurgic way, from the position of the Higher Spiritual Power of Authority. We wonder: Has there ever been, or is there, such a Spiritual Authority in Freemasonry?

As an analogue to the magic chain, as we have already mentioned, there is the symbol of the "chain of brotherly unity", which, according to René Guénon, is embodied in the cord surrounding the Masonic temple at its upper part. This is the rope used by Operative Masons to outline the contour of the building; however, this does not exclude the symbolism already mentioned, since symbols have multiple meanings and different contexts. The "Chain of Unity" has twelve knots corresponding to the signs of the Zodiac, in which the planets are arranged, and for that reason, it forms the "outer casing" of the Cosmos, which may also be called the *"celestial vehicle frame"*. The function of this "vehicle frame" is to "connect" the elements included in it, which is the content of the term "Chain of Unity". As a matter of fact, as is well known, the very word *Cosmos* means exactly that: an orderly and harmonious system. In this sense, the Masonic temple represents systematical orderliness, as opposed to the chaos outside it. At a deeper level, it can be assumed that the "Chain of Unity" is the "Vehicle Frame of the Temple", as part of God's Chariot – the universal vehicle of movement throughout the Worlds. Thus, the temple represents itself a specific kind of *Merkaba*[43] of the Masonic Lodge, through which Brothers are able to accomplish astral journeys during the Initiatic Rites. However, to achieve this, knowledge and experience are needed, which unfortunately do not exist in Freemasonry. We will dwell on the essence of the *Merkaba* in the further exposition of this book.

We now proceed with the cord symbolically encircling the Masonic temple. Each of the knots represents the point where forces act, determining one or another state of manifestation. Thus, it could be said that this "knot" holds the Creation in a certain state of being, so its undoing would be equivalent to "death" for that state. This, namely, is also the meaning of the concept of the *"vital knot"*. The knots, as well as the links of the chains, are the core essence of that which connects these states of being not only with each other, but also

---

43  *Merkaba* (from Hebrew: "Chariot of God") – a school in Judaic Mysticism of the 1st century AD, based on the first chapter of the *Book of Ezekiel;* a Kabalistic technique for ecstatic experience – *AN*.

with the very Primordial Principle. In this case, the thread, the rope or the chain have an "axial" meaning, so climbing upwards along them embodies the process of returning to the Primordial Principle. For humans, however, depending on the degree of their spiritual development, this state of being in which they are may become a form of attachment. This attachment enchains them and forces them to believe that the necessity to leave this state of being is a misfortune, making them unhappy. The rupture of the shackles is regarded as cutting the Gordian Knot (the vital knot), or as the death of the state of being to which they are attached. In this way, the mechanism is triggered of the fundamental subconscious fear of death as a principle. In order to surmount this fear, it is necessary to recognize death as transformation, and also, to view this getting out of a certain state of being not as a rupture of the chain associated with death, but as a transmutation of *"that which enchains in shackles"* into *"that which unites"*. In this sense and context, namely, the following Masonic maxim should also be understood: "We break the chain of hands, but the chain of hearts remains joined forever!"

Death is a gate to other worlds and a different way of existence. However, in order to become aware of this, and to free ourselves from the fear of death, we must symbolically experience death while still in life, and then be born again. The Mysteries of Death are the greatest *Sodallias* (from Hebrew: *sod* – "secret") in all spiritual traditions, including the Masonic one, where it is no coincidence that the Master's Initiation, namely, is the Initiation into Death.

The Masonic knotted cord can also be likened to the *"Chain of Worlds"*, which is usually depicted in the form of a circle. If each world is viewed as a cycle and is symbolized by a figure of a circle or sphere, then its full manifestation can be called the *"cycle of cycles"*. Thus, the chain can be passed without any interruption, from the beginning to the end, and then again, and again, always in the same direction but already on another level, and so on, infinitely. The circle represents evolution, so the end of one circle along the spiral turns into a new beginning *(Initiatio)*, just as the second *He* represents *Yod* in embryo, the beginning of the next unfolding of God's Name. In Freemasonry, this initiation that we must go through in order to be raised to a new level is the beginning, which must not break the connection with the end, forming and maintaining Infinity. That is why all Freemasons ought to carry, each within their own consciousness, the *white apron,* no matter what kind of an apron they have tied to their waist. The idea of the infinite beginning is embedded also into the white apron of the Grand Master, which, unfortunately, is seldom seen already accomplished, since it is a trial, above all, for the ego.

The mathematical roots of the idea of Infinity are in Ancient Hellas, 6th century BC, in the writings of the great philosopher, mathematician and Magus – Pythagoras. To him, numbers are living *eidoses,* they are Divine, and they are embedded into the very foundations of the whole Creation. He considers the number 1 to be the "father" of all numbers, because, when one integer is added to another, the result is a bigger number, and so on, to infinity. Therefore, at the basis of the Pythagorean system, there stands the Divine Nature of integers, and under the influence, correlation and attitude of this Divine Nature, the visible Universe emerges and is maintained. A discovery of one of the disciples of Pythagoras, Hippasus of Metapontum, however, breaks down this mathematical and logical system. This is the discovery of irrational numbers: namely, that there are numbers which cannot be represented as a ratio of two integers. Irrational numbers are non-recurring; and, if such a number is to be written, infinitely many digits have to be written, which is practically impossible. The discovery of irrational numbers shakes up Pythagoras' theory that every single *thing* (which is to be understood as *number*) represents a ratio of two God's *entities (numbers).* The existence of irrational numbers was kept in absolute secret, and, moreover, only within the circle of the Pythagorean Initiated Disciples. In any case, the idea of the Divine Nature of integers is fading away, whereas the theory of space as being composed of infinite straight lines, curves and planes, is speeding up. Perhaps the most revolutionary discovery in this direction is the so-called *Riemann sphere:* it shows us how infinitely many points in a plane can be made compact by adding a "point at infinity" to the sphere. The Riemann sphere represents a two-dimensional plane, with its north pole playing the role of a "point at infinity"/ *"attractor"* in the Theory of Chaos, towards which all the straight lines and points in the plane tend. Thus, instead of positive and negative infinity (the two ends of a real one-dimensional straight line), now there is an entire plane, which, using the sphere as a matrix, curves around itself, tending to a point at infinity from each direction (all directions leading to the north). If an analogy is made with Kabala and the Sefirotic Tree, then each Sefira has a "point at infinity", an unattainable point – and this must be the Core Essence of God, expressed through the specific God's Name of this Sefira. If that point is in the north, the symbolism of which is coagulation – a quality of the negative pole, then it should be concluded that God, as Infinity, represents shrinking, a negative sign (minus), but in the aspect of attraction. Of course, the above stated would not fit into the esoteric paradigm as perceived by conceptual minds; but nevertheless, plenty of minds which are tuned on the Sefira *Bina,* if they had not questioned the scientific paradigms, would not have made the greatest epochal discoveries.

In view of the above exposed, when discussing again the topic of the "Chain of Worlds", the point at which the chain is joined is incomparable to any other points because it does not belong to the sequence of manifested states of being. The beginning and the end coincide, and, in reality, they are one the same thing. This is because they are situated beyond the limits of the last point (knot, link, grain, sphere), representing themselves the point at Infinity of the Chain at the very Primordial Principle. This is the *Alpha and Omega, Alef and Tet, All and Nothing,* the "Circular Asar", "the snake biting its tail".

After this necessary straying from the subject, we return to the magic chain again, in order to make the transition to a concept related to it: *egregor.*

## Egregor

On the Law of the Magic Chain, the creation of entities known by the term *egregor* is based. When the principles of the magic chain act persistently in the course of some period of time, being the representatives of a large society, the members of which adhere to certain guiding rules, and direct their own willpower towards a specific goal, then, on the astral plane, a self-dependent entity is formed, representing itself a sum of those convictions and goals. This sum is something like a spiritual principle of the newly created entity called *egregor.* After acquiring a sufficient reserve of forces through the members of this society, the egregor begins to live a self-dependent life. However, egregors do not have completely free will, as their existence is limited by their own principle, which consists of the goals this egregor has to achieve. However, on the other hand, the egregor itself influences the members of the society who created it, urging them to serve the goals of this principle. In this way, an interaction arises between the egregor and the society that has formed it. In the struggle between such societies, their egregors fight as well, initially starting a war themselves, and then engaging also people in this war. This is so as a result of the principle that "Noumena generate phenomena" – or, in other words, things first occur in the subtle worlds, and then manifest themselves in materiality. In the dissolution of a society, its egregor keeps on existing for a very long time, endeavoring to accomplish the goals of that society. For example, after the defeat of the *Order of the Temple,* or better known as the *Order of the Knights Templar,* its egregor continued to exist and became manifest in Rosicrucianism and Freemasonry. The two largest and most significant Universal Egregors are those of Good and Evil. In Kabala, the former is called *Michael,* whereas the latter – *Samael*.

Thus, we have come to the *Masonic egregor,* which is one of the most powerful egregors of any Initiatic society, since it has not interrupted its activity over the centuries. Despite being polluted by the energy of Modern Freemasonry, its archetypal nature holds it within the parameters of the Universal Egregor of Good.

Whenever a Mason pronounces with faith the words or uses the symbols and signs serving as some motto of Freemasonry, he attracts to himself and in his favour its egregor, which, as has become clear, is on the side of Good. The impact of the Masonic egregor is, above all, unconscious on those who are connected with it, and therefore they are determined by it, willingly or unwillingly. Whenever its action is used consciously, through the magic chain, it is not possible to go drastically outside the scope of the Egregor of Good. Therefore, the statements that Freemasonry is the "evil genius" of humankind cannot be entirely true. It is actually a fundamental mistake to attribute to Freemasons any power of authority along the horizontal line, because their true power, if still any, is along the vertical line, and, moreover, within the bounds of Good. We do not claim that there are no deviations at all – on the contrary; however, we do believe that they do not go beyond the above pointed limits. Besides that, we do not consider that this knowledge is being used consciously and purposefully, because of the profaning of Freemasonry in general and its alienating from its own esoteric roots and from the *Royal Art,* which is one of the definitions for *Sacred Magic.* In this sense, and in the context of the above said, it is imperative that we focus more essentially also on the *art of magic.*

# V
# NAOS

## 5
## Magic and Freemasonry

> *Magic has the power to experience and fathom things which are inaccessible to human reason; for magic is a remarkable secret wisdom, just as reason is a remarkable obvious folly.*
>
> **Paracelsus**

Initially, magic uses intuitively and subconsciously the Laws of the Universal Edifice of Creation, characterizing itself as the first primitive science. Through gaining experience, it begins to study and apply these laws, using methodology, which transforms it into veritable science, whereas the rest of its content turns it into an art. Magic is the first form of human thought. Humans were unable to think otherwise than through concepts of magic. Thus, magic encompassed the totality of the mystical and the scientific life of people. Religion stemmed from the faults and failures of magic. When realizing that one's own thoughts and actions meet resistance from the world, one ascribes mysterious powers to this world – powers, appropriated by itself. Thus, humans deify these forces and no longer compel them but integrate them through adoration, sacrificial offering and prayer. A magician forces and compels, while religion brings peace. A magic ritual has direct impact and does not require the mediation of an active cleric, while its effectiveness is a prerequisite. *In magic, knowing something means being capable of doing it!* Its core essence is operativeness based on the method of *induction,* which represents that operation of the mind, by which we conclude that what is known to us in some case or in several specific cases will be valid in all others that are similar to the first one. Induction is a matter of logic and is based on the Axiom of Order and Regularity in Nature. Magic uses these correlations, which can be reduced to three inductive laws if counteraction is also included in the term *induction.* These are the Laws of *Contact,* of *Likeness,* and of *Opposites:*

"Things that once have come into contact continue to interact"; "Likeness attracts and generates likeness"; "Opposites act upon each other".

Humans give birth to ideas, which, if not accomplished, turn into reveries. Therefore, an important role of the one giving birth to a certain idea is to focus its energy by directing the mental flow through the willpower, and then to dress it in astral forms through the desire and restrained passion, and finally, to bring it into action (to accomplish it) on the physical plane. *In this sense, magic is a science of embodying ideas.*

Once we have co-created an idea (we do not accidentally use the word "co-created", for we do not create the significant ideas by ourselves), we must mentally shape it in a concrete form so that it acquires a clear content and purpose. Then, the intention and the willpower to accomplish it are needed, by channeling and concentrating this mental energy. The process continues on the astral plane, where it is necessary to harness the energy of the desire ignited by the astral fire of the already mastered passion. Finally, we have to transform all the accumulated energy from potential into kinetic one, and transmit it into the material world. Such is the path of any idea, from its emerging to its implementation, without considering the possible obstacles on the material plane. In magic, this interval between the desire and its fulfilment is either absent or very short, so we would liken it to an *accelerator* of mentally and volitionally controlled processes, and, in this sense – having the characteristics of anticipation.

A magic ceremony generates a transformation process through certain implementation formulas and magic keys. An implementation formula is a symbolic sentence consisting of "words of the Force", a symbolic outlining or gesture, which embody a particular idea through the willpower and desire. Each ceremony related to embodiment of ideas has to end with an affirmative phrase or word putting an authoritative accent on the relevant work or action. Such words are most often *Amen* (coming from the Egyptian tradition and meaning *The Hidden One*), *Verum est* ("So be it!") and *Hallelujah* ("Praise the Lord!").

We will now illustrate a magic formula compiled and used by *Philippus Aureolus Theophrastus Bombastus von Hohenheim*, known as *Paracelsus*[44] – a physician, scientist, philosopher, alchemist, astrologer and Magus. Like every great Magus, he also had a motto that could serve as one of the defini-

---

44 *Paracelsus* means "equal to" or "greater than" *Celsus*, referring to the 1st century Roman encyclopaedist *Aulus Cornelius Celsus*, known for his treatise on medicine, *De Medicina*, in eight volumes. *Paracelsus* begins to use this pseudonym around 1529 as a symbol and a sign that he has surpassed even *Celsus* himself – *AN*.

tions of magic: ALTERIVS NON SIT, QVI SVVS ESSE POTEST. Literally translated, it means the following: "He does not belong to another who can belong to himself." If we paraphrase it, the motto would have the following meaning: "Do not be another one when you can be yourself!"

**Figure 4**

## The Magic Implementation Formula Pentagrammatica Libertas

*Faith ought to support imagination and be supported by imagination, since faith creates the willpower. The resolute willpower is the beginning of all magic actions. It is precisely because humans are unable to develop perfect imagination and absolute willpower that the results of their magic actions are doubtful and inaccurate, otherwise they would always be entirely credible.*

**Paracelsus**

This magic implementation formula was inscribed with secret symbols on the Trident of Paracelsus – *Tridens Paracelsi,* where he encoded it because of the Inquisition, and especially because of the profane and the malevolent people, since the first rule in magic is to understand what you do and pronounce so that it possesses implementation force. The formula can be seen in his book, *Archidoxis magicae,* which was first published in 1569 in the city of Krakow, 28 years after the death of Paracelsus himself. The publication and translation into Latin are due to Adam Schröter; and subsequently, all other editions in various languages ensue from this one. It is a classic version of a magic incantation, which should always begin with a reference to the Divine Authority that the Magus relies on in the corresponding magic work. The formula, as we have already said, is encoded on the Trident, which consists of three flat triangular blades forged from horseshoes, with a handle made of insulating material.

On the handle, there is an inscription with gold letters reading: FATO. VLIDOX.P.P.P. However, the words are intentionally shuffled, and their true sequence should be as follows: P.P.P.VLIDOXFATO. On the right blade, there is an inscription reading: *Imo,* and on the left one – *Obito.* So this formula will take the following form:

*In nomine Pentagrammatica Libertas Trinitate, In Dox et Fato! Imo, Obito, Archedosel! Verum est! Amen!*

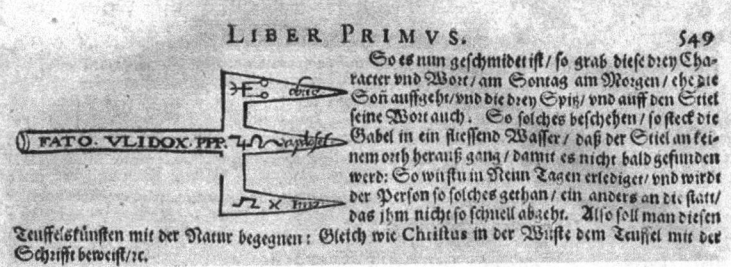

**Figure 5**

We proceed to the clarification of this inscription. The triple Latin "P" is an indication towards the triple pentagrammatic freedom (on the three planes), which is the basis upon which to proceed to the implementation of the formulas written on the three blades of the trident. It is this freedom that will unlock and form the willpower, owing to which the corresponding idea will be accomplished.

The sign "V" might denote the Roman numeral 5, as a confirmation of the idea of the pentagram. However, it is unlikely that a magic formula would require a confirmation of something already written in this very formula. It may also be reasoned that this is a sign of the unity of the trinity, but this logic could not stand either, since the three "P"s are present on the handle uniting them. Rather, we have to assume that the sign "V" stands for the Latin *VIS – Force.*

DOXFATO – *Dox* is probably an abbreviation of the word *Doxa;* and, according to Medieval Latin, it means *magnificence, glory, splendour, light.* In the Gospels, the Greek word δόξα is used 167 times in its various contexts, but mostly as *Glory.* It obviously refers to the *Glory of the Lord,* an expression that is usually an indication towards one of the Kabalistic Worlds – *Atzilut.*

*Fato* (from Latin) means *oracle, prophecy, prediction, fate, karma, death, end of life;* and, in the context of the formula under consideration, it should be interpreted as *Fate* and *Karma*. Following the line of the various meanings of *Fato,* the word *Doxa* would have the meaning of the *Force that shapes and determines Fate and Karma.* The latter two concepts, however, are not identical in our opinion, since *fate* represents *irrevocable karma* as opposed to the revocable one, and this is of significance for the further unravelling of the formula. The Force that structures fate is called *Providence* and is situated in the *Bria* World of the Kabalistic Tree. In the Kabala section of this book, we will dwell on the latter in more detail, but here we need to bring some more clarity on the subject. Divine Providence is situated in the so-called *"Makom"* ("Place") in the Sixth Heaven, in the *Bria* World of the Kabalistic Tree, from where Creation is generated and where the Will of the Almighty God, the Masonic Great Architect of the Universe, manifests itself, and therefore, it is also known as the *"Palace of Will".* In this sense, Providence is the Force designing and outlining things – and they can only be changed through God's Will. *(See Fig. 23 on p. 186.)*

Ultimately, DOXFATO – these are Providence and Fate, on which the life of humans depends. Providence is above Fate, governing it, whereas Fate, in its turn, rules over the souls. No one is free from the Supreme Fate as irrevocable karma – *Fortuna,* but the revocable one can be controlled and cleared, so we have to be vigilant regarding it. In the same line of thoughts, LI, abbreviated from *Libertas,* means that pentagrammatic freedom refers and is directed to revocable karma rather than to *Fortuna.* In the picture of the Tenth Arcanum of Sacred Magic, the Wheel of Fortune *(Rota Fortunae)* is presented, and above it is the Sphinx as a symbol of Providence setting the parameters of *Fortuna.* We can in no way escape from *Fortuna* and from what is allotted to us by Providence, but we do have the choice to either be in unison with God's Providence and not go against it, in the sense of "Your Will be done!", which will lead to our Liberation – or to accumulate karmic debts and rotate continuously in the Wheel of *Samsara.*

Therefore, what is inscribed on the handle of the trident should mean: *"In the name and with the power of the triple pentagrammatic freedom, Providence and Fortuna!"* The authority we should rely on, namely, the force we ought to use and the laws we must observe in the materialization of the idea, are all indicated.

On the right blade, the word **Imo** is inscribed, which is literally translated from Medieval Latin as *on the contrary, despite, regardless of, contrary to.* Therefore, this part of the formula will refer to all crucial circumstances, and its meaning should be *"despite Destiny",* as reversible karma, but not despite, i.e. against *Fortuna.* The logogram preceding the inscription is a symbol of the Sun's force, of the *Solve* expansion corresponding to the alchemical *sulfur* and the astrological sign *Leo.* In Latin, the word *Imo* has also the meaning of *inner, deep, the deepest intimate innermost part*, as well as the *"I"*, the *Self*. We shall dwell on this last meaning later. The Latin sentence *Ab imo pectore* – literally, "From the bottom of the heart", undoubtedly identifying the *Sacral Self*, is also a confirmation of this.

The inscription on the left blade is **Obito**, meaning *death*, and also, *to go towards something, to reach*, as well as *to live*, in the sense of *to dwell*, but in this particular case, it means *(you have to) subdue, (you have to) accept*. We can judge about this by the logogram preceding the inscription, this logogram being a symbol of the receiving negative Moon force *Coagula*, corresponding to the alchemical *mercury* and the zodiac sign *Cancer*.

On the central blade, the complex formula **Ardosel** is written, consisting of three separate words. The first one is **Ar**, an abbreviation of the Greek ἀρχή *(Arche)*, which is an indication of *Archetype, Primary Cause, Supreme Spirit*. The second is **Do** and may be an abbreviation of the word *Doxa*, which, as we have already understood, means *Providence*. The following question arises: What is the point of writing *Doxa* twice – once on the handle and once again on the middle blade, which represents a continuation of the handle itself? According to Éliphas Lévi, the positive pole of the astral light OD – the *odic fluid* – is encoded in *Doxa*. However, if we accept Lévi's assertion, then OD should be inscribed on the right blade because it is a positive, expanding force, while on the middle one, in this context, the balanced astral light OR should be present – and it is indeed present, the testimony of which is the logogram preceding the inscription, in the form of a serpent, the biblical symbol of the astral world.

To get to the truth the closest we can, we need to define what the trident actually represents: whether it is a kind of magic dagger or sceptre, or a combination of both. With that end in view, the point of reference must be the function of the trident. We believe that there is no dispute regarding the fact that in magic the sword is used to inspire respect into the various disembodied entities, whereas the sceptre is used to transmit and implement the will of the Magus. The inscriptions on the trident definitely lead to the conclusion that it has the function of a magic sceptre; whereas, the presence of the blade – that it should act as a dagger as well. It also serves as a healing appliance, but we will discuss that later.

Having the function of a magic sceptre, eventually, DO represents an encoded sign of the positive pole OD of the astral light OR – an indication that the operating Magus is definitely obliged to be of a masculine gender, no other. This also becomes clear from the names of the First Arcanum of Sacred Magic – *Magus* and *Vir* – respectively *magician* and *man*, which we will discuss in detail when viewing the Arcana Knowledge. If a Magus wishes to transmit his willpower, then he should use that force, and it is quite normal for it to be marked on the central blade, which is an extension of the handle, which, in turn, is an extension of the hand, the conduit of willpower. In this sense, assuming that the term *"odic fluid"* did not exist at the time of Paracelsus, then we must assume that DO is the Latin verb *DO*, which is translated as *to send, to initiate, to illuminate,* and also *free will*. All these meanings can be related to the final Latin word **Sel**, meaning *salt*, which is the alchemical symbol of Earth and crystallization, materialization, as well as of the material plane where the idea is to be conducted, transmitted, and, ultimately, implemented.

In the context of the inscription on the handle indicating the authority which the Magus relies on, the blades contain the actions through which his intention will be accomplished. However, the written on them seems incompatible with the clarifications given. On the right, there is the inscription *Imo*, which means *on the contrary, despite, regardless of,* and on the left – *Obito*, which means *to submit to, to accept*. These two contradictory actions should be reconciled by the middle blade, through which the Magus conducts and materializes the Supreme Will, joining and balancing the forces of the lateral two ones – *Coagula* and *Solve*. However, the following question arises: Despite what should we go and what should we obey? The inscriptions on the three blades would not have a meaning of their own unless they are connected with the meaning on their handle, thus making the complete magic formula sound like this:

*"In the name and with the power of the triple pentagrammatic freedom, Providence and Fortuna! Despite Destiny[45], submit your will to the Supreme Force and materialize it! So be it! The Concealed One!"*

In this form, however, the inscription possesses the nature of a clarifying instruction, not of a magic implementation formula that must be pronounced by a Magus in the first person singular. Therefore, it is undoubtedly more appropriate to use the other meaning of *Imo* – *"I"*, as an indication that the action is performed by the Magus, with the power and will of his authority, resting on the Divine Authority. In view of this, also the instruction for the use of the *odic* force in this action can in no way be not present in the formula as well. In this way, the antagonistic meanings of the inscriptions on the two blades, in the context of "despite" and "to subdue", are also avoided. Thus, the final form of the formula would look like this: **In the name and with the power of the triple pentagrammatic freedom, Providence and Fortuna! I, through the forces of the astral light, affirm the Supreme Will on Earth. So be it! The Concealed One!**

In this sense, the other meaning of *Obito* – *to live*, not existentially but as action, also fits neatly into the written above: instead of *I affirm*, the phrase

---

45 Here, *Destiny* is in the sense of *revocable karma* and is different from our understanding of *Destiny* as something that cannot be avoided – *AN*.

*I live according to the Supreme Will* should be used. The latter phrase, however, has the characteristic of constancy, unlike the other one, which refers to a specific action, as is the principle of magic formulas.

Anyway, the point of Paracelsus's formula is that a Magus obeys Providence and Fortuna, while ruling over Destiny and implementing his own ideas and intentions despite the crucial circumstances, as revocable karma.

How would all this, however, be interpreted according to the Kabalistic Tree? It is obvious that we can look for an analogy between the three vertical Pillars of this Tree and the handle with the three blades of the trident. In this order, the Central Pillar of the Tree, which illustrates consciousness and willpower on the microcosmic plane, will correspond to the handle and the central blade. Therefore, we should independently inscribe the text on the pillar formed by them, as follows:

**P.P.P.VLIDOXFATO and Ardosel** *(Fig. 6)*

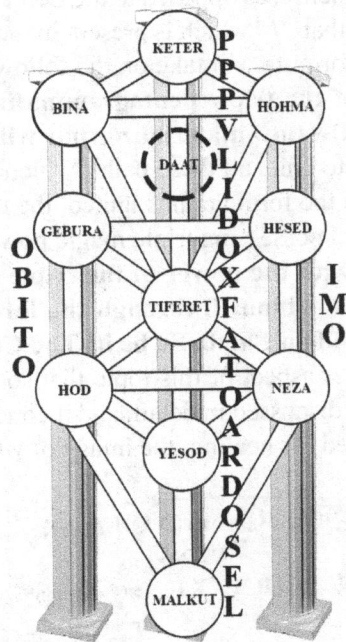

**Figure 6**

In accordance with the interpretation already mentioned above, of these two texts, each taken separately, when we merge them into one, the following sentence will be obtained: **In the name and with the power of the triple pentagrammatic freedom, Providence and Fortuna, the Spirit, through the Sun's force, keeps on creating!**

The text, thus joined, is an indication towards the Middle Path of the permanent creative forces of the Spirit through which the Spirit builds worlds. This is a continuous process – and, according to the trident, we have several choices related to it. One is that the Magus ought to flow into this path, becoming part of it, and use its power. An indication towards this should be the phrase on the left blade – *Obito,* which, in this sense, and also as an incantation, would mean *(you have to) subdue,* or rather, as we have said, *(you have to) receive and transmit* the things and processes of this creative building solar force, and this should be the path corresponding to the Left Pillar of the Kabalistic Tree. Then the formula would look like this: **In the name and with the power of the triple pentagrammatic freedom, Providence and Fortuna, receive and transmit the creating force of the Spirit!**

The other choice is dictated by the inscription on the right blade – *Imo,* meaning *on the contrary, despite,* and therefore it is analogous to the Right Path of the Tree. In this sense, as opposed to the Left Path, the above indicated meanings are used, not that *"I"* which is present in the final version of the formula. In this way, the formula will take on the following form: **In the name and with the power of the triple pentagrammatic freedom, Providence and Fortuna, despite Destiny, materialize your will!**

The third choice is to unite all these paths, which is obviously the idea of the trident, and through the formula thus united, the trident turns into a combined sceptre-and-sword possessing triple magic power:

**In the name and with the power of the triple pentagrammatic freedom, Providence and Fortuna! I, through the forces of the astral light, affirm the Supreme Will on Earth. So be it! The Concealed One!**

There is also another aspect of this topic that so far seems to have only been mentioned but not discussed in detail, and it concerns the reverse side of the trident when it is used for healing, the image of which is shown in *Fig. 7.*

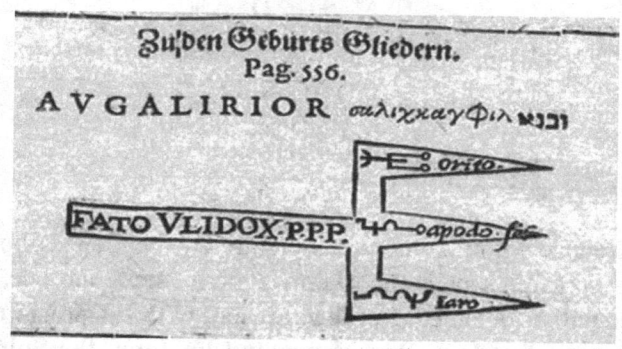

**Figure 7**

It is immediately noticed that the inscriptions on the three blades are different from those we have viewed so far. In order to understand their meaning, we must first decipher the inscriptions above the trident, which are mostly re-encoded through combinations of Greek and Latin words, forming something like a title of the corresponding topic. Knowing from other authors that the trident was also used to treat male impotence, it is relatively easier to unravel the first inscription – AVGALIRIOR.

We start with the Greek αυγά – AVGA, literally meaning *eggs* – or, in this case, *testicles*. We then proceed with our familiar LI, abbreviated from the Latin word *Libertas*, or *liberty*, and we end with RIOR, from Latin PRIOR – *before, prior state*. Thus, the word AVGALIRIOR literally acquires the following meaning: "To liberate the testicles into their prior state" – in the sense of "before impotence".

There follows a word written with Greek letters, which in Latin would be written as SALIXKAGFIL. We proceed to unravel it as well. In the beginning is the Latin word SALIX, meaning *medicine, remedy, cure,* but in this case, *remedy from willow bark*. There follows the Greek word κάγ (ώ) – KAG (O), which is the conjunction "and", and finally – FIL, which in Latin means *ray of light, hope*. Following these clarifications, the two words together, AVGALIRIOR SALIXKAGFIL, written above the picture of the trident, would have the following meaning: **"To liberate the testicles into their prior state through remedy from willow bark and through the ray of hope."**

After these clarifications, we now proceed already to the inscriptions on the blades. On the left blade, where the *Obito* inscription is present, we now see the word *Orito* on this side of the trident. It consists of the Latin words *Ora* – *to pray, prayer,* and *Ito* – *to do in order to make sth work/ function;* and, as a whole, it would mean "to make a prayer". As we have already explained, the left side is the receiving and obeying one, so it is perfectly well-grounded here to have the prayer as part of the complete formula.

On the right blade, where the word *Imo* was inscribed, now the word IARO is written, which we interpret from Greek ιαρός/ Ιατροσ as *Divine Healer* or *Divine Healing*.

Finally, on the middle blade, there is an inscription *Apodo.Sel,* consisting of two Latin words: *Apodo* means *to connect,* and regarding *Sel,* we already explained that it means *salt* – the alchemical symbol of Earth and crystallization, as well as of the material plane where the intention is to be conducted and transmitted so that it is ultimately accomplished. Thus, the whole inscription *Apodo.Sel* would mean "I connect for the materialization of the intention."

To us, there is no other alternative than joining the inscriptions on the blades with the written on the handle P.P.P.VLIDOXFATO, thus recreating the whole formula: **In nomine Pentagrammatica Libertas Trinitate, In Dox et Fato! Orito, IARO, ApodoSel! Verum est! Amen!**

Translated into English, it would look like this: **In the name and with the power of the triple pentagrammatic freedom, Providence and Fortuna! I direct my prayer towards the Divine Healer** (mentioning His name), **so that my wish be materialized** (specifying the wish)**! So be it! The Concealed One!**

As we have already mentioned, this formula is present on the trident that is drawn under a heading indicating that it concerns the treatment of impotence. However, we believe that this formula is universal and that the trident, in this sense, should be used for any treatment.

Quite purposefully and at the risk of boring the reader, we have made a decoding of this magic formula to illustrate once again the importance of knowing the inner sense and meaning of symbols, and also how they are utilized.

In conclusion, we will make the following generalization: *Tridens Paracelsi* represents itself a multifunctional magic device, as it is modernly called, combining a magic sceptre, a sword and a healing appliance. From all that has been said above, it is necessary to conclude that there exists a type of magic which is not connected with any traditional rituality but is carried out within a certain ceremony. It is called *Ceremonial Magic* and is the operative core essence of Sacred Magic. As is well known, in Freemasonry, rituals are widely practiced, so, in the context of what was exposed above, rituality possesses magic nature, and that is why it is called *Royal Art* – a term related to Ancient Egypt, where magic was the official religion. *Pentagrammatica Libertas* is a powerful magic implementation formula that could be acknowledged formally by Freemasonry without the use of *Tridens Paracelsi,* because it is characterized by universality. In principle, the sceptre is present in the Masonic rituality, but this sceptre is far from being magical, neither is it used as such. Our reason for using this magic formula in Freemasonry is that, through it, the Will of the Almighty God, the Great Architect of the Universe, is ultimately affirmed. With some pity, we remind that the modern Masonic Rites do not possess the Art of Magic, so the purpose of this book is to revive it – and, as we know, art always has its manifestations in the material world.

## Reality and Evil

*There is, to be sure, no evil without something good.*

**Pliny the Elder**

As it is, in the material world, if you want something, then, in order to receive it, you have to sacrifice something else; and, if you want everything – you ought to sacrifice everything. Such is the Law of Sacrifice. However, this law is not valid in the Spiritual World, because, as Rumi says, "A candle loses nothing from its light by lighting another candle." Nevertheless, the harmony in the physical world is maintained by the dynamic equilibrium of opposite forces. Whenever you receive without giving, you violate this harmony, and therefore it must be restored by taking away something from you. Giving and taking are mechanisms for maintaining equilibrium, the difference between them being that, in the former, positive emotions are being experienced, while the latter is perceived as punishment. If we learn to perceive the enjoyment of the taker, then giving will turn into supreme bliss. Egoism is formed in a consciousness conditioned by non-giving, so, in order to restore the harmony, Love has to be placed as an opposing force. *Egoism* and *Love* express the two initial and mutually opposing forces – the centripetal and the centrifugal one. Egoism preserves the wholeness of the point, whereas Love allows the circle to expand. Thus, the harmony of the *Creator-Creation* configuration is preserved. These two forces are embedded in the foundation of both the *Dark Lodge* and the *White Lodge*. The former serves only for personal self-perfection and egoistic purposes, while, in the latter, everything is subordinate to Love, to creative expansion, to the principle of the good fruit. A relatively flexible equilibrium between the two forces is necessary, since harmony is a function of their opposition. The Great Architect of the Universe is the Head of the *Grand Universal United Lodge* and directs both the White and the Dark Lodge. Therefore, concepts like *good* and *evil* are to be viewed in terms of Absolute Truth and relative truth. In the exoteric aspect, which must be assigned to relative truth, everything manifested is reality, so good and evil are also realities. However, is everything manifested real? Historically, in philosophy, under *reality,* the very Existential Being of the essential in everything was meant. We would further develop this definition to the extent of something most inherent to the core essence[46] – and, as such, reality is constant, unchanging Existential Being. In view of this characteristic, the real is only inherent to God, Whose Core Essence is the Eternal and Absolute Truth. The Core Essence of God is Non-Caused (Acausal), He is That Which IS in Itself, and therefore He is *Immanent* and at the same time *Transcendent.* This is the Non-Manifested God standing behind everything – and, as such, He represents the substantial reality. God's Might limits itself within various forms so that it is not destructive. Each form, however, is subject to time and space, and therefore it is impermanent, fugitive, changing. The Non-Manifested God as substantial reality is the One who IS, while, in the manifested forms, He is the constant Change as the only constant of materiality.

---

46 The core essence is assumed to be something immutable – *AN.*

At this level of reasoning, the manifested is not real, because it does not have the characteristics of the Absolute, of Eternity. Therefore, God is Eternity, Perpetually Manifesting Itself, and yet, He is Non-Manifested Reality. In this sense, everything manifested is Illusion. However, it should not be forgotten that the principle of opposites acts in everything. As a result, the Truth has two poles: the *Absolute* and the *Relative*. One aspect of this principle is the *Law of the Divine Paradox*. From the point of view of the Relative Truth, in the context of the Divine Paradox, every single thing should be viewed at the level of its manifestation. From the angle of our finite mind, the Divine Paradox in the physical world is that "Although the world does not exist, it still exists" – it is actual.

"It is truth without any lie, it is certain, and it is truthful" (veritable, authentic, actual) – this is how the *Emerald Tablet* of Hermes Trismegistus begins. *(Fig. 8)* The first is equivalent to *real*, whereas the third is all-encompassing, containing both the illusory and the real, only from the aspect of the relative. To paraphrase, what Hermes has said means: *We can behold this in the Spirit, feel it through the soul, and see it embodied into matter.*

**Figure 8**

Actually, at this level of reasoning, the following conclusion should be drawn: The Manifested in which God's Providence is contained is Relative Reality, while everything else is Illusion. There is no Evil but rather non-evolved Good, and there is no darkness but rather lack of light – these are degrees of one and the same thing. There is no Evil except that which is done inside the human soul. At another level of knowledge, we would say that the ancients were right, considering the World to be Illusion – "Maya"; and we would add also: The only reality in the Manifested is Change – πάντα ρεῖ (Panta rei)[47].

## Oneness

*Everything is One, whereas the Attitude towards it produces the Differentness.*
**Sabaor Abu Avira**

Oneness is perhaps the first archetype of Creation and the process of Building the Edifice of the Universe because they are formed by one Creator, in accordance with one and the same principles. Therefore, Oneness is a vivified analogy. *Identity,* in the sense of *sameness,* means absolute coincidence not only with something else, but also with oneself. Since factuality is changeable, there exists no absolute identity (sameness) with oneself. Identifying things, in this sense, requires that they be distinguished in advance, as a reference point, and that is why no sameness exists between them either. So, each identity (sameness) of phenomena "at first glance" is illusory, and it has the characteristics of similarity or analogy, and is therefore relative, so only their change is absolute. Identity (sameness), like any other thing, should be viewed in accordance with the Principle of Opposites. In correspondence with it, if the Non-Manifested God is a constant quantity: the Absolute, and therefore, also – the Substantial Reality, then He is identical with Himself, or Immanent. Hence, God's qualities as being archetypal are identical with themselves. In this sense, absolute identity (sameness) exists, yet it is immanent, which is why it is by definition unknowable and inherent to God alone. In all that is manifested, there is a relative identity (sameness), which is an illusory, speculative concept insofar as it is a comparative degree of illusory things. In the *Emerald Tablet* of Hermes, quoted above, the Law of Analogy is formulated as follows: "That which is below is like that which is above, and that which is above is like that which is below, to perform the miracles of

---

[47] From Greek: "Everything flows" – Heraclitus ("Everything flows, everything moves, nothing stays in the same place, and you cannot not step twice into the same river.") – *AN*.

Oneness." Analogy represents the comparative category replacing identity (sameness) in the material world, and it is also an instrument of acquiring knowledge of the subtle worlds.

The understanding that *"You are my other Self"* is an achievement affirming one of the most ancient ethical principles. It does not mean: "I am identical with you." It means: "We are consubstantial." There is an analogy existing between us all because we are God's creation and we are all alike because we are Humans. This is the core essence in the words of Jesus: "I and My Father are One." (*Holy Gospel of John* 10:30, *NKJV*)

Even products originating from one and the same mould, being perfectly alike, cannot be identical because their informational saturation is different. Identity (sameness) in the material world, as we have already explained, is a speculative concept, meaning complete likeness, but of illusory symbols, and is therefore relative. *Real* is everything stemming from the Spirit in which the Creative Will of the Divine acts, and therefore it has the characteristic of Eternity. On the contrary, *illusory* is everything in which the Spirit is absent, and it is therefore temporal and relative. This gives us the confidence to affirm that Love is eternal, whereas hatred is its temporary opposition.

In order to understand what Oneness represents, we need to clarify the terms *likeness* and *analogy*.

*Likeness* denotes such a connection and correlation between things in which one thing contains in itself several attributes and qualities of another.

*Analogy* is the highest form of likeness – an especially strong relation between certain things, and, above all, the presence of an archetype. In view of what has been said about magic, we can add that magic is the art of seeing and using the relations of analogy, yet not for self-interested or utilitarian purposes. Magic is the ability to build and awaken analogies, and trigger them to resolve unresolved binaries. Following these clarifications, we can define *Oneness* as "the result of a manifested analogy, when things are revealed and when they penetrate each other, during which their energies are mixed, but without any loss of identity". Oneness implies self-identification – and the formula for that is: *"I am this"*, with the ending: *"but this is not my "I"*. Oneness is a vivified analogy, and, as we have said, it is the first archetypal idea of the Creator.

# The Fall and Divisiveness

> *We are sinful not only because we have eaten of the Tree of Knowledge, but also because we have not yet eaten of the Tree of Life.*
>
> *Franz Kafka*

The Unity of Oneness before the Fall is represented in the Old Testament by the Garden of Eden, inhabited by the human who is consubstantial with God and the Universe. The *Tree of Knowledge of Good and Evil* is the tree of involution, so it grows downwards. It symbolizes the *Decalogue* of Moses, containing the Ten Commandments which are prohibitive and indicative. Knowledge shapes the perceptual world of human empiricism that builds the paradigm of divisiveness. The Tree of Knowledge is the modus of transition from the consciousness of consubstantiality to a differentiation marked by the binary code of the categories of *good* and *evil*. It is necessary to get out of the three-dimensional reflective space and to obtain an informational picture beyond the traditional cause-and-effect experience and binary thinking. The operative algorithm for this is the other Tree in the Garden of Eden, the *Tree of Life,* which is evolutionary and therefore grows upwards. It symbolizes the broken Tablets of Moses containing the Laws of the Universal Edifice – the Tablets that were lost by humans.

The fruit of knowledge transforms the primordial, synthesis consciousness of humans into analytical, conceptual thinking. Thus, in terms of philosophy, from an object, the human being turns into a subject in relation to Eternity, and becomes mortal in relation to materiality. Sinfulness is the alienation of humans from God through divisive thinking, while innocence is a symbol of their consubstantiality with Him. Thus, the "Fall" of humans is the loss of their "innocence", so they begin living in "sin" – *separated from God at a maximum degree.* Divisive thinking forms a mental binary world, conditioned by contradictory categories of differentiated consciousness. The human "I" represents the synthesis attitude towards these contradictory principles, whereas the human Ego perceives them as differentiation. The way out of this contradictoriness cannot be found at the level of the very differentiated consciousness: it will be accomplished through the transition from the Tree of Knowledge to the Tree of Life, from the illusion of knowledge to the reality of Life. In a Kabalistic key, this is implemented by upturning the Sefirotic Tree within humans.

## The Ego

> *The one who conquers oneself*
> *is the mightiest warrior.*
> **Confucius**
>
> *Ego says: "Once everything falls into place,*
> *I will find peace."*
> *Spirit says: "Find peace –*
> *and everything will fall into place."*
> **Zen**

Following all that has been said so far, we should view egoism as illusory reality – the primary foundation of the Fall, of the Original Sin. Sin does not affect the innermost nature of humans, which is consubstantial with God, but rather affects the shells of their personality, which are the masks hiding them from their Heavenly Origin. However, as Seneca says, *Nemo potest personam diu ferre.*[48] Sooner or later, humans have to remove their own masks, and then each will be floodlit by the radiant light of one's own "I". Humans ought to let their "conceptual mind" be "stolen" so that they be transformed into Jubrān's mind-less "madman"[49], because this is the only way they will come close to the Truth. "Pilate said to Him, "What is truth?" – and when Jesus replied with *Alta silentia*[50] (*Holy Gospel of John* 18:38, *NKJV*)[51]. In the apocryphal *Gospel of Nicodemus*, however, Jesus answers to this question with the words: "Truth is from Heaven." Pilate asks, "Is there no Truth upon Earth?", and Jesus replies, "Watch closely how those who speak the Truth are judged by those who have power of authority upon Earth." The concreteness of this answer, emphasizing the injustice regarding those who speak the Truth, does not ignore the very core essence of the Truth. The Truth is as IT IS, no matter to what extent it does not fit into paradigms. Fiction needs credibility to be liked and accepted, unlike the Truth, which takes no interest whether it is liked or not. In this sense, namely, is also the Latin phrase *Credo, quia absurdum*[52], and

---

48 From Latin: "No one can wear a mask forever" – *AN*.
49 Jubrān Khalīl Jubrān (usually referred to in English as *Kahlil Gibran*) is a Lebanese poet, writer, philosopher and painter, a Maronite Christian. In his creative work, he combines elements of Eastern and Western Mysticism, and he becomes famous for his aphoristic poetic works, one of which is *The Madman* – *AN*.
50 From Latin: "Profound silence" – *AN*.
51 In the Gospel, the Greek word used is ἀλήθεια – *alétheia*, which has the meaning not only of "pronounced truth", but also of "Divine Truth revealed to humans". In Ancient Greek, this word was used as an antonym of *illusion* – *AN*.
52 "I believe because it is absurd" – *AN*.

also, as Heraclitus says, "Unless you expect the unexpected, you will never find the Truth." And yet, who can tell what the Truth is, when even the Son of God answered in silence? He has bequeathed to us, however, the Nine Beatitudes of the Gospel, pronounced in His sermon on Karn Hattin Mountain, Palestine, the first of which is: "Blessed are the poor in spirit, for theirs is the Kingdom of Heaven." (*Holy Gospel of Matthew* 5:3, *NKJV*) We would translate this Beatitude from the New Testament as follows: "Blessed are the poor in reason, for theirs is the Kingdom of Heaven", because the word *bina* ("reason") is used in the Hebrew text. The text is an indication that humans have to sacrifice their own conceptual mind, the product of the ego, and become an *"empty cup"*, free from the haughty pride of education and the arrogance of knowledge; that they have to first and foremost be disciples sitting in anticipation on the unhewn stone in front of the pillars of Solomon's Temple, a symbol of Wisdom. Using Christian symbolism, we will say that Jesus dies, while Christ is resurrected, which means that the mind has to die so that the consciousness may be resurrected. We cannot get to know the Truth but we can build up our Soul as a Temple, forging an altar from our ego, on which Truth is to perform the Sacred Rites.

The term *Ego* means *"I"*. It has a sacral meaning only in the expression *Ego sum (I am)*.[53] In Ancient Hebrew, it is pronounced as "Ehyeh", and this is the Name of God given to Moses. Outside of this formula, the ego is the "false self" of personality, its individual accomplishment, called in Hinduism by the term *ahamkara*. It is the complex of false notions of the very personality about itself, as well as the judgments of others about it, which it has perceived and which are part of its introjection. These notions may be conscious or unconscious, but anyway, they are the ones that shape, to a great extent, humans such as they wish to be. However, they are their false image, the way they liked themselves, unwilling to change; yet, as Seneca has said, *Animum debes mutare, non caelum.*[54] This is the essence of the ego, whose basic tool is the conceptual mind. It does not brook any differentness – and, whenever any differentness appears, humans fall into cognitive dissonance leading to the breaking of the correlation between reality and the already built cognition. This causes psychological discomfort motivating the maintenance of a consonant cognitive construct. This means that the ego and the

---

53 *"Dixit Deus ad Mosen: Ego Sum Qui Sum"* (*Exodus* 3:14, *Latin Vulgate*) – "And God said to Moses, "I AM WHO I AM." *(NKJV)* According to the Holy Bible of the Bulgarian Orthodox Church, "God answered Moses: I am the Eternally Existing One." – *AN*.

54 From Latin: "You ought to change your spirit (i.e. state of mind), not change the Heaven." – *AN*.

conceptual mind adjust reality by using axiomatic apperception, which has formed already accepted conceptions and notions that are not contestable. In this way, true reality is replaced by a conformist subjective reality, which, however, is not in dissonance with the false self of personality. This is how comfort is maintained in the bimodal consciousness while reflecting the inner and the outer world, at the expense of the illusory nature of the latter. These attitudes alienate humans from their true Core Essence which constitutes their immortal "I" and is referred to as *Ego sum, Ehyeh,* whereas, in the Egyptian esoteric tradition, it is called *Issy*. After flying off from the Primordial Matter, which is the Boundless Primordial Light, Issy is incorporated into a biological body – a vehicle, and starts its mission in the physical world. The fulfilment of this mission leads to transformation and reincarnation. An ancient Egyptian priestly text reads: "I have turned into Khepri – the God of reincarnations." *Kheprer* is the very process of transformation, as we have already mentioned, while *Khepri* is the sacred beetle – scarab, and means *to be, to become,* which is symbolically associated with the "becoming" and "being" of the Soul. On a very particular, concrete plane, Khepri represents the transforming force through which, for example, in the pupa, the organs of the caterpillar undergo histolysis, and then the new organs emerge of the imago, which breaks the shell and flies away, reborn for a new life. This phenomenon contains the symbolism of the ascending transformation of the human form, and, in the Egyptian tradition, it is represented by the scarab – a beetle that rolls a dung ball, the latter constantly expanding and enlarging itself in this process. Egyptians symbolically depict the sacred beetle rolling the solar disk along its celestial path. Behind the Sun, *Ra,* there stands *Atum,* the Spirit of the solar force, the latter called *Aton* by Pharaoh Ehnaton. This is *Amen* – the concealed principle of all solar religions that affirm the solar energy *solve* underlying the basis of expansion and transformation.

The anatomical correspondence of the Sun is the solar plexus where the Sefira *Tiferet* of the Microcosmic Kabalistic Tree is positioned. There the Sun "rises", and the Sacred Beetle begins to "roll" it upwards through the levels of consciousness. The spiritual principle is *Issy,* with its manifestation in the solar plexus, where sunlight becomes visible, similarly to the solar disk *Ra*. Kheprer is the power of "becoming" and transformation raising the consciousness up along the path towards the Spirit – our true Self, our true "I", which is consubstantial with everyone else.

The notion of the "other one" is the illusion of the ego, reflected in a multitude of mirrors. Because of their own ignorance, humans see their own reflection in them but recognize it as the "other one", who is our spiritual mirror – so, if we do not like this "other one", then we do not like ourselves.

In the ego, there is no true willpower, because, after all, the ego obeys the body and the influences of the natural and social environment. Illusion represents one of the main reasons for the lack of true willpower in the ego. Therefore, the Sefira *Yesod* of the Kabalistic Tree (on the Microcosmic Tree, it is positioned in the genital area), where the ego is located, is called the "dim mirror" because it reflects things blurred and in the "Sfumato" style. What is seen in the mirror is believed to be actual reality; however, it is distorted by the type of experience and the many delusions of the ego, as well as by its striving to preserve the status quo. Therefore, in the Masonic Rites, the ego is being symbolically covered with the apron, to show that it is ignored, and in the temple, the personality is dropped out, and all become one whole. The proper state of being of the ego is its service to the true "I", situated in the Sefira *Tiferet* (the solar plexus), where our spiritual heart is located. In the Old Testament, Joseph (the ego) only prospers in the obedience to Pharaoh (the "I"). Then, ascension of the consciousness begins towards its Divine Nature. A large part of all humans are on the "shore of their animal inner essence", while very few have set foot on the "bridge" leading to their Divine Core Essence. This "bridge" is the very human, because it connects two extremes: the animal and the Divine; and yet, like any other bridge, it contains tension in itself. Therefore, one never resides in stillness. The bridge is to be crossed; however, humans have built a home on it. Therefore, Christ, too, says that our Home is not here, that we have no Home in this world, and that our Home is elsewhere. Stopping permanently and finally on the bridge is pointless, because anyway humans are predestined to walk beyond, onto the shore of their Divine Nature, to climb the biblical *Ladder of Jacob*. One can achieve this with the help of a Spiritual Master, of spiritual teachings and spiritual societies, Freemasonry being one of them. With the help of the esoteric science, the Worshipful Master and the Brotherhood, a Freemason ought to sacrifice his ego on the altar of the "I", and to become aware of the delusions of *Set* (the conceptual mind). Then *Anubis* (the distinguishing mind) begins to be formed in him, and through this mind, he begins to distinguish Truth from illusion, to winnow the grain from the chaff. So, in the end, *Horus* is born – the enlightened mind that will transform him into the reassembled *Osiris* – the whole human. The analogue of the ego in Masonic symbolism is the unhewn stone, which must be dressed in order to become the Chief Cornerstone – the "I".

One can attract Khepri, the Sacred Beetle, the God of reincarnations, only by becoming aware of one's triune core essence, by becoming a likeness of God's Temple. Then in *Tiferet* (the solar plexus), the dung ball is transformed into a Spiritual Sun. It is only then that Khepri comes flying and starts rolling up the "Inner Sun" so that it "rises" and "sets", upwards along Jacob's Ladder, enlightening the levels of consciousness buried in darkness. Only then does Anubis lead humans to Horus so that they merge with their Divine Nature, and thus, illuminated by the Spiritual Light, they will probably exclaim, just like Jubrān's mindless madman: "Blessed, blessed are the thieves who stole my masks!"

**Figure 9**

# 6
# Christ and Golgotha

*Golgotha is, in its essence, the faith in Golgotha!*
**Sabaor Abu Avira**

The reason why it was necessary for the Logos to penetrate into the souls and free them from egoism is in order for them to get to know the Spirit as Sublime Reality which they have to aspire to. Christ is the thread of Divine Wisdom that leads the human mind out of the enchanted vicious circle of matter, into the Light of Truth. Jesus reveals the immortality of the Spirit: He shows that death is contained in birth, so unless you are Born Anew, you cannot enter the Kingdom of God. The birth from the Spirit takes place during the Sacred Initiation when the veil of the Holy of Holies, the *Paroklet,* is lifted, and you rise to face the Truth. If an unprepared person lifts this veil, that person will be burnt to ashes by its mighty fiery power. This preparation took place only in the temples under the guidance of Masters. During the Sacred Initiation in the Ancient Mysteries, one sacrifices one's old illusory inner essence, which dies so that the true "I" may be born. The "I" in each person is the incarnation of Truth, and the Truth is the only reliable, authoritative Law of God. Our Spirit – this is God inside us, and He is the Supreme Lawgiver of Truth that makes us free. This is also the deep meaning of the Masonic maxim "Only the Law will give us Freedom."

A Great Spirit – Christ, in the hypostasis of Jesus, comes to Earth to show that the Truth is to be lived as the Path – the Way. Therefore, He says, "I am the Way, the Truth, and the Life" (*Holy Gospel of John* 14:6, *NKJV*) – and therefore He does not give Pilate a definition of the Truth: because He came not to define the Truth but to embody it in life. The attempt of getting to know Christ through the binary consciousness means either failing to understanding Him or misunderstanding Him.

The story of Jesus, called *Christ,* has been the one occupying the minds of humans in the utmost degree over the millennia, so in the context of knowing the Divine, we will dwell on specific facts. The name *Christ* comes from the Greek Χριστός, which, as we have already explained, means *The Anointed One*. Anointing was performed with crocodile fat and is a tradition inherited from Ancient Egypt.[55] This term was used regarding anyone who was subject to performing the anointing ritual. The Babylonian *Tammuz* was being called *Christ*, or *Holy King,* and such a nomination applied to all pre-Christ figures analogous to "Jesus". Outside of the New Testament texts, there is nothing written anywhere about the existence of Jesus. It is known that more than 40 chroniclers recorded the events in Judea at the time when Jesus was said to have lived, and none of them mentions Him. On the other hand, in ancient times, before Him, there were stories, myths and legends about the Son of God saving humankind. A whole millennium before Jesus appears, the myth of the "pagan saviour" Virishna existed in the East, who was born by a virgin through Immaculate Conception with the intervention of the Holy Spirit. There exist also many other pre-Christian Deities about whom the same story was told. Birth in a barn or cave is a recurring theme in myths related to the Sun because the cave symbolizes the "dark place" where the Sun was believed to "die" during the winter solstice, and "be born" again 3 days later, on December 25. It is for this reason, namely, that the ancient Gods were given this

---

55 *Messeh* means "Holy Crocodile", as well as "anointment with crocodile fat". From this word, *Mashiach* ("Messiah") derives – *AN*.

birthdate, 3 days after the winter solstice (December 22). The Virgin Mother of the Son God is also an old theme that can be found all over the world. It refers again to the myth of the Sun, which, at certain periods of time, rises along with the constellation *Virgo*. On December 25, the Romans celebrated the *Natalis Solis Invicti*, the Birthday of the Invincible Sun, and this epithet coincides fully with the one used by the Persians regarding the Divinity worshiped under the name of *Mithra*. The Persian Mithra chooses 12 followers to whom to convey His teaching. Three days after His funeral, He comes back to life through resurrection. He is called *"The Truth and the Light"*. More than three thousand years ago, at the annual celebration in honour of the Resurrection of the Persian Mithra-Saviour, the priests proclaimed in a solemn voice: "Rejoice, mourners! Your God has come back among the living!"

Many of the mythical solar Deities were crucified because of the sins of humans, just as it is described as having happened to Jesus. It is an ancient ritual in which the "Son" on the cross represents the Sun during the spring equinox. The cross itself is not a unique Christian symbol: it had been used for millennia before. In Persia, there was a ritual in which a young man pretending to be dead was "resurrected". They called him "Saviour" and proclaimed that his sufferings would bring salvation to people. The same was said as well in Egypt about Horus, and also in India about Krishna, long before the birth of Christian faith.

The miracles performed by Jesus, in one form or another, are present in still more ancient traditions. In the Egyptian *Book of the Dead*, a picture can be seen in which it is illustrated how the imperfections from which the soul wants to break free take the form of pigs and are banished by Thoth who symbolizes Sublime Wisdom. This is reminiscent of the scene of Jesus casting out demons. We can give also many other examples, the impossible synchronicity of which gives reason to believe that Jesus is a fabrication; however, exactly these examples make us not have doubts, according to the maxim: *Certum est, quia impossibile est.*[56]

There is an evident paradox that conceptually seems insoluble. On the one hand, it turns out that Christianity has adopted as its basis the ancient symbolic history of the Sun, as well as many other accompanying myths, legends and stories, historically presenting them as something that really happened. On the other hand, the canonized and the apocryphal Gospels, some of which were written by the disciples of Jesus, are testimony to His real existence. This contradiction cannot be resolved through ordinary human analytical thinking. Therefore, humans do not recognize the Deity in Jesus, so He

---

56 From Latin: "It is certain because it is impossible" – Tertullian *(regarding the Resurrection of Christ) – AN.*

does not represent any interest to the historians and chroniclers of His epoch, because, to them, He is not unique, He is one of many. The numinous cannot be grasped through the mind: it can only be reached through Faith. Only through Faith, it is possible to surmount and transcend the divisive conceptual thinking. Therefore, Faith is the way to resolve the Divine Paradox, and is contrary to the conceptual mind. The cross is a universal symbol of the Unified Oneness, and it is the modus of the new synthesis thinking. Upon it are being crucified the Transcendent and the immanent, the Divine and the human, the Eternal and the temporal, the Imperishable and the perishable, which are ultimately the characteristics of Life and death. Resurrection is a symbol of renewal and victory over death through the sacrifice on the cross and the acquisition of Eternal Life. This is precisely what the mission of Christ is: to atone for sin and restore the innocence of humans by proclaiming their consubstantiality with God, and also to reveal the Truth as Life, triumphing over death.

The truthful growth of personality stems from inner processes, not from external sources. The appearance of Jesus to Paul might not have happened if he did not know about the existence of Jesus, but anyway, the vision is the fruit of the unconscious of Paul himself. This is one of the testimonies that Christ represents the supreme symbol of the concealed Immortal within the mortal human. In mythology, this duality is shown through the immortal twin. The commemoration of the ritual sacrificial death of Jesus is not only a recurrence of a historical event, but, each time, it is an experience of an eternal process of renewal. Golgotha is a moment of Eternity in time.

Therefore, it is not so important whether Jesus the Nazarene is a real historical personality and one of the greatest Initiates who has received the Spirit of Christ, or whether He is a Divine allegory. It is also of minor importance whether He is the Son of God Who is Born of Unity, or he is just a human son playing some *"esoteric show"* so that the *"written"* in the Old Testament actually takes place; as well as whether the Magus Jesus exteriorized his soul and, after being taken down from the cross, brought it back into the body that was buried after some time somewhere near the Dead Sea, nor the circumstance that Jesus might be a fabrication giving credence to deep esoteric secrets and truths. Whether all this is true is not so important. What is more important is that the "tree" named *Jesus* has given fruit; and the fruit is the only criterion for the Truth, as this same Jesus teaches us: "You will know them by their fruits." These fruits are Love and sacrifice that are the Way, the Path towards the Truth. What is important is the Path which we ought to identify with, in order to become the very Path.

## The Path

> *Each long journey*
> *begins with a single step.*
>
> **Lao Tzu**
>
> *Your "I" is the final destination*
> *of your journey.*
>
> **Chinese proverb**

The ancient thirst of each and every Soul to get to know the Secret and to experience the Holiness of the Sacrament, which inspires everything exquisite created by humans, can fit into the esoteric concept of the *Path*. Being upon the Path and being the very Path is one and the same, because you cannot walk along the Path and not become this very Path. There is nothing more important in life than the Path, so we ought to be travellers along the Path. This means that we should not identify ourselves with anything, nor try to hold and keep anything else except the very Path. In this Path, everything unnecessary will be taken away from us but we will be given things, regarding which, at one point, we will become aware that they are a gracious boon, and also that the breath (the Spirit) is our only property. According to Rumi[57], "To be able to reach one's Home, one has to leave many temporary dwellings." The fundamental work of all spiritual schools, Freemasonry being one of them, is to unite the souls to walk together along the Path, and become conscious of this Path. Blessed are those who have embarked on the Path, for they have come closer to the gates of the Kingdom of Heaven!

However, as Seneca has said, *Non est ad astra mollis e terris via* – "There is no easy way from the Earth to the stars". It must be known that this Path is a joint, shared Path, because no one enters the Kingdom of Heaven individually, "For where two or three are gathered together in My name, I am there in the midst of them", Jesus says. (*Holy Gospel of Matthew* 18:20, *NKJV*) However, we believe, like *Ramana Maharshi*, that one has to find one's own path which is connected with a particular spiritual circle, tradition, religion, without being compelled: "All who seek God should be let to follow their own path." First of all, most important is the *motivation* along the Path, which can be defined essentially as follows: The Freemason's Path is that of spiritual transformation and raising the consciousness towards Wisdom and Truth. As for whether this actually happens, each Brother should answer for himself. It

---

57 *Mevlânâ Jalāl ad-Dīn Muhammad Rūmī* is a Persian poet and Sufi mystic. He was born in 1207 in the city of Balkh, in present-day Afghanistan, at that time Eastern Persia. Because of his authority, Rumi is called *Mevlânâ* – a Guide and Master of his disciples. He teaches philosophy, religion and law, and writes poetry – *AN*.

can be said that motives are the core of human personality. They stand behind the psyche and determine the personality's behaviour and actions. The word *motivation* derives from Latin[58] and means *to move, to set in motion,* or most generally – *action*. However, it is about some inner movement, which is a process of the psyche, as opposed to the *stimulus,* which is entirely external. The word *motivation* has rather an ideal connotation, whereas the word *stimulus* – primarily a material one. The motivational sphere is hierarchically structured and is not constant, which is why the priority motives are constantly changing. Therefore, the motivation of those who have embarked on the Path has to be a mental and energetic expansion leading to spiritual transformation. God is dynamic. He keeps expanding, and along with Him – the whole Creation; but still, His Core Essence remains unchanging. Thus, also Wisdom, which is God's Will, keeps on expanding, but its substantial reality does not change. The scope of our consciousness also keeps expanding, our personality keeps being transformed, but the laws underlying them remain. The ancient Magi have formulated it in the following way: "I am this, but this is not my "I", whereas Jesus Christ has formulated it by the words: "I and My Father are One." (*John* 10:30, *NKJV*)

The term *expansion of consciousness* should be understood as that purposeful and focused spiritual transformation that is the result of the esoteric knowledge of God's Laws and their unconditional observance through Wisdom. This is what any disciple (apprentice, fellow craft) has to aspire to at the very beginning of the Path in every Initiatic society. We have already explained that the Master Teacher in Freemasonry is the *Worshipful Master*[59]. He cannot give all the knowledge but actually his task is to help the Brothers recall. This is the transmission of *"Baraka",* of Initiatic force, of awakening force, of gracious boon from a Master to a disciple. *Baraka* is a term used by Sufis and means *force, food* and *Grace,* all at the same time. The force and the gracious boon not only flow into the soul of disciples as into a receptacle in order to fill them, but they have also the quality of an awakening stream. Knowledge is inside humans: it only has to be driven out of the abyss of oblivion, and also, the Law of Lack of Understanding ought to be overcome, with the help of the Master. By turning one's glance inward and sinking into the depths of silent speechlessness, we can extract the old experience and knowledge from our sub-consciousness. However, this can only happen if the inner chatter of the mind stops. The mind is like a wild horse throwing away

---

58  From Late Latin, *motivus* – "movable", deriving from the verb *movēre:* "to move", "to set in motion", and its past participle, *motus:* "motion", "change", "sth that is in a position to, or capable of, moving or being moved" – *AN*.
59  One of the titles of the Master of the Lodge – *AN*.

every thought that wants to harness and ride it for more than a few seconds. However, the greatest vice of the unenlightened mind is falsehood, telling lies. The pain in a cut finger is actually in the pain centre of the brain, but our mind deludes us that it is in the finger. What is the guarantee, then, that it does not lie to us about subjective and objective reality, presenting some events as unreal (internally, we imagine that we see a horse), while others – as real (outside of us, we see a real horse)? This question arises because of the lack of any answer to the following question: According to what criterion do some facts appear to us as being inside us, whereas others – as being outside us? That is why the great mystic[60] of the 8$^{th}$ century Shantideva has said: "If you manage to tame only your mind, then everything else will be tamed by itself." The mind can only be tamed through the power of the Will, which is acquired through the discipline and self-discipline of spiritual disciples.

## The Spiritual Discipleship

> *A student is not a vessel to be filled, but a fire to be kindled.*
>
> ***Plutarch***

David's *Psalm 23* is a psalm about Spiritual Discipleship. In it, the Path of Disciples is given: "Though I walk through the valley of the shadow of death, I will fear no evil; for You are with me; Your rod and Your staff, they comfort me." (*Psalm* 23:4, *NKJV*) The power of anchored trust and the mystical experience of the Soul are conveyed: "He restores my Soul; He leads me in the Paths of Righteousness for His Name's sake". (*Psalm* 23:3, *NKJV*) A spiritual disciple walks along the Path of Righteousness, unceasingly attaining the Secret of God's Name. However, this is possible only in union with the Truth and the Incarnate Wisdom, while the aspiration towards them must not only be dictated by a desire to achieve egoistic results, or become a goal itself. Disciples are initially enticed by the brilliance of the boons that the spiritual teaching promises to them, just as a savage is enchanted by the glitter of gold and diamonds. A savage learned to use a shovel and finally realized that he did not need whatever had been buried in the ground, and he began to love the shovel more than the treasure. The same is the meaning of the text in the Gospel: "The Kingdom of Heaven is like treasure hidden in a field, which a man found and hid; and for joy over it he goes and sells all that he has and buys that field." (*Holy Gospel of Matthew* 13:44, *NKJV*)

---

60  *Mystic, mysticism* – these terms derive from the Greek μυστικός *(mystikós)*, which means "related to the Mysteries of the Initiatic cults". Another word that is closely related to it is μυστήριον *(mysterion)* – "mystery", both having one and the same root: μύστης *(mýstēs)* – "initiated" – *AN*.

Jesus says: "For where your treasure is, there your heart will be also." (*Holy Gospel of Matthew* 6:21, *NKJV*)

The Path is to love our discipleship and the shovel more than what we dig out. The shovel in spiritual teachings is a symbol of Wisdom and of the Soul's constant aspiration towards it.

Speaking of the field, which is the symbolic image of the Soul, we will quote also another passage from the Gospel: "Another parable He put forth to them, saying: "The Kingdom of Heaven is like a mustard seed, which a man took and sowed in his field, which indeed is the least of all the seeds; but when it is grown it is greater than the herbs and becomes a tree, so that the birds of the air come and nest in its branches." (*Holy Gospel of Matthew* 13:31 – 32, *NKJV*)

Mustard is a weed, spreading everywhere without sowing, and in the Middle East it is believed to cause insanity and is therefore not used. The following question arises: Why would anyone sow a weed in one's own field? It would be for purely agricultural reasons, on the one hand – to let the soil rest; and, on the other hand – to enrich it. At a deeper level, however, the idea of natural fertilization means that part of our consciousness must remain unsown. Thus, this part represents the field into which God's Seed will be sown. Besides that, the Hermetic Law of Rhythm is illustrated in a specific way. The antithesis contained in this text, in the image of the mustard seed, which is "the least of all the seeds" but which becomes larger than all cereals, when spreading as a plant, is clearly distinguished. What does this opposition mean, according to which the Kingdom of Heaven is both the small and the great? This means that the transition from the lower to the higher, from the material to the spiritual, contains in itself, by analogy, the reverse process. Just as the image of an object in the mirror is reverse, the same way *"the greatest"*, at the level of the Primordial Beginning, is in the end *"the least"* as its mirror image, its visible image at the level of Manifestation. Even the smallest contains the Divine; and when we are aware of this, it will turn into the greatest again.

The idea of the seed, as a symbol of Oneness and of the Primordial Beginning, is contained in many traditions. Such is the seminal syllable *OM,* through which the Universe is created. Such is also the tenth letter *Yod* of the Hebrew alphabet, on the basis of which all other letters are created, and as such, it illustrates the One Unified Primordial Beginning. From a Macrocosmic perspective, the Primordial Beginning is the Centre of the World, which in Kabala is called *Holy Palace* and is virtually the centre of every Creation, which, in the Microcosmic aspect, is symbolized by the heart and is the innermost point of contact with the Divine. The letter *Yod,* with its meaning of the Primordial Beginning in which Everything is included, represents a grain in which Everything is also contained on the material plane. According to the Hermetic Law of Analogy, from a transcendental and immanent point of view, they are equalized within the unified synthesis of the Universal Harmony.

Masonic symbols are like mustard seed: they contain Everything contained in the Primordial Beginning as an archetype. These symbols, which have been objects of reflection, contemplation and operative handling of generations of Masons, have sealed in themselves the imprints of certain information and ideas.

In the Lodges of Ancient Masonry, *apprentices,* or *disciples,* as they called them, only *listened,* and the word of the Master (Teacher) was a Law. The title of the *Upanishads,* the Ancient Indian collection of mystical and philosophical writings, is literally translated as *"Listening at the Feet of the Master Teacher"*. Thus, initially, the participation of any apprentice (disciple) in the "construction of the temple" was limited to listening only. After becoming a fellow craft, each Mason, besides listening, ought to already reflect on the heard, meditating, because meditation is a continuation of reflection, although in another state of mind. When meditating on Masonic symbols, one gets access to their astral clichés and reaches their core essence without even having verbal or written information about them. Moreover, as Paramahansa Yogananda says, "By the practice of meditation, you will find that you are carrying within your heart a portable Paradise."

The Path of a Freemason is a gradual one, consisting in the successive construction of the Temple of Wisdom. The construction material is delivered in stages, and experience is acquired slowly and persistently during the process of *Building the Edifice.* This is the slow "chewing of bread" of Wisdom, leading to transformational change. This transformation is expressed, in the first place, in smoothing and calming the mental stream. This stream is chaotic and marked by peaks and dips. The states of joy and euphoria are replaced by despondency, sadness and depression. When an apprentice realizes that these states of mind, though tangible, are nevertheless illusory, and that only the aspiration towards Wisdom and compassion leads to true happiness, then his mind will find peace. He will liberate himself from the fetters of circumstances and will cease fighting against them, so that he may be truly free. True freedom is the *freedom from any choice* – when there is no longer any necessity for you to make any choice, when you have already chosen the Right Path, and you follow it steadily, without paying attention to crossroads.

The next stage in the work on *Building the Edifice* is the acquisition of implementation power of authority. This happens when the Spirit begins to perform Holy Sacraments in the altar of the Temple of the Soul. Then the psychic powers of the Soul are released and can be governed by the willpower. Finally, qualities and abilities are acquired which other humans lack. They are strictly individual and diverse – but one of them is the direct knowledge of numbers and the proportions of the Temple.

However, the process of *Building the Edifice* is accompanied also by trials. In the first place, these are the spiritual trials, part of which consisting in the task given to Brothers: to learn humility and patience. Still, the most important trial is the Brotherhood itself, which includes both patience and humility. Without true brotherly interrelations, the work on *Building the Edifice* is impossible. Pythagoras places friendship between disciples as the basis of the joint Path.

At the cross, Jesus Christ conveys His essential messages to humankind, one of which is the power of the spiritual bond. He addresses His mother, pointing at John, saying: "Woman, behold your Son!" And, to John: "Behold your mother!" (*Holy Gospel of John* 19:26 – 27, *NKJV*) This means that the spiritual bond is stronger than the bond of blood, which is why the Spiritual Brotherhood in any Initiatic society is "above all", and it is the "Chief Cornerstone" of Freemasonry. The emblematic example of this bond is the so-called *brotherly chain* in Freemasonry, which we have already discussed. The solidity of a construction work is determined by the strength and indestructibility of this bond, which, however, requires willpower. All can be achieved through willpower, which represents the main tool of a Freemason. This tool cannot be bought but must be forged through the fire of Truth and the hammer of spiritual practices leading to mystical ecstasy, characterized by the highest vibrations of the mind. In this way, merging with God's Mind is achieved. Therefore, in Medieval Gnosticism, *ecstasy* was called *"Merging"*. Egyptians called it *Hetep* ("rejoicing", "bliss", "spiritual happiness"), Sufis – *Baraka,* in Tibetan Buddhism it is known as *Pirna,* whereas in the Kabalistic tradition – *Shehinah.* The modified state of consciousness, which is obtained in the process of spiritual practice, leads to mystical experience – the ability to recognize God's Providence everywhere and in everything.

The purpose of every spiritual process and training is to achieve mystical ecstasy; and this purpose must be pursued to the end, because, as Seneca says, *Melius non incipient, quam desinent.*[61] The state of *spiritual ecstasy* is expressed in merging the mind of the mystic with God's Mind. This is achieved through spiritual practice, representing purposeful focused performance of exercises and meditations that develop the willpower and self-control, increasing the clarity of consciousness.

Freemasonry is undoubtedly a mystical teaching, but it has lost its spiritual nature long ago. However, we mean Freemasonry as a human presence, not as a teaching that cannot in any way lose its mystical nature, but is nevertheless dead and incomprehensible at the present moment. Its ideas, rites, signs, symbols and secrets should be vivified so that their magical power may be utilized for the higher good. The adjective *magical* should not startle us, for Sacred Magic is a science of the noumena, of the hidden forces behind the phenomena,

---

61  From Latin: "It is better that you shall never begin rather than stop halfway" – *AN.*

and the ways of their conscious management. A Master Mason once used to be a Magus – and a confirmation of this is the emblematic engraving where he is depicted with a head like the Sun, pointing upwards with his right hand, holding a set square; while his left is pointing downwards, holding a plummet. *(Fig. 10)*

**Figure 10**

This is the posture of the *Magus* from the First Arcanum of Sacred Magic, which is a symbol of Oneness because it connects the three worlds, residing simultaneously in all of them: the mental world, the world of the psyche, and the physical world, thus embodying the Law of Analogy postulated by Hermes Trismegistus.

# 7
# The Soul – a Temple of Wisdom

*All Supreme Wisdom comes from the Lord and abides with Him forever.*
**Book of Supreme Wisdom of Sirach 1:1**

Through the Brotherhood and the willpower, a Freemason has to build his own Temple of Wisdom just as Hiram built Solomon's Temple. In the Old Testament, in the *Book of Proverbs*, Solomon's wisdom is conveyed by the following symbolic text: "Wisdom has built her house, she has hewn out her seven pillars; she has slaughtered her meat, she has mixed her wine, she has also furnished her table. She has sent out her maidens, she cries out from the highest places of the city, "Whoever is simple, let him turn in here!" As for him who lacks understanding, she says to him, "Come, eat of my bread and drink of the wine I have mixed." (*Proverbs* 9:1 – 5, *NKJV*)

In Ancient Hebrew, the word *home* is written with the second hieroglyph, *Beit*, which literally means *home,* but also *wisdom* and *soul.* The Home built by Supreme Wisdom is the Soul of the human being. Wisdom is the womb of Truth, whereas the home of Truth and Wisdom is the Soul. Hiram built a temple – the Temple of Wisdom; for Solomon symbolizes Wisdom. Who are the servants of Wisdom in Solomon's text? These are the Sons of God, for it is said, "Blessed are the Peacemakers, for they shall be called *Sons of God."* (*Matthew* 5:9, *NKJV*) By *Peacemakers* here it is meant "Builders of the World". In the original text, the word *shalom* is used, which is translated as *peace.* War destructs, while peace builds – and therefore Peacemakers are Builders of Worlds. The word *Shalom* means also *Incarnated Truth,* because first in it is *Shin* – the hieroglyph of Fire, which is tangible non-existence. That is why the "Builders of Worlds" are the ones who continually give existentiality to the Truth, making it tangible and comprehensible, like fire. This text of Solomon says also: "Come, eat of my bread!" (*Proverbs* 9:5, *NKJV*) The word *lehem* is used, which is translated as *bread,* but it also means the *food of knowledge.* Or, the Bread of Wisdom is the knowledge of the Laws of Nature, whereas understanding these Laws and becoming aware of them is the very Wisdom. The Temple of Solomon is called *Beit Lehem,* or the *Temple of Bread,* and the builders of that Temple were Masons.[62] Hence, the conclusion is imperative that Masons are Builders of the Temple of Truth, which makes them Peacemakers – Sons of God.

Everyone has to gradually build one's own Soul as a Temple of Wisdom, in which the Truth acts in a sacral way, performing Sacred Rites. This process of *Building the Edifice* in the ancient esoteric teachings is symbolically called *The Path.* The beginning of this Path is the aspiration towards Wisdom, while the ultimate goal is the merging with the Truth – the Primordial Light. When we have finally built the Temple of our Soul, it means that we have implemented the Self according to the ancient esoteric tradition. This represents the attainment of the wholeness of the mind, which includes pure Reason, Wisdom and Truth. These are the three forces sustaining the human Spirit. Reason, through esoteric knowledge, ought to reach the Paths and Laws of the Creator. Wisdom is needed so that we do not deviate from them, so that we can feel the taste of Truth. It is a universal Path, and is therefore the Path

---

[62] In the broadest sense of the term (builders, stonemasons), not as an organizational structure – *AN*.

of every Freemason leading to Initiation and to the connection with the Great Architect of the Universe. The Truth is a flame in which everything burns that has not become the Path. This Path in the Masonic tradition is called *Building the Edifice* and is symbolized by the three pillars in the Temple, the three Pillars of Freemasonry: *Wisdom, Glory* and *Eternity*. As for the hewn stone (or, the "ashlar stone"), it is the altar on which we are to sacrifice our ego. It is said of the sacrificial offering given by Supreme Wisdom: "She has slaughtered her meat." (*Proverbs* 9:2, *NKJV*) The first sacrifice of a person who has embarked on the Spiritual Path is the self-abnegation of the ego – the false image of oneself and of the World. Such a sacrifice is a purposeful, deliberate and conscious suffering, and therefore unlocks the might of the potential force inside us. Therefore, we must become conscious of the great and transformative power of suffering, which, if wisely organized, turns into a mighty weapon. Wisdom is primordial and inherent to our Soul. Wisdom stands before Time, but yet, even before Wisdom, Truth stands, which is the Primordial Light. Faith will lead us up to Love towards our neighbour and towards God. Faith is the Life of Truth within our Spirit. Love is an expression of the power of God's Will through which God has created the World. Thus, the three forces that will help us along the Spiritual Path are *Knowledge, Faith* and *Love*. Through Knowledge, reason turns into a transmitter providing access to the inexhaustible Wisdom of God. Wisdom is the ability for a spontaneous and true judgment of every phenomenon and event in our lives, in the context of God's Providence. However, it is only through the heart, not through the reason, that we can attain Wisdom. The Old Testament says: "The heart of fools is in their mouth; but the mouth of the wise is in their heart." (*The Book of Supreme Wisdom of Jesus the Son of Sirach* 21:26).

Only the wise are able to make full-value use of God's gift of freedom of will. Wisdom and freedom of will have an inseparable dialectical bond. This freedom, however, is only possible under the conditions of the "invisible" Lord. The more God manifests Himself, the more our freedom diminishes. Therefore, bestowing God's creatures with freedom of choice marks the transition from their unity with God to the second stage – disunity with God. Unfortunately, the first manifestation of freedom of will is expressed in the form of a denial of God. The dividing line between God and humans is the very consciousness of dividedness. Freedom builds the individuality of every living creature of God, which in the final stage of its evolution is transformed into a personality. The evolution of God's creatures is the evolution of their individuality, which is a karmic category, unlike the personality we ourselves represent in a particular life.

# Freedom of Choice

> *What really interests me
> is whether God had any choice
> in the creation of the World.*
> **Albert Einstein**

Humans are free in their choice, and this is their greatest temptation and trial in the Garden of Eden, as they face the abyss of absolute freedom. The limit of this freedom was delineated by the prohibition of God, but after being overstepped by humans, they come to stand before the dreadful abyss of this freedom already having a "Sfumato style" nature. Elimination of the fear of the unknown and of the irrevocability of death can only be achieved through faith in God and the Immortality of the Soul. Through prohibition, one becomes aware of the existence of the category of freedom, but by violating the prohibition, people already experience it. *The mind, denying, always affirms its own freedom.* Perhaps the purpose of the first prohibition in Paradise was precisely to be violated so that, in this way, humans become aware of freedom and probably also acquire the separative, analytical thinking which they will need in their forthcoming *"descent"* into the material binary world.

The choice between good and evil penetrates every single instant of human life. It is our Divine Gift, our sacred right to make errors, to have delusions, to hurt another person and even to take his or her life. The very choice represents itself one of the most powerful karmic energies. At the moment of choice, either karma is being resolved, or negative karma is created – or liberating and constructive karma. Very often, when we choose in accordance with our heart and conscience, we simultaneously resolve and dissipate old karma, building new creative one. Personalities who have attained true mastery differ from non-evolved souls in the fact that they have the ability and the willpower to give up what they desire in the name of the Path of their spiritual growth, but above all – in the name of the universal good. The most striking example of this is Christ's prayer in the Garden of Gethsemane, ending in the following way: "... but as You will!" However, before we reach Christ's Consciousness, we have to learn to be free from the influence of temptations and contradictions by rising above them. Most contradictions are not a choice between good and evil but a choice between one or another illusion, lie or falseness. In this way, the soul and the mind end up trapped in illusions because we are trying to choose between left and right, not between up and down. The great art consists in stopping before the choice is made (this is what the Sixth Arcanum of Sacred Magic teaches us), in order to raise the mind above it transcendentally, because the commonly practiced choice represents horizontal binarity: left – right, forward – backward; however, we have to rise upwards. Only a prominent mind is able to make the right choice. However, the more we ascend towards the Spiritual Worlds, the more the need for choice drops out. This can be illustrated by the six-pointed star known to us as the *Star of David*, or the *Seal of Solomon*. In the middle of this star, there is the astral choice between good and evil. *(Fig. 11)*

**Figure 11**

From this line, going down, humans have the right to choose between evil and greater evil. At the lower apex, where the densest matter of nature is, there is no choice. When rising from the middle line upwards, the choice is between one good and another one, and, at the spiritual apex, the choice drops out. If we suppose that human beings, in principle, want to eliminate evil so that good may triumph, and that they also do so, then their development should be from good to better and still better. Or, if evil gets the upper hand, then they will strive for greater evil. This is so because, otherwise, stagnation would occur, and this cannot happen in any way, since we know that, in the material world, the only constant is change. Therefore, whether for better or for worse, development is inevitable. In both cases, however, the comparative degrees of these concepts drop out, unless, as a reference point, there is a dividing line between good and evil. There is no way to differentiate better from good unless the category of "evil" exists. Some will ask themselves: What is the obstacle for humankind to grow in development within the frames of good without this category? Maybe this will be possible in the conditions of another structure and organization of our world; however, in the present matrix system, the binary code is embedded, so this code predetermines the existence of various categories and levels. In this context, the expression *necessary evil* finds its reason; although, even if it does not exist, *good* in comparison to *better* will take the principle position of *evil*, albeit different from its present inner essence. It means that the relative category of *evil* will always exist, in the sense of *opposition* as an engine of development, regardless of the various characteristics of this concept, and it also applies equally to the category of *good*. Thus, choice occurs between relative realities, and therefore True Freedom is present whenever the need for choice drops out.

The culmination of the evolution of freedom of will is the act of self-abnegation and loss of our identity, just as rivers lose their name and image, flowing into the ocean. The main consequence of the freedom of will is that God does not interfere into our affairs unless we wish for it. In the beginning, He gives us the gift of limited freedom of will, due to the initial stage of our evolution, which is fundamentally connected with the transformation and expansion of the individual. This process represents the essential meaning of every Initiatic society, as is the Masonic one as well. The transformations of a Freemason along his Spiritual Path are marked by formal initiations and Sacred Initiations. The means for that is contained in the formula *"Grace and Regeneration"*, which we have already discussed. It involves accepting the Grace of the *Sekhem* of the Masonic symbols, and resurrecting Master Hiram inside every Initiate who has a renewed mind and soul. It is the Worshipful Master who ought to lead the Brothers along the Spiritual Path, and to transform their souls with the power of Masonic Art[63].

The Path towards the Truth is, in its essence, the Path towards our Soul and the Spirit living inside this Soul. The Truth is the Sun dazzling the unprotected one. Just as the Earth's atmosphere protects us from the burning influence of the Sun's rays, the same way the Truth is covered with veils protecting the seeker from any direct contact with True Knowledge. These veils represent themselves the Arcana System that safely reveals the Truth, consistently lifting veil after veil.

Wisdom is the Home of this Truth, and this Home is being gradually built through knowledge, willpower, and sacrificial work. In the beginning, we have to sacrifice our hitherto existing way of life, our illusions, our stereotypes and our shells of personality, our habits and comforts – everything that is formed by our false self: the ego. The struggle with the ego continues throughout our whole earthly existence. This is the meaning of the Masonic motto: "Life is a struggle: slaves struggle for freedom, free ones – for perfection." As Publilius Syrus put it: *Qui totum vult, totum perdit*[64]; and we will

---

63 Uniting all esoteric teachings – *AN*.
64 From Latin: "One who wants everything loses everything" – *AN*.

declare still more explicitly that self-sacrifice is the beginning of the Exodus from slavery, because the Law of Sacrifice reads: "If you want something – then you sacrifice something; if you want everything – then you sacrifice everything!" According to the Christian doctrine, God Himself sacrificed His Only Begotten Son Who is Born of Unity – and, on the esoteric plane, we would say that He sacrificed His Breath because He "exhaled" the World.

## The Breath

> *Breathing is the bridge connecting life with consciousness, connecting our body with our thoughts. Each time your mind gets distracted, use breathing as a means in order to bring it back into your hands.*
>
> **Zen Master**

Life represents breathing. It begins with the first breath of air when the newborn cries, and ends with the last exhaled breath of the dying one. Just as the take-off of an airplane, the initial breathing is also "manually operated", after which it goes on autopilot until the very last breath, unlike the manual landing of the airplane. Animals and humans uninfected by civilization are constantly on autopilot, and their flight is accompanied by a serene, sunny and cloudless sky. In their normal state, humans breathe naturally and properly. For people, however, civilization is like a storm with flashes of lightning, which necessitates switching to manual control in order to take control of the "life-flight". We all have to switch to manual mode, in the person of willpower, through which we ought to begin to learn to breathe properly. Why is this necessary? This is because, to the body, breathing improperly is like a storm to the airplane: there is a danger of damaging it and ending its flight catastrophically.

If we stop identifying ourselves only with our body, we will come to the understanding that the Self, the "I", through the mind and willpower, is the body's operator. Thus, through it, we can consciously manage all the processes in our body and keep it in perfect balance. One reacts mentally but also biologically to everything experienced. Thinking, along with making sense of it, is mental, and the body naturally responds to the thought. All this can be explained through the Law of Materialization, since there occurs an emanation from the brain outwards, which is being imprinted into the astrosome, and from there, it is projected on the physical plane.

Ancient esoterists knew that there is a certain force in the air from which life ensues. This force has been called by different names in different times and epochs, but perhaps the most common and known name, even to this day, is *Prana*. The word *prana* comes from Sanskrit and means *absolute energy*. The Breath of God, the Great Breath, is a Force, Eternal Movement, the Wave of Life, the Universal Energy – and all this is *Prana*.

In relation to the above said, it can be ascertained that, in the first chapter of the *First Book of Moses, Genesis* in the Bible, a clear distinction is made between the atmospheric air and the mysterious mighty active Principle contained therein. This book speaks of *Neshemet Ruah Hayim*, which, translated, means the *Breath of the Spirit of Life*, where *Neshemet* means the "ordinary atmospheric air", *Hayim* means "life" or "lives", and *Ruah* means the "Breath of Life" or the "Breath". *Spirit* in Latin is pronounced *spiritus*, which means *breath*. In Greek, *spirit* is πνεῦμα *(pneûma)*, which, in addition to *spirit*, means also *breath* and *wind*. The most common use of this word is in the sense of *God's Spirit*. It has the same meaning as the Hebrew *ruah* and the Aramaic *ruha*, meaning at the same time *spirit, wind, air* and *breath*. When speaking about the *Holy Spirit (Breath)*, we need to know what the meaning of the word *Holiness* is in Aramaic – the language of the Bible. The Aramaic word for *Holy* is *Quadash* and consists of two roots: *qd* – a pivot point around which everything rotates, and *ash* – a circle expanding from that point and acquiring strength and warmth. Or, *Holiness* means "creation, vacating of a place for the pivot point of the axis around which life is formed and shaped, and keeps rotating". Therefore, the first step towards *Building the Edifice* is to open a free space; and when the pivot point is already built in there, the space becomes holy. If we find the "Holy Centre", then we have opened a gate towards the Divine. In this sense, *Holy Spirit (Breath)* means "Force accomplishing all of the above mentioned". The meaning of the word *Quadash* resembles that of *nahash*, the astral world, and gives us the connection with *aor* – the astral light. The other Aramaic word for *light* that we already know is *shem*, but it means also *holiness*. Thus, the general meaning of what has been said in this context is that wherever there is Holiness, the Creating Light enters and acts in a sacred way, performing Sacraments. That is why Jesus, as we have already mentioned, used the healing magic term *El-Fatah*, literally meaning *Be open (to God)!*

In the Kabalistic tradition, it is interesting to make an analogy with the second hieroglyph of the Holy Tetragrammaton – *He*. Therein, it symbolizes the feminine principle of God, the resemblance being clearly seen to the exhaling sound "HA" and the inhaling sound "SA" in Hinduism. The letter *He* is also the fifth hieroglyph in the Ancient Hebrew alphabet, and its meaning is *Love*. It is already clear that the Divine He is God's Breath in the form of the feminine aspect, which, by its nature, is expanding, all-pervading and giving birth to life. If God can be represented as the first archetypal geometric figure – a central point in a circle, then, in the context of the exposition so far, the Spirit, the masculine aspect of God, is the central point, as concentrated energy of God's Consciousness, while the circle, implying expansion, is the Breath of God, the feminine aspect, which is the receiving one and is the circle of creation, being the Mother in relation to the Creator, and yet, on its own part, represents also an active principle of a new creation.

God's Love, being is the *"Fifth Element"* in the creation of the World, is identical with God's Breath and the *"Quintessence"* (the essence of the five). This Love is born of the great "exhaling" done by God, and it gives life to the Universe. Breath, let us recall, is called *ruah* in Judaism, and therefore, in the word combination *Ruah Elohim*, it means *God's Breath*. Breath is the fundamental force of life, which is the core essence of blood. The sacred element in blood is *Love;* and, in order to multiply this element, we need to consciously connect ourselves with the power of Divine Breath that is the bearer of Universal Love. Breathing is life – however, humans have detached themselves from their own Divine Nature and do not breathe properly, which is why their life is short and accompanied by various diseases. The process of breathing is unconscious and automatic – although, as we said, it can be consciously controlled through willpower: specific breathing exercises within the various esoteric traditions teach us exactly this. There are no breathing or meditation practices in Freemasonry; and yet, it does not mean that they have never existed outside of the Rites known to us. The lack of such applications in Modern Freemasonry significantly hinders the process of physical and spiritual transformation of its members. The so-called *Masonic Workshop* should include all sorts of esoteric work outside the frames of all Rites, not the Brotherhood being fixed only within the canonical form of established Rites. To some, it may sound heretical, and still, the form should serve the Spirit, so whenever any form becomes a prison of Spirit, it has to be destroyed and replaced with a new one. Naturally, in this process, care must be taken not to replace old chains with new ones. The conclusion is that we must not turn into slaves of the form, but rather be able to sacrifice it, continually renewing and updating it, yet without going beyond the verges of archetypes. In our World, everything is born of form and abides in form. Gods are also born of a womb, and yet, to emphasize their difference, the womb is that of a virgin. Therefore, in order for the *God-Child* to be born in us, an "Inner Mother" is needed to conceive immaculately – or, in another transcultural esoteric context, the *"sleeping beauty"* has to be awakened by the *"kiss of the prince"*.

# 8
# The Secret Kiss of the Master

*Men in black gather together from all sides.
The temple is lit by the silvery light of the full Moon.
The channels of spirals stand out against the square,
well-hewn stones. They seem to come to life, vivified
by the torch flames. The men utter the secret word
and enter the Temple of the Virgin. The Rite begins,
filled both with solemnity and mysticism. Symbolism
and Wisdom intertwine like two snakes around the
body of the chosen one. The culmination reaches
its peak when the Master kisses the initiated one at
the base of his spinal column, kneeling in awe and
reverence.*

This is probably how one of the Rites of the Order of the Temple looked like. It is related to honouring the Virgin giving birth to our true Divine Core Essence. The energy equivalent of this "Inner Mother" was called *Kundalini* by the ancients. Of the Rite described, only the kiss is not imaginary, and this shows that external help is needed for Spiritual Birth.

The Gematric value of the *Serpent* in the Garden of Eden, as we have already explained, is the same as that of the *Messiah*. The cunning Serpent, as a tempting creature, is *Kundalini* – the source of the illusion of divisiveness. However, when the *serpent force* is awakened and sublimated, it becomes the means of salvation. In other words, what leads to our downfall is the same through which we may rise again. The national genius put it another way: "Fight fire with fire."

Just as the human embryo undergoes the various evolutionary phases, the same way specific energy has to pass through the chakras, to activate their bodies and their respective levels of consciousness in order to attain Oneness. This is reality, represented by the Sanskrit word *yoga* ("union") or the word *religion*,[65] from the Latin *religare*. This is the connection of the individual

---

65 The term *religion* has no clear etymology. According to Cicero, it comes from *relegere*, which means *to pass, to pass through, to read again more carefully* – reviewing the things that relate to the worship of Gods. According to Lucretius, though, it is derived from *re-ligare*, in the sense of "linking people to certain practices", which, at a later stage, is regarded as "connecting with Gods". According to the Italian historian of religions *Enrico Montanari*, this word in no case comes from *religare* – "to connect face to face with Gods". This interpretation of the word's origin is a Christian one, and it is simply ascribed also to the ancients, which is not true – *AN*.

with the Whole. It is the inner movement – and, as any movement, it needs energy. In this case, however, it refers to a potential spiritual energy that resides in the body in a latent state.

## Kundalini

> *"... Be wise as serpents and harmless as doves."*
>
> **Holy Gospel of Matthew 10:16, NKJV**

In the thousand-year-old Indian tradition, this energy has been given the name *Kundalini*, which in Sanskrit means *coiled around itself*. It is coiled three and a half times around its axis and is located in the sacral bone – the *sacrum*, above the first chakra, *Muladhara*, corresponding to the earth element. In Sanskrit *dhara* literally means *support, base,* and it is the foundation upon which the sacrum is established, whereas Kundalini is the "guardian" of this sacred place. Kundalini is a spiritual God-co-creating energy, and therefore it can be awakened only through Divine energy in the form of *God's Grace* – the esoteric name of the energy protective capsule enclosing the colossal energy and might of God's Names. Blissful are those who are able to receive directly the energy of God's Grace: they ought to be prepared for this, because it is destructive for the unprepared. In most cases, a mediator is needed who is a pure transmitter of God's Force. Whether directly, or through a mediator, God's Grace has to meet Kundalini so that an ignition takes place. When Kundalini awakens, it draws with itself in its ascension the Shiva Spirit – a reflection of God within the heart, with whom Kundalini unites in the *thalamus*[66] in *hieros gamos* – sacred marriage.

In the "matrimonial room", yoga occurs – the union between the two energies, after which, in the *Sahasrara* crown chakra, *Samadhi* bursts out. This inner state is called *Nirvana* in the Indian tradition, and it is the ultimate goal of the ascension of Kundalini. Sahasrara is the verge beyond which we cease to exist such as we are. Thus, the path of Kundalini extends from the sacrum to the crown chakra, the Kabalistic correspondence of which is the Sefira *Keter*. This is the distance between the circle and the central point in it – from the world of forms to the world of unified formlessness. The ultimate goal is not the awakening of Kundalini but rather the Union of Oneness.

---

66  From Greek, literally: "matrimonial room" or "bedroom" – *AN*.

# Twice-Born

*Those who do not die before dying
disappear when they die.*
**Jakob Böhme**

In the Christian religion, the union with the "I" is the "Second Birth" of which Christ speaks: "Jesus answered and said to him, "Most assuredly, I say to you, unless one is born again, he cannot see the Kingdom of God." (*John* 3:3, *NKJV*)

In India, any accomplished Soul is called *Dvija*[67] – Twice-Born. In Sanskrit, *dvija* means *bird*. Birds are born once in the egg, and the second time – at the breaking of the egg, when their true life begins. It is no coincidence that the main attribute during the Sacred Initiation in the Ancient Orphic Mysteries was the bird egg, also known as the *Orphic Egg*. It is depicted with a snake coiled around it. In the esoteric sense, the egg is a symbol of the *Universum*, of Life, and the snake is the force breaking the shell, though not to swallow the bird but to release it, to give it a chance for a true Life. Many ancient peoples have combined the bird and the snake. Thus, Quetzalcoatl, the feathered serpent, was the Supreme God in the Mayan Pantheon. In Kabala, the egg is also a symbol of the *Universum*. The four sections of the egg symbolize its four worlds. According to the Chinese mythology, at first, the Universe represented complete chaos and had the form of a chicken egg. The One Who created the Cosmos came out, breaking the egg, and so on.

Feathers symbolize the Spirit rising in Heavens, whereas the snake changing its skin represents the physical body and the soul being reborn again and again. Therefore, the symbol of the Holy Spirit in the Christian tradition is the *dove*. Since we are talking about "Second Birth", it means that the Principle of Mother and Father is necessary. However, the point here is about a Spiritual Birth only, an "Immaculate Conception", which takes place with the help of Kundalini – the Virgin, the Inner Mother.

So this is how the cult of the Knights Templar to the Virgin Mary is explained. Their statutes, written by Bernard of Clairvaux, are entirely dedicated to the Holy Mother of God. In the period of their might, the most remarkable Gothic cathedrals, fruit of the Masonic genius, all of them glorifying the Holy Virgin, were built. A pretext for the cruel persecution against the Templars is the kiss at the base of the spinal column during the Sacred Initiation Rite, considered by the Church to be an expression of pederasty. Actually, by performing this kiss, the Master awakened the future Knight's Kundalini located

---

67  From Sanskrit: *dvi* – "two", "twice", and *ja* – "born" – AN.

in this area. Therefore, the most important Christian holiday for the Templars was Pentecost: the day on which the Apostles celebrate the Holy Spirit – the awakening of Kundalini. The spiral, being wound three and a half times, is a fundamental symbol in the Order of the Temple. Even now, in France and Ireland, temples and chapels with a spiral image in a triangle (the sacrum) can be seen. In Freemasonry, the symbol of the awakened Kundalini is the wavy-bladed sword, the attribute of the sentinel, the Guardian of the Threshold (the Sefira *Yesod*).

And yet, the most widespread symbol of latent energy concealed inside the human nervous system is the snake. This may be due to the fact that it possesses many Kundalini-related qualities, mostly the crawling movement experienced upon its awakening. The snake is a symbol of Wisdom, so it never causes harm unless it is alarmed and perturbed. In this sense, Jesus's phase, "Behold, I send you out as sheep in the midst of wolves. Therefore be wise as serpents and harmless as doves" (*Matthew* 10:16, *NKJV*), may also be correlated to Kundalini, which is also as wise as a serpent and as harmless as a dove. However, it can be very dangerous if it is disturbed in a wrong way. Kundalini is like an electric current, which is why it is necessary to unblock all the channels so that it flows freely through them, otherwise blockages lead to diversion from its path, and to ill-being.

Since ancient times, the snake has also been a sexual symbol, indicating that there is a connection between sexual energy and Kundalini. The very fact that it is located above the first chakra, in which sexual energy is stored, means that, when raised under control, this energy can awaken Kundalini. At the same time, it must be known that it has nothing to do with sexual energy, because the first chakra is the only one that is not in the path of this snake.

The rise of Kundalini leads to a multitude of transformations and changes in the chemical composition of the body, to chemical harmony. In this way, unity of body, soul and Spirit is achieved – and, according to Alchemy, the burning fire of Kundalini in the *athanor* (alchemical furnace) synthesizes in humans the *Lapis Philosophorum* (Philosophers' Stone); and, when it comes to a *stone*, there is no way of speaking outside the context of Freemasonry.

As we have already noted, Kundalini is usually associated with a vertically standing snake, as it moves upwards towards the parietal chakra. However, there exists also another very ancient symbol: the snake biting its tail. This symbol shows us that when the awakened Kundalini develops to its fullness, it coils itself like a hoop, forming its own, inner, energy circle. If one remains as a straight line, the awakened energy leaks out, figuratively speaking. If, however, the two poles merge, and a circular motion is formed, then the centripetal and the centrifugal force preserve the energy.

On the pediment of the Temple of Delphi, there was an inscription: γνῶθι σαυτόν – *"Know Thyself!"*, which is present also in the Masonic Rites. It means "Get to know your Soul, and merge in one with it!" True knowledge represents *merging*. This is why also it is said in the Bible: "Adam knew Eve." (*Genesis* 4:1, *NKJV*) True knowledge comes when the snake's head unites with the tail. The two ends of the snake carry different polarities. In men, from the symbolic point of view, the snake's tail is the feminine principle: then the snake has bitten its tail, part of it hanging from its mouth. In women, the tail of the snake is the masculine principle, and then the tip of the tail only touches the head slightly. The union of the two poles, of the masculine and the feminine principle, leads to completeness, symbolized by a snake *engulfing its tail*. In this context, the expression *"Adam knew Eve"* is not to be understood in the traditional sexual sense, but rather as a merging of the Spirit and Soul within the frames of the body. Knowing ourselves, we will get to know God, as one Sufi aphorism says: "Seeking God, I found myself. Searching for myself, I found God."

These ideas are present also in the Ancient Egyptian esoterism and find expression in the symbol of the circular Asar. Osiris is depicted with a body curved in a circle, with the toes touching the back of the head. According to the Egyptians, cyclicity is not linear, with a beginning and an end, but rather a series of transformations in which events occur simultaneously at the various levels. The Spiritual Powers – the *Neters,* are the Eternal Noumena, who, although unnoticed, are embedded in the foundation of the manifested visible world. Through transformation, a link with them is accomplished, and death is the beginning of another cycle, at another level. Life and death represent the fundamental rhythm of a stream, consisting of the active and the passive forces of nature, which are involved in a joint transformational circle, the synthesis of which is to be found in the symbol of Asar. The *Osiris-Consciousness* is the immutable participation in the complete cycle of nature passing through life, death and each transformational consciousness.

*"Know Thyself!"* – the purifying fire of Kundalini, leads to opening the gates of consciousness towards the Unified One. Christ has said all this quite simply: "Jesus answered them, "Is it not written in your law, 'I said: You are gods!'?" (*Holy Gospel of John* 10:34, *NKJV*) In *Psalm* 82:6, we read: "I said: You are gods, and all of you are children of the Most High." *(NKJV)* In the *First Book of Moses, Genesis* 1:26, it is very clearly written: "Then God said, "Let Us make human beings in Our image and likeness." *(NCV)*

## Image and Likeness

> *Gods are immortal humans,*
> *and humans are mortal Gods.*
>
> **Hermes Trismegistus**

The human being is a copy of God in miniature – God in development. By getting to know ourselves, we shall get to know God. We are His "deputies" in the physical world. Humans are multidimensional beings residing simultaneously in the various worlds, and representing themselves a link between those worlds. *As above, so below* – and in the middle is the human being uniting them. As Confucius says, "Humans are the middle ground, centred between Heaven and Earth."

Testimonies of the Likeness to God can be found still in the dawn of human civilization. We can give as an example the Sumerian Pantheon, headed by God *An,* the Father of all gods, known by His name, *Anu.* He had countless nameless sons – the *Anunnaki,* and two sons with given names – *Enlil* and *Enki.* However, there was another Supreme Deity – a Goddess called by many names, the most common of which is *Mami.* According to the Babylonian *Epic of Atra-Hasis,* the Anunnaki were sent to Earth where they worked too hard, beyond their strength; however, at one point, dissatisfied, they rebelled. Then the Supreme Gods decided to create a being to replace the Anunnaki – the human being: "Create *"Lulu"* (primitive humans), and let them bear the yoke. Let the humans bear the burden of the Gods!" According to another Babylonian epic written on clay tiles – *The creation of the human being by the Mother Goddess,* the fourth Supreme Deity, Mami, is charged with this task. Before that, however, the Supreme Gods mixed clay from the blood and flesh of the gods: "God and human were mixed together from clay." From it, Mami – the casting form, creates seven boys and seven girls by means of seven pairs of wombs. Then the epic goes on: "The *Mother Womb* brought them together in pairs. They handed the pickaxe into the hands of the blackheads, to hold it." Thus, the beginning of humankind is laid down, in the person of *NamLuLu* – the blackheads.

**Humans and God are of one and the same substance!**

According to the esoteric science, any God's creature, having reached the end of its evolutionary path, is known by the name *Spirit-Monad.* As the name itself shows, it is a combination between a Spirit – a particle of the Holy Spirit, and a Monad – a totality of the Three Personifications of God: Father, Mother and Son. The Spirit-Monad represents a *Quaternary* – the manifested, spiritualized and creating content of God, being the parent of all creatures of God, and, in this capacity, giving birth to seven pairs of Soulmates – seven masculine and seven feminine. Each of them is incorporated into a biological body.

"Nature created seven androgynous humans in accordance with the *Septenary Principle;* and they moved in the air." *(Corpus Hermeticum)*

Initially, Soulmates were one whole, bearing the esoteric name *Androgyne*. Subsequently, for the purpose of its own evolution, this whole is divided into a feminine and a masculine polar Soulmate. Being created in the Archangel World, the body of an Androgyne is subtle – and therefore, as Hermes says, "it moves in the air". The end of the earthly evolution is when these two Soulmates unite into one joint consciousness and become Peacemakers, called *Sons of God* in the Gospels.

As a result of the spiritual catastrophe, Atlantis sank, leaving the island of *Poseidonis,* which subsequently sank as well. The memory of this is preserved in the writings of Plato and Solon. The spiritual elite, amidst whom was one of the first among God's Sons, *Thoth,* moved to Egypt, where they laid the foundation of the Egyptian civilization.

From what has been said so far, it becomes clear that there are a certain number of Initiates, an Inner Circle of humankind, known in the Kabalistic tradition as *L'amed-Vav* ("The Thirty-Six Ones"), who kept and passed on the torch of spirituality and knowledge in the various civilizations. They have preserved also the esoteric knowledge of the creation of humans. Naturally, part of this knowledge has found its place also in the Judaic religion, in particular – in *Books of the Law and the Prophets,* known to us as the *Old Testament.* Let us see, in the context of all that has been said so far, what the content of the "Image and Likeness of God" is. The word *image* literally means *flesh and blood,* at a deeper level being understood as *Consubstantiality with God.* As Jesus said, "I and My Father are One". *(John* 10:30, *NKJV)* At an even deeper level, *God's Image* means that we are an incarnate part of the Holy Spirit. The Image of God within all of us is God's Spirit: "Do you not know that you are the Temple of God and that the Spirit of God dwells in you?" (*First Epistle of St. Paul to the Corinthians* 3:16, *NKJV*)

If the Spirit of God is God's Image, then our Soul should be the very Likeness of God – or, more precisely speaking, of His Soul. This means that we are a Likeness of God not in form, but in essence. God has endowed us with the potential of His Core Essence, which we, through the Soul, have to develop along the path of evolution, reaching as close as possible to Him. Hermes emphasizes: "And, if you do not become a Likeness of God, then you will not be able to get to know Him, because only the like can get to know the like." Peter Deunov adds: "To be a Likeness of God means to give an opportunity to the Divine within you to manifest Itself." So, if we are essentially a Likeness of God, as a Soul, then, to what extent are we equal to Him as an Image? Can we say that our Spirit is identical with the Spirit of God? Insofar as we are within the Manifested, we cannot be identical, as we have already clarified; whereas, in relation to the Non-Manifested, the same is valid, because the Non-Manifested is Unknowable. In this case, however, the most important is to be identical with ourselves as a Spirit, which means that we are God-like – so, along the path of evolution, we can become an incarnate Image of God, identical with our Selves and analogous to God, or – Sons of God.

The development, the improving towards perfection, and all the transformations, until the very transfiguration of a human being into a Son of God, is called, as we have said, *Spiritual Path*, or just *Path*. The energy equivalent of this Path is the path of Kundalini through the chakras, whereas its beginning is the awakening of the Virgin who will give birth to the Consciousness of the Higher Self.

The Master's kiss, if it ever immediately awakened Kundalini, subsequently became symbolic. This is a sign that seekers ought to awaken the latent energy that will transform their body into a perfect instrument of the Soul and Spirit. The snake is the one that will break the shell of the envelopes of personality, and release the Spirit so that the latter may fly out towards the Light. Therefore, one of the fundamental symbols in Egypt is the solar disk combined with the feathered serpent. Another symbol is *Khepri* – the sacred beetle rolling the inner Sun to illuminate the various levels of consciousness. In this context, it is appropriate to quote what the Buddha has said: "Do not seek other Suns but rather shine with the Light of your own Sun."

Kundalini is the God-co-creating energy embedded in the esoteric name of the human being. This is the energy we need to invest in order to pay off, to repay our energy credit from God, and fulfil our mission. Our evolution depends on how much we have activated our chakras through Kundalini so that we may charge them with Prana, and, as a whole, to charge the energy accumulator Merkaba. We have the freedom of will to fulfil our mission, thus paying off our energy credit through the use of this God-co-creating energy – Kundalini. The ultimate purpose of our mission is to become consubstantial with God and God-co-creators, for it is said, "Blessed are the Peacemakers, for they shall be called *Sons of God*." (*Matthew* 5:9, *NKJV*) One of the ways for us to become Sons of God is the Path of God Thoth.

# 9
# The Arcanorum System

## Ad Fontes[68]

### The Path of God Thoth

The *System of Magic Sacraments* (Latin: *Sistema Arcanorum*) is a term adopted during the Middle Ages by the Magi and Initiates, to denote the Egyptian system of Initiations, also known as the *Path of God Thoth*. Unfortunately, it is mostly recognized as *Tarot Cards*. According to one of the hypotheses, these mysterious cards originate from Ancient Egypt, and their hieroglyphs are, in their original form, images on the pillars supporting the Temple. Papus says: "The Tarot doctrine is the Ancient Egyptian Kabala." According to the same author, "... the most ancient Tarot images were medals from which they made talismans afterwards. The 'Small Keys of Solomon' consisted of 36 talismans, with 72 imprints analogous to the Tarot hieroglyphic figures."

The exceptional coincidences with the elements and details of the Kabalistic Tree also enforce another thesis: namely, that the word *Tarot (Taro)* is an anagram of the word *Torah (Tora)*. There are opinions according to which *Tarot, Taro* is a derivative of the word *rota* (Latin: "wheel") and represents a "path" towards knowledge. An analogy is also drawn between the Tarot symbolism and that of *The Ancient Egyptian Book of Thoth,* an esoteric guide to the Mysteries of the world.

This statement – that the Tarot cards are of Egyptian origin, as well as the interpretation of the Arcana in the spirit of Kabala, are both owing to the French Protestant pastor and Freemason, Antoine Court de Gébelin. In his article, he compares the allegoric figures of the famous *Tarot of Marseilles* with the religious symbols of Ancient Egypt. Many researchers are of the opinion that these cards were carried by Gypsies[69] and Arabs during the 14th century, first to Southwestern Europe, and then spread throughout the whole continent. Legend has it that the Egyptian priests, seeing the barbarian conquerors destroy their sanctuaries that were full of ancient knowledge, sealed the secrets of their teaching into drawings and hieroglyphs on metal plates[70] – the origin of the Tarot. They hoped that, through them, vice and gambling would preserve this valuable knowledge better than any temporary virtue. Indeed, by the 19th century, these unusual cards were used exclusively for the *Tarocchi* gambling game.

---
68  From Latin: "Back to the wellsprings", or "Back to the primary sources" – *AN*.
69  In the Middle Ages, they were considered to be descendants of the Egyptians – *AN*.
70  According to some, the original source of Tarot cards are pictorial paintings on a temple colonnade – *AN*.

# Core Essence

> *Tarot cards can work miracles if you don't let your mind interfere... Logic is how the mind knows reality; intuition is how the Spirit experiences reality.*
>
> **Osho**

According to the theory of Fabre d'Olivet, in his book, *La Langue Hébraïque Restituée (The Hebraic Tongue Restored)*, after deciphering the Tarot hieroglyphs, a word is obtained with the meaning of "Secret knowledge of the foundations of the World". The Tarot deck, in its complete form, consists of 78 cards, divided into two groups: *"Major"* and *"Minor"* Arcana (Latin: *arcanum* – "secret", "mystery", "sacrament"). The Minor Arcana contain 56 cards called *"keys"*, divided into 14 in each of the four suits corresponding to those of today's game cards. The Major Arcana represent a group of 22 cards with symbolic figures and inner meaning that become the object of magic science, occultism and esoterism only after the 18th century. These cards are called "Twenty-Two Arcana of Sacred Magic" and correspond to the letters of the Hebrew alphabet.

Esoterists view Tarot as synthesized Kabala related to several teachings. The assertion of Gérard Encausse – Papus, is that "Tarot is contained in the hieroglyphic book *The Thirty-Two Paths"*, and his brief explanation can be found in the book attributed to Abraham and called *Sefer Yetzira (Book of Formation)*.

From the esoteric point of view, it can be said that the "Arcana System" is the humankind's most ancient school of thought, since it structures all the knowledge about God, the World and the Human Being in a harmonious all-embracing picture. It is a method of expressing systematically the Laws existing in the Universe and the human Soul, and also a way to become aware of their action. The "Arcana System" represents Knowledge, Wisdom and Truth, arranged in such a way that they represent a unified, complete and adequate picture of the triune world. Thus, we begin to understand these Laws at the level of the mind, of the Soul and of the flesh. The mind of the personality, grounding its position on intellectual conceptions, is called *conceptual*. Such a mind is fruitless. The "Arcana System" is not conceptual. It is called *system* because knowledge relies on logic and dialectics, and mostly because it has methodology at its disposal and utilizes it. The logical constructions of the Arcana are filled with moral content and are life-orientated. That is why the Arcana are called "school of thought", "way of life" and "mode of action" – because they are vivified by Wisdom. The "Arcana System" represents the *living eidoses* of humankind. All ideas with which the collective spiritual mind of humankind can operate are presented in the Arcana in an orderly and systematic manner. The Sacrament System, the System of Mysteries, is neither a way of soothsaying through Tarot cards, nor merely a deck of cards, though cards have stemmed from the Arcana System. In Ancient Egypt, *"Sacraments", "Mysteries"* were how they called the Pillars of Wisdom, the Pillars supporting the Temple. It can be said that these Mysteries are not a teaching but a state of being. The Sacrament as a Spiritual Initiation is a supreme gift. In order to receive it, you have to spare no effort, nor anything else, and be prepared to sacrifice everything. *"Faith is not to be acquired but rather given from Above whenever one is ready to receive it."*

At a certain level, the "Arcana System" manifests itself as supreme psychology, while at another – as releasing the inner forces and qualities, which is called *implementation power (of authority)*. This implementation power is willpower which is active, conscious, liberated, and polished by knowledge, and is also the fruit of Wisdom inside the Soul. The images of the Arcana are a visual expression of their ideas, being themselves mirror images, and turning out to be, in relation to us, the mirror in front of which we stand.

In the achievement of the 22 Sacraments, in particular the First Arcanum, the spiritual practice that helps us acquire the qualities of the Arcana is the so-called *practice of becoming a likeness*. Each symbol (sentence, image, sign, and incantation text) has many symbolic contexts; and the art of seeing all of them in their correlation in the implementation of a certain idea is called *"implementation power of the mind"*. One ought to aspire towards awareness and maximum degree of implementation power that are attained through Sacred Initiation. The very Sacred Initiation is based, namely, on the Arcana.

Arcana can be narrated, written down in ordinary language or symbolized. The ancient Initiatic schools have chosen the third type for conveying the Arcana – depicting through symbols. Basically, three types of symbolism can be systematized: that of colours, which is predominantly inherent to the black human race; another one, of geometric figures and images, property of the red human race; and a third one – that of numbers, characterizing the white human race, whose motto is "Everything is number, measure, and weight." The Arcana symbolism is that of the Egyptian *(bronze)* human race, in which the three types of symbolism are united.

Figure 12

## The First Arcanum

The First Arcanum is the beginning of the system of Sacraments and is at the same time a Teaching of the Perfect Human, a Teaching of the Perfect Oneness and of the Perfect Might that can be given to the human Spirit here, on Earth. That is why (and not just because it is the first one) we will dwell on it essentially, in order to present the system and the way in which the *"Major Arcana"* should be viewed. The Teaching of the First Arcanum clearly distinguishes between the notion of magic as a set of everyday practices, and the Higher Teaching, which, in fact, the Royal Art represents itself. In the First Arcanum, we are introduced to keys and symbols that will later serve as landmarks for the process of "becoming a likeness". They will be in front of our inner vision and will guide our lives, gradually turning into the form, path and method of our "becoming a likeness" of the Magus from the Arcanum. However, this requires a sacrifice that represents a voluntary act in which we ourselves determine its level and volume. Anyone who wishes to *"sacrifice"* one's entire life will turn into a Magus. The First Arcanum, however, is not a generous promise of something concrete, and is not just a pretty picture. It makes us think about the motivation behind our actions. Spiritual practice is not some romantic experience. On the one side of the scales is *serving,* and on the other is the *desire* to benefit or to gain something. A choice needs to be made. In the Brotherhood, motivation is the Brotherhood itself. No studied images or paintings should ever turn into an object of attachment. Part of our motivation has to be the aspiration towards Wisdom, which, however, does not belong to any human but is beyond humans and beyond time, as Solomon says. If we embark on the Path of Wisdom, then, at one point, Wisdom will come to us itself – however, we cannot obsess, rule or control it; we can only devote ourselves to Wisdom.

God's Path is from up downwards, while the Path of Humans – from down upwards; and, at some point, these paths meet at the cross. **Blessed is the one who resides in this point.**

There are treasures awaiting us along the Path; and still, we should know that they will be revealed to us slowly and gradually so that their contents do not blind us and so that we do not go mad, like a beggar who suddenly realizes that he is immeasurably rich. The most precious treasure along the Path is our spiritual liberation. It is not hidden from anyone and is not buried, but it is to be acquired through persistent practices, the first of which being patience. If we cultivate the tree of patience, which bears the fruits of humility and the thirst for Wisdom, we will accomplish everything in the Path. No one will do for us whatever we have to do for ourselves – to recognize ourselves as a Spirit, as a particle of God's Spirit.

As a state of the Spirit, *Magus* means *Enlightened*. An Enlightened human is not necessarily a magus, in the sense of performing magic work, but rather a Magus at an inner level. The most fruitless activity, however, is trying to judge who is Enlightened and who is not. The very Magus, if asked whether he is Enlightened, will answer that he is not. Therefore, as we have already said, what is important is the motivation – and the evidence of it consists in our actions along the Path, as well as is the Path itself.

The First Arcanum can be called *"The Secret of Human Unity"* – one of the great secrets of the Royal Art. To attain this Secret, it is not enough to merely know what triunity in itself is. You need to become such a triunity; and the greater the effort and sacrifice to achieve this goal, the more we will become a likeness of the Magus from the First Arcanum. In its image, two teachings are concealed: both the teaching about Humans and the teaching about the implementation power, the conscious will, the magic art, the elements and the control over them, about the Laws of Unity, of Analogy, of the Ternary, which are embedded in the foundation of the Sacred Initiation of the Master Mason, who, by definition, is a Magus. Therefore we will dwell a little more on the First Arcanum only, without any pretence to exhaustiveness, and will only mark some of the other Arcana, since the Arcana knowledge is not the main topic of this book.

Before that, however, we should present the principle algorithm of the "Arcana System".

## The Arcana Algorithm

> *Nothing stands still:*
> *everything moves, everything vibrates.*
> **Kybalion**

The Arcana represent themselves pictorial images that are visual expressions of their own ideas; and, as such, they represent combined multifaceted symbols – glyphs. The Arcana, in the context of their ideas, may be objects of meditation, but, above all, they are a means of initiation. Thus, they have meditative and initiatic methods for understanding the Sacred Initiatic picture of any Arcanum, this picture being the artistic and symbolic image of its *eidos*.

Each Arcanum has five titles that give it certain differentiated characteristics and are a means of penetrating into its *eidos*. The first title reveals the meaning of the Arcanum on the spiritual plane, as well as its core essence. The second title shows its meaning on the astral plane, at the level of energy and soul. The third one reflects the manifestation of the Arcanum on the physical plane, or how the previous aspects manifest themselves specifically and visibly in matter. The fourth title is called "general esoteric" one: it is located at the top of the picture and reveals the contents of the Arcanum on the three planes. The fifth one shows the most important symbolic context, represented by the expression of its numerical value and the corresponding hieroglyph of the Hebrew alphabet.

The titles of the First Arcanum are the following ones:

1. *Divina Essentia (Divine Essence)* – an active part of the Archetype;
2. *Vir (male person, chief leader)* – an active part of Humankind;
3. *Natura naturans (Creating Nature)* – an active part of Nature;
4. *Magus*.
5. The hieroglyph of this Arcanum is *Alef*, and its numerical value is 1.

We will try to give brief explanations of these titles.

*Divina Essentia (Divine Essence)*. This is the Primordial Foundation, the Archetype, the concentrated thought of the Divine, the pure thought, the thought in itself, the pure mind.

*Vir (male person, chief leader)*. The male person is presented as the active part of humankind, since he possesses positive, creative energy. On the astral plane, however, exactly the opposite is true: the woman is in the active position.

*Natura naturans (Creating Nature)*. This title indicates to us that it is about Nature in itself. The effect of Creating Nature is that our flesh and our whole physical organism are to become conscious, perceiving and accepting the transforming Light of Truth.

*Magus*. The fourth title teaches us that a Magus is one who is able, first and foremost, to control one's body. All kinds of chaotic processes disappear in an obedient body because it obeys the mind and the willpower.

The symbolic contexts (meanings) of this Arcanum are: Spirit – Divine thought; Magus – male person – master; willpower – implementation power; the posture of the Magus – the Law of Analogy; Alef – the Law of the Ternary and the Law of Analogy; Unity, Oneness – the sign of Humans; the smile of the Magus – the smile of the Sphinx (the Initiated Soul); the gaze of the Magus – transcendence, etc.

The symbolic order of the whole picture of the Arcanum represents a successive activation of all its symbols and images through which we get an idea of its *eidos*. The analysis of the symbolic order of the picture of the First Arcanum can be called "revealing the attributes of the magic operation".

The symbolic picture of the First Arcanum consists of the following attributes, represented as symbols: 1. the Magus; 2. the posture of the Magus; 3. the purple garment of the Magus; 4. a silver belt, in the form of a snake biting its tail; 5. a gold hoop upon the head; 6. a sign of infinity above the head; 7. a wand (scepter) in the right hand, raised above the head; 8. the smile of the Magus; 9. the gaze of the Magus; 10. a cubic altar, and upon it – 11. a sword; 12. a cup; 13. a pentacle.

# 10
# The Posture of the Magus

> *Only the great sages and the great ignorants are immutable.*
>
> ***Confucius***

The posture of the Magus is a symbol of the science of symbols, of the relation between them and the Archetypes, of the Law of Analogy, of Triunity, of the Law of the Ternary, of the implementation power, of the active willpower – a symbol of the active attitude of the Magus towards the surroundings. *(Fig. 12 on page 136.)* All of this is within the core essence of the letter *Alef,* without exhausting it.

The posture of the Magus is the explicit and conscious expansiveness regarding the surrounding world, which actually constitutes the activity of the Spirit ruling over the Soul; the positive spheres of the Soul rule over the negative ones; and the Soul, thus united, rules over the body and its physical manifestations. Such is the inner hierarchical structure of the Magus's power of authority embodying the Law of the "Ankh" and objectively implementing his will. The posture of the Magus enables all the energy and volitional characteristics of the human to reach high mental intensity and expansiveness. It expresses inner psychological unity. All parts of the fragmented Self, of the fragmented consciousness are firmly united in the Magus around a single unified centre. The Magus is the reassembled Osiris, gathered together in one piece; he is the Master Mason, the crown of the Initiatic hierarchy, present and commanding by his will in the three worlds.

Here is the place to dwell also on the Law of the Ternary symbolized by the hieroglyph of this Arcanum – *Alef,* and also by the Magus himself, who represents their embodiment.

## Binary – Ternary – Quaternary

> *Evolution is the Law of Life.*
> *Number is the Law of the Universe.*
> *Unity is the Law of God.*
>
> ***Pythagoras***

*Binary,* translated from the Latin word *bini*[71], means *duality, doubleness, polarity.* A typical example of a binary, in the context of the First Ar-

---
71 The adjective *binarius* means "containing or consisting of two things" – *AN.*

canum, represent the two hands, which, without the torso, create the illusion of dividedness, although actually, along with the torso, they make the unity of the ternary. The *eidos* of the ternary is vast, and there is no way we can embrace it, all the more that this is not our intention. For our purpose, we will only mention that, from a formal point of view, *ternary* means *triplicity, threefoldness, triunity*, with its numerical expression and designation being the number 3. The idea of triunity is archetypal because it is generated by God Himself, with His three hypostases, and is affirmed through the univeral Law of the Ternary. Therefore, this law underlies all processes in the Manifested Universe and is conveyed by the symbolism of their expression in the various traditions. We shall give as an example a fundamental symbol of this type – that of the Holy Trinity, which is present in various modifications in the pantheons of deities and in the religious doctrines.

In Freemasonry, the basic Degrees are also three, and the "3 x 3 salute" is an indication towards the unfolding of the Divine Trinity to the ninefold incarnate human core essence. Jesus Christ led humankind to *"9 o'clock"* – the hour of Truth[72], hence the Masonic "9 o'clock salute". However, humans have to walk alone, by themselves, without a Messiah, the rest of the way *"up to 12 o'clock"*[73], but they ought to be brought up to there by the Initiatic societies, the Masonic society being one of them. Therefore, in the latter it is necessary to have also a "12 o'clock salute" – the hour of the turning point and the change.

If we are to postulate the Law of the Ternary, in relation to what has been said about the binarity of our world and thinking, this law reads as follows: "Every binary can be transformed into a ternary." Paraphrased, it means that each binary is a non-manifested ternary – or, in other words, a ternary is a manifested binary. In both cases, the binary contains a potential ternary, which will sooner or later manifest itself, and the binary will turn into a ternary. However, the manifested binary is illusory because it is a ternary in its very essence. Therefore, binaries can be *unresolved* (conditional, illusory) and *resolved* – joined into a ternary. According to this law, there is no insoluble binary, so sooner or later it becomes a ternary.

---

72 *Truth* in Hebrew is the word *Emet*, the Gematria of this word being the number 9, just like that of the word *Adam* – AN.

73 Literally – 9 o'clock, marking ¾ of the clock dial, the last ¼ of which, in order to close the circle, has to be walked by humankind. An analogy is also made with the ninth hour of the daily worship services of the Christian Church, after which the evening service begins, which reproduces the world at the time of Creation, and symbolically represents the end and the new beginning – AN.

There exist also static and dynamic binaries, as well as polar and hierarchical ones. The polar ones include opposites: good – evil, light – darkness, hot – cold, plus – minus, contraction – expansion, whereas the hierarchical ones include subordinate quantities: Divine – human, Cosmic – earthly, etc.

As a consequence of the Law of the Ternary, the following rule ensues: "Not every ternary produces a quaternary." Thus, this law acquires the following general formulation: "Any binary can become a ternary, but not every ternary is able to produce a quaternary." The quaternary is the productivity and ultimately – the fruit of the ternary, which, in the greatest extent, is actually the very human being. Naturally, a lot can be written about the manifestations of the quaternary as part of the *eidos* of the number 4, of the square, of the four qualities of the Sphinx, of the four Living Entities from the "Chariot of Ezekiel", of the four elements, of the four directions, and generally, as a symbol of form and materiality, but we are going to stop at this point for now. However, we must point out a deeply esoteric key opening the most covert gate of the First Arcanum, leading to its duality. It is expressed in the bipolar essential characteristic of the Magus, who manifests himself as both a "white" magus and a "dark" one. However, we assume that they are part of the core essence and the various contexts of the First Arcanum, so we will not view them as independent Arcana. In the same way, Kabala speaks of the Sefirot and their antipode entities called *Qlifot*. We will no longer set ajar this gate, but we will only clarify that the difference between a "white" and a "dark" magus is solely in the motivation of their actions.

What has been said is a small amount of the knowledge about the First Arcanum; and still, it is an illustration of how one should penetrate into its *eidos*, as well as into the *eidoses* of all the other Arcana. We have already said that the topic of the book does not include a thorough representation of the "Major" Arcana, much less of the "Minor" ones. That is why we have only focused on the emblematic First Arcanum, which, through the figure of the Magus, coinciding with that of the Worshipful Master, unequivocally shows the connection between the Arcana knowledge and the Masonic science. We believe that the 22 Arcana of Sacred Magic represent the "Egyptian Kabala", as Papus claims, which we believe was most probably called *Ka-Ba-Ra*, or the "Divine Double of Ra". Not only are they correlated, but they also represent themselves the fundamental basis of the Masonic science. The very Arcana have interconnection between each other that can be expressed in multiple combinations and numerical correlations, revealing various ideas from their *eidoses*.

# The Path of the Arcana

*The mind is the great slayer of the Real.*
**Helena Blavatsky**

The manner and the sequence of walking the Arcana paths, however, basically depend on whether it will be done self-dependently or as part of the Kabalistic Tree. In the second option, the path of initiations follows the "Path of the Serpent", *Nehushtan,* which is the evolutionary Path of Wisdom, beginning from the 22$^{nd}$ Path and successively reaching the first one. The traditional path of the Sefirotic Tree is the so-called *Path of the Lightning Flash,* which starts from the First Arcanum and reaches the 22$^{nd}$ Arcanum, yet without successively crossing all paths, and since it is *involutionary,* it can in no way be Initiatic. There are also other involuntary paths, such as that of *"magic"* and that of *"revelation",* as well as the *"straightforward path",* on which we will not dwell now before clarifying the core essence of Kabala. However, they are also not Initiatic but magic ones, and are used by those who are already Initiated.

Walking the whole Path of the Arcana on one's own is traditionally presented in a sequence, from the First to the Twenty-Second Arcanum. Formally, there is some logic in this – whereas there is no logic, at first glance, in starting from the last one backwards. On the other hand, it seems more normal to become a Magus at the end of the Path rather than at the beginning.

We will not comment and give further judgements in this context but we shall rather dwell on a specific algorithm of passing through the Arcana that should be connected to Masonic initiations. This connection, though not accomplished in Modern Freemasonry, is dictated by the circumstance that in the Cosmogony of Hermopolis[74], God Thoth played the role of a Demiurge, as is also the Great Architect of the Universe.

This method involves walking three whole paths within the 22 Arcana. The First Path, called the *Horus Path,* starts from the Third Arcanum; the Second Path is called the *Isis Path* and starts from the Second Arcanum; and the Third Path starts from the First Arcanum and is called the *Osiris Path.* The sequence of all three paths is through two Arcana. The beginning of the Horus Path, as we have said, is at the Third Arcanum, which most generally symbolizes *"birth"* in all its aspects and contexts; and it is truthful that this is the path

---

[74] *Hermopolis* – in Greek Ἑρμοῦ πόλις, meaning the "City of Hermes", an equivalent of God Thoth. In the Egyptian language, this city was known as *Khmunu* – the "City of the Eight Gods". There are two legends connected with Thoth in the role of a Demiurge. In one of them, Ibis (Thoth) lays an egg, from which Ra is born. In the other one, Thoth creates Himself through the power of His own Word (as in the *Gospel of John* 1:1, *NKJV* – "In the beginning was the Word...") – *AN*.

of the apprentice who, from a *"seeker"* in the world of the profane, is *"born"* in the world of Freemasonry. Then apprentices embark on the Isis Path – the path of the fellow craft; and, after the successful walking of this path, they continue along the final path – the Osiris Path, which is the Path of the Master.

The Horus Path, which we would call the *Son's Path*, is the introductory Initiatic Arcanum Path that a *"newborn"* apprentice has to embark on, in order to be protected to the maximum extent and to sufficiently *"entrench his roots"* before continuing along the other two paths. If we are to describe it concisely, it begins, as we have understood, with the *"birth"* of a Freemason in the Third Arcanum, followed by the Sixth Arcanum, where the "choice" is to be made whether to continue along the path; then, in the Ninth Arcanum, the apprentice is given a protectorate from the Heavenly Hierarchy; and, in the Twelfth Arcanum, he has to become aware of the Law of Sacrifice. He is then awaited by the trials of the Fifteenth Arcanum, entitled "The Devil" and subtitled "Logic". It hints that the biggest enemy along this path is logic, which is also reflected in the sign of the apprentice through which the head is symbolically cut off. Therefore, the Entered Apprentice's Step is with the left foot, which means that we ought to follow our heart and intuition, while the metaphorical cutting of the head is an instruction to ignore logic and conceptual mind. This is so because an apprentice has no accumulated knowledge which to analyze and use logically. He further encounters duality in the Eighteenth Arcanum, in order to find out that duality is illusory, as well as to get rid of the past, which leaves, in a crab-like manner, a bloody trail in his consciousness. Finally, this path ends in the emblematic Twenty-First Arcanum entitled "The Fool" and denoted by the Hebrew letter *Shin*. Since this Arcanum is also of a dual nature, as is the First Arcanum, and having in mind the fact that it is perhaps the most mysterious, we will therefore dwell a little more on it as well.

**Figure 13**

# The Fool

*Omnia mea mecum porto*[75]

According to some, this is not the Twenty-First Arcanum but the Zero Arcanum, and it is named "Joker" because it looks like the joker in a deck of cards and can be present anywhere in it. We accept the Zero Arcanum thesis only in the context of the zero, which, situated between two integers, represents an infinite space filled with transcendental numbers. This is therefore a symbol of the Spirit whose characteristic is Infinity, just as the zero is itself an infinite circle, a symbol of Eternity. The foregoing explanation finds support also in the meaning of the letter *Shin*, the first in the *Alef-Beit* and meaning *Fire*, which is indisputably the essence of the Spirit. On the other hand, however, one of the titles of this Arcanum is "Matter", which contradicts the above said. This contradiction is resolved if it has a binary character and represents a *binary code,* which means that it is both the Zero Arcanum and the Twenty-First one and that, depending on its manifestation, takes the place of the one or the other. Therefore, its title as the Twenty-First Arcanum should be "Matter", while, as the Zero Arcanum – "The Fool", thus symbolizing the residing of the Spirit in the material. Indeed, in this sense, in the eyes of the profane, those through whom the Spirit manifests look like fools because they do not fit in the ideas and paradigms of the profane, and, in general, in their way of thinking: such persons are naïve, and they confide in others despite everything experienced – they are being cheated, and still, they trust; they are being cheated again, and they trust again, and this is repeated over and over again. Their trust is infinite and so pure that no one can deprave them, and only an evil dog can tear their garment. Those who deceive such a person, as well as anyone who would deceive him, taking advantage of his innocence, tell themselves, "This one is a complete fool: he does not learn from experience." His actions are nonsense to others because they judge these actions through their mind; however, he has "lost his mind" because he relies on intuition and God's Providence. He never laments over his fate because he has become aware of what is contained in Rumi's words: "I was sad because I had no shoes, until I met a man who had no feet." That is why we would eventually call the Zero Arcanum "The Mind-less Human", whereas the Twenty-First one – "The Fool".

It is no coincidence that in Solomon's *Book of Proverbs,* which we have already cited, Sublime Wisdom appeals: "Whoever is simple, let him turn in here!" (*Proverbs* 9:4, *NKJV*) In this case, "simpleness" is to be understood in

---

[75] From Latin: "All that is mine, I carry with me" (Cicero) – *AN.*

the sense of the conceptual mind, not the Spiritual Reason – the quality of the Sefira *Bina* of the Kabalistic Tree, which we shall view further on. Since we mentioned a tree, the Mind-less Human, just like an age-old tree, has no doubt in God's Providence. Ever since the moment the tree was a little seed, it has never thought about not sprouting. Sometimes the seed falls on a stone, while other times it is trampled on by humans, or it is dug out by pigs, and yet it grows again because it trustfully serves the Great Deed. Both the tree and the Mind-less Human are bearers of purity, innocence and trust. Mind-less Humans do not surround themselves with walls of knowledge, and therefore they are fools. Whatever experience comes into the life of Mind-less Humans, they let it happen, and they go on, so they are fools. Even if they are deceived, swindled and robbed, they allow it to happen because they know that what is truly yours cannot be taken from you, and therefore they are fools. They own with an open palm facing upwards from which anyone can take, so they are fools. Mind-less Humans know that every time they do not allow the situation to embitter and deprave them, their inner wholeness becomes even more fortified, but they are therefore fools. They do not care that the dog is pissing on them and that they themselves are heading towards a precipice full of crocodiles, because Mind-less Humans are convinced that at any moment, when necessary, they will be granted the support of the Spiritual World, where the guides are trust and innocence, not skepticism and experience – and yet, that is why they are fools. Thus Mind-less Humans become pilgrims, developing the ability to walk the whole Path towards Home in darkness and without any guides, alone, relying on the protectorate from the Heavenly Hierarchy. At some point, sooner or later, they embark on this Path, because in the earthly world they are exiles. They illuminate the present moment with the lantern, its light being completely sufficient for the instant, and darkness cannot grasp it. Nothing is able to sway and distract them from the Path, for their trust has become inner confidence, and their faith has been profoundly anchored. They have tasted the outward gloss of this world and have already realized that all is vanity, and still, this has not embittered them, it has not made them cynics. Putting on the mantle of compassion towards the world, Mind-less Humans are walking towards the Home that is not on Earth – so therefore they are fools.

    Here we can make an even deeper analysis of the Arcanum entitled "The Fool", explaining that the Initiated Master adorns with the joker's hat those over whom he plans to operate as over a passive principle, although, when necessary, he is able to duly put it on himself, imitating the Fool. Being aware of the illusory nature of the physical plane, he occasionally becomes bored with his own body shell and the delusional pleasures it supplies; however, he is not entitled to reject that shell before completing his mission. His karma has outlined a program of trials and sacrifices in the present incarnation, so the course of life has to cover this program in its entirety. It is exactly in these moments that the Master ought to be able to close his eyes to the imperfection of the physical plane, to be able to integrate into life, becoming absorbed in his trinkets; he has to be able to immunize by himself the "ghost" of happiness, having in mind that, strictly speaking, happiness cannot be found on Earth. Such an immunization would be a complete imitation of the "Fool" – a total and voluntary abandonment of what was acquired through Initiation. Can we nowadays liken a Master Mason to the "Fool" of the Twenty-First Arcanum?

Becoming a child again, yet after acquiring the knowledge of experience, going back to the state of innocence after getting to know good and evil, is the very "Second Birth"[76] of the "Mind-less Human" who is ready to become consubstantial with the Twenty-Second Arcanum – "The Universe". It is no coincidence that the Eastern term *lao* means both an *old man* and a *child*. A Masonic apprentice, however, is not yet ready for this, so he must walk also the whole second path, the Isis Path, in order to reach the Twentieth Arcanum, where this "Transformation within Time" will be fulfilled, and he will be drawn by the "Divine Attraction".[77] Thus, the apprentice is already transformed into a fellow craft, but he is not yet ready to become part of the Universe, for he must walk one last path to the end – the Path of Osiris, the Master who, before finishing with the Twenty-Second Arcanum, goes through the Nineteenth one, to learn "The Truth of Humans" and to synthesize the "Philosophers' Gold".[78]

*Truth* in Hebrew is denoted by the word *Emet*, and its Gematria is the number 9, the same as the Gematria of the word *Adam*. Nine is the number of Truth and the number of Humans (144 000 people will be saved, and maybe they will save the Earth, and maybe Truth will save Humankind). This is the Sacred and Mystical Nine (144 000 = 9), which is immanent; and whatever we multiply by 9 still equals 9, because it is part of the Truth, because even if we assume that something is false, it is still part of the Truth about the untruth. Jesus Christ leads humankind to the Ninth Hour when on the cross He says the popular words: "My God, My God, why have You forsaken Me?" (*Matthew* 27:46, *NKJV*), and then yields up His Spirit with His last breath. We have already explained that the path from this hour to the Twelfth Hour should be walked by humankind by itself, so if Masons consider themselves to be the enlightened part of this humankind, they must be in the lead.

Everyone walks the whole path from 0 to 9, from the Mind-less Human to the Pilgrim, and steps into the Path of Truth leading to our Home that calls

---

76   The Twenty-First Arcanum (2 plus 1 equals 3) is correlated with the Third Arcanum, entitled "Birth" – *AN*.
77   These are two of the titles of the Twentieth Arcanum – *AN*.
78   These are part of the titles of the Nineteenth Arcanum – *AN*.

us – and this call is stronger than everything else. Then humans add to themselves the number 1, the Primary Cause, and become a 10. This is how *Rota Fortunae* spins, and *Hermanubis* takes us upwards through the abyss of *Daat* towards a new dimension, towards a new Heaven, a new Earth, a new circle and a new Zero. Thus, the Mind-less Human walking along the Path adds to his 9 also "one more thing and another", until he turns into the "Fool" of the XXI Arcanum, consubstantial with the "Omnipotence of Nature", credulously walking towards the precipice. He becomes the old dotard of a Zen parable who had forgotten everything, even who he was, and yet, wherever he passed, the sour cherry trees burst into blossom.

The path of humans through rebirths passes from 0 to 21, and always before the next integer in succession, there is 0, because each spiritual transformation bringing us closer to God requires a Mind-less Human.

# 11
# Kabala

**Core Essence**

*It is forbidden to anyone to study Kabala for any other purpose than spiritual elevation.*
**Talmud, Sanhedrin**

Getting closer to God is the goal of all great religions, where Oneness with Him is being experienced as mystical ecstasy; and in all spiritual traditions, this state is achieved through the Mysteries. *Mystery* in conversational speech means *something secret and inexplicable*. In the religious sense, however, it is the Truth that is revealed only by God. The Mysteries represent Schools of Sacred Initiation. The tradition of Western Mysteries is rooted in Ancient Egypt, although it has reached us through Judaism, the goal being the achievement of *Religare* and Yoga. The mysticism of the Ancient Hebrew tradition represents the basis of modern Western esoterism. According to the Hebrew tradition, the *Torah* is the skeleton of the Judaic religion, while Kabala is its Soul. The *Torah* was set up before Creation and constitutes the Great Name of God expressing the concealed Divine Core Essence. The order of the *Torah* is the order of Creation. Moses wrote down the *Torah* (the *Pentateuch*) following the system of the secret teaching of Egypt, which is why it has three meanings: *exoteric* (explicit), *indirect* (symbolic), and *esoteric* (concealed). Kabala constitutes the concealed section of the *Torah*. According to tradition, Moses received the *Oral Torah* but penetrated into the mystical *Written Torah*, which continues to be concealed for the uninitiated ones. The *Written Torah* is viewed as a symbol of the active sphere of the Divine, whereas the *Oral Torah* is a symbol of the passive sphere. Thus, it can be said that there are three different types of *Torah*: *undisclosed, oral* and *written,* the latter being the *"white fire"*, whereas the oral one – the *"black fire"*. Initially, there was a primordial, undisclosed *Torah,* in the Sefira of "Mercy", and from this *Torah*, the one written in the Sefira of "Harmony" ensues, and then, from the latter, on its turn, the *Oral Torah* emerges, in the Sefira of "Action". The *Written Torah,* concealed in the white light, is revealed through the *Oral Torah* arising from the black light. From the Sefira *Tiferet*, under the impact of the Light of the *Written Torah,* processes occur in the Sefira *Malkut* which leave impressions forming the so-called *Oral Torah*. Only through the latter can we acquire true un-

derstanding. After all, according to some rabbis, only the *Oral Torah* exists, while the *Written Torah* is a mystical concept embodied in a sphere accessible only to prophets, whereas the *Primordial Torah* remains undisclosed! The words in the *Torah* are words of Wisdom, and they are the thoughts of God. That is why they are religious Truths that are beyond the capabilities of the *"conceptual"* mind which gets lost in the labyrinth of its own reasoning. The *Logos* is limited within the form of words; however, they cannot fully express its core essence. There is a certain limit beyond which words are powerless. This is where the symbolism of intuition begins. Mystics transmit their own mystical experience through the symbolic language of the subconscious. Symbols possess and express the Truth, whereas words lead us far away from it. Just as we cannot step twice into the same river, so with the same word we cannot pronounce twice one and the same Truth, because it has already changed, it has already flowed away. In the manifested world, everything changes, and the only constant, as we have noted, is the very change.

Behind the ostensible appearance of the physical world, there are Divine Powers and Principles; and Kabala gives us a method for getting to know them, through a composite symbol known as the *Tree of Life*. Since we have objections regarding the uniform use of this name, we will henceforth use the term *Kabalistic Tree*. This glyph (combined symbol) is a way of reducing, to a single diagram, each force and every factor in the manifested world and in humans, connecting them with each other and illustrating them on a diagram so that the correlations between them can be seen. The Kabalistic Tree is a symbol of the human being and the Universe.

According to some, in addition to the established meaning of *"oral tradition"*, Kabala also means *"to receive"*, and hence the conclusion that its mastering requires the development of a teacher-student (Master-disciple) relationship. The etymology of the word *Kabala* is usually derived from the Hebrew word *kibel (kebel, kabel)*, meaning *to collect* or *to receive*, and is translated as *received lore (tradition);* it corresponds to the mission of the Master in the Masonic tradition, formulated in the phrase "Gather what is scattered". *Kabala* also means *correspondence,* which comes from the Hebrew word *nakbalah (analogy, parallel, correspondence),* because it deals with the correspondences of things by examining their spiritual roots that connect them to Heavens. This principle is a modification of the Hermetic Law of Analogy. However, some researchers believe that the word *Kabala* has a non-Hebrew origin. The standpoint is maintained that it may have an Indian root, where, in Sanskrit, it consists of two words: *ka* ("nature") and *bala* ("force"). *Kabala* is also imparted with some other semantic meanings: *Secret Wisdom, Inner Wisdom, Ultimate Truth, Science of Truth, Path of Truth*. There is still another, little known meaning: *Might and Spreading of the Thirty-Two*.[79]

## Linguistic Clarifications

Before proceeding to a concise presentation of the history of Kabala, we will make some linguistic clarifications. There are discrepancies in the bibliographical sources, in the use of the Kabalistic terminology. This is due to the varying transliteration of the Hebrew terms into both Latin and Cyrillic letters. Most Bulgarian books on this subject are translated from English, which is why the terms are influenced by the Latin transliteration, as well as by the Western esoteric tradition, which differs from the purely Hebrew one. Thus, for example, according to the latter, *Wisdom* is written as *Hohma/ Hokma*, whereas, according to the Western tradition – *Chokmah/ Shokmah; Bina – Binah; Gevura – Geburah; Neza – Netzah/ Netzach; Malkut – Malhuth/ Malchuth*. Some Hebrew and non-Hebrew authors write *Hod* as *Od*, and *Zohar* as *Zoar*, etc. It is important to pay attention also to the difference in the spelling of the ten emanations of God, called by many authors "Sephiras". This term can be seen in plenty of different variations: *Sefira* (singular), *Sfira* (sing.), *Sfiras* (plural), *Sefirot* (pl.), *Sfiroth* (pl.). However, we believe that it is most correct to vowelize this term as *Sfara* (singular) and *Sfarot* (plural). This is because, contrary to all concepts, we derive the word *Sfara* from the Sanskrit word *Ishvara*[80], meaning *Lord, Supreme Lord, Supreme Master*. Discrepancies are noticed also in the spelling of the word *shell: Qelifa – Qlifa* (sing.), *Qelifot – Qlifot – Qlippot* (pl.), as well as of the words *Bria – Beria, Vau – Vav, Yod – Yud*, etc. The spelling of Kabalistic terms from now on will be according to our views; however, if there is any invariance, it will be in order to cover the diversity of information described. Besides, we should also point out the Kabala methodology, including *Gematria* (a doctrine of substituting words and letters with numbers), *Notarikon* (a doctrine of determining the influence of signs), and *Temura* (a doctrine of combinations, correlations and transformations).

---

79 This relates to the 32 Paths of Wisdom in the Kabalistic Tree. The word *Kabala* is written with the Hebrew letters *Kaf* (meaning *might*), *Beit* (having the numerical value 2), and *Lamed* (meaning *spreading* and having the numerical value 30) – *AN*.

80 And also the designation *Sarah*, which turned into a term for *tsar (king)* in other nations – which is a confirmation that *Sarah* is a title, not the name of Abraham's wife, who was evidently a matriarch – *AN*.

# Origin

> *Who can imagine a world*
> *that is not filled by the Creator?*
> ***Talmud, Shabbat***

After this clarification, we can now proceed with the history of Kabala, which is shrouded in enigma and legends. According to one of them, Kabala is a Divine Revelation given to Adam at the very Creation of the world, and later written down by Moses and conveyed orally in secret from one Initiate to another. Another belief narrates that the Archangel Raziel conveyed Kabala to Adam after his expulsion from the Garden of Eden. According to a third legend, this was done by the Archangel Metatron. In still another one, Abraham is identified as the first Kabalist and the author of *Sefer Yetzira*. Perhaps the most widespread version is that Moses received the authentic Ten Commandments that made up Kabala; however, after he came down from Mount Sinai and saw the Hebrews worship the Golden Taurus, he destroyed the tablets. Then he climbed the mountain again and returned to his people with the already familiar to us *Decalogue*. The authentic Ten Rules of Kabala were orally transmitted to Aaron, the High Priest and Moses's eldest brother. Thus, Kabala was passed on from one priest to another in the tribe of the Levites, and later – from one Initiate to another, turning into an oral tradition. The ancient Kabalistic Mysteries are considered to originate from the Egyptian ones, being a continuation of them, because Moses was initiated into them. In this sense, there are claims that the Egyptian esoteric knowledge was called *Ka-Ba-Ra* ("The Divine Double of Ra"), after which was named *Kabala* by the Hebrews. In this way, the Egyptian God *Ra* was replaced by the Hebrew hieroglyph *L'amed*, which symbolically means "spreading". The Mystery tradition of Kabala is grounded, to a great extent, also upon the visions of the biblical prophets, who, according to the deep esoteric science, were the Initiated representatives of humankind reincarnated in Israel.

Kabala became known for the first time to Western civilization perhaps through, if not the greatest, the most famous Kabalist who has ever dwelt on Earth – *Yeshua ben Miriam*, known as *Jesus Christ*. Thus, the tradition of Western Kabala was gradually established, which differs from the Hebrew one and combines in itself Freemasonry, Rosicrucianism, Martinism, Astrology, Sufism, Magic, Christian Mysticism, and Hermetism. A major contradiction between the two systems is that the Hebrew Kabalists do not acknowledge any connection between the 22 Major Arcana of the Tarot cards and the 22 Hebrew letters, and hence, consequently – the presence of the former as "Paths" in the Kabalistic Tree.

Many researchers believe that Abraham was the founder of the oral tradition, whereas, the first to write it in *Sefer Yetzira* was Rabbi Akiva in the 1st century AD, adding to it also the teaching of God's Chariot – *Merkaba*. Views are also maintained that *Sefer Yetzira* originates from still more ancient Egyptian and Mesopotamian sources, because it also contains certain Alchemical tradition, which we shall dwell on further. However, we will now try to essentially present the teaching of Western Kabala. We say *essentially*, which may also have the meaning of either *abridged* or *incomplete* in this particular case, because that teaching is not the subject of this book.

## Fundamental Terms and Clarifications

> *The Torah is concealed. It is only revealed to those who have reached the level of the righteous.*
>
> **Talmud, Hagiga**

The *Universum*, which is an emanation and a final product of the Logos, is actually a mental form, a mental image in God's Consciousness, which is brought to its materialization in the physical world. Our consciousness and God's Consciousness are analogous, and therefore it is called *con-sciousness* (from Latin, literally "with-knowledge") – because we are *con-scious* with God but not identical with His Mind, because God's Mind is Alone in Himself, within Himself, it is immanent. Thus, our consciousness is at the basis of a mental entity, mental matter, which is manifested, in a very small part of itself, in sensuous beings such as we are. For the most part, it is free and exists in the astral space. Blavatsky calls this mental matter *Akasha*, while, according to Papus, it is "reflective ether". This "reflective ether", or "Akasha", extends from the Sfara *Yesod* of the single Kabalistic Tree, where its root is, to the Sfara *Neza*, where its upper layer is. The Akashic Records, or the "Memory of Existence", is that mental matter whose canvas is consciousness and which creates the particular forms of thought comprising the matrix made up of the etheric lines of force. The *Universum* is the final product of the seminal "ejaculation" of the thought of the Logos, while the Kabalistic Tree is the symbolic representation of the algorithm of its creative work. The core essence of Kabala is concealed precisely in this Tree. It is composed of the Thirty-Two Paths of the Divine Emanations, consisting of the Ten Sfarot, arranged in a specific way and connected to each other by lines called *Paths* (22 Major Arcana) and corresponding to the 22 letters of the Hebrew alphabet. *(Fig. 14)*

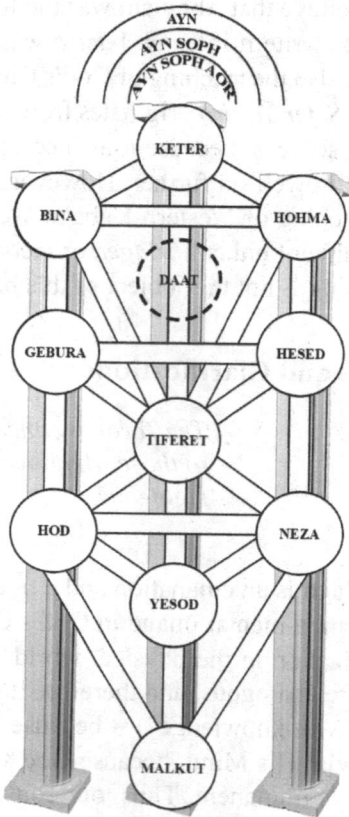

Figure 14

## The Sfarotic Tree in Its Traditional Form

The Sfarot are a stage in the emanation of God's Spirit (respectively, the Human Spirit) in its development from a Noumenon to its existence in the world of phenomena. Each Sfara represents a degree of this development, whereas the core essence of each Path (Arcanum) can only be understood if the nature of the Sfarot connected with it in the Tree is taken into account. The teaching of Kabala is clothed in illustrative form, because it is the only language understood by the subconscious. The symbol of the Kabalistic Tree is synthesized by the individual sub-consciousness as a projection of the Universal Consciousness, in order to express the hidden forces of the Universe. It also represents itself a glyph of the Macrocosm and the Microcosm, so analogies can be drawn between them, since they are derivatives of involutionary identities, in the mathematical sense. Certain aspects of consciousness have been developed in accordance with certain stages of the involution of the Spirit, and for that reason, they express one and the same principles. Each symbol on the Kabalistic Tree expresses some cosmic force or factor. When the mind concentrates on this glyph, the practicing one makes contact with this force, gradually building the unity with it and acquiring magic abilities. The Sfarot are macrocosmic, while the Paths are microcosmic by their nature. The Sfarot are created in a numeric order, and this is illustrated by a flash of lightning symbolizing the Divine Emanations of involution. The Paths, as a microcosmic symbol, indicate the successive stages of unfolding the human consciousness. They are often depicted as a snake coiled around the branches of the Kabalistic Tree. This snake is traditionally called *Nehushtan* and is a symbol of Wisdom and Initiation. *(Fig. 15 on p. 159.)*

"Western" people have sunk deeply into the dense matter and seek to possess it, while "Eastern" people wish to escape from it into the Spirit. Denial of the earth level is part of the evolution of "Eastern" people, whereas the conquest of the material world is recognized by Western civilization as its own mission. Esoterists of the West seek to spiritualize matter by bringing down the Divine Power among humans, while mystics of the East strive to spiritualize themselves under a tree in the mountain. The common between them is that they both aspire to a conscious connection with God. Such is also the aspiration of Hebrew Kabalists, and their way is up along the Kabalistic Tree and the merging with Ayn Soph, without being interested in any returning. To "Western" Kabalists, returning is vital, so they attach great importance to the "rooting" into matter.

According to Kabalists, there are four levels of the Manifested and three levels of the Non-Manifested.

The four worlds of the Manifested are as follows: *Atzilut* – the World of Emanations, *Beria (Bria)* – the World of Creation (the mental world), *Yetzira* – the World of Formation (the world of the psyche), *Assia* – the World of Action (the physical world, the world of matter). *(Figs. 20 and 20ᵃ on p. 168.)*

The levels of the Non-Manifested are the following: *Ayn* – "without" (the Negation), *Ayn Soph* – "without limit" (the Boundless, the Infinite), *Ayn Soph Aor* – "light without any limit" (the Boundless Light). The very presence of this Tree in all worlds confirms the Law of Analogy and the fact that one and the same law rules in all worlds: "As above, so below." *(Fig. 14 on p. 152)*

According to Kabala, the whole existence comes from *The Nothing* called *Ayn Soph;* and the followers of Dao call it *Wu Tsi* ("without Tsi", "no-Tsi"). According to Daoists, everything is *Tsi* (also *Chi, Qi*) – *Universal Energy*. However, *The Nothing* cannot be defined by any words: it is beyond all definitions, qualities, and states of being. Therefore, namely, only IT *IS* – the Substantial Reality.

The Divine World *Atzilut* means in Ancient Hebrew *to be near to* (in immediate proximity) – in this case, to Ayn Soph. As such, it represents a direct reflection of His Will. Some Kabalists perceive this world as a human figure, as is the case with Ezekiel's fiery vision. It is known as *Adam Kadmon* – the Primordial Human, the First Human, the Cosmic Human, the Human in Principle – the Image of Divinity. Others call this Divine figure *Kavod – God's Glory*. In his vision, Isaiah beholds Him in the Temple sitting on a huge throne. The "fallen" human, on his part, is called *Adam Belial*.

In the *Bria* World, the *Seven Days of Creation* are accomplished. This World is the energy centre of Existence, the Breath of Life, or *Ruah ha-Kodesh* – the Holy Spirit.

The next world is the World of Formation, and it is called *Eden (Paradise):* the place where Spiritual Entities, through the diversity of forms, take on a certain appearance. This is a "water world" where the whole life cycle takes place simultaneously.

Below this World of *Yetzira*, which, besides Paradise, contains also Hell, the "kingdom" of physical manifestation is situated – the *Assia* World, where physical Time is linearly distributed into past, present and future. These characteristics of space and time, however, are determined by the binary code of our separative consciousness, as well as by the consensual reality determining their constant perception within it. As we have already explained, the alienation of humans has led to their attitude towards the world as towards an object, which results in an interval differentiated by that measure, the parameters of which are time and space. For the sake of clarity, we will explain the illusory nature of the measure of time and space through the following example. Let us imagine that we are travelling by train through a field, the beginning and the end of which we will mark with A and B. Looking through the limitative frame of a window, we perceive the indicated distance in the form of a sequence of film frames within a certain time. The first film frame is the present; however, displaced by the second one, it becomes the past; and all the rest following them represent the future, successively becoming the present and the past. Thus, the view we see through the train window is the present, whereas the one that has passed by and the one which we are about to see are the past and the future. In this way, we perceive the segment between A and B, divided, for example, into twenty-five film frames, and for the same number of minutes. However, if we open the window and pop our head out of it, we will see the whole distance at once, and we will see both the beginning and the end simultaneously. Then space and time are transformed into one whole regarding our perception – and the illusion of their separateness disappears. People travel in the illusion train, unaware that its window can be opened; as for those who know, they have no power to open it. This knowledge and this power can be gained when walking along the Spiritual Path. *Initiates are able to open the window.*

We need to clarify the meaning of three more emblematic terms: *sefer:* signs, book, script, letters, or generally – *forms; sefora: calculation, computation, number,* or generally – *measure; sipur,* meaning *speech, sound,* or generalized – *vibration.* That is why it is said in *Sefer Yetzira* that the world was created through the three *Sefarim: sefer* (forms), *sefor* (measure) and *sipur* (sound). In the Bible, this knowledge is present in the inscription "Mene, Mene, Tekel, Uparsin", which was interpreted by the Magus of all magi, the Prophet Daniel. (*Book of Prophet Daniel* 5:25)

It can be said that the Sfarot are "bisexual", which means that each Sfara is both active (giving) and passive (receiving) at the same time. The Sfarot are also called "Kelim" – *receptacles,* because they are able to receive both positive energies (being "pure") and negative energies (being "polluted" and called *Qlifot*, which literally means *shells* or even *harlots*). Some believe that the Qlifotic Tree is the shadow of the Tree of Life projected to the left of it, while others maintain the view that it is a tree turned upside down from the Sfara *Malkut* downwards. However, in view of the above explanation, we believe that the Sfarot are being "polluted" by the negative energies of our personality shells, resulting in the formation of solid shells that encase the Sfarot. Thus, the Qlifotic Tree is the already familiar Kabalistic Tree, only with "polluted" Sfarot. When one purifies one's negative energy, then the personality shells come off like old skin – or, in other words: the shells are destroyed and the Sfarot flash like lightning.

The two-dimensional model of the Kabalistic Tree is unfolded in vertical projection; however, in the three-dimensional space it can be represented in a spherical shape, as is done in *Sefer Yetzira*. In this model, Ayn Soph represents the concealed centre of this system; the First Sfara being the central point, and the Tenth Sfara – the periphery, where the Creative Logos manifests Himself as the Incarnate Word of God. Thus, we are again faced with the emblematic figure of the *central point in a circle,* and its archetypical nature is again confirmed by what has been said. The sphere can unfold (i.e. a process of involution) from the First Sfara to the Tenth, and vice versa – to fold up itself (i.e. a process of evolution), in which lies the core essence of the initiation of personality. One of the methods, in the first case, is *incantation,* while, in the second one, the method is *prayer*. According to other concepts, however, Ayn Soph is in the periphery, and by collapsing, an empty space opens up, in which the manifested worlds unfold in the form of the three-dimensional model of the Kabalistic Tree.

From Ayn Soph, Primordial Oneness is born – the place where no opposites exist; and in Kabala it is called *Keter.* This is the point in the Manifested as the only accessible form of the Unknowable God for our finite mind. Each manifested form is generated by opposites, which is why *Keter* emanates its two opposite aspects: *Hohma* (Wisdom), or the positive masculine aspect, and *Bina* (Understanding), the negative feminine aspect. They are the Father and the Mother which, in triunity with *Keter,* are called the *Three Heavenly Ones* (the *Supernals*) and are the most powerful forces from which All is created. In the Daoist tradition, they are analogically called the *Three Pure Ones: Tai Chi, Yang* and *Yin.* The Heavenly energy is *Yang,* the earthly energy is *Yin,* and the mediator between them is *Tai Chi* (Unity, the point of equilibrium). In Kabala, these three elemental forces were called the *Three Mothers,* represented by the hieroglyphs *Shin, Alef* and *Mem.* According to *Sefer Yetzira,* the creation of the world was accomplished through the letters of the Hebrew alphabet. They represent symbols illustrating the actual sounds – commands coming from God. Each letter contains a different type of information. *Keter* is the Androgynous All-Father, *Hohma* – the Father, and *Bina* – the Mother. Between them and the lower six Sfarot, the Abyss is situated, in which *Daat* (Awareness, Knowledge) is located. The secret Sfara separates the three Divine Sfarot, which are not within the capabilities of human knowledge, from the next six Sfarot – the *Small Countenance,* which are accessible to the finite human mind. *(Fig. 18 on p. 163.)* These three Sfarot and their mysterious fourth one refer to the head, which, in the Human Archetype Adam Kadmon, symbolizes the highest level of consciousness. According to some Kabalists, only the First Sfara – *Keter,* in the single Kabalistic Tree, constitutes Adam Kadmon and the *Atzilut* World. *Daat* is the result of the interaction of *Hohma* and *Bina,* in which Wisdom is combined with Understanding, and Awareness is obtained. According to these Kabalists, they also together form the *Bria* World. Others believe that Adam Kadmon and the *Atzilut* World do not coincide and are separate worlds. *(Fig. 17 on p. 161.)*

    *Daat* is associated with the nape, the point at which the spinal column connects to the skull, the place where the development of our primitive ancestors took place, forming the most ancient brain – the *medulla oblongata.* *Daat* represents the consciousness in another dimension and is symbolized by the Sacred Mountain in the esoteric tradition of nations. The consciousness descends along the path of involution, following the route of the flash of lightning, and it ascends back towards the Spirit along the path of evolution and begins to manifest, level by level, only when the opposite Sfarot are in equilibrium. Therefore, the consciousness is projected onto the Middle Pillar, while the magic powers are at both ends of each pair of opposite Sfarot. The Path of Initiation follows the Spiral of the Serpent on the Kabalistic Tree, whereas the Path of Enlightenment follows the Central Pillar. This is the path of mystics, different from that of occultists, because it is freed from the temptation of unbalanced force, but it does not grant any magic powers. *(Fig. 15)*

**Figure 15**

The Fourth Sfara *Hesed* (*Love* or *Mercy*) is in equilibrium with the Fifth – *Gebura* (*Justice* or *Severity*), and they both represent the two poles of Divine Love and Divine Nemesis. The Sixth Sfara *Tiferet* (*Beauty* or *Harmony*) is the one balancing *Hesed* and *Gebura*. It is the place where all the "lower" Divine Forces are in perfect balance. In *Tiferet* is the Enlightened Consciousness known as *Christ Consciousness*. The next pair of Sfarot are *Neza (Victory)* and *Hod (Glory)*. The former is the force that fills the whole Creation and is considered to be the abode of intuition, feelings and emotions; while *Hod* illustrates the notion of form and structure. It is the archetype of logic and rationality. These two Sfarot of logic and emotion are balanced from the upper side by *Tiferet (Harmony, Beauty)*, while from the lower side they are balanced by *Yesod (Foundation)*. It is the archetype of sub-consciousness and unconscious thinking, and it illustrates the sexual force in the Universe. The Tenth Sfara is *Malhut (Kingdom)*. It symbolizes the physical world, the world of matter. The ancient world was mainly subconscious, while the modern world has developed the consciousness. When the two worlds merge, they will synthesize the Super-Consciousness which Initiates aspire to. *(Fig. 14 on p. 154.)*

In addition to the symbols of the lightning flash and the serpent on the Kabalistic Tree, there is another fundamental symbol – the *Pillars of Manifestation*. According to Kabala, the whole Manifestation is based on dualism. The traditional view of Western European Kabala is that the Right Pillar is positive, or masculine, while the Left Pillar is negative, or feminine. This duality is in everything and grounds the Principle of Opposition. This is how Force and Form are differentiated – the two elements of Manifestation. *Hohma* is at the top of the "Pillar of Mercy", whereas *Bina* is at the top of the "Pillar of Severity". Between the two pillars, there is a third one, the "Pillar of Equilibrium", balancing the pillars of action and expressing the very consciousness. Thus, in the Right Pillar, the three Sfarot Forces are situated, whereas, in the Left Pillar – the three Sfarot Forms. *(Fig. 14 on p. 154.)* Each Sfara is negative, i.e.

feminine, with respect to its predecessor, from where it receives the Divine influence, while being positive, or masculine, regarding the one following it. Therefore, namely, we said that any Sfara can be defined as "bisexual". If we use the Kabalistic Tree as a subjective symbol, then the Three Pillars are the three channels of Prana according to the Yoga tradition: *Ida, Pingala* and *Sushumna*. According to Chinese philosophy, on the other hand, they are equivalent to *Yin* and *Yang,* and the balance between them – *Dao*. The Central Pillar corresponds to the spinal column, along which the Kundalini energy rises that is wound in a spiral in the Sfara *Yesod*. In the Yoga system, the consciousness expands when Kundalini rises along Sushumna, just as the Kabalistic magic operation for ascending through the levels of consciousness is also performed in the Central Pillar of the Kabalistic Tree. In addition to the vertical ternary, three horizontal ternaries are also formed in this Tree, and they consist of Sfarot grouped into triads, from up downwards: the first triad is the so-called *Heavenly Trinity* – *Keter, Hohma* and *Bina;* then below it comes the second trinity, called the *Triangle* of *Ethics* – *Hesed, Gebura* and *Tiferet,* and the third triad, or the third triangle, is the so-called *Astral Triangle* including the Sfarot *Neza, Hod* and *Yesod*. Here is the Masonic "Three times three". *(Fig. 16)*

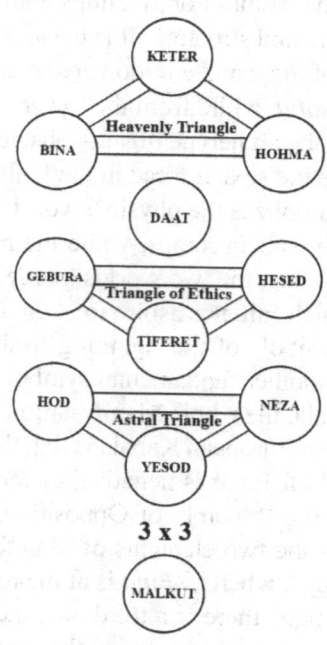

**Figure 16**

We have already mentioned that there are also other designations of these three horizontal ternaries, as well as another horizontal differentiation of the Kabalistic Tree. We noted that, according to some, the Sfara *Keter* is independent and that it represents Adam Kadmon. The following triangles below *Keter*, in this classification, form the energy worlds described above: *Hohma, Bina* and *Daat,* constituting the *Atzilut* World; then there follows a triangle formed by the Sfarot *Hesed, Gebura* and *Tiferet,* constituting the *Bria* World; the next triangle is composed of *Neza, Hod* and *Yesod,* which are in the *Yetzira* World; and finally, there is the Sfara *Malkut,* situated in the *Assia* World. The five "final" forms of some Hebrew hieroglyphs correspond to this classification of the worlds, from up downwards, as follows: *Kaf Final, Mem Final, Nun Final, Pe Final, and Tsadi Final.* Through the same classification, the five degrees, or the five levels of penetration into the *Torah* can be represented, the first letters of which form the word *Pardes* (Paradise): *Peshut* (literal), *Agada* (myth), *Remez* (instruction), *Derush* (interpretation, analogy), *Sod* (secret). On the microcosmic plane, this classification corresponds to the energy envelopes of the human body *(kuf)* – *Yehida* (personality, indivisible monad), *Haya* (life), *Neshama* (breath), *Ruah* (Spirit, breath), *Nefesh* (vital soul). *(Fig. 17)*

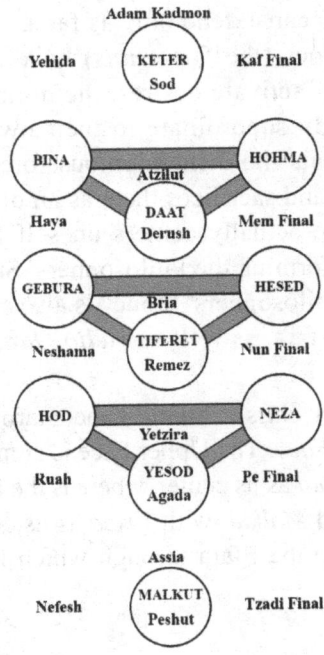

**Figure 17**

The five-degree classification is also repeated in the so-called *Gardens,* or *Faces* of the Extended Kabalistic Tree, which we will dwell on when describing the Tabernacle.

It is noteworthy that *Malkut* is always separate and does not fit into any triad, and therefore it is called the *Kingdom* – because it is a self-dependent sphere, which, however, corresponds neither to the earth element nor to the planet Earth, but it corresponds to the physical embodiment of Creation – to matter with its four elements: *air, water, fire* and *earth.* Non-harmonious forces are called *Qlifot* by Kabalists. They are the dark side of each Sfara, so negative forces are in there. The *Six Sfarot* (*Hesed, Gebura, Neza, Hod, Yesod,* and *Tiferet*) in the Old Testament are personified in the *six kingdoms of Edom,* associated with the unbalanced force, with the passions of the disharmonized humans, who are actually the "fallen human" – *Adam Beliel.* The six unorganized kingdoms of Edom are defeated by Abraham, who is a symbol of reason and logical thought. He gives tithes to Melkitsedek, a symbol of God's Will (Wisdom), and the latter, on his part, gives Initiation to Abraham. The author or authors of the Old Testament tell us that unorganized forces can extend only as far as the Sfara *Hesed* because the Three Heavenly Ones (the *Supernals*) have no vices. In the "fallen human", when instincts activate desires, the mind implements them, and thus humans are already subordinate to their own animal nature. When reason (Abraham) defeats the disharmonious forces (the kings of Edom) through the willpower, and sacrifices them as an offering to God's Wisdom (Melkitsedek), then one actually centers oneself in the Sfara *Tiferet,* the point of Harmony, and forming the Philosophers' Stone, is transformed into Adam Kadmon. The "Philosophers' Stone" is also called *Eloah Gabal,* after the name of the Sixth Sfara, as well as *Helio Gabal*[81], because its symbol is the Sun.

There is still another classification of the Sfarot in the Kabalistic Tree: *Upper Face* and *Lower Face.* The Upper Face is comprised of *Keter, Hohma, Bina* and *Tiferet,* with *Daat* as its center, whereas the Lower Face is composed of *Tiferet, Neza, Hod* and *Malkut,* with *Yesod* as its centre and the foundation of the whole Tree, being the Sfara through which forces can move up and down. *(Fig. 18)*

---

81 "Solar stone" – *AN.*

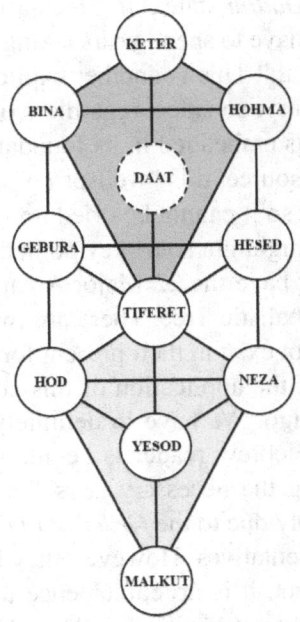

**Figure 18**

The traditional representation of the Sfarot, as has been already understood, is upon the glyph of the Kabalistic Tree; however, there is still another older symbol preceding it – and this is the candlestick known as *Menorah*, which is a generalized symbol of the Hebrew spiritual tradition. The original *Menorah* is with seven branches, and it stood in the Temple of Solomon, representing the Ten Sfarot through the symbolism of its construction. In front of the altar of Solomon's Temple, there were ten such candlesticks, which represented the Ten Sfarot. This is an indication that, in each Sfara, there is one Kabalistic Tree, and in each Sfara of the latter, there is still another Tree, and so on, endlessly. Misunderstanding the symbolism of the Kabalistic Tree leads to a deviation from the True Path and straying towards the *Qlifot*. After the death of Moses, the caste of the priests strayed from this Path and from its teaching. As a result, many people could not reach the fruits of this Tree except its shells only.

In completing the schematic representation of Western Kabala, we must emphasize that it is *"practical"* in relation to its original source – Hebrew Kabala. Therefore, it is impossible for us not to dwell on the latter, especially since Z'ev ben Shimon Halevi, the respected by us Kabalist, in his book *The Way of Kabbalah,* writes the following about the ritual form as a dynamic approach to achieving the *Gadlut* state: "In Freemasonry, a European offshoot of Kabbalah, a man may have to spend years taking part in a ceremony before he is allowed to conduct it." This is another explicit definition of the Kabalistic nature of Freemasonry; so since, regardless of the different varieties of Kabala, Hebrew Kabala is embedded in its foundation, we ought to stop our journey and stay by this source, this "wellspring". However, it is inexhaustible as the very Creation, so it cannot be dried up – moreover, that is not our purpose, so we will only highlight some key points. As we have noted earlier, Hebrew Kabalists do not have the 22 Major Arcana with their designations upon the Paths in the Kabalistic Tree. There are two reasons for this: firstly, because these cards did not exist in their present form in Judea; and secondly, because the beginning of the application of this correspondence dates back to only a few centuries ago. We have to definitely pay attention that what is presented to the non-Hebrew reader is "epidermal", having a "Sfumato style" nature, and lacking the necessary keys for understanding. Shedding light upon Kabala is largely due to the *Order of the Golden Dawn,* in the person of its brightest representatives. However, they have laid the foundations of Modern Kabala, and yet, it is no coincidence that it is called "Western" Kabala because it is clearly not identical with the Hebrew one. In this sense, we must emphasize that, in the latter, the Truth is veiled, and in some cases – deliberately distorted or spared, so as to prevent the profane from reaching it. That is why there is so much contradiction between the various authors in the Kabalistic literature, including regarding the Paths in the Kabalistic Tree and their situating between the Sfarot. We believe that the most reliable method for establishing their proper location is the "energy analysis", which we will dwell on while explaining the so-called *Masonic Regularity of the Temple.* Here, however, we cannot but point out the key knowledge that, within humans, the Microcosmic Tree is *turned mirror-like* with regard to the left-right horizontal line, as opposed to the Macrocosmic one. This, of course, affects only the two lateral vertical columns, which exchange places. This key is very important for "unlocking" the Tree of Life within the human being, and it has played a bad trick on many "Kabalists".

## More Keys

We have already explained that in each Sfara there is one Kabalistic Tree, and in each Sfara of the latter, there is still another Tree, and so on, endlessly. This is important in the Sfarotic analysis, in which we have to reach at least the *"sub-subplane of the subplane of the plane".* For the sake of clarity, we will give the following example. If we qualify a person as "cruel", it is not enough only to decide that this person has a problem with anger on the *Gebura* plane. Knowing that, in this Sfara, there is another Kabalistic Tree, which represents its subplane, we must analyze it as well (for example, we find the presence of the vice of the Sfara *Hesed – envy*). Then, taking into account that, on this subplane, there is also a Sfarotic Tree, which represents its sub-subplane, we should analyze it as well (we find out the vice of *Yesod – greed*). Thus, in the end, the conclusion will be that this person is cruel, because the negative qualities prevail in the Sfara *Yesod* on the sub-subplane, in the Sfara *Hesed* on the subplane, and in the Sfara *Gebura* on the highest plane, and therefore it is necessary to act in these Sfarot for the removal of those negative qualities. In this way, according to the given example, at the deepest level, greed generating envy is rooted into the researched person, which in turn awakens anger, which in turn grows, being objectified into cruelty as a final result. As we have already clarified, the subtle generates the gross, meaning that negative energies ruin not only the soul but also the body.

The conclusion is that, if we do not win the fight with greed, then we will not succeed in the fight against cruelty either. Thus, by healing the soul, we will cure the body as well – and, in this way, we can reach the cellular and the subcellular level. This key, however, is universal and can be used to analyze and explain any action or event in our and other Worlds.

**Figure 19**

## The "Ladder of Jacob"

> *Then he dreamed, and behold, a ladder was set up on the Earth, and its top reached to Heaven; and there the Angels of God were ascending and descending on it.*
>
> **First Book of Moses – Genesis 28:12, NKJV**

In this sense and for the purpose of our exposition, however, it is impossible to not dwell also on the unfolded Kabalistic Tree, symbolized in the Old Testament by the "Ladder of Jacob", which differs from the more widespread single Tree. Before that, though, first let us examine the symbolism of the ladder in principle.

The ladder is a very widespread symbol as an analogue of the Sfarotic Tree and has an *"axial"* meaning, quite like the Tree itself. The "axis" of the Universe is a ladder, along which, a constant movement of ascent and descent is taking place. The railings of this ladder correspond to the duality of the Tree of Knowledge, or the two lateral "Pillars" of the Kabalistic Tree, already familiar to us, which is an indication that it is incorrectly referred to as the *Tree of Life*. The latter is an illustration of the *Atzilut* World, where there is no duality, and which is characterized by the Names of God.

The ladder can also be viewed as a symbol of change. In some ancient depictions of Osiris, he is portrayed as the *Lord of the Ladder,* a symbol of his metamorphosis, crowned by his rebirth into Horus.

The symbolism of the Tree of Knowledge is explained in a different way. Some view the tasting of the fruits of this Tree as an attempt to test and experience evil in practice, others interpret this symbol as establishing ethical norms independently of God, while still others – as a symbol of power of authority over the world, asserting itself independently of God and making its source not His Will but the human will. That is why the Serpent, namely, promised the humans that they would be "like Gods". We shall add that the Tree of Knowledge is the Tree of Death, for through it, people become mortal. They have never had access to the Tree of Life – neither in the Garden of Eden, nor after their expulsion, since a Seraph with a fiery sword is placed to guard the access to it, which is why we will use the common, unifying term *Kabalistic Tree*, or *Sfarotic Tree*.

After this digression, now we return to the *ladder* again, as a symbol of the Kabalistic Tree. Its *steps* are analogous to the Middle Pillar of this Tree and represent the aforementioned "axis" of the worlds. Thus, the ladder is a "vertical" bridge, rising through all the worlds, with the steps being the different levels of the Universal Manifestation. This meaning is evident in the biblical symbolism of the "Jacob's Ladder", along which Angels ascend and descend. It is also known that, at the place where Jacob had this vision, he placed a stone which he "raised like a pillar", also symbolizing the "axis of the World", and in some way replacing the ladder itself, which ought to stand with its lower end upon the Earth, which means that the world of humans is the "support" from which the ascension must begin. Whenever a ladder is used in some of the Initiatic rituals, its steps are considered as an embodiment of various Heavens, such as the Seven Heavens in Kabala. Thus, in the Mysteries of Mithra, the ladder had seven steps, which were in relation to the seven planets and were made of metals that were correlated to these planets. Surmounting these steps symbolized initiation to the corresponding degree. This seven-step ladder is also found in some other Initiatic societies, including in the High Degrees of Scottish Freemasonry. There are also seven steps in front of Solomon's Temple, which are depicted on the carpet of the so-called *Blue Freemasonry*. The usage of the Sfarotic Tree in the sense of a ladder, the steps of which are the different levels of manifestation or worlds, is the most important Kabalistic key to interpreting and penetrating into the *eidos* of Things. The difference is that, in the unfolded Tree, each of the four worlds contains one Kabalistic Tree. However, there is a contradiction in the views regarding the manner of its unfolding. One claim is that *Malkut* appears as *Keter* on the next Tree. *(Fig. 20 on p. 168.)* We support the thesis that the unfolding begins with *Tiferet*, which represents *Keter* of the next Tree. In this way, the Lower World of the Upper Tree is superimposed over the Upper World of the Lower Tree, and this also has its own meaning and significance. *(Fig. 20ª on p. 168.)*

The point of support for the mutual penetration and overlaying of the Worlds can be found in the alchemical symbolism of the Fourteenth Arcanum. It depicts the Archangel Michael stepping with one foot into a lake. The Kingdom in which Michael is situated is *Bria*, but he has dipped his toe into a lake symbolizing the human psyche – the *Yetzira* World. *(Fig. 21 on p. 169.)*

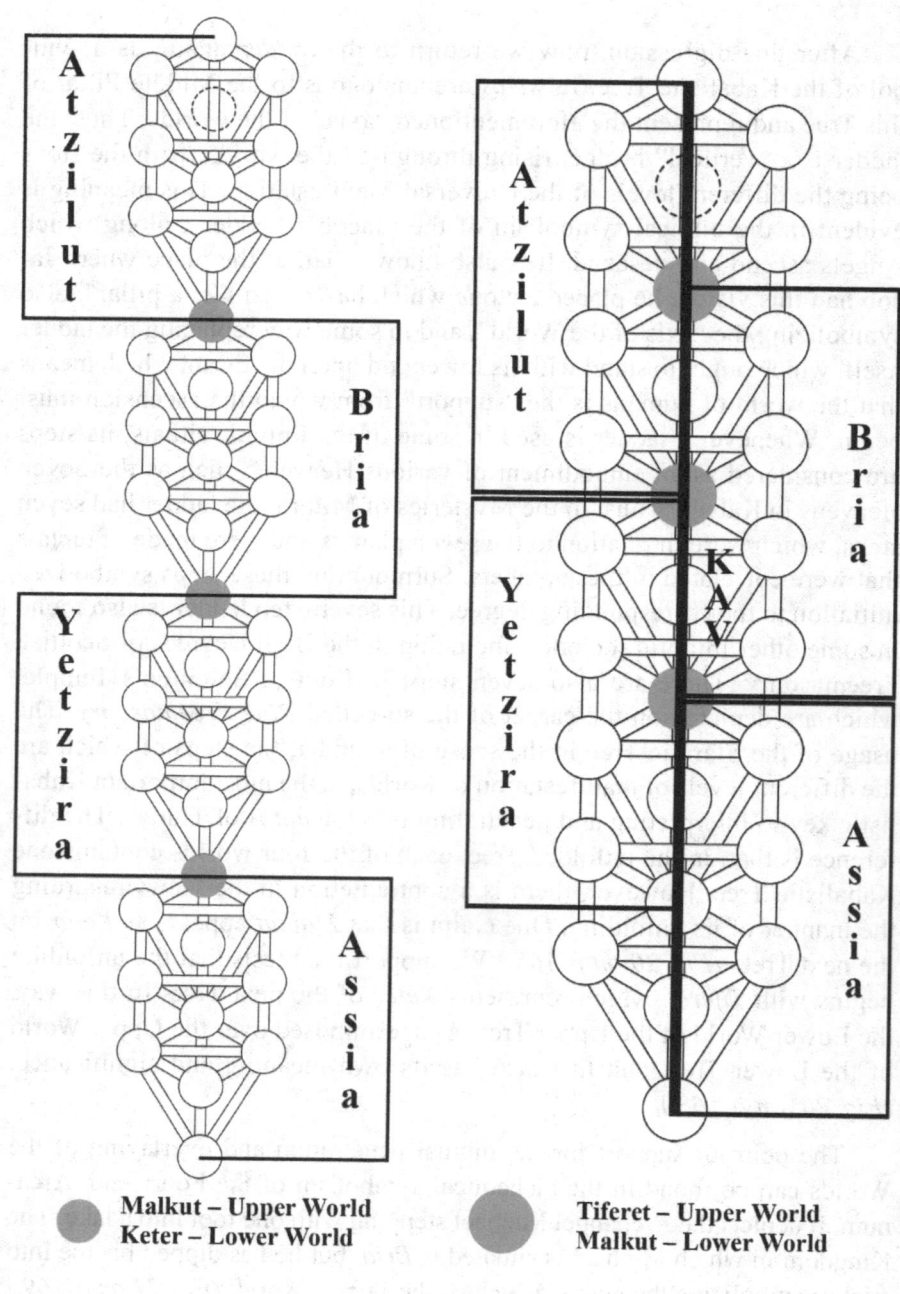

Malkut – Upper World
Keter – Lower World

Tiferet – Upper World
Malkut – Lower World

Figure 20

Figure 20<sup>a</sup>

**Figure 21**

This is an indication that the Lower World of *Bria* is in contact with the Upper World of *Yetzira*, and they are overlapping one another. In the microcosmic aspect, though, it is a sign of the immanence of the collective (archetypal) Self in our astral body. *(Fig. 22 on p. 181.)* Thus, the partial overlap of the four Worlds accomplishes the link between them through the Sfarot *Daat* and *Yesod*, and builds the Great Tree uniting the entire Universe. The vertical line, extending from the highest level down to the lowest one, so as to form the backbone of this Tree, is called *KAV* in the Kabalistic tradition. *(Fig. 20ᵃ)*

This deep esoteric key is important because, when viewing and analyzing any Sfara, we must always keep in mind in which World (in which Sfarotic Tree) it is situated. It makes difference, when talking about the Sfara *Yesod*, whether it is situated in the Tree of Life in *Atzilut*, where the Great Architect of the Universe resides, or in the Kabalistic Tree of *Yetzira*, where the ego is. In the context of the example of cruelty given above, the aforementioned negative qualities are in the corresponding Sfarot, which are situated in the Trees of *Yetzira* and *Assia*.

The Extended Tree model finds its footing in *Sefer Zohar*, and yet, we are obliged to point out that models also exist grounded on *Sefer Yetzira*, on the basis of which the *Merkaba*, the Divine Chariot, is formed.

Many more points from the so-called *Hebrew Kabala* can be specified, key points at that; and still, in this book we examine the Kabalistic knowledge only with respect to its preliminary nature and its correlation with Masonic science. We will only mention the existence of a certain school of Hebrew Kabala – the *Lurianic Kabala,* named after its creator Yitzhak Luria, and popularized by Michael Lightman nowadays. We will not dwell on it even essentially, since we consider it to be rather a philosophy and something like an "art within the art", a "white square on white canvas", and therefore it is not substantially correlated with Masonry, which is more operative.

We have also no claim to the essentiality of the exposed so far, because the most concentrated presentation of Kabala is contained in the *Lord's Prayer ("Our Father").* In compensation, we will try to analyze and interpret the prayer itself, which may be an expression of the Christian Kabala, but anyway, its basis is the Hebrew Kabalistic knowledge.

## 12
## The Lord's Prayer
## ("Our Father")

*When His disciples asked Him
to tell them how to pray, Jesus said to them:
"In this manner, therefore, pray:
Our Father Who are in the Heavens!
Hallowed be Your Name;
Your Kingdom come; Your Will be done
On Earth as it is in Heaven.
Give us this day our daily bread;
And forgive us our debts,
As we forgive our debtors.
And do not lead us into temptation,
But deliver us from the evil one.
For Yours is the Kingdom and the Power
And the Glory forever.
Amen."*

***Holy Gospel of Matthew 6:9–13***

We will start with an exoteric commentary on each verse in this prayer, which begins as follows:

**Our Father Who are in the Heavens!** (The words of this prayer are taken from the *New King James* version of the Bible, the only difference being that we have replaced the words "in

Heaven" with the phrase "Who are in the Heavens", which is a more precise translation of the original Hebrew text – *AN*.)

For the first time, unlike the God of Moses, Who is a cruel and vengeful tribal God and Who has introduced *Lex talionis*[82] – "Eye for eye, tooth for tooth", Jesus, on His turn, offers a different countenance to this God, calling Him *Father*. Quite naturally, there is much more sacral and theological essence in the word *Father*, but it still means *paternal parent, familial father*. By saying "our", Jesus makes it clear to understand that it is not only about the tribal Hebrew God, but the God of all. This conclusion can be drawn from Jesus's entire behaviour directed towards moving out of the esoteric circle of knowledge. During the Palaeolithic Age, the Mother Goddess was at the head of the pantheon of gods. However, there comes a moment when the Aryans and the Semites introduce the masculine principle. Following this line, the Hebrews, in the person of Moses, inheriting the pantheon of the Sumerian and Akkadian gods, adopt this already established understanding of the dominion of the masculine principle, and proclaim a tribal God, a patriarchal God. The Mother Goddess disappears; She is no longer present. At a later stage, Christianity adopts all this, in order to establish the Doctrine of Trinity – yet, a masculine Trinity: the Father, the Son, and the Holy Spirit. Christianity has given an incorrect interpretation – or perhaps such was the policy of the Church – of the Kabalistic symbolism in which the Holy Spirit is spoken of in the feminine gender. In the *Zohar*, which is the reference book of Kabala, the Holy Spirit is referred to as "She, the Holy Spirit". The Holy Spirit is, in its core essence, the feminine, creative, formative principle of God, though distorted by the Judeo-Christian tradition, and crossed out. In the canonical prayer "Our Father", inclusively, the feminine principle does not exist either. In the apocryphal *Gospel of the Perfect Life*, however, Jesus says the following: "From now on, you shall pray: Our Father-Mother Who are above and within, hallowed be Your Name." So Jesus has left His message in this Gospel (though not canonized by the Church) that there is a feminine principle present in God – and that we, as His image and likeness, also have a masculine and feminine core essence. Therefore, in the context of the above exposition, the designation *Father* bears the content and form of Supreme Androgynate. In support of this, the Aramaic word for *father* – *abwoon*, has the meaning of *personal father*, but also of *spiritual parent*, without any gender differentiation.

It must be paid attention that it is said, "Our Father Who are in the Heavens!" – not in *Heaven*, but in *the Heavens*. What does that mean? Jesus re-proclaims the One United God, Who, however, manifests and objectifies

---

82  From Latin: "Law of Retaliation" – *AN*.

Himself through His ten essential qualities, and Who is the God of All. This universality obviously corresponds to the Freemasons' Great Architect of the Universe, regardless of their personal faith or religion.

The prayer goes on as follows:

**Hallowed be Your Name...**

Which is the Name that ought to be hallowed? God has Ten Names corresponding to the Ten Sfarot in *Atzilut,* and still, there is One Concealed Name that is pronounced only once a year during a special ceremony, and very quietly at that, just as in Freemasonry certain names are uttered in a whisper. This Name is the *Great Tetragrammaton: Yod-He-Vav-He,* pronounced *Yahve,* or more commonly – *Jehova.* According to the Kabalistic tradition, the Secret Name of God which consists of 72 letters derives from this Divine Name. Furthermore, in practical Kabala there are 72 names of Genii, each composed of the attribute of the Genius and one of God's Names – *Yah* or *El.*

These Names are formed from three verses in *Exodus* 14:19 – 21 of the Old Testament, which contain something unique that is not repeated anywhere else in the Bible. The Names are formed through a certain "technique", each of them containing 3 letters. Thus, 72 trigrams are formed, that is, 72 roots of 3 letters each, constituting 72 Names which express the Divine qualities.

According to tradition, those who know these 72 Names become God-like and are able to create and destroy worlds. Therefore, it is said that only 70 Names were given to Mohammed, since the last two are not to be revealed to anyone, because otherwise humans would be equal to God. The 72 Names are also known by the popular designation *Shemamforash* meaning *Circle of Invulnerability,* from the Hebrew "Shem ha Mevorah", literally "the Name that is not to be pronounced", and perhaps more precisely from "Shem ha Mufrash" – the "Locked Name". According to the Hebrew esoteric tradition, only the *L'amed-Vav* know this Name and are able to operate it. We must point out, however, that God's Name *Ehye,* which is translated as "I Am", is the Name by which God reveals Himself to Moses; and since it is the Name of the Sfara *Keter,* where the All-Father, from Whom Everything originates, is situated, therefore it also represents His Primordial and Supreme Name. Its meaning is "Forever and Ever", and it expresses the Eternal Core Essence of God-Father.

We will now make an analogy with the four elements, regardless of the fact that they are in *Malkut,* while we are now referring to *Keter.* There is a Kabalistic maxim which reads: "*Keter* is *Malkut* of Ayn Soph", whereas, according to the Hermetic Law of Analogy: "As below, so above." That is why it is not illogical to discuss the four elements here. In order to get the physical body purified, we call upon the *Angel of Earth;* we summon the *Angel of*

*Water* so that our heart may be washed; we invoke the *Angel of Air* so that our mind may be uplifted; and, in order to hallow anything, it would be through the *Fire of Light*. Only where there is pure Light can we speak of hallowing. So "Hallowed be Your Name" means that we have to hallow God's Name through the Fire of Wisdom and the Light of Reason. This means to reason, to meditate upon God's Name from the position of *Bina* through the power of *Hohma*.

The prayer continues:
**Your Kingdom come...**
Very interesting – the Kingdom, this is *Malkut*. Where should the Kingdom come, since it is already down in *Malkut*? Obviously, it has to come at a much higher arc, because *Malkut* is the accomplished form, while *Bina* represents the idea of the form, and *Daat* is *Keter* of the form. Within *Daat* is the state in which first the form is manifested, and then – the force, unlike *Bina*, where the force is first manifested that gives rise to the idea of the form. That is why the concealed Sfara *Daat* is *Keter* of the form, so *Malkut*, the Kingdom, ought to come here, in *Keter* of the form. It means that the accomplished form should be manifested in *Daat* through awareness, which, in turn, is an indication that the fallen Sfara *Daat* must be restored, and we will discuss this in detail further on. The Kingdom, however, can come when there is a desire – and it already represents itself astral energy embracing the heart centre. Therefore we have to understand, become aware of, and hallow the Name of God through our Spirit, and then wish for His Kingdom with our heart.

If we refer to the Aramaic version of the term in view, *Teete Malkutakh*, we will find still another aspect of its interpretation. The last word is translated as *Kingdom*, though it rather expresses the *Principle of Reign*, in the sense of *governing*. The word *Malkutakh* is in the feminine gender, and it derives from the same root as the word *malkatu*, which has been used in the Middle East for many years as a designation of the Mother Goddess, as Her title. In this sense, it is obvious that a "feminine kingdom" is meant, which Jesus uses quite often in combination with "Shemaya" or "Shamaya" – *Heaven*, or "Heavenly Kingdom".

Then it is said in the prayer:
**Your Will be done...**
The Will is the energy of the Sfara *Hohma* because Wisdom represents conscious ethical willpower in action. Without the Will of *Hohma*, we cannot implement our ethical ideas, intentions and desires. The *Three Heavenly Ones* (*Keter, Hohma* and *Bina* – the *Supernals*) constitute God's Mind, as well as our mind. Usually, when talking about the *mind*, people imagine the brain, which, however, is only a tool of the mind. The *Ternary of the Mind*

is synthesized in *Keter*, at the summit of the Heavenly Triangle, where faith is situated. Its "thesis" is the Sfara *Hohma*, where the Will resides, which constitutes the positive pole. The negative pole is the Sfara *Bina* where the imagination, or the "antithesis", is situated. When talking about *Bina*, it is not just about intellect and logic but about spiritual reason, which means that it aspires towards Wisdom. As such, reason also has poles, with intellect being the negative pole (−), its creative manifestation being the active part, which is actually the imagination, representing, in this case, the positive pole (+). *Hohma*, on the other hand, also has polarity, with the willpower, as we have said, being the positive pole, while the negative pole is compassion. When the positive poles of *Bina* and *Hohma* are in perfect harmony, then Faith is accomplished as the most supreme quality, for Faith is above reason and above Wisdom. When we accomplish the imagination and willpower in perfect harmony, then we acquire Faith and the so-called *Ternary of the Mind*. Imagination, willpower and Faith, polished through adequate spiritual practices, form the enlightened mind. These practices are: *listening, reflection, meditation, penetrating insight, awareness, mastered will, restrained passion*. This is the path towards attaining the Ternary of the Mind and its synthesis – Faith. In the basis of this path, there is the yearning, and as the Law of Sacrifice reads: "If you yearn for something, then you sacrifice something; if you yearn for everything – you sacrifice everything." In this case, the "yearning" includes the idea, the intent, the aspiration, the desire and the will for implementation. The implementation power of authority is the willpower materializing each of our ethically and consciously motivated intents, which we have to distinguish from any desire, in the context of what Rumi has said: "This world is a trap, and desire is its bait." If we can make an analogy with grapes, the symbol of the "Great Mysteries", then the *ideas* are the seeds, the *intent* is the husk, and the *aspiration* is the process of swelling of the fruit, of growth of the idea. Intents are situated on the mental plane, they represent mental desires, *desires* in the mind and through the mind. Aspiration, as dynamic, effective development of the intent for implementation of the idea, also represents mental energy. The path, however, goes further through the astral desire, which represents the physical juice of the fruit, while the *willpower* is the vital force of that juice. All these elements have to be welded together through the energy of Love flowing from the source of the heart, because this energy of Love is the *quintessence*.

The *ether*, as a type of matter, is the fifth element on the physical level, because the ether is a type of matter, and, on the spiritual plane, the quintessential element is Love, which is the connecting element, just as the ether is the connecting element for the other four elements.

Let us continue with the prayer, where the general definition of place follows:

**... On Earth as it is in Heaven.**

If we assume that the earthly world is imperfect, full of unbelievers and blasphemers inveighing against God, it follows that this world is not dominated by God's Kingdom and God's Will, and therefore the latter must be established also on Earth as they are established in Heaven.

There are affirmations related to God so far in this prayer: "Hallowed be Your Name", "Your Kingdom come", "Your Will be done" – but after that, there come human-related requests:

**Give us this day our daily bread...**

The requests are for ourselves, starting with bread, which is no coincidence at all: it symbolizes physical food but it is also an even greater symbol of *Spiritual Food*. Therefore, when the devil tempts Jesus, saying, "Now when the tempter came to Him, he said, 'If You are the Son of God, command that these stones become bread!" (*Holy Gospel of Matthew* 4:3, *NKJV*), Jesus answers to him: "It is written, 'Man shall not live by bread alone, but by every Word that proceeds from the mouth of God'." (*Holy Gospel of Matthew* 4:4 *NKJV*) "But Jesus answered him, saying, 'It is written, 'Man shall not live by bread alone, but by every Word of God'." (*Holy Gospel of Luke* 4:4, *NKJV*) This conviction of Jesus is also evident from His other words: "Do not labour for the food which perishes, but for the food which endures to Everlasting Life, which the Son of Man will give you, because God the Father has set His seal on Him" (*Holy Gospel of John* 6:27, *NKJV*), and also: "Not what goes into the mouth defiles a man; but what comes out of the mouth, this defiles a man." (*Holy Gospel of Matthew* 15:11, *NKJV*)

Therefore, when He says, "Give us this day our daily bread", He is referring in particular to Spiritual Food besides physical food; because humans need the physical nourishment but are even more in need of the Spiritual one, and this is the first condition for existence – "Give us this day..." Unfortunately, judging by the state of being of humankind, Jesus seems to have indicated a principle, not a real assessment.

The next request is:

**And forgive us our debts...**

Again, the idea of the compassionate and all-forgiving God is upheld, unlike the God of Moses, Who is vengeful, jealous, and cruel. One of God's Ten Commandments is "You shall not kill!", and it was given through Moses to the Hebrew people, whereas that same God commands them to conquer the land of Canaan: "You shall dispossess the inhabitants of the land and dwell in it, for I have given you the land to possess." (*Fourth Book of Moses*,

Numbers 33:53, *NKJV*) Jesus "revises" Moses and affirms the merciful and all-forgiving God in the continuation of the above verse:

**... as we forgive our debtors.**

The Law of Karma is undoubtedly also embedded here – we will only be forgiven if we forgive as well, because, if we do not forgive, we will not be forgiven. Of course, this passage has also a profound moral and ethical message that derogates the Law of Moses "Eye for eye, tooth for tooth."

The following words give rise to the question of whether God can tempt:

**And do not lead us into temptation...**

We learn from the *Holy Gospel of Matthew* 4:1 that: "Then Jesus was led up by the Spirit into the wilderness to be tempted by the devil." We understand that it was the Spirit who led Jesus, not anyone else, which means that the temptation implemented through the devil is a necessary trial, testing the faith and anchorage, and sent to us by God. What are God's temptations about which we pray not to be given to us? We can summarize them in one temptation: When we are given the Grace of God, to become *haughty* – the devil's favourite sin.

The prayer goes on with the seemingly, at first glance, illogical phrase:

**... But deliver us from the evil one...**

There exists a possibility that the translation of this phrase may not be correct or that it has been distorted over the centuries from "And do not lead us into temptation, *AND* deliver us from the evil one" to the illogical "And do not lead us into temptation, *BUT* deliver us from the evil one". However, if we assume that this phrase is relatively authentic, then it means: "Yes, God tempts us because He loves us, but let Him save us from the temptations of the devil." It refers to the temptations of our individual devil – the ego. Thus, the word *BUT* is no longer outside the logical context. And still, the plea to God is not to send us trials, but rather in the sense of Jesus's plea in the Garden of Gethsemane: "O My Father, if this cup cannot pass away from Me unless I drink it, Your Will be done!" (*Holy Gospel of Matthew* 26:42, *NKJV*)

We will now proceed to the research of the Sfarotic correspondence of these request verses. The phrase "Give us this day our daily bread" is a symbolic designation of the Sfara *Tiferet* – the Sun, because we receive everything from the Sun, and it is "our daily bread" without which we cannot exist.

By the next sentence: "And forgive us our debts, as we forgive our debtors", forgiveness is introduced for the first time, and this is an indication towards Mercy – the Sfara *Hesed*. Mercy, however, needs to be balanced, which is understood by the following words:

**And do not lead us into temptation,**
**But deliver us from the evil one.**

This means that without the Severity and destructive power of *Gebora*, we cannot cope with temptation. We have to learn to balance Mercy *(Hesed)* with Severity *(Gebora)*, because otherwise Mercy will turn into pity, whereas *Gebora* – into cruelty. This is how we attain balance – "And forgive us our debts, as we forgive our debtors", expressed in harmony and beauty in the Sfara *Tiferet*, because here is the centre of the Kabalistic Tree, as well as "our daily bread".

Finally, the prayer ends as follows:

**... For Yours is the Kingdom and the Power and the Glory forever.**

There are discrepancies in the interpretations regarding the Sfarotic correspondence of the words *kingdom, power, glory,* and *forever*. The Initiatic Ascension in the Kabalistic Tree is accomplished along the Path of the Serpent, and it crawls from *Malkut* to *Yesod*, *Hod* and *Neza*. Thus, the phrases pointed out above should correspond to the sequence of these Sfarot.

The Kingdom, of course, is *Malkut*, where the Creator's idea is accomplished. However, in order for this to take place, a certain transformation of astral energy into physical energy ought to start, which occurs in the Sfara *Tiferet*. Descending into *Neza*, forces begin to condense for the first time, and then in *Hod* they acquire some concreteness so that the matrix is elaborated in *Yesod*, and then Creation is accomplished in the patrix of *Malkut*. In order for any force to be productive, it has to be closed into form, but it is limited there, so sooner or later the form becomes retrograde. Likewise, birth is the gate to death, which is why *Malkut* is called "the door of death", "the door of tears", for it carries "death". As long as the Spirit is not closed into form, it is immortal; but when it becomes clothed in form, it "dies" for the Spiritual World. When we come here, we *die* regarding the Spiritual World, and we *are born* regarding the physical one; and, when we die here, we die regarding the physical world, and are born regarding the Spiritual World. Thus, *Malkut* is also called the "Lower Mother", the "Prolific, Luminous Mother", while *Bina* is the "Higher, Dark, Sterile Mother". *Bina* is the archetype of form, whereas, in *Malkut*, Creation has physical dimensions and is the World of Action. In the Egyptian esoteric tradition, this has found expression in the dual aspect of Isis, who is the Fertile Mother who gave birth to Horus, though at the same time sitting on the throne of the Sterile *Bina*. Or, these are Nephthys and Isis, the crying and the weeping one, the higher and the lower soul, who seek their brother, the true King Osiris (the "I"), dismembered by his brother Seth (the Ego) into 14 parts. Both of them, together with Anubis *(the distinguishing mind)*, Horus *(the enlightened mind)* and Thoth *(Wisdom)*, find the parts and reassemble Osiris – the complete, whole Human. It is clear that these gods have their Sfarotic correspondences, which we will not dwell on here.

So the "Kingdom" is *Malkut*, and the "Power" should logically be the next Sfara along the Path of the Serpent – *Yesod*, and also because its very name, *"Foundation"*, has the emanation of Power, of Might. In addition, *Power* is the other name of this Sfara, for the Name of God corresponding to this Sfara is *El Shadai Hai,* which is translated as "Almighty Living God" (G.A.O.T.U. – The Great Architect of the Universe). The Angelic Host (Angelic Order) is *Kerubim* and means "Mighty Forces". Also, its image is of a "handsome and very strong man". One of its correspondences in the Tarot cards is the *Nine of Wands* named "Great Strength". Apart from this, the very essence of *Yesod* is the etheric template, in which the images produced by *Hod* are already being constructed as a final matrix in *Yesod*, which has to "strike" the patrix of *Malkut*. In *Yesod* are the lines of force forming this template and this matrix. All of this undoubtedly leads to the conclusion that the correspondence of the "Power" is the Sfara *Yesod*. This is precisely where the *vital force* resides which gives life to our physical body. The creative forces of nature are in *Neza* – and, condensing, they acquire some concreteness in *Hod*. This concreteness is given a matrix correspondence in *Yesod*, whereas its very imprint is the material world in *Malkut*. Therefore it is said "Power" *(Yesod)*, not "Powers" *(Neza)*.

The natural Path of the Serpent, as we have already noted, after the Sfara *Yesod* goes on through the Sfara *Hod*, its name meaning "Glory", hence, also in the literal sense, it is the Sfara corresponding to the phrase "... and Glory..." in the prayer.

To what has been said so far, we can add laconically that this is the Sfara of coagulation, hence also of magic as an act of materialization, and therefore its symbol is also the apron, an attribute of craftsmen – creators of forms. In Symbolic Freemasonry, the apron covers the Moon Centre, *Yesod,* where the genitals and the ego are, and we believe that this needs no explanation.

Finally, we come to the last word, the ultimate point of the prayer – *forever* (for all eternity), which, following the Serpent of Wisdom, refers to the Sfara *Neza*, whose name means "Victory" but its other designation is "Eternity". The expression *forever* (in the sense of "for all eternity") reflects, both in the end and in the beginning of the prayer, the essential quality of God – *Eternity.* Thus, this prayer closes a whole circle, following the inner sense of "I am the Beginning and the End", *"Alef* and *Tav" (Alpha* and *Omega),* "All and Nothing", repeated by Jesus.

All this means that the Power is primordial and eternal, but Its manifestations have found different expression in the existing traditions and cosmogonies. The prayer "Our Father" expresses the synthesis of the unfolding of the Power through the 10 Divine Emanations (Sfarot) according to the Kabalistic tradition and science, as well as its ascension, accomplishing the levels of consciousness. In polytheistic religions, this is accomplished through the core essence of different Deities, which can also be related to the Sfarot. *The Power is one; only the approach and the viewpoint regarding It are different.*

## "Our Father" and the "Ladder of Jacob"

> Then Jacob awoke from his sleep and said, "Surely the Lord is in this place, and I did not know it." And he was afraid and said, "How awesome is this place! This is none other than the house of God, and this is the gate of Heaven!"
>
> **First Book of Moses – Genesis 28:16 – 17, NKJV**

We will try to elucidate the prayer also from yet another Arcanum (angle) of Hebrew Kabala, which will give us the opportunity to penetrate deeper into its secret (concealed) nature. However, this can only be done if we use the glyph of the unfolded Kabalistic Tree, symbolized by the "Ladder of Jacob", which has 72 steps. *The method of "climbing up the tree" (towards God) by converting the Upper Face of the Lower World into the Lower Face of the Upper World is regarded as "Returning to God". The Hebrew word for this process is "teshuvah" – "repentance".*

As we know, this prayer begins with the specific form of address "Our Father", and we have found out that it is undoubtedly a reference to the Sfara *Keter*. However, in view of the unfolded Tree, the following question arises: *Keter* of which Tree (in which World) is meant in this reference? The answer is perhaps concealed in the next verse, "... Who are in the Heavens!" In Hebrew Kabala, the word *Heavens* (plural) is associated solely with the "Seven Heavens" that are situated on the Sfarotic Tree in the *Bria* World. In Hebrew, the phrase used in the discussed verse is *shevashamayim*, *sheva* meaning *seven*, and *shamayim* meaning *heavens*. The Seventh Heaven, called *Arabot*, is the Heaven of Heavens and is situated in the supreme triad *Keter-Hohma-Bina* of the *Bria* Tree. However, as we have clarified, the Upper Face of *Bria* coincides with the Lower Face of *Atzilut*, the Sfara *Tiferet* of the latter figuring as *Keter* of the supreme triad of *Bria*, where Creation begins from. (Fig. 20$^a$ on p. 168.) The Father Who is in the Heavens ought to be precisely in the Crown of Heavens – *Keter* of *Bria*. However, the Archangel Metatron is there, as *Bria* is the Archangel World. Then who is the Father and what is His Name? To answer this question, we must mention also some specific and more unknown Names of God, situated on the Central Pillar of the Kabalistic Tree: "He" for *Keter,* "You" for *Tiferet,* and "I" for *Malkut. (Fig. 22 on p. 181.)*

We now already have enough keys at our disposal to decipher the Kabalistic information in the phrase:

**Our Father Who are in the Heavens!**

The specific form of address "Our Father" answers the question: "Who?", whereas the next phrase gives us the very answer: "Who are in the Heavens." This answer represents information that, here, *Keter* of the *Bria* World is meant – the Crown of Heavens. It is also an indication towards God's Name *You* (in some translations of the Bible, perhaps this phrase is by no coincidence "*You* Who are in the Heavens"), and in this way, we understand that the Sfara *Tiferet* is also referred to – yet, in which world, we will find out from the next verse:

**Hallowed be Your Name...**

To this end, we will refer to the final words of Jesus on the cross, which, according to the *Vulgate* and the *Septuagint,* are the following:[83]

"Eloì, Eloì, lamà savahtanì?" (*Mark* 15:34)

"Ilì! Ilì! lamà savahtanì?" (*Matthew* 27:46)

These words are usually translated as "My God, My God, why have You forsaken Me?"

Many scholars believe that Aramaic was the language spoken by Jesus, and therefore it is the language embedded in the Gospels. According to these scholars, the words "Eloì, Eloì" in Marco's text are the exact words pronounced by Jesus, whereas, in Matthew's text, the words "Ilì! Ilì!" have been adapted into Hebrew.

According to many New Testament analysts, Matthew tried to write his Gospel in a style similar to the Old Testament style. For this reason, it is believed that he changed the Aramaic word *Eloi* to coincide with the text of *Psalm* 22:1 in the *Psalter,* where the Hebrew word *Ilì* is used: "Ilì! Ilì! lama azavtani" – "My God! My God! [hear me;] Why have You forsaken Me?" (*Psalter, Psalm* 22:1).

Since the two evangelists were not under the cross to hear Jesus's words, there are various analyses and opinions which we will dwell on later. Now we will make only a few clarifications in the Kabalistic context of our exposition.

---

83 There are discrepancies in the spelling of this phrase in the various Bibles. In the *Vulgate,* this phrase is *Eli, Eli, lema sabacthani?,* in *King James* it is *Eli, Eli, lama sabachthani?,* in Greek it is Ἠλὶ ἠλὶ, λιμᾶ σαβαχθανί (*Eli, Eli, lima sabathtani*), in Russian it is *Илù! Илù! Ламà савахфанù? (Ilì, Ilì! Lamà savahfanì?),* whereas in Bulgarian – *Илù! Илù! Ламà савахтанù? (Ilì, Ilì! Lamà savahtanì?)* – *AN.*

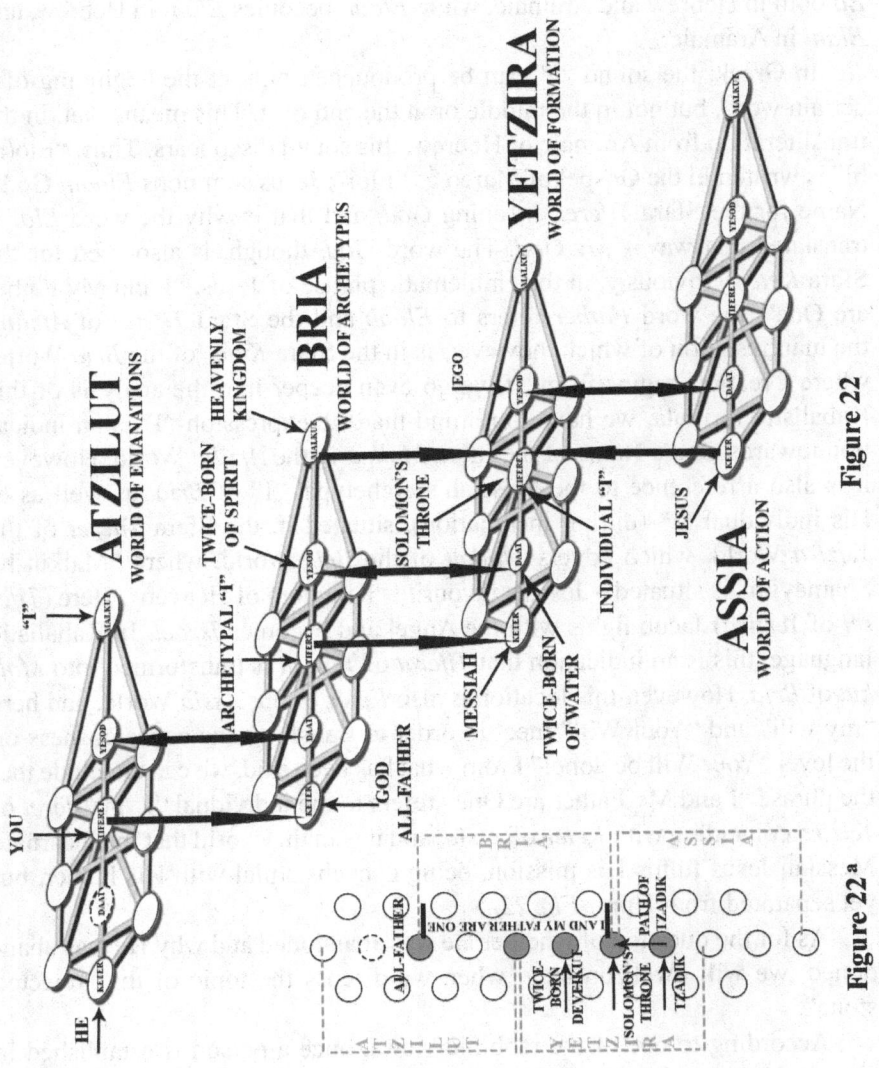

Figure 22

Figure 22 a

In both Hebrew and Aramaic, to refer to God, the words *Eloah* and respectively *Elahi* are used, as well as the main word for the two languages: *El*. To say "My God!", the letter *Yod* is simply added to *El*, and the result is *Eli* both in Hebrew and Aramaic, while *Eloah* becomes *Elohi* in Hebrew, and *Elahi* in Aramaic.

In Greek, the sound "h" can be pronounced only at the beginning of a certain word, but not in the middle or at the end of it. This means that, in the transliteration from Aramaic or Hebrew, this sound disappears. Thus, "Elo(a)hi" is written in the Gospel of Marco as "Eloì": Jesus summons *Eloah*, God's Name for the *Sfara Tiferet*, meaning *God*, and that is why the word *Eloì* is translated that way – *My God*. The word *God*, though, is also used for the *Sfara Keter*. Obviously, in the emblematic phrase of Jesus, "I and My Father are One", the word *Father* refers to *Eloah* and the *Sfara Tiferet* of *Atzilut*, the manifestation of which, however, is in the *Sfara Keter* of the *Bria* World, where Creation begins from. If we go even deeper into the analysis of this Kabalistic formula, we have to remind that the expression "I" is an indication towards God's Name of the *Sfara Malkut* in the *Atzilut* World. However, it is also a reference to the Messiah's archetypal "I" of *Bria*, as well as to His individual "I" (during incarnation), situated in the *Sfara Tiferet* of the *Yetzira* World, which covers *Malkut* of the *Bria* World, where "Malkut ha Shamayim" is situated – Jesus's favourite "Kingdom of Heaven". Here (*Tiferet* of *Yetzira*) Jacob fights with the Angel and becomes *Israel*. In Kabalistic language, this is an indication that *Tiferet* of *Yetzira* is transformed into *Malkut* of *Bria*. However, this location is also *Keter* of our *Assia* World, and here "my will" and "Your Will" meet in order to transform the consciousness on the level "Your Will be done!" From what has been said, we can conclude that the phrase "I and My Father are One" refers to the individual "I" in *Tiferet* of *Yetzira* coinciding with *Keter* of *Assia*, and it is in this world that the incarnate Messiah Jesus fulfils His mission, being consubstantial with His Father, but yet separated from Him. *(Fig. 22)*

As for the question of whether He was abandoned and why He was abandoned, we will dwell on later, when we discuss the topic of the "rejected stone".

According to one of the rabbinic views, once a person is established in *Yesod* of *Yetzira*, this person is also on the *"Path of Tsadik"*. The purpose of this Path is to attain *Tiferet*, which is also *Malkut* of *Bria* – the Kingdom of Heaven. *(Fig. 22ª)* What is specific here is that walkers are willing to keep their own balance along this Path without moving away from it, neither to the left nor to the right.

The left side is often associated with obedience to the commandments of the *Torah*, while the right side – with the desire to do things for God. Whenever one within the *"Tsadik Path"* maintains oneself in equilibrium and correctly applies the *Torah* in all spheres of one's life, this one will reach the level of *Tiferet* of *Yetzira* – the starting point of the Kingdom of Heaven (*Malkut* of *Bria*). This Sfara is also called the *Throne of Solomon* because of its key position connecting the three Worlds: *Assia, Yetzira* and *Bria*. Solomon himself was called "The human who knows the three Worlds". *(Fig. 22)*

Those who have reached *Tiferet* have access to *Daat* of *Yetzira*, which is *Yesod*, the foundation of the spiritual sphere of *Bria*. This is the precise middle of the extended Tree. Here one passes from the state of *"getting closer to God"* to the state of *Deveikut* – *"communion with God/ closeness to God"*. *(Fig. 22ª on p. 181.)* This location connects the Lower Face of *Bria* to the Upper Face of *Yetzira*, because they overlap at one and the same place in the extended Tree. To make this connection means to be *"Twice-Born"*, *"of Water"* – *Yetzira*, and *"Spirit"* – *Bria*, thus attaining the *"Kingdom of Heaven"*, which Jesus speaks of, and this is a confirmation of the Kabalistic reading of His words. *(Fig. 22)* The verb "hallowed be", besides what was said initially, is another indication that God's Name *Eloa(h)* is referred to, because *Tiferet* is also called "The Holy One, blessed He be". However, we cannot but mention, when speaking about the Names of God, also the existence of a notion that the *Pentateuch* constitutes God's Name, which extends from the first letter in the *First Book of Moses, Genesis,* to the last word in the *Fifth Book of Moses, Deuteronomy,* in the Old Testament. Finally, we can conclude that by *Father,* on the Kabalistic plane of this prayer, the Sfara *Tiferet* of *Atzilut* should be understood, with the Name of God *Eloah,* the manifestation of which is *Keter* in the World of Creation. *(Fig. 22)*

In the context of the present exposition, already from the point of view of the single Tree, we can add about the verse **"Your Kingdom come"** that the designation "Kingdom" is used not only for the earthly but also for the Heavenly Kingdom, which is situated, as it became clear, in *Malkut* of the *Bria* World, and which has to be established upon *Assia*'s Earth. The concept of "God's Kingdom" in any field of manifestation is reduced to the supposition of the existence, in time, of maximum prosperity, harmony and functional adaptation at a given moment and in a given sphere. The "Kingdom of God", for any planet, is the epoch of its supreme blossom in the mentioned sense. "God's Kingdom" for any subject will be the epoch of the most sublime harmony of the totality of the subject's perceptions and manifestations. If we assume that these are the manifestations of the Spirit, then we can paraphrase this part of the prayer in the following way: "May the Kingdom of Spirit come." In an even deeper Kabalistic reading, the phrase "Your Kingdom come" is correlated with the so-called *Fall* that is associated on the epidermal level with the expulsion of Adam and Eve from Paradise. The "Fall", however, means that the Sfara *Daat* (Knowledge, Cognition) has "fallen" into the position of the Sfara *Malkut* (Kingdom) and has become invisible. *(Fig. 34 on p. 282.)* The transition from one World into another takes place through the connection (the tunnel) between the Sfara *Daat* of the next World and the Sfara *Yesod* of the previous one. *(Fig. 32 on p. 272.)* At the "Fall" of *Daat,* the connection with the *Bria* World is broken, and *Yetzira*'s Adam turns into *Assia*'s human. As we noted in our initial review of the topic (in the context of the single Tree), *Daat* turns out to be *Keter* of form, which means perfect unity. Since we are speaking of *form,* it means that this is the World of Formation, or that we are talking about the Sfara *Daat* of *Yetzira,* where the Tree of Knowledge is situated. Here, in addition to the form, the consciousness is also whole and non-alienated, and the knowledge of the world is not illusory. By "falling" and merging with the Sfara *Malkut* of the *Assia* World, the consciousness becomes differentiated and detached from the Spiritual World of *Bria,* which is why it denies its existence, or, in the last resort, accepts it, though as a world separate from the material one. Thus, humans fall into the binary illusory world, in which they always wander between two poles, between two extremes, just as the profane wander between the pillars *Jahin* and *Voaz* in front of the Temple. The phrase "Your Kingdom come... on Earth as it is in Heaven", in this Kabalistic key, means to restore the original state of being, with *Malkut* rising into *Daat,* and the latter becoming a "visible" Sfara. This, of course, is not to be taken literally but as an indication that those residing in the Kingdom of *Assia* will already have the full, non-differentiated consciousness, just as the one they had in the *Daat* of *Yetzira* before the "Fall", thus building a connection with the Spiritual World.

In the initial interpretation of the verse **"Your Will be done"**, we presented sufficient grounds for asserting that willpower, as a mental force based on the Divine Moral and Ethical Platform, is an attribute of the Sfara *Hohma* – Wisdom; and this is so in principle. However, in particular, from the position of the unfolded Kabalistic Tree, without any contradiction, things are getting specific. There are Seven Heavens situated entirely in the *Bria* World. The Sixth Heaven is called *Makom* – the Place from which Everything originates. Since it coincides with and covers the Lower Face of *Atzilut,* here is the location of the action of the Will of *El Shadai Hai* (*Yesod* of *Atzilut*), Who is the Great Architect of the Universe, which is why this Place is also called the *Palace of Will,* where contact is made "face-to-Face" with the *Almighty El Shadai.* *(Fig. 23 on p. 186.)*

From the point of view of the extended Tree regarding the verse "**on Earth as it is in Heaven**", we have to point out that the Sfara *Yesod* in *Atzilut* coincides with *Daat* of *Bria* where *Bat Kol* resides – the Voice of the Holy Spirit through which *El Shadai Hai* operates. *(Fig. 23)* The very name *Almighty Living God* indicates that this is the operative core essence of the Manifested God, Whose action extends throughout both Heaven and Earth. It should be noted that in this part of the prayer, in all the initial major translations and versions of the Bible, the word *Heaven* is used in the singular, as opposed to *Heavens* in the phrase *"Who are in the Heavens!"* In Hebrew, in both cases, the word *Shamayim* is used, which is in the masculine plural, because *Heaven* is always used in the plural form. We will not comment on whether this is due to the imperfection of the translation or not, because, anyway, it refers to the *Bria* World, one of the characteristic names of which is *"Heavens"*. To us, however, the use of the word *Heaven* in the singular, whether voluntary or involuntary, means an indication towards the presence of boundaries, of the boundary between the "Heavens" and the "Earth". Without going into detail about how *Elohim* created the "expanse" and called it "Heaven", and then gathered together the waters beneath it, and the dry land emerged, which He called "Earth" (*Genesis* 1:6–9, *ESV*), we will point out that the boundary between them is *Tiferet* of *Yetzira*, coinciding with *Malkut* of *Bria*, the First Heaven of all, and with *Keter* of *Assia*, from where the physical world starts unfolding *(Fig. 23ᵃ on p. 186.)*. From there downwards, the Upper Earth begins, in the Lower Face of *Yetzira*, where Adam ("earthly being") was created out of dust from the ground, reaching the Lower Face of the *Assia* World – the Lower Earth, where Adam and Eve were cast out, and they slipped on animal skins (physical bodies).

Here is also the place to note that, according to some Kabalists, just as there are "Seven Heavens", the same way there are "Seven Earths", as well as "Seven Hells". The "Seven Earths" are situated in the *Assia* World, with the uppermost comprising the "Three Heavenly Ones" ("Supernals") and being called "Aretz" – earth (the earth element), whereas the lowest comprising *Yesod* and *Malkut* and being called "Tebel". In the Sfara *Hesed*, "Adama" (earth) is situated – this is where we are. In *Gebura*, the earth called "Arka" is situated, containing the "Seven Hells". From *Tiferet* to *Malkut*, there are earths inhabited by humans which are not descendants of Adam. *(Fig. 23ᵃ)* After what has been said so far, it can be concluded that God's Will probably does not reach all the earths listed, and therefore in the prayer it is affirmed "Your Will be done on Earth as it is in Heaven", which includes also the lowest earth.

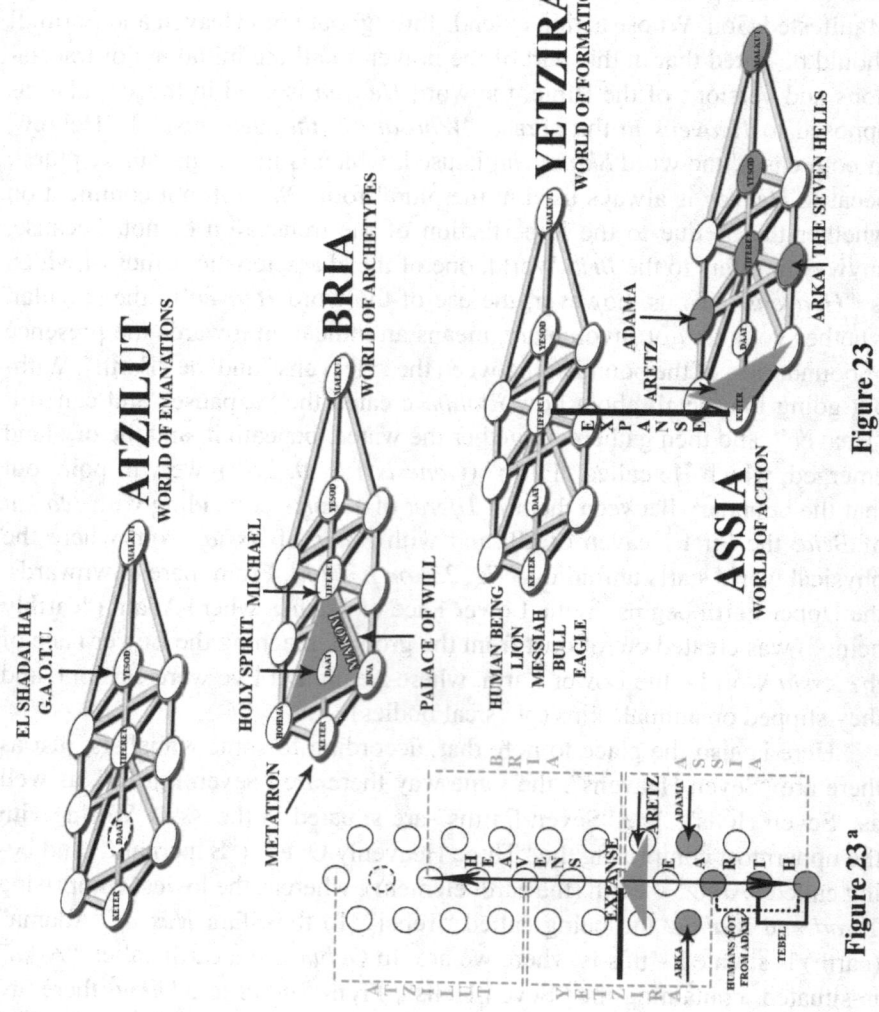

Regarding the next verse, **"Give us this day our daily bread"**, we have already commented that the request in it is related to *bread* as a symbol of physical food, but more so of the Spiritual Food which we ought to take daily. We also pointed out that this is the symbolic designation of the Sfara *Tiferet* – the Sun, because we receive everything from it. The physical and the spiritual Sun are our daily bread without which we cannot exist. Here we need to further develop this subject, mentioning that the Sfara *Tiferet* is called *Solomon's Throne*, whereas its Temple – *Beit Lehem* ("House of Bread"). King Solomon is a symbol of Wisdom, so *Tiferet* represents the throne of *Hohma*, and indeed there is a shortcut between these Sfarot in the Kabalistic Tree, denoted by the hieroglyph *Vav*. This same Solomon says, "God's Wisdom had been before time was", which means that this Wisdom is beyond Time and, as a quality, exists for all Eternity. The Buddha, on the other hand, speaks of the "Arrow of Wisdom darted from the Truth". Truth is before Wisdom and before Reason, and is called *Primordial Light (Keter)*. It cannot be known, yet through the power of the Soul's inspiration and of beauty *(Tiferet)*, its breath can be sensed; whereas, through the Light of Reason *(Bina)*, its dazzling splendour becomes comprehensible. Through Reason, we penetrate into esoteric knowledge in order to reach the Paths and Laws of Truth, while Wisdom *(Hohma)* is there so that we do not deviate from them, and having set foot on the Path, to become the very Path. To an accomplished human being in flesh, the Primordial Light can be comprehensible on the highest level of *Keter* of the *Yetzira* World of the unfolded Tree where the Messiah (Messiahs) and *Hayot ha Kodesh* are situated – the Four Living Beings of Holiness. As we have clarified many times already, in its descending unfolding, *Keter* of the next Tree begins from *Tiferet* of the previous one. That is why *Keter* of the *Yetzira* Tree is *Tiferet* of the *Bria* Tree emanating it, and there is the place of the Archangel Michael. It is said that humans are able to "ascend" even "above" the Angels and Archangels, and legend has it that Enoch the son of Jared even sat on the Throne in the "Crown of the Heavens" and became the Demiurge of the manifested worlds in his capacity of Metatron. So, in this sense, a human should be able to ascend to the "Seventh Heaven"; and it is no coincidence that there is such an expression: "He is in the Seventh Heaven from happiness." We will discuss this attainment further.

However, now is the time to dwell more deeply on the knowledge about Karma. Regarding the verse **"And forgive us our debts, as we forgive our debtors"**, we explained that the practice of forgiveness has been introduced as a fundamental method for clearing the karmic debts. It is about asking for forgiveness and giving forgiveness, in this case the request being directed to

God. Without delving deep into the vast topic of Karma, we must note that it is not understood well enough, and this leads to misunderstandings.

There are many biblical expressions in which we can clearly see indications towards the causal regularity of the Karmic Law: "Eye for eye, tooth for tooth", "With the measure you use, it will be measured back to you", "Whoever digs a pit will fall into it", "Whatsoever a man sows, that shall he also reap", "All who take the sword will perish by the sword", etc. As these messages reveal, there is a Law of Retribution that restores the balance and harmony of matters and relations. The Law of Harmony is a great, fundamental law, and a number of other laws are subject to its action: the Law of Conservation of Energy, the Law of Action and Reaction, the Law of Cause and Effect, all of them more or less expressing the Law of Karma. Whenever this harmony is broken, it is restored, though at the expense of the one who violated it.

## Karma

*Keep your thoughts positive
because your thoughts become your words;
your words become your behaviour;
your behaviour becomes your habits;
your habits become your values;
your values become your destiny.*

**Gandhi**

The term *karma* literally means *action* (from the Sanskrit root *kri* – "to act"), but it also includes in itself the *fruit*, the consequence, the result of this action. Each and every action – mental, verbal or physical – creates a *subtle imprint* upon our unconscious mind. These imprints are called *"samskaras"* in the Yoga tradition, and they arise as a result of our actions, the latter being themselves motivated by the subtle imprints. This creates a circle formed by actions creating *samskaras*, which, in turn, direct our actions. This circle is the Law of Karma. It is useless to search for the beginning of this circle, because, like any circle, it is beginningless. It is important to know how to get out, how to break free from it, and achieve "Moksha" – *Liberation*.

According to ancient scriptures, there are three types of karmic currents: *dormant, active,* and *potential*. Wise people have described dormant karmas as arrows in the quiver, active ones – as arrows flying towards the target, whereas potential ones – as arrows that are not made yet, even though their components are ready. A triggered karma is a darted arrow, so at this point it is already hard to change anything. Active karma means "already in the process of fruit production" and is known as *Fate (Fortuna)*. We are not able to stop the course of events triggered by Fate, and yet we are free to either accumulate the fruits of our karmas or renounce them. The preservation of fruits creates an environment for further binding and for the creation of the so-called *potential karmas* that are to be accomplished. Our actions create subtle imprints within the unconscious mind, and our attachment to them gives them the strength to reactivate themselves continuously and to be generators of new actions. If we accept our fate with wisdom, without any attachment, and if, on the egocentric plane, we renounce the fruits of our actions, then we will not create any potential karmas. One of the ways to free ourselves from all karmas is *dispassion*, or "non-action within action". This means that we should not get attached to the outcome of our actions but rather simply *do* things. This practice of *non-attachment*, however, is a passive and precautionary measure. It works only with weak karmas. In order to neutralize the impact of powerful, dormant karmas, intense spiritual practice is required. Active karmas determine when, where and how we will be born, how long we will live in this body, and what major events will take place during our life. Not much can be done regarding this karmic current. However, with respect to potential and dormant karmas, we have to practice non-attachment and dispassion. The lack of dispassion causes us to cling tight to our desires and form potential karmas feeding the karmic cycle.

Nothing in this world belongs to us. There is a Zen piece of wisdom telling us: "Make your Spirit like the wind that passes above all things without attaching itself to any of them." We use the objects offered to us by Fate, but at the same time we ought to be able to leave them and move forward. Those humans possessing true Wisdom are free: to them, gain and loss are all the same, they are indifferent to both because they are beyond and above them. Even sages, however, obey the Law of Fate. In Bhagavad Gita, even Lord Krishna does not dare change Arjuna's fate but uses the human skills of a chariot driver instead. In history, there is not a single example of a Great Master Teacher trying to change his own fate. They usually changed the karmas of their disciples, but only in unison with God's Will. We can do nothing with fate unless we are connected with Divine Providence that works beyond the Law of Karma.

However, there is nothing in our fate that is not created by ourselves. We possess the freedom of choice to do only beneficial actions that shape our future fate, our future destiny. Devoting ourselves to this type of action for an extended period of time is called *Spiritual Practice*. It is precisely this practice that makes us perfect. Whenever we undertake positive actions, we create positive potential karmas that serve as an antidote for the negative ones. That is why there exists not only bad but also good karma, the essential wording of which could fit into the Latin phrase *Do ut des* – "I give so that you give back." However, this is not a matter of reciprocity, and also, the purpose of giving should not be to receive. We ought to love the other one for the sake of Love and for the sake of this other one, whether or not the other person will share our feelings. Love does not set any conditions; Love does not possess and does not want but only keeps giving. Unfortunately, humans ceaselessly only want and want more, and they want and ask not from themselves but from others and from God; and when they do not receive, they are grumpy; and, as Rumi says, *"Everything in the Universe is within you. Ask all from yourself!"*

According to the various teachings, there is no entirely personal karma. This is so because each action involves at least two sides: one performing the action and another one with respect to which it is performed. Each side has its own independent destiny, but also a shared group destiny. The main destiny of a person functions as the secondary karma of another person and vice versa. In this way, we are entangled in a complex karmic network. Without karmic connections, we could not exist. Karma is a necessary burden, and its solution is a *great teacher*. The karmic connection between people is accomplished within the physical, the astral and the causal dimension, or, in the Kabalistic language – in the *Assia, Yetzira* and *Bria* Worlds.

The Buddha teaches that those dimensions of reality ought to be attained which stand above good and evil. Since the mind gives a judgement of a certain action, then the very mind is itself manifested karma, and therefore only deliberate acts turn into *samskaras*. If an action has no connection with good or evil, then it cannot generate karma. Or, after all, *deliberate* actions are recorded, while undeliberate ones are not. In order not to be misunderstood, we will clarify that our *attitude* makes things good or bad, and ultimately conditions the karma.

If a general essential conclusion is to be drawn, it will be that attachment to the ego creates karma. The ego desires the result of the action. This desire creates attachment, whereas attachment, in turn, creates karma. Whenever the ego does not work, there is no desire for results, hence no attachment and no karma are created. This is the main key to cancelling and outgrowing karma. This means action without any interest of or attachment to the result. Along the path of renouncing one's ego, one merges with higher and higher levels, which are manifested through one's actions, thus gradually rising above the Karmic Law. In order to achieve liberation, we must give up both the ego that performs the action and the ego that desires a certain result. Therefore, all participants in any spiritual community, including Freemasonry, have to answer themselves the question about the motivation behind their own participation and also behind the actions related to it.

Thus, in the material and the astral dimension, the Law of Karma acts, because in the *Assia* World (the physical world), there is the action itself, along with its fruits, while in the *Yetzira* World (the world of the soul), there is the emotional *attitude* towards them. However, the law works also in the causal dimension, or the *Bria* World, because, as we noted above, *the mind, by giving its judgements,* creates or triggers the karma. Still, karma can only be cleansed in the World of Action. In the context of this prayer, "asking" and "giving" is the action, whereas forgiveness itself is the "attitude", being astral energy; as for who our debtors are, we "judge" this through our mind, so this is already mental energy.

If we ask for forgiveness, and if we ourselves forgive *(Gebura – Hesed),* and if we pay off our karmic debts, not accumulating any new ones, then we can embark on the path leading to the Sfara *Bina* in the *Bria* World. It is ruled by the Twenty-Four Elders, Masters of Karma, in whose hands all destinies are. Absolute freedom is obtained only here. *Bina* is a narrow gate. Whoever slips through it leaves its skin there, exactly like a snake, which, in order to shed its old skin and be freed from it, wriggles through between two rough stones. This door corresponds to each person in a specific way; so, in order to pass through it, one must be without any clothing and any material valuables, just like any Seeker in Freemasonry. Having passed through that door, one discovers the treasury of Wisdom.

## The Eye of a Needle

> *"It is easier for a camel to go through the eye of a needle than for a rich man to enter the Kingdom of God."*[84]
>
> **Holy Gospel of Mark 10:25, NKJV**

The symbol of the "narrow gate" is analogous to the "needle's eye", and it is in this sense, namely, that it is mentioned in the Gospel text cited above. The needle in the vertical position, with its perforated extremity upwards, can be considered as an image of the World Axis. There is an exact coincidence between this position of the "eye" of the needle and the position of the "eye" of the dome, which will be discussed when clarifying the fundamental symbolism of the stone. Here we will paraphrase what René Guénon has said, since we fully agree with him.

---

[84] Jerusalem was entered through several gates, and the narrowest was called the "Eye of the Needle", because, in order to pass through it, you had to leave your saddlebags – *AN*.

In ancient epochs, needles were not perforated as they are now, but simply bent over at one end, in such a way that they formed something like a loop through which the thread was passed. The loop corresponds to a lasso that is thrown and tightened around an animal's neck. Hence the connection with the primary idea of the knot is drawn, and especially of the "tightening knot".

Just as a sliding loop tightens, the same way people are bound by conditions restricting them that hold them in their particular state of manifestation of their existence.

In order to get out of this "loop" state, they need to free themselves from their own determinations and attachments, and to pass through the sliding loop in such a way that the latter would not tighten around them. This is equivalent to the fact that such persons will pass between the "jaws" of death so that the latter do not shut around these persons. The loop is another aspect of the "narrow gate", just like the "thread passing through a needle's eye", representing the passage through the "solar gateway", by means of which the "exit" from the karmic world is accomplished, so that one can finally be "delivered" from the bonds of one's own existence.

There is also another important aspect of the symbolism of the "needle's eye" in its meaning of a "loop" referring to the "vital knot", which we have already mentioned in connection with the "chain of worlds". Actually, the "vital knot" represents the bond between the various constitutive elements of individuality, so that it retains the human being in its "loop" state, because, whenever that bond is broken or weakened, there follows a disintegration of the elements joined through it, and this disintegration represents the death of individuality, entailing the transition of the human to another state of being.

This is transposed with reference to the ultimate "deliverance", so we can say that when a person is able to pass through that loop so that it does not tighten, it is equivalent to a situation in which this loop has got loose and untied because of this person – moreover, quite definitively and finally. The "untying" of this "vital knot" is, in its essence, another equivalent of the passage of human beings through the "needle's eye", symbolizing the "narrow gate", in order to free themselves from the "wheel of rebirth", which is actually equivalent and can be compared to the untying of the karmic knot, leading to the cleansing of karmic dependencies.

The primary basis of the "narrow gate", however, can be found in the Ancient Egyptian esoteric tradition, in the meaning of the word *uzi*, which is present in the Dendera Temple, and its meaning is a *narrow opening* towards the Kingdom of Heaven, the point at which the Human and the Divine touch each other, or perhaps a passage between two universes.

We continue with this topic; and, as we have already said, in a Kabalistic key, these gates are situated in the Sfara *Bina* and are called the *Fifty Gates of Intelligence*. When one is ready, *Bina* opens its Gates. After passing through them, the Karmic Law is no longer working, and one enters the Sfara *Hohma*, in which the *Thirty-Two Paths of Wisdom* are revealed. They correspond to the thirty-two teeth of humans, and through them Initiates chew and nourish themselves on Divine Wisdom. That is why it has been said in the tradition that the "Bread of Wisdom" has to be chewed slowly. Here, in the Sixth Heaven, Divine Providence is manifested by the Palace of Will, where it arranges the puzzle of things that will be manifested in the lower worlds as karma.

From here on, tradition again says that only eighteen Initiates can ascend and return back to Earth. Only those survive there who have been chosen centuries ago and are called upon to fulfil a grand mission on Earth. Their bodies are transformed into luminous ones (not in the literal sense), which is the very purpose of Rosicrucian Alchemy and Masonic Royal Art. If a Being from this dimension comes down to Earth as a Messiah, this is as a result of this Being's own wish, not of any karma, so this will not be a rebirth but rather a *Divine Emergence*.

Thus, through one sentence in this prayer, the Law of Karma and the Key to Liberation from its power are presented essentially. Since this is a law of continuity, it is invariably correlated with rebirth.

## Rebirth

> *Those who clearly understand that my births and actions have a Divine Origin, after leaving their body do not fall into the trap of rebirth, but attain Me.*
>
> **Lord Krishna (Bhagavad Gita 4:9)**

We have already clarified that, contrary to conventional views, the lack of faith in God is something irrational and unconditioned by experience. The conviction that humans irrevocably and forever cease to exist after death leads to the idea of the meaninglessness and emptiness of life, which is why the only goal is pleasure. This approach and way of thinking makes people identify themselves only and solely with their bodies – the most tangible and obsessive tool for enjoyment. Thus, life is reduced to the existence of the body and the satisfaction of its needs and desires. Accordingly, the dream of immortality is associated with immortality of the body. However, in order for something to exist eternally and immutably, it must be perfect. Are our bodies perfect? Are they not just physical bearers of our Divine Core Essence, which is immortal regarding the Spiritual World? However, the path towards it goes through the material world, so until we learn its lessons and achieve self-awareness and non-attachment, and also until we clear our karmic debts, we return here again and again through rebirth.

Rebirth is not a process we can observe. There is a certain reality of the psyche which we attest by verbalizing our experiences, so in this way, there exists rather a fact of the psyche than a reality on the physical level. Rebirth is one of the most ancient noumena in the world, and it is archetypal by nature, which is why there are similar expressions for *rebirth* in the traditions of various nations.

Usually *rebirth* and *reincarnation*[85] are considered as fully identical, which is inaccurate. It is necessary to distinguish between these two concepts. *Reincarnation,* known from the Yoga system, is called *avatara* ("descent") and is the fruit of intense practice, which, however, has not led to the desired goal in one life only. Such souls reincarnate, going on with their development in the next life from where they have stopped. Thus, the series of reincarnations leads, at a certain moment, to achieving the goal – the *Accomplishment of the "I" (of the Self)*. These are Adepts who are no longer part of the reincarnation cycle. They have taken off their karmic load and have passed through the "narrow gate". If, by God's Will, they are to return to this world, this takes place through the so-called *"Divine Birth"*, or more commonly known as *Birth through "Immaculate" Conception*. Yogis call it *"Divine Emergence"*. This is how Rama, Krishna, the Buddha and Jesus emerged, and their death represented leaving the body. Unlike the reincarnated souls, the *reborn souls* are those who did not aspire towards ascension, so for them the Sanskrit term for rebirth is "born again" in the sense of "unfortunately". Such people die and are reborn *unconscious*. At birth, they identify themselves with a particular body, unlike the Masters and Adepts who "emerge", because they do not identify themselves with the body in which they reside.

And yet, does rebirth exist, or are we just one-day butterflies? Can there be any evidence and proof in support of rebirth? There is certain historical information regarding rebirth. In Hinduism, for example, there is a belief in the rebirth of personality, whereas, according to Buddhism, the Divine, impersonal core essence is reborn. The *Vedas* are dominated by faith in the afterlife. In the later *Upanishads,* the doctrine of *Samsara (Wheel of Rebirth)* appears, liberation from it being possible only with the help of the priests. The Buddha revised it, saying that salvation can only be achieved through becoming aware of the cause of each and every suffering – *passion*. Zoroastrism is based on

85   From Latin: *re* – "again", and *carnis* – "flesh", or: "again in flesh" – *AN*.

the doctrine of rebirth. In Egypt it is also present, while in Judea and Ancient Hellas, the idea of *metempsychosis* is professed. In Tibet, after the death of each Dalai Lama, lamas immediately begin their search of the boy into which he is reborn. The theory of rebirth was professed by Hermes, Orpheus, Pythagoras, Jesus, Confucius and Lao-Tzu, Plato, Plotinus, Paracelsus, as well as by the Druids (Celtic priests), the Druze in Lebanon, the Islamic mystics – the Sufis, and the Judaic communities. Theosophy and Anthroposophy are also based entirely on the doctrine of rebirth.

The official Christian theology does not accept the doctrine of karma and rebirth, since this doctrine preaches self-salvation instead of salvation through Christ. Yes, but Jesus Himself says that we shall reap whatsoever we have sown. The question arises as to why the Church is so afraid of rebirth and of the Law of Karma, denying them. On the one hand, Christ declares that each one must pay for what this one has done, while, on the other hand, the Church preaches repentance and granting absolution through its ministers. It is obvious that the Church is willing to maintain the monopoly on absolution of debts. It is quite natural that, according to the Church, this should happen in the one and only life, because otherwise it risks the weakening of its influence and authority. Anyone could say, "I will not respect the Church now, but in some of my next lives I will ask for forgiveness and absolution." Therefore, retribution will come, according to the Church, not in the next life, but in the permanent Hell of the hereafter beyond. Nevertheless, the Church could not completely avoid the idea of the existence of a Karmic Law, since, according to the dogma of the "original sin", we have to expiate certain guilt that does not come from our present life. Yet, according to the theory of rebirth, the "original sin" is the karmic burden that we bring with us into our earthly life.

However, if we still accept that the Church does not belong to Paul the Apostle, but to Jesus Christ, about Whom Paul himself says that He is the "Chief Cornerstone" of the Church (*Ephesians* 2:20, *NKJV*), we have to accept what He has bequeathed to us: "And forgive us our debts, as we forgive our debtors." (*Holy Gospel of Matthew* 6:12, *NKJV*), as well as His explicit statement regarding John the Baptist: "He is Elijah", and also: "Judge not, that you be not judged." (*Holy Gospel of Matthew* 7:1, *NKJV*) – all of these being obvious indications towards the existence of karma and rebirth. The temptation for humans to *judge*, however, is huge, and hence the plea towards the Father: "And do not lead us into temptation but deliver us from the evil one."

Regarding this part of the prayer, in addition to the above said, we can add that the temptation from God is the temptation of *our own Self* in *Tiferet* of *Yetzira*, who, when accepting God's Grace, might develop a specific kind of *spiritual ego* and fall into the mortal sin of haughty pride. This is the subtlest and most inconspicuous temptation, to which, according to the Gospels, even such an Archangel as Lucifer has succumbed. Therefore, we ask God to not lead us into this temptation, because we will hardly cope with it. The temptations of the Wicked and Cunning One are the temptations of the ego (*Yesod* in *Yetzira*), our "individual devil" lurking on the path towards our Self, our "I". We send these requests – and yet, as stated above: **His Will be done!**

Rebirth is implicitly related to death, which is the greatest mystery in this world. It is no coincidence that the idea of *dying and rising through resurrection within the framework of life* is embedded at the foundation of the Master's Degree Rite. According to Goethe, "As long as you do not have within yourself that which is dying and rising, you are nothing but a silly guest on the tenebrous Earth." Jacob Böhme, on his part, believes that "Those who do not die before dying disappear when they die." We also believe that the ritual experience of death is a powerful transformational initiation for those walking along the Path. Therefore, we cannot but dwell essentially also on the core essence of *death*.

## Death

*The secret of life consists
in the knowledge of death.*
**Yogic Wisdom**

There are two immutable things in our lives: birth and death. Birth through the womb clothes us in a body, whereas death liberates us from it. This is very well illustrated by Rumi through the following words: "We arrived naked; we dressed; we undressed; and left." Birth gives us the gift of life in the material world, but also the gift of death – an experience we can only gain here. Therefore: *Blessed are humans with death.* The material world, as the utmost emanation of Creation, can only be experienced through the physical body: it experiences the most powerful sensations in this world – pain and pleasure. Each and every second, we sense our body, and through our body – everything around us. People identify themselves with their body, considering it to be a framework of existence and a symbol of life itself. The fear of death is a fundamental fear generating all other fears. Most people's view is: "If my body dies, I die, too." Hence, the consciousness of this *one-off nature of life* is formed: a life that has to be lived as well as possible, regardless of the cost. This is also the reason why the Law is not inside humans but outside them, which is why there exists a striving towards breaking the law, and even the fear of death cannot stop them, but nevertheless, it does not make them free – *Nemo liber est, qui corpori servit*[86]. The Masonic maxim: *"Only the Law will give us freedom"*, in its profound esoteric core essence, refers precisely to the Inner Law resting on the moral and ethical platform of personality, built according to God's Laws.

Death is a universal trial experienced by humans and by all other types and forms of existence. However, humans are the only living beings able to think of death as of some inevitable event – *Nascentes morimur*[87]. Throughout the various epochs, cultures and religions have viewed death in a heterogeneous manner, so this has been manifested in their funeral ceremonies and rituals. Regardless of the different approaches, however, the fear of death prevails, and it is mainly generated by the pain during death and by the unknown after it.

The topic of the beyond is fundamentally covered in all religions, esoteric teachings and philosophical systems, and many comparative analyses and studies have been made on this subject, which is why we will not dwell on it. We would like to only point out that views on the subject are under development, including those of the Catholic Church. The following statement from 1998 by Pope John Paul II during a general audience in Rome is quite indicative of this: "In any case, one should not believe that life after death begins only after the resurrection of the dead after the Last Judgment. It is actually preceded by that condition in which every human being is placed since the moment of their own physical death. I mean a phase of transition in which the decay of the body is opposed to the further existence of a spiritual element possessing consciousness and willpower so that the Self of this human continues to actually live in the meantime, deprived of its complete corporeality."

For thousands of years, humans have been trying to achieve immortality referring to corporeality; however, residing eternally in one and the same body, and being one the same personality is rather a punishment than a gift. With the sacrifice at Golgotha, Christ showed that human beings are immortal because they are Spirits not subject to death, while the body is only an envelope of the Spirit. Living with faith in the immortality of the Spirit, the fear of the unknown will drop out inside humans, and they will accept death as liberation. As Aristotle says, "Only those who have overcome their own fears will be truly free."

There might be bodily pains at the deathbed, so perhaps it is these pains that we are mostly afraid of. We are fighting these pains by all possible ways so that they may be reduced or eliminated. For the sake of this, euthanasia is

---

86  From Latin: "No one is free who is a slave to one's own body" (Seneca) – *AN*.
87  From Latin: "Being born, we are dying" – *AN*.

substantiated and justified, despite the fact that it does not remove the suffering itself but the suffering one. Of course, this is a profane approach, while it is necessary here to consider what the message is which is carried by that pain, and where the causes of the pain originate from. Very often, they are complex, with emotional and spiritual pain at the basis. If we understand the message it carries to us, and if we change, we may also change the very pain, transform it and transcend it. In medical science, this phenomenon is known as "Hering's Law". However, at the very moment of death, all bodily pain disappears, and we carry into the afterlife only the mental, emotional and spiritual impressions from our lives. Although we reside there without the body, the experiences of grief and delight are preserved because they are a state of the mind, which is an instrument of the immortal Spirit.

In all beliefs, the afterlife beyond is identified with Hell and Heaven as places of punishment or reward for what has been done during the life on Earth. Of course, the delights of Heaven are preferable to the torments of Hell, and yet, even the fear of punishment does not seem to make us better. Still, we wonder: Do Heaven and Hell actually exist? According to religions, the answer is "Yes", but according to Yogic science, it is both "Yes" and "No". If we believe in them, then we will, through our own beliefs, form various realities in our mind. Those who see things dually, in black and white, and expect a reward or punishment, will build their own heaven and hell, and after death they will go there. Those who are aware that their own actions, unlike the conceptual mind, are not entirely black or entirely white, will go into a sphere known in the Christian religion as *Purgatory*. In the Yoga tradition, each one of those residing there is called "preta". Hell and Heaven are located in the astral realm, so our journey to Heaven is not the goal and end of our development towards perfection, because, if we have not achieved awareness and dispassion, there will be suffering there as well. Unprocessed feelings of jealousy, sense of superiority or depreciation, and also irresistible desires, create within the soul an inner hell, even while being in Heaven. Even from the standpoint of the finite mind, the differentiation of experiences in Heaven would lead such souls to dependency and jealousy. According to Yogic science, souls keep going to Heaven until their good karmas are exhausted, and respectively – to Hell until the bad ones are exhausted. This means that thoughts at the moment of death are crucial to our journey beyond and to getting out of the wheel of rebirth. If, through our willpower and determination, during death we think of the Divine, then the Sacred Cow will appear – the ray of light that will illuminate our way through the darkness of our unconscious mind, so that we merge with the Primordial Light.

As for the dangers stalking inside our own unconscious, and how to deal with them, all of this is described in great detail in *Bardo Thödol,* or "Liberation Through Hearing During Bardo", which is the other title of the so-called *Tibetan Book of the Dead,* which is actually also called "Secret Teaching of Spontaneous Liberation on Peaceful and Wrathful Deities". Very often this book is referred to simply as *Bardo* – the famous term for the intermediate state between the physical death and the subsequent rebirth, or between physical death and liberation. The *Tibetan Book of the Dead* contains an authentic teaching of what happens to the consciousness after a person's physical death. Carl Gustav Jung authored a remarkable commentary on the *Tibetan Book of the Dead,* in which he defines it as being "in the highest degree psychological in its outlook", stating that "we have nothing in the West that is in any way comparable to the *Bardo Thödol*". According to Jung, life is a means of attaining higher perfection, with the spiritual summit marked at its end, at the moment of death, when the immersion into Bardo takes place. As Goethe says, "Life is the childhood of our immortality."

The guide map for disincarnated souls is the so-called *Egyptian Book of the Dead*[88], the Ancient Egyptian title of which is actually "Spells of Going Forth by Day (into the Light)" and relates to the notion of revival and new life after death. However, all the knowledge and experience of this book ought to be learned while still living on Earth, so that the soul may easily and unimpededly reside in the world beyond. Naturally, such books exist also in other traditions, such as that of the Maya peoples, indicating that the Ancients possessed knowledge shaping an attitude and understanding of death other than those of today.

This topic is perhaps endless and not in the focus of our main presentation, yet in conclusion we will have to render the human body its due in order not to leave the impression that we ignore it. The body is the physical vehicle of the Spirit and the Soul – the means of their residing in the material world and of its full perception. However, the most important reason for residing of humans within bodies is the full accomplishment of their true Self and the unfolding of their veritable Divine Nature. When this takes place while the person is still alive on Earth, *liberation* from the wheel of Samsara is attained, so one rises in the Spiritual Realm and is not reborn again here anymore unless when having a mission. However, if this does not happen at the time of being alive on Earth, it may be accomplished during death or after a certain

---

[88] This title was used by the German Egyptologist and linguist Karl Richard Lepsius in the publication of one of the Turin Papyruses in 1842. Since it is the first scientific edition of this work, the title *Book of the Dead* (in German *Das Todtenbuch*) is widely spread and preserved until present day – *AN*.

period of time following it. It is death that determines the way and the form of our further existence. Death, unlike any profane understanding, represents beneficial Grace, and the first of the possible boons it gives us is that, if our Primordial Nature (our true "I") is not awakened, then during death it receives the most powerful impulses in order to wake up. This can be triggered even while still being alive on Earth through the ritual dying and a new birth, embedded in the Mystery traditions.

After this long digression, we come to the last verse of the prayer:

**"… For Yours is the Kingdom and the Power and the Glory forever." (for Eternity)**

This prayer so far outlines the involutionary path of the Kabalistic Tree from *Keter* to *Malkut*. Through the last sentence, the evolutionary path is initiated from *Malkut* up to *Keter* through the levels of consciousness, encompassing the parameters of the so-called *Spiritual Path*. Along this Path in the single Tree, following the Sfarotic correspondence, one reaches *Neza*, the characteristic of which is *Victory* and *Eternity*. In this context, "Victory" and "for Eternity (forever)" is an emblematic ending of this path. However, if we have a look at it, we will see that this ending in *Neza* is at a very low place in the single Tree – in the astral triangle, below the ethical one. The following rhetorical question then arises: Do evolution and the "Glory" of the Creator reach only as far as there? That is why some people, having in mind how Christians make the sign of the cross (touching their shoulders), position the *Power* and the *Glory* in *Gebura* and *Hesed* respectively, whereas that quality which is named *Eternity* is associated with the Kabalistic Tree as a whole. And yet, how will the above said be correlated to the unfolded Tree? It is most logical that the "Kingdom" and the "Power" and the "Glory" correspond to the three Worlds – *Assia, Yetzira* and *Bria;* whereas Eternity, of course, is a quality of *Atzilut*.

As for whether everything we have said about the prayer *"Our Father"* tastes like Truth, we shall leave it to the very reader to sense.

## Kabala, Rosicrucianism and Martinism

Now we have to present Kabala also in the light of the Rosicrucian and Martinist tradition, which is indisputably related to the Masonic one. To this end, we will make use of the knowledge that the Rosicrucianist and Martinist Gregory Ottonovich Mëbes of the early 20th century has left to us, by presenting the Ten Sfarot of the Kabalistic Tree as one family. In this family, Hebrew Kabala distinguishes, as follows: *Supreme Androgyne (Keter)*, or *Macroprosopus* ("with an extended face"); *Father (Hohma); Mother (Bina),* and their *Child,* represented by the set of the next six Sfarot (4, 5, 6, 7, 8, 9), bearing the name *Microprosopus* ("with a small face"). The centre of its functionality is the sixth Sfara *(Tiferet),* whereas the instrument of its activity is the ninth one *(Yesod).* The Spouse or Bride of the Microprosopus is the 10th Sfara *(Malkut).*

However, any closed family in the chain of causality should be preceded by another family, and so on, right to the Primordial Source. The Hebrew Kabalists have only reached the family of the Initial Sfarotic System of the Universe, considering this system to be a Manifestation of some Unattainable Core Essence, called by them *Ayn Soph* (literally "Without Limit" or "Unattainable"). They did not allow any analysis of the very Ayn Soph.

In the Rosicrucian tradition, however, members of the family are also present, this family being placed by Rosicrucianists between Ayn Soph and the Manifested Family through the Sfarotic system of the Kabalistic Tree. Thus, two Divine Families are present in the Rosicrucian diagram. The Unattainable is manifested through the letter *Yod* in the Holy Tetragrammaton; and this Non-Caused Primordial Principle is the Transcendental Love, which is the Father of the First Family. This Father, through His aspiration (bearing the character of radiance), will determine the existence of some Passivity, strictly commensurate with His Activity. This Passivity will be the first letter *He* in the Holy Tetragrammaton, which, in turn, represents the Mother in the First Family and is defined as *Transcendental Life.*

This element, as an antipode to the Radiant *Yod,* is bound to have some "shadowy" character. This is something that is darkened, ready to accept in itself the Radiant Influx of the Unattainable – hence, its Latin designation, *Restrictio:* Shadow Limitation in the midst of the Infinite Light. Thus, the Transcendental Love – *Yod* (the First Father), fertilizes the Transcendental Life – *He* (the First Mother), and they both conceive and generate the Logos – the Transcendental Word, *Vav* (the Son), the Great Architect of the Universe, "without Whom nothing can be what it IS".

The Logos emanates the second *He* of the Holy Name within the First Family, which is already manifesting itself through the Ten Sfarot that form the Second Family through the first of them – *Keter,* the Macroprosopus of the Universe. Next there come the other nine Sfarot of the Second Family in the diagram of the so-called *Four Worlds,* which does not differ essentially from the already known to us and described diagram within the single Kabalistic Tree.

The *World of Emanations (Olam ha Atzilut)* contains in itself the Androgynous Crown (Macroprosopus), balanced Mentality, manifesting, on the one hand, as the totality of *That Which is able to know* (the Sfara of Wisdom –

*Hohma*), and, on the other hand, as the totality of *That Which is able to serve as an object of knowledge* (the Sfara of Reason – *Bina,* limiting the former one).

In the *World of Creation (Olam ha Bria),* on the one hand, the active Sfara of Mercy *(Hesed)* is situated, being a reflection of the expansiveness of the second Sfara (Wisdom) as the thirst for knowledge, and, on the other hand, the passive Sfara of Severity (*Pehad/Peshad,* or *Gebura*) is situated, limiting Mercy as a result of the extremity in the realm of objects of knowledge (i.e. by virtue of the limitedness of Reason).

These Sfarot are neutralised through the Splendour of the Radiance of the Sfara *Tiferet* – the World Harmony, the Universal Beauty.

*World of Formations (Olam ha Yetzira):* it contains Victory of good over evil, of the spiritual over the material, of the light over the dark, of the active over the passive – the seventh Sfara *Neza,* in which Initiates reside, unmistakably choosing the correct path in the Sixth Arcanum. The active aspiration towards choosing the proper paths, however, does not exclude the need for calm movement along the path already chosen, without feverish thirst for or expectation of new choices. After all, we need to walk at least a few steps along the chosen path, to calm down for at least a minute after the victory, to rest at the position achieved, to wait for the fruits of the sown good to come.

This mighty Sfara ought to be limited by the passive Sfara of Glory or Peaceful Stillness *(Hod).*

Victory and Glory are neutralized by an androgynous, complete Form and Foundation *(Yesod),* for each particular concreteness.

Indeed, for any form to exist, we have to put it aside, to choose it. Victory is the choice of a path in such a manner so that we stop ourselves upon it (Peaceful Stillness, Glory). This is also the process of conceiving and generating the Ninth Sfara *Yesod,* which is projected into the...

... *World of Action (Olam ha Assia),* as the Sfara of Kingship, of Kingdom – *Malkut,* i.e. the embryonic state of a particular world inhabited by us.

So far we have tried to essentially present the Kabalistic knowledge, knowing that this is impossible in principle, only to illustrate clearly that Kabala is essentially present in both the Masonic and the Rosicrucian traditions. In support of this, we will quote Éliphas Lévi, who, in his book *The History of Magic,* writes: "That great Kabalistical association known in Europe under the name of *Masonry* appeared suddenly in the world when revolt against the Church had just succeeded in dismembering Christian unity." Some would immediately say that this does not apply to Freemasonry as a whole, but only to "extensions" and "superstructures", some of which include Rosicrucianism and Kabala. However, if we assume that the Master's Degree is the crown of the Initiatic hierarchy, as Oswald Wirth claims – and we agree with that – then how can we possibly exclude from it any knowledge within the scope of Masonic science in general, and even more, such fundamental knowledge as that of Arcana and Kabala? In addition, the term *Master* in all Initiatic traditions and arts (including martial arts) is used to designate one who has attained perfection in them. Also, the title *master* is used for anyone who, best of all, knows and is able to do something in a particular segment of the manner of living and life in general. We shall ask, then, the following question: Those Masters who say that esoterism in Freemasonry is only meant for separate esoteric Lodges or for out-building structures, and is not its core essence, what Masters are they, and, as such, are they really the "crown" of the Initiatic hierarchy? After all, Initiates are those who preserve and convey to humans the Truth about God, about the World and about the Human Being.

## 13
## The Spiritual Centre

*Seeking drives you outside;*
*seeking takes you away from yourself.*
*When all seeking stops, you are suddenly*
*at the very center of your being.*

***Osho***

There is a place in the earthly world where this Truth is preserved as a tradition of non-human origin, through which Wisdom is conveyed. According to Hinduism, the holy point of this centre is *Manu,* being the embodiment of Cosmic Intelligence, and present among ancient peoples in the form of different pronunciation variants – *Min, Menes, Minos,* etc. In the context of designating Universal Intelligence, Manu is the Principle of the thinking being. Regardless of the personality in which it is reflected, the Core Essence possessing the qualities and attributes of Manu is at the head of the Spiritual Centre of the Earth, and constitutes the Supreme Pontifex Power. The word *pontifex* is definitely charged with Masonic connotation because it means literally a *bridge builder.* Through this spiritual bridge, the connection is provided between the earthly world and the Heavenly one. Here is perhaps the right place to dwell briefly on the *symbolism of the bridge.*

It represents a link between two different points, usually referring to the two banks of one and the same river. Each of these banks symbolizes two different states of being, whereas the bridge itself is analogous to the "central axis".

One of the two ends of the bridge starts from the state of being in which the person is, while the other is the Primordial Realm. One of the river banks is the sphere of death, where everything is subject to change, whereas the other is the sphere of Immortality.

In relation to the "axial" meaning of the symbolism of the bridge, we must note its connection also with the arc. The symbolism of the arc is very complex and is manifested in various aspects, the most important of which is perhaps the one relating to the snake, which is found in many traditions. It is known that one of the fundamental symbolic meanings of the snake is correlated to the cosmic currents, which are an expression of forces emanating from Heaven and Earth. The likeness between the arc and the serpent is in complete conformity with the generally recognized nature of the rainbow arc as a sign of the union of Heaven and Earth. In this context, the snake is most commonly associated with axial symbols such as *tree, wand* or *sceptre*.

We believe that, in this sense, Manu is an expression of the core essence of this symbol, and, as such, resides in the centre of the Edifice of the Universe, and governs the Universal Motion. In any case, it refers to the pole of existence, so the *swastika* is one of its symbols, i.e. a cycle around a certain centre. One can clearly see the indisputable essential identity with the meaning of the Aramaic word for *holiness*, which we have already explained. In the Masonic tradition, all this is included in the phrase "most luminous and most pure place", which also applies to the Lodge itself. This centre provides stability, balance and harmony between the destructive and creative forces manifested in the ethical world of relationships as justice and peace-lovingness – the Sfarot *Gebura* and *Hesed* in the ethical triangle of the Kabalistic Tree. To ensure all this, the Supreme Pontifex has the regulating function of the Sfara *Tiferet*, where the King of the World is born. Hence, the conclusion that, in addition to being the Head of the Spiritual Centre, Manu is also the King of the World, so he is both a *priest* and a *king*. This duality of the power of authority was a rule without exception in the ancient peoples.

## The Wise Men

> "Now after Jesus was born in Bethlehem of Judea in the days of Herod the king, behold, wise men from the East came to Jerusalem, saying, "Where is He who has been born King of the Jews? For we have seen His star in the East and have come to worship Him."
>
> *Holy Gospel of Matthew 2:1–2*

The notion of *king-priest* is also embedded in the foundation of Christianity in the form of the mysterious kings, the *Wise Men*, or the *Magi*, who offer gifts to the newborn Jesus. According to the exoteric interpretation, one of the Wise Men is *white* and *presents gold* – symbol of Life and Light; the *black* one gives the gift of *myrrh,* image of Death and Night; the *brown* one – *frankincense,* symbol of Divinity, conciliator of the two other principles. It is evident that the principle of royal authority, the symbol of which is gold, and that of spiritual authority – frankincense, are separated, so the scene with the Magi shows that a process of merging of the royal and the spiritual authority in the person of the newborn Jesus is forthcoming. However, the exact meaning of the word *Magi* in Bulgarian – *влъхви [v'ləhvi],* in the esoteric aspect, is derived by its spelling with the Ancient Hebrew hieroglyphs *Bet-Ayin-L'amed (Bal)* and *He-Vav-Yod (Havi),* or *Baal-havi,* but with time, in the transcription of its vowelizing, it has become the Bulgarian word *влъхви [v'ləhvi].* The exact meaning of *baal* is *ruler, master* or *lord,* whereas the vowelized variant *He-Vav-Yod* is, according to some, the word *havayod,* and so the result is *the ones ruling over (the masters of) havayod – baal havayod.* There are views that *havayod* is the name of the devil, because the places of *He* and *Yod* in the Tetragrammaton are exchanged, with the hieroglyph *Yod* (the active, the positive, the Spirit) is positioned at the end, whereas the letter *He* (the passive, the receiving, the negative) – at the beginning. We believe that the correct pronunciation of *He-Vav-Yod* in combination with *baal* should be *baal-havi,* which, as we have mentioned, in Bulgarian has turned into *влъхви [v'ləhvi]* – the kings-priests known as the *Wise Men,* or *Magi.* The names by which the Magi are known are *Emanuel, Melchior,* and *Balthazar.* The middle one of the Magi (not coincidentally in the middle), presenting gold, is called *Melchior,* a vowelized variant of *Melki-or,* where *melek* means *king,* and *or* – *astral light,* or *King of light.* The name *Balthazar,* on its part, is derived from *Baal-asar,* the one mastering the Mysteries of Osiris (of life and death) and presenting myrrh, whereas *Emanuel* consists of *Manu* and the suffix for Divinity, *-el.* From what has been said so far about Manu, it becomes clear that this Magus symbolizes religion and connection with God, hence he offers frankincense. It is no coincidence that the three *Masters of havayod* bow down before the newborn Jesus, Who symbolizes the path of the *"Son"* (*Ben,* in Hebrew), which is the middle path, indicated by the Middle Pillar in the Kabalistic Tree. The path of *Baal-havi* is that of the Serpent, *Shatan [ʃa'tan],* containing the temptation of the unbalanced force of the two extreme columns of the Tree. Thus, the biblical scene of the Magi bowing down before the newborn Jesus means that those who are Masters of the path of Shatan, or Satan, acknowledge the supremacy of Ben – the central, balanced, safe Path, freed of all temptations. On the other hand, the occult path is unbalanced and full of dangers for the uninitiated, and therefore it is the embodiment of Satan, who has gained the regrettable notoriety of the Devil Tempter, symbol of Evil.

Here is perhaps the place to mention also the meaning and origin of the word *wizard* in Bulgarian – *вълшебник [vəl'febnik]*, known to us as *someone working miracles*, or *sorcerer*. However, the etymology of this Bulgarian word from Hebrew is the familiar to us *baal*, and *shem* ("name"), or *baal-shem*, meaning *Master of the Name*. It refers to the Great, Formidable, and Secret Name of the Lord, through which the one who has mastered it becomes a Creator – a topic which we shall dwell on especially.

## Melkitsedek – the King of Justice

> *An eye for an eye – and soon the whole world will be blind.*
> 
> **Mahatma Gandhi**

Clarifying the etymology of the names, we come to the mysterious Melhisedek, laconically mentioned in the Old and the New Testament. *Melhisedek (Melchisedec)*, or more precisely, in Hebrew – *Melki-tsedek*, is the title of the person performing the function of "King of the World" in the Hebrew tradition, analogous to *Manu*, as a governing spiritual principle. In Christianity, this function is assigned to Jesus Christ. In Ancient Hebrew, *Melek* means "king", while *Tsedek* means "justice", "righteousness". He is mentioned in the Bible as "Melchizedek/ Melchisedec, king of Salem" *(NKJV/ KJV)*. Literally translated, it means "King of Justice" ("King of Righteousness") and "King of Peace", in the sense of "King of the World". We are faced with the figure of a king and priest at the same time, combining both attributes of the "King of the World" – justice *(Gebura)* and peace-loving *(Hesed)*. The word *Salem* means *City of Peace*, though it has never designated a real city, for example Jerusalem[89], but is a symbolic designation of the dwelling of Melkitsedek, which on the Kabalistic plane is the Sfara *Tiferet*.

As is well known, the Temple of Jerusalem, which is the "heart" of this spiritual abode, was built by Solomon, whose name in Hebrew, *Shlomo*, is derived from *Salem* and means *Peacemaker*. Melkitsedek blesses Abraham, and Abraham acknowledges this seniority, separating a tenth part of what he gained in defeating the kings of Edom. Melkitsedek is said to be a priest of *God Most High (El Elyon)*, Who is higher than the God of Abraham – *God*

---

[89] One of the early names of Jerusalem, according to some, was *Ariel* – "The Lioness of God." (*Book of the Prophet Isaiah* 29:1, *NKJV*: "Woe to Ariel, to Ariel, the city where David dwelt!") – *AN*.

*Almighty (El Shadai);* and, after the blessing, which is actually a Sacred Initiation into the ancient spiritual tradition, Abraham acquires a bond with the God of Melkitsedek.

"Now, beyond all contradiction, the lesser is blessed by the better." (*Hebrews* 7:7, *NKJV*)

According to the Gematria Kabalistic method, *El Elyon* is the equivalent of *Emanuel* ("God in us") – one of the Magi; and if El Elyon and Emanuel are similar, it becomes clear what tradition Melkitsedek passed on to Abraham: the Birth of God within us. That is why also Christ is a priest forever according to the hierarchical order of Melkitsedek – because He introduces the Spiritual Birth of humans through the Eucharistic rite of communion with bread and wine.

"For He testifies: "You are a priest forever according to the order of Melchizedek." (*Epistle of St. Apostle Paul to the Hebrews* 7:17, *NKJV*)

Real royal blood, a condition for this Sacred Initiation, is symbolically replaced by wine – the Mystery is open to all who are ready for it.

Melkitsedek does not know death, neither does he know the end of days, for his origin is inhuman, insofar as he is the primordial archetype of humans, and the image and likeness of the Divine Word in this world: "… without father, without mother, without genealogy, having neither beginning of days nor end of life, but made like the Son of God, remains a priest continually." (*Hebrews* 7:3, *NKJV*)

Melhisedek is "first… 'King of Righteousness', and then also king of Salem, meaning 'King of Peace'." (*Hebrews* 7:2, *NKJV*) – and therefore his attributes are the *scales* and the *sword*. The same attributes are inherent also to the Archangel Michael, as being the Angel of Justice. According to one of the traditions, Melkitsedek was ordained to the priesthood precisely by the Archangel Michael in the earthly Paradise. To Alexandrian agnostics, Melkitsedek is the "Great Collector of Eternal Light", which is analogous to Manu, who absorbs the rays of Intelligent Light emanating from Ayn Soph. Melkitsedek is the earthly spiritual pole that is connected through the axis of the world to the *Heavenly Spiritual Pole* – Metatron. *Metatron,* in an exoteric sense, means *Angel of the Face.* The two opposite faces of Metatron are Zadkiel – the light one, and Samael – the dark one, Melhisedek being the embodiment of their equilibrium aspect on Earth, combining *royal and pontifical power of authority.* According to the Kabalistic tradition of the Sfarotic Tree, Metatron is the Archangel of the Sfara *Keter,* as well as of the Sfara *Malkut,* in the image of his cousin, the Archangel Sandalphon. The difference between the names is so that the Law of Analogy may be taken into consideration, meaning that *Keter* and *Malkut* are similar but not identical. Because of being the "Angel of the Face", Metatron should be present in both the *Macroprosopus* (The Great Face) and the *Microprosopus* (The Small Face), like Sandalfon, because: *What is below is similar to what is above, and what is above is similar to what is below, to perform the Miracle of Oneness*. Metatron and Melkitsedek are correlated in the same way, thus revealing the relationship between the human being, as a Microcosm, and the Macrocosm, whereas "That" which is between them is denoted in Kabala by the Ancient Hebrew word *asher*, which expresses everything contained between *Ehyeh* (I Am) at the top – *Keter*, the Crown, and at the very bottom – *Malkut*, the Kingdom. Above and below them is the Nothing from which Everything stems. The Miracle of Oneness, however, is accomplished in the Sfara *Tiferet* – the point of equilibrium of the Sfarotic Tree, where Pythagoras's "Harmony of the Spheres" is attained and where eight channels flow in and out – the so-called *Paths*. Michael is the Archangel of this Sfara. The innermost concealed meaning of his name is "merging the flows in one". This is an indication that in humans, the union of the flows of the psyche takes place in the centre of their own Microcosm – the solar plexus. The inactivated spiritual heart of the "fallen" human, *Adam Belial*, is located there. The temple is not yet built in him; however, when he builds it, he becomes *Adam Kadmon*, the "Primordial" Human. The solar plexus, as an embodiment of the "spiritual heart", is activated in the sixth Sfara *Tiferet*, through the synthesis of *El Gabal* – the *Divine Stone*, known mostly as the *Philosophers' Stone*, and in more rare cases – as *Eloah Gabal*.

In the Hebrew tradition, the Divine non-incarnate presence on Earth is *Shekinah (Shekhinah)*[90], whereas Melkitsedek is the embodied aspect of the Spiritual World. The large vertical binary in the Kabalistic Tree, *Metatron – Melkitsedek – Shekinah*, connecting the Worlds *Bria*, *Yetzira* and *Assia*, is a synthesis between *Keter*, *Tiferet* and *Malkut* of these Worlds. From a Kabalistic point of view, Shekinah represents the totality of all Sfarot. Traditionally, the Left Pillar of Severity corresponds to Justice, while the Right Pillar of Mercy corresponds to Peace, and the two unite in Shehinah, who resides in *Beit-Din* ("House of Justice") – a synonym of the Spiritual Centre of the Earth. The connection between *Malkut* and *Tsedek*, between royal power and justice, is most accurately reflected in the name of *Melkitsedek*, who embodies the energies and the core essence of the Sfara *Tiferet*, balancing the energies of *Gebura* and *Hesed* through their attributes, the *Sword* and the *Scales*.

---

90  The archetype of Shehinah is *Asherah*, a local Goddess whose symbol is a lioness, worshiped as Jehovah's Wife. Asherah was a symbolical image of the power of life and was summoned during birth and sowing. She was later disguised under the form of *Shekinah* – the Holy Spirit. In the Bible, she is mentioned in the *Fourth Book of Kings* 17:10: "They set up for themselves statues and images of Astarte on every high hill and under every green tree." In Arabic, she is called *Shakina*, meaning "The Great Peace-Lovingness" – *AN*.

In this way, he figures as deputy of Metatron, reigning Justice in Peace, just as the Archangel Michael performs the same functions in the Spiritual Worlds. It is all about Justice bringing equilibrium and stable harmony in *Tiferet,* not Justice in the sense of *Gebura* (Severity) and *Din* (Judgment). Shekinah, being in exile, resides in the "Lower World" and is personified by the tenth Sfara *Malkut,* into which the energies of all the Sfarot flow. It represents the receptacle of the waters of the Higher River – Shekinah. *(Fig. 24)*

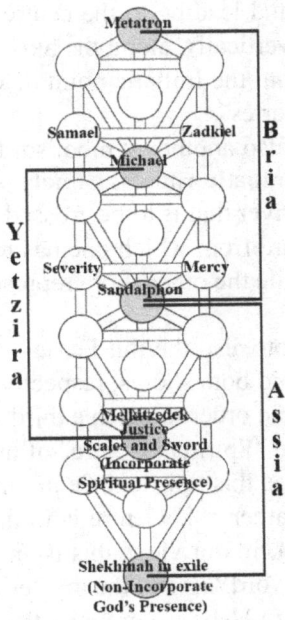

**Figure 24**

## The Heavenly River

*If we move the stones, then even the river will change its course.*

**Zen**

The river is a primordial esoteric symbol of the "Heavenly River" descending onto Earth and giving Life. In the Hebrew Kabala this "River of Life" finds its correspondence in the "channels" of the Sfarotic Tree through which the influence of the "Upper World" is transmitted to the "Lower World", which marks *the descent of Shehinah,* equivalent to the Hindu *Shakti.* Thus, the waters "flowing downwards" represent the foundation of the waters "flowing upwards" – an expression illustrating the returning towards the Heavenly Source by inverting the direction of the flow itself. This "inversion" was represented in the Vedic rituals through inverting a ritual vessel, but it should in no case be associated with the symbolism of the "Inverted Tree".

The "Heavenly River" (which can be equalled to the Kabalistic Tree), reaching the terrestrial Paradise, spills horizontally in the form of four rivers in all four directions of the world, forming a cross. The "rising of waters" can be viewed as being attainable in two stages: the first one – accomplished on the horizontal plane and leading to the centre of this world, and the second one – implemented vertically, along the axis. Thus, these two successive stages can be likened, from the Initiatic point of view, to the "Small Mysteries" and the "Great Mysteries".

We should mention also another symbolism that is present in almost all traditions and in some Initiatic rituals, namely – the crossing of the river, most often by boat. The river that is to be crossed in such a way is the "River of Death", where the shore from which one has to sail away is the sphere of manifested existence, while the other shore represents a state of being, finally liberated from death.

Finally, we should note also the third case – "descending downstream", which clearly aims to avoid both shores, respectively, the "world of humans" and the "world of Gods", in order to reach a third world – the "world of Initiates", which some call the "Spiritual Centre" of the Earth.

According to Hebrews, this Spiritual Centre in *Malkut* is the Mount Zion (heart of the world), or rather, this Centre is in the abode of Shekinah – the Temple of Zion. However, in our view, this is an exoteric concept. The esoteric one is related to the word *Luz* and the mysterious city bearing that name. An *almond tree* (also *luz* in Hebrew) grew by the walls of this city: the only entrance to the city was at the roots of this tree. This is the place called by Jacob *"Bet El"*, where he fights the Angel, as a symbol of the struggle between the ego and the "I", after which he receives the name *Israel,* meaning "He shall rule as God". This is the "Holy Place" and the first step of the ladder he beholds in his dream, along which Angels ascend and descend, and where he places the stone, which is to be the altar of God. The word *Luz* ("almond pit", "nut", "walnut" or "bone") means *something internal, secret, concealed, invulnerable. Luz* also denotes the indestructible body particle in which the Soul resides until the Resurrection. *Luz* is a receptacle of potential elements needed for the Resurrection of the human being. It is the core of Immortality in humans – and the Resurrection of the dead begins with it. It is thought that *Luz* is located at the bottom of the spinal column, next to the caudal bone, where, according to the Hindu tradition, *Kundalini* resides, and we have already clarified the core essence of the latter. Upon awakening of

Luz-Kundalini, one returns into one's primordial state of being and acquires a feeling of Eternity. *Luz* is at the lower part of the human organism and corresponds to the separate "fallen human", while, for the whole totality of the terrestrial humankind, it is equivalent to moving the Higher Spiritual Centre into the "subterranean world". The alchemical aspect of the macrocosmic reservoir of Kundalini is called the *Laboratory of the Holy Spirit,* whereas Initiation – the *Deed of the Holy Spirit.* The place in the human body where this Kundalini energy is located is called *kanda* in the Yoga tradition, while in the Alchemy tradition it is called *athanor* – the alchemical furnace in which the processes towards activating this energy must take place. These processes are treated by the *Art of Alchemy,* which is not alien to the Masonic science, because it underlies the foundation of the Royal Art, as is also by definition Freemasonry itself.

# 14
# Alchemy

*Alchemy serves to separate
the true from the false.*
**Paracelsus**

*What is covert must be made overt;
and what is overt must be made
covert: that is the task of the wise!*
**Bernardo Trevisano**

Alchemy is not only the practical side of Western European Kabala, but it can also be said that it is part of the Templar and the Rosicrucian Initiatic tradition, which is why it is impossible for it not to be present also in Freemasonry, as their successor. Alchemy is called *Royal Art* because it originates from Egypt, and in an esoteric sense, it means that it is a path of ascension of the "True King" – the "I", in the realm of human psyche. Alchemy is not a privilege of Medieval Europe because it is contained, in one form or another, in all esoteric traditions – for example, in the Tibetan *Vajrayana (Diamond Way),* which is the alchemical core of Mahayana Buddhism. The Tibetan teachings related to Alchemy are also the *Six Yogas of Naropa.* Daoism, on its part, is the Chinese form of Alchemy. We should not miss also the Arabic tradition, which actually gives the name *Alchemy.*[91] The main source, however, is Hermetism, and most of all – the *Emerald Tablet* of Hermes Trismegistus.

---

91  From the Arabic word *al-khimia – AN.*

Regardless of the various religions and traditions, all mystics are in the "central point of the circle", speak one and the same language, and form a community known by various names: *The Great White Lodge, House of Israel, School of the Holy Spirit, School of Immortality.* Rosicrucianism, which is one of the esoteric forms of Christian Kabala, is a transmission of this tradition into Freemasonry. According to Kabala, as we have already mentioned, *L'amed-Vav* represents the *Thirty-Six Righteous Ones* who are the "Inner Circle" of Humankind. Alchemy, as a part of practical Kabala, represents the *Yoga of the West*. The purpose is one and the same: union of the subject and the object of existence. This supreme Self-Accomplishment in Alchemy is called *Accomplishment of the Great Work,* and is represented as a snake devouring its tail, symbolizing the Hermetizing of consciousness. This completeness is also hidden behind the alchemical term *AZOT.* It consists of the first and the last letter of the Hebrew alphabet (*Alef* and *Tav*), and also of the Greek one (*Alpha* and *Omega*) and the Latin one (*A* and *Z*).

The most emblematic notion about Alchemy is the transmutation of lead into gold, which has been taken literally, although it is symbolic and concerns our own being, which means that the lead of imperfection is sublimated into the gold of perfection. The Great Work is comprised of two main levels: the *White Work* and the *Red Work.* Together, they lead to the alchemical Gold of Completion. The White Work deals with the subtle vehicle of the soul, whereas the Red Work – with the physical body. Naturally, the Great Work is illustrated and clothed in substance through the transmutation of metals, all the more so that it is subject to the Hermetic Laws, and above all – to the Law of Analogy.

The fundamental view of alchemists about metals is that the whole set of known metals can be positioned within a progressive scale with bipolar nature, with the one pole of perfection corresponding to *silver,* whereas the other pole – to *gold*. In these two metals, two principles are perfectly connected: the principle of *sulfur* (the Sun) and the principle of *mercury* (Mercury), where inside silver this connection is accomplished in the most perfect way for manifesting the properties of Mercury, while in gold – to manifest the properties of the Sun. The remaining metals are regarded as compounds which have not reached their own perfection, up to silver in the negative pole direction or up to gold in the positive one.

Thus, in any metal (even in any simple body) the connection of the Sun with Mercury has been accomplished; however, in gold and silver, it has been hermetically implemented in a perfect way. In order to transmute another metal into silver or gold, we must first break the imperfect bond established in that metal, to separate the subtle (sulfur, fire) from the dense (Mercury,

mercury), and then build a new perfect union. The *Emerald Tablet* tells us precisely about this separation of the subtle from the dense.

The sulfur principle (the Sun), together with the mercury principle (Mercury), are neutralized by the salt principle, and, through a special mineral (called *Magnesium of the Wise*), the so-called *AZOT of the Sages* is synthesized, also known as the *Universal Solvent* and the *Mercury of Philosophers*, or may be referred to as *Astral Light,* in the form of condensation of double-polarized vortices. The obtaining of AZOT from magnesium is carried out through a mysterious operation by application of personal magnetism – the *Philosophers' Magnet.*

The metals *gold* and *silver* are subjected to the action of the *AZOT of the Sages* in order to release from them the *Living Sun* (metallogenic sulfur) and the *Living Moon* (metallogenic mercury). The resulting substance mass is being enclosed inside a container, which is slowly heated on low fire in a special egg-shaped furnace. This furnace is called *athanor* – a word derived from the Arabic *at-tannūr* and the Hebrew *tannur,* meaning *furnace.* In the Alchemical tradition, this word is associated with the Greek *A-Θάνατος, (Thánatos),* meaning *death,* but the preceding letter *A* adds to it the meaning of *without,* and hence a new content – *immortal.* This word has given the name of a secret Brotherhood – "Order of the Immortals"; however, we will dwell on the topic of Immortality further on.

We shall not analyze in detail the phases of these processes; and yet, in the context of the present book, we shall mention only that the process called the *Head of the Crow* begins with carbonizing the material, after which it blackens completely and the so-called *Kingdom of Saturn* begins, in which it "dies" in order to be reborn, much like a Freemason in the Rite for receiving the Master Degree Initiation. The mass evolving inside an egg is called *rebis*[92] and is different depending on whether we wish to perform white or red transmutation, whereas, as in the so-called *Kingdom of Apollo,* red stone is being synthesized which has many synonyms but is mostly known as the *Philosophers' Stone.* Apollo is a solar deity, which indicates that, on the Kabalistic plane, the "Kingdom of Apollo" where the *Philosophers' Stone* is synthesized is the Sfara *Tiferet.*

This is followed by the stage of *Growth of the Stone,* during which the procedure is done as described, using a certain amount of gold. The new "Red Stone" is ten times stronger than the previous one regarding their transmutation properties, and with it, the final phase is at hand, called *Stone Projection,* in which base metals are transformed into silver or gold.

---

92  From Latin: *res* and *bis* – "dual matter", "double matter", "two things" – *AN.*

From what has been said so far, the fundamental maxim in Alchemical Work is drawn: *"In order to make gold, you must have gold."* Metaphorically, it means that in order to transform the lead of egoism into the gold of Enlightenment and Self-Accomplishment, you must first become conscious of your Primordial Divine Nature. Or, as Éliphas Lévi says, all vital forces, represented symbolically by the six metals, must be transformed into a Sun – that is, into Truth and Light. This is the most important task of the Great Work; and whoever has mastered the principles and analogies of Nature is able to make material gold as well.

In the context of the *Emerald Tablet,* Sulfur is the Father, Mercury – the Mother, whereas Salt – the Androgynous Child; or Osiris, Isis and Horus in the Egyptian tradition. Isis, the Feminine Core Essence, before conceiving, has to reassemble Osiris's body, uniting the consciousness divided into fourteen parts, in order to give birth to Horus – the Enlightened Consciousness, the Buddha Nature. The Father of Virtue will be the activity of the subject (the Sun); the Mother will be the subject's passivity (the Moon); Virtue will be carried by the wind of the astral environment; it will be nurtured by Mother Earth because it can manifest itself in the world of sacrifice – in the world of the Zodiac. However, only the *magnetism* named *"Telesma"* by Hermes, which represents the sheath of will-power, is able to provoke the process of its birth, the process of its carrying within the womb, and the process of application. All of this means that the key to the fruitful Truth is given through a three-stage Initiation, such as the Templar or the Masonic one.

The final phrases of the text of the *Emerald Tablet* affirm that the *"Work of the Sun"* has ended, i.e. that it has been accomplished not only on the two higher planes, but also on the physical plane, and also that the power of authority of Hermes extends also over the three planes. Thus, the Great Tablet of Egyptian tradition affirms Alchemy as a universal science of perfecting the nature of matters, and mostly of humans.

As we have pointed out, the *"Red Work"* is related to the physical body. However, the main influence acts upon the *astro-etheric body,* so through the changes within it, the impact is indirectly upon the subconscious mind (the object of the *"White Work"*), which actually controls the physiological functions. This is precisely the purpose of Magic, which includes also Alchemy: to create the form ourselves, only without falling into its shackles. When visualizing something in our microcosm with the help of imagination, and then projecting it outside of ourselves, we perform an ancient practice representing a fundamental technique in Alchemy. It is the means by which we separate the subtle from the gross, as Hermes Trismegistus says, whereas Jesus defines it as *"winnowing the grain from the chaff"*.

Symbolism is the language of the subconscious used in sleeping dreams and visions. We have access to the entire system of symbols contained in the collective subconscious. In Kabala, this system of symbols is attributed to the *Yetzira* World, on the Ladder of Jacob, and to the Sfara *Yesod*, on the single Tree, and is called the *Treasury of Images*. The Arcanum entitled *Twilight* symbolizing meditation is denoted by the Hebrew letter *Tsadi* meaning "a fishing hook". This is an indication that, in meditation, the hook with the "bait" chosen by us descends into the "sea" of our subconscious, after which we draw out the "catch" and illuminate it within our consciousness. The subjective subconscious is part of the collective subconscious, which represents the other name of the astral plane. Carl Gustav Jung calls it the *collective unconscious* – and this is the "covert order", the cause for everything happening within the "overt order". In this way, immersing into the subjective subconscious, we establish a connection with the astral plane, with the "covert order", so we can foresee and control whatever is happening in the world of noumena. On the alchemical plane, the above described means having access to and operating with *quintessential matter*.

## The Holy Grail

*The worth of a cup*
*depends on its contents.*

**Chinese proverb**

One of the great alchemical symbols is the *Cup of Perfection,* which has found its historical and literary expression in the *Holy Grail*. The Quest for the Grail is a symbol of walking along the Spiritual Path. Attaining the Grail is the *Liberation* from death and rebirth, while finding it, in the context of Alchemy, is a metaphor for *Attaining the Quintessence*. In the Masonic tradition, the Quest for the Grail corresponds to the *Quest for the Lost Word,* while its finding symbolizes the *Sacrament of True Initiation.* Judaism also does not seek any lost object but rather the pronunciation of the True, Great, Terrible and Secret Name of the Lord. This analogy shows the common centre of all Initiatic brotherhoods and traditions. The "Sacred Vessel" is present in the various myths, under different names, through which the energy of the "Upper Worlds" can be retained in *Assia* – the World of Action. The Grail is a vessel held by pagan goddesses. It is the cup carved from Lucifer's emerald, the Moon Cup of Atlantis, the cup full of wine brought by Melhisedek, who initiates Abraham into Kabala, and, according to *Sefer Yetzira,* introduces him into alchemical practices. There we read the following: "Know, think and imagine that fire sustains water." Initiates will recognize in this sentence one of the Daoist alchemical practices of "Kan and Li" – *water* and *fire*. This inner alchemical formula, in its microcosmic aspect, for both the Daoistic and the Kabalistic system, is quite mysterious, for in both systems, *fire* is above (respectively the heart and the head), whereas *water* is below (respectively the genitals and the abdomen). The "Kan and Li" formula exchanges the places of these two elements: *water* rises in Dan Tien, which plays the role of a boiler, while *fire*, which in this case is the universal solvent AZOT, descends beneath it and heats it. Water forms "steam", which is the transforming inner alchemical agent representing the Universal Innovator – INRI. In Kabala, this technique does not even require such a shift, since it is related to the Kabalistic Tree, on which the "Lower Fire" *(Neza)* heats the "Upper Water" *(Hesed)*, which begins to "evaporate" and circulate in our body within the great circle, between *Neza, Hesed, Gebura* and *Hod*. This is the fundamental formula of Inner Alchemy – and, as we have learned, it is present in Kabala, so it should not be alien to Masonic Art. *(Fig. 25)*

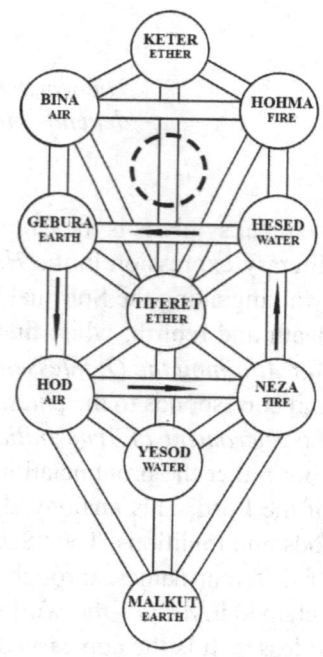

**Figure 25**

The above said obviously applies also to the symbolism of the Grail. According to alchemical interpretations, when the "Cup" is filled with "Living Water", the body begins its transformation, and subtle changes occur in the bloodstream. This phenomenon is observed before completing the Great Work and is one of the signs of the rise of Kundalini. We have already noted that the Grail is a symbol of our true Self in the Sfara *Tiferet*. On the other hand, however, the Kundalini energy is located in the sacrum, above the first chakra – a place related to the Sfara *Yesod*. The sacrum itself has the shape of a cup, and, in principle, in the context of the Kabalistic Tree, when speaking of a *cup* as a *vessel for collecting liquids,* we mean the Sfara *Yesod*. It is the foundation where all the streams flow into, which is why it can most reasonably be likened to a cup. It should as well not be forgotten, however, that the currents of the upper part of the Tree flow into *Tiferet,* and therefore this Sfara can also be likened to a cup, just as the Grail is presented to us in its most widespread version. After all, what does the Holy Grail represent itself actually? Are we talking about a stone, a cup, or the womb of Mary Magdalene, carrying the Sacred Blood of Jesus, or about the Vedic *soma,* the Hindu *amrita,* the Greek *ambrosia* – all of them *drinks of Immortality,* or perhaps about a Sacred Book? Also, what is its analogue to the Kabalistic Tree – the Sfara *Yesod* or the Sfara *Tiferet?* In general, are the Holy Grail and the Philosophers' Stone identical on the material and the spiritual plane, or maybe they represent differentiated realities? Can it be said that it is all about a Spiritual Core Essence with different material symbols and contexts depending on a given exoteric and esoteric tradition? We think that it is most likely the case. A cup, a stone, or a drink, as symbols of the Grail, all contain the characteristics of Immortality and Eternity, yet not in the physical sense but rather as immutability of the spiritual heritage from the First Times. The loss of the Grail symbolizes the loss of the initial Spiritual Centre, in the person of the Garden of Eden, and the loss of the sense of Wholeness and Eternity. Finding the Grail represents the establishment of a substitute for Heavenly Paradise by restoring the Primordial Spiritual Tradition, through which the Original State of Being is attained, and the "feeling of Eternity" is acquired. However, this can only be achieved through sacred union with the Immortal Spirit, representing our true "I", which is positioned in the Sfara *Tiferet*. The purpose of this Great Work is that the Supreme Spirit manifests Himself into matter in full power and spiritualizes it. It is the symbol of the Advent of the Messiah, the attainment of Buddha-Consciousness and the enlightened mind of Horus. In the *Emerald Tablet* of Hermes, the completion of the Great Work is called the "Work of the Sun".

All the energy and all the forms on Earth represent specific adaptation of the Sun's force retransmitted through the human being. That is why the secret name of humankind is the *Heart of the Sun*.

The Gematria of the word *Shemesh* (*Sun* in Hebrew) is the same as that of the phrase "My cup runs over" used in the *Psalter, Psalm* 23:5 *(NKJV)*, "You prepare a table before me in the presence of my enemies; You anoint my head with oil; my cup runs over."

The core essence of this phrase is identical to that of the Masonic one: "I am pleased: I have received my wage at the column on the left", which is proof of the existence of adapted alchemical symbolism in Freemasonry. The Divine inside us represents a certain potential that we ought to discover, unfold and manifest. Naturally, for all Freemasons, the veritable Grail, as a symbol of the manifested Divine presence in *Tiferet*, is the stone – "Eloah Gabal", the "Philosophers' Stone", the "Stone of Wisdom", on which we will dwell in detail when viewing the topic of the dressed stone. *Shemesh* is a projection in the Sfara *Tiferet* of the Spiritual Sun, which for our planetary system is the star *Sirius*, bearing the esoteric name **The Tear of Isis**.

The star *Sirius* is associated with the Mother Goddess Isis and her older archetype, Hathor. The fact that in Egypt and Babylon the beginning of each new year was associated with the heliacal rising of Sirius speaks of the important role of this star in the culture of these peoples, and at a later stage – also upon the Hellenes and the Romans. This is the moment when Sirius, the Sun and the Earth line up in the Cosmos. In Egypt, almost all the temples, as well as the direction in which the Sphinx looks, were aligned along this straight line. It has been established that our Solar System moves in the Cosmos in a stretched spiral because it is attracted by the star system *Sirius*. Actually, we are connected with Sirius in a sacral way, and Sirius is the Spiritual Sun whose manifestation is our Sun which is familiar to us. In addition to our Solar System, such a spiral motion is also observed between *Sirius A* and *Sirius B*. According to scientific research, this spiral motion is a reminiscent of the DNA molecule.

It is no coincidence that the followers of Master Beinsa Douno hold their annual gathering in Bulgaria every year around August 19th, when the heliacal rising of Sirius occurs, and this moment of the year has been a sacral point in the culture of all ancient civilizations. There is a lot of information about Sirius, so whoever wishes can get acquainted with it; therefore, we stop here, with a recommendation to winnow the grain from the chaff.

**Figure 26**

# 15
# The Chief Cornerstone

> *God sleeps in the rock, dreams in the plant, wakes up in the animal, and knows that He is awake in the human.*
>
> **Asian proverb**

## The Cornerstone

In the book already quoted, Jean Palou writes the following: "The Christian tradition, one of the fundamental esoteric forms of which is Freemasonry, attaches great importance to the *Cornerstone* and its symbolism. The fundamental in this tradition consists in the following sentence: 'The stone which the builders rejected is become the Head of the Corner'." Then he continues: "The symbol of the Cornerstone is one of the hardest to explore, for, willingly or unwillingly, authors confuse it with the foundation stone because of the famous *Gospel of Matthew* (16:18): 'And I also say to you that you are Peter, and on this rock I will build My Church, and the gates of Hades shall not prevail against it.' From a Christian point of view, this is the origin of a very annoying confusion of this stone with Christ, Who is the *Cornerstone,* not the *foundation stone* of the Edifice." Palou further grounds this statement, explaining that "... the cornerstone is the keystone of the vault – and, because of its shape, it can only be placed at the summit, in this sense representing the 'Stone come down from Heaven': an expression befitting Christ and also being a reminiscence of the 'Stone of the Grail'." In support of this, he quotes René Guénon, who, according to Palou, "quite rightly points out that the *cornerstone,* taken in its true sense of a 'summit stone', is called in English both *keystone* and *capstone. Capstone* derives from the Latin *caput* ('head'), which brings us back to the name of this stone as the 'head of the corner'; it is probably the stone that completes, or crowns a building". After that, the author puts a sign of equality, or rather of interchangeability, in the sense that when there is no cornerstone (keystone), there is the *oculus* (Eye of the Lord) – an opening through which light enters the church. In support of this, he gives as an example the plumb-line in Freemasonry, which symbolizes both the oculus and the keystone. Also, quoting the Apostle Paul that Jesus represents Himself the "Chief Cornerstone", Palou identifies the *cornerstone,* the *keystone,* and the *summit stone* with the "Chief Cornerstone", which represents itself the "Head of the Corner".

Unfolding this topic, Jean Palou mainly uses the developments in the works of René Guénon literally, which is why we shall also dwell on them in more detail when discussing the esoteric side of this question. Here, however, we will have to quote Palou again, in view of the designation of another stone: "The first stone of the building is always placed at the northeast corner, performing a ritual typical of each region. In the same way, in Speculative Freemasonry, the newly initiated – a symbolic foundation stone of the future building – is placed at the northeast corner of the Lodge." From this text we learn that there is also a "first stone" that is placed facing the northeast. Thus we understand that there are such terms as *first stone, cornerstone, stone in the foundation, foundation stone, chief cornerstone, summit stone, stone as the "head of the corner".* That is why we are about to analyze each one of them in order to understand both its functional and symbolic meaning, and especially its esoteric one. Since, according to Jean Palou, "The Christian tradition attaches great importance to the *Cornerstone* and its symbolism", let us see how this stone is present in this tradition in the form of laying the first stone in church buildings. In Latin, the laying of the first stone is referred to as *Lapidem primum ponere* or *Fundamentum ponere.* It is interesting to note that sometimes the first stone is replaced by laying precious stones or gold in the foundations. Such is the case of Petershausen Abbey, Germany, where, in

983, four gold coins were laid in the foundation of the future building. In the same way, in 1136, precious stones were laid in the foundation of the *Basilica of Saint-Denis* in France. It is not uncommon for the first stone in the form of a cross to be laid in the foundation. Symbols written on the first stone were also present, such as in the *Church of St. Michael* in Hildesheim, Germany (1015), and the *Strahov Monastery* in the Czech Republic (1297) with the inscription JESUS CHRISTUS. In La Couronne, Angoulême Abbey, France (1171), special round signs and a middle inscription, reading PAX HIC, are laid in the foundation. Beneath the cathedral in Speyer, Germany (1030), there are 12 foundation stones with the names and portraits of the Apostles, along with one of the Madonna with Child. However, there is no indication anywhere of the place of laying the first stone or its analogues.

An ancient Bulgarian custom, which has left deep traces into the psychology not only of the master builders but also of the whole nation, is "walling a human shadow" into the construction, so that it ensures the strength and durability of the construction. This is a reminiscence of the much more ancient offering of human sacrifice. It was later replaced by a sacrificial animal, usually a hen or lamb, which was slaughtered in such a way as to spray the first stone with its blood. This custom is still practiced in some parts of the country even nowadays, and it is believed that the sacrificial blood will protect the occupants and visitors of the building against misfortunes and diseases.

Another custom, analogous to the above one, can be found also in the Masonic tradition. In the archives of the French Research Lodge, *Villard de Honnecourt,* member of the *Grande Loge Nationale Française* (Grand National Lodge of France), in the third section, related to Rites, there is a 1981 article by Pierre Girard entitled *Extant Operative (Rites) in England and Scotland.* On page 107, we find the following regarding the "Ceremony of Laying the Foundations of the Temple in Jerusalem": "... During the celebration, a Brother was chosen to be the 'human sacrifice'...", because, in ancient times, "it was believed that a human should be sacrificed by burying this human into the centre of the building between the four corners, otherwise this building would not remain stable". The ceremony is described as follows: "A table, 6 feet (1.8 m) long, is covered with white fabric to look exactly like a large white stone block, and at the time of laying the stone, six men lift the 'block' and place it upon the 'sacrificed one', after which the ceremony continues, examining the stone with the set square, the level and the plumb-line in the usual way".

The examples given so far show the symbolic character of the first stone rather than any constructive or functional meaning.

Since the laying of the first stone is an object of Masonic ceremonies, let us see how they proceeded in a time closer to the present. Such ceremonies were held during the construction of the most important buildings in the USA. For example, on September 2, 1885, when the Capitol Building in Georgia had been under construction for almost a year (November 13, 1884), it was decided to lay the "first stone". The place for that was the northeast corner of the building. The ceremony was performed in the presence of nearly 10,000 people, with hymns and orations praising the importance of the building to the "New South", as well as a Masonic ceremony involving water and oil. The stone was hollow, with a time capsule inside, containing the Bible, national state documents, and memoirs from 1885. It was made of marble, unlike any other in the building.

The same can be said also of the Capitol Building in Nevada, the first stone of which was laid on June 9, 1870, upon other stones previously placed. A brass box, acting as a time capsule, was put inside the stone. Sometimes there was more than one ceremonial stone, as in the case of Truro Cathedral, England, in 1880, when one stone was laid by Freemasons facing the northeast, and another – by officials towards the east.

From the esoteric point of view, the time for laying the first stone had to be chosen very carefully, taking into account the position and influence of the stars. In this way, the building that is in the beginning of its construction process will have the chance to be "born" under the influence of the best possible position of the stars. Thus, on the day of the laying of the first stone of the Capitol by George Washington, the star Sirius rose shortly before the Sun. This phenomenon is called *heliacal rising*, and it marked the beginning of the New Year in Ancient Egypt, and also was embedded in the foundation of many important Egyptian and Masonic rituals. The first stone of the statue of George Washington and that of the Pentagon building were placed during the heliacal rising of Sirius. This is proof of the importance attached to this stone in Freemasonry, both in the symbolical and the operative aspect.

All these examples impose the conclusion that the first stone has a symbolic core essence rather than a purely functional one, in its capacity of a cornerstone.

There is information about the cornerstone mostly of an exoteric nature, which can be reduced, in the first place, to a purely constructional aspect of this concept. This is a large stone lying in the corner of the groundwork (foundation) of a building. It is laid in such a way that through it the two walls are connected to each other. There is no specific text about the cornerstone in the "Foundations" section of Marcus Vitruvius Pollio's manual *De Architectura (Ten Books on Architecture)*. Then, let us see what the definition is in some modern dictionaries.

The *Cambridge Dictionary* states that *cornerstone* is:
- *a stone in a corner of a building, especially one with the date when the building was made or other writing on it*
- *something of great importance that everything else depends on*

In the *Oxford Dictionary*, the definition of *cornerstone* is the following:
- *a stone that forms the base of a corner of a building, joining two walls*

The *Collins Dictionary* states almost the same:
- *a stone at the corner of a wall, uniting two intersecting walls*

In the context of this functionality of the *cornerstone*, we must clarify that in any masonry building, the wall is load-bearing, i.e. the foundation of the very wall is important, not the foundation in general. In the middle of the building, there is practically no need for any foundation. That is, the cornerstone is a supporting stone in the foundation, under the wall, where the construction process begins, because the building (most often a rectangle) is determined by its four endpoints. The construction process starts from one corner, where the cornerstone is placed, which is why it is also called *"first stone"*, *"chief cornerstone"*, *"foundation stone"*, *"fundamental stone"*, *"stone which lays the foundation"*, *"stone in the foundation"*.

Literally, the name *chief cornerstone* comes from the circumstance that it represents the edge of corners. In the classic square or rectangular base, there are four corners, hence there are four stones. However, the term *chief cornerstone*, as a stone in the corner of the foundation, refers to a cornerstone that is clearly different from the other three ones. We will dwell on this specific feature later, in the context of the analysis regarding the topic of René Guénon. Before that, however, we have to view this topic in the light of the various traditions.

## Eben ha-Shetiyah

> *When the Holy One, blessed be He, was about to create the World, He detached one precious stone from underneath His Throne of Glory and plunged it into the Abyss; one end of it remained fastened therein, while the other end stood out above. Out of the latter, the World started, spreading itself to right and left into all directions.*
>
> ***The Zohar***

According to the Judaic view, the "stone in the foundation" or the "chief cornerstone" is embedded in the foundation of the Universe, because it is with this stone, namely, that the Lord begins the Creation of the world. Upon this stone, at the time of the First Temple (967 BC – 586 BC) the Ark of the Covenant was placed, with the Ten Commandments of God. During the Second Temple period (515 BC – 70 AD) the stone was used for placing incense. On the Jewish holiday Yom Kippur, the high priest could not place his censer there because the visible surface of the chief cornerstone was extremely uneven, i.e. in the metaphorical and philosophical sense, every initial idea is like a rough, unpolished stone, such as the chief cornerstone obviously is. In Hebrew, the term for *Chief Cornerstone* is *Eben (h)ashtia,* which literally means "the stone (foundation) of drinking", since it is the stone of "Living Water".

The Rabbinic tradition reveals that remarkable events took place around it: God created Adam and Eve; there stood Noah's Ark at the time of the flood; this is the place where Abraham was ready to offer as a sacrifice his firstborn son Isaac; on this stone Jacob fell asleep and dreamed of the Ladder between Heaven and Earth, with Angels ascending and descending, after which he named the place *Beit El (House of God),* raised the stone like a pillar and *anointed it with oil.* According to legends, King David rediscovered this stone while digging the foundations of the Temple, and after the construction of the Temple by his son Solomon, that stone was placed as an altar for the Ark of the Covenant in the Holy of Holies. It is a synonym of *Zion,* and it is the centre from which blessings flow out for the whole world.

In the *Jewish Heritage* magazine, it is written that the Tannaitic term *eben ha-shetiyah* was interpreted in two ways during the Talmudic period: "the stone (or rock) from which the world was woven", and "the fundamental stone". Both meanings stem from the belief that the world was created from the Holy of Holies of the Jerusalem Temple, representing its centre. This concept is closely related to the notion of Jerusalem and the Temple as being located at the "navel of the world". The Holy Ark was placed on this rock, and during the Second Temple period, the high priest, upon entering the Holy of Holies on Yom Kippur, placed the fire-pan upon this stone. The Muslim tradition identifies this place with the "Dome of the Rock" which was built on top of it.

The idea of a sacred stone symbolizing the "navel of the world" is *archetypal* because it is present in the mythology of peoples in different parts of the world. Each ancient civilization considered the place from which it originated to be a specific centre of the world. This place was the most familiar to each of the civilizations and became the *sacral centre* of its existence. In this centre, a stone was placed, a remnant of a much more ancient cult to Nature. This stone was considered sacred and was called "navel", most probably because it symbolizes the connection with the Primordial Origin – the Source of Life. In the Inca civilization, which has left the most noticeable trace on the South American continent, the idea of the centre of the world is present in the name of the capital of the ancient empire called Cuzco, which, translated from *Quechua* (local/ indigenous language) means "navel of the *Earth*", in the sense of the

*Universe*. They believed that this was the place where the underworld and our world connect with each other. It was from here, from the central square of the city, that all the roads in the empire started.

The locals of Easter Island have always called this island *Te Pito o Te Henua*, or "Navel of the World". In southern Turkey, 15 km northeast of the city of Şanlıurfa, the temple complex Göbekli Tepe is located (in Turkish – "Belly/ Rounded Hill"), also known as the "Navel Hill". According to scientists, an impressive temple towered at that place, towards which worshipers flocked from all over Mesopotamia, the Euphrates, Cappadocia, the area of Lake Van, today's territories of Iran and Iraq.

In ancient Babylon[93], the place where all languages were mixed was also considered to be the "navel of the world" by its founders. Here was the temple of Marduk, the chief God of Heaven and Earth; this temple was marked with a stone similar in shape to the Greek *Omphalos*.

In Ancient Greek mythology, the term *Omphalos* appears – *navel, sacred stone*, considered to be the Centre of the Earth. According to the most widespread legend, Zeus released two eagles from different edges of the Earth, to determine with their help the Centre of the world, the sacred place where order was born out of chaos. Zeus marked with a *stone omphalos* the place (in Delphi) where the birds met.

The Romans considered the cosmic centre to be the so-called *Mundus – World, Universe, Heavens, Humankind*. According to Plutarch, when Rome was founded, Romulus dug a pit in what is now called the *comitium*[94] ("meeting place"), and threw the first fruits of each plantation there. This pit was called *Mundus* by the Romans – the same word used to describe Olympus. Hence, the ancient tradition of the Romans, before building a new city, to dig a hole representing the centre/ navel of the city, which also played the role of connection with the afterlife world beyond, of contact between the world of the living and that of the dead. In the Roman Forum, a conical building is preserved from a much later era: that of Emperor Septimius Severus, called *Umbilicus Urbis Romae* – the navel of the city of Rome, having the same meaning of the Greek *Omphalos*.

To the three monotheistic religions, Jerusalem represents the holy city that Christians and Jews still venerate as the "navel of the Earth" up to this day. The "Omphalos" itself is Mount Moriah. The *Talmud* says that Palestine is in the centre of the world, whereas the city of Jerusalem – in the centre of Palestine, the Temple – in the centre of Jerusalem, the Holy of Holies – in the centre of the Temple, and the Ark of the Covenant – in the centre of the Holy of Holies.

---

93  *Babylon* derives from *Bab-ilu – Door of God, Gate of God*. The Hebrew word *valal*, or *balal*, means *to mix (up), to confuse, to stir, to rub* (Genesis 11:9) – *AN*.
94  The *Comitium* was situated at the northeast corner of the Roman Forum and represented the political centre of Rome until the Late Republican era, when the Forum took over its functions – *AN*.

To Christians, Mount Tabor, located southeast of Nazareth, also has an important meaning. In Hebrew, *Tabor (Tabur)* means *navel*. The shape of the mountain resembles a hemisphere towering majestically in the middle of Galilee.

In Jerusalem, on Mount Moriah, the *Qubbat As-Sakhrah* ("The Dome of the Rock") Mosque is situated – a sacred place originally considered the "navel of the world" by the Muslim world before being replaced by Mecca, the sacred *Kaaba*, which, according to legend, was built by Ibrahim (Abraham) and Ismail. The *Kaaba* embodies the ancient pre-Islamic cult to the stones of the ancient Arabs. The *Black Stone* of the Kaaba is a very old sacred relic, revered long before the emergence of Islam, and being the main object of worship and a symbol of the Might of Allah. The "Sent Stone" shone with its whiteness, so bright that it could be seen from a distance of a four days' journey away from the *Kaaba*. However, gradually, because of all the human sins, it began to darken until it became completely black. According to a belief, when the Last Judgment comes, the Black Stone will turn white again.

There is a Hebrew legend that the Divine Name, יהוה *Yod-He-Vav-He*, was inscribed on the fundamental stone. According to this legend, the sages were afraid that someone would learn the Holy Name from the stone, which is why they created two bronze lions at the entrance of the Holy of Holies. In case that anyone penetrated into the sanctuary and learned the Name, the lions would roar so loud that this Name would be erased from the person's consciousness.

According to the Muslim tradition, on the other hand, the Rock, an analogue to the "stone in the foundation" and the "chief cornerstone", originates from Paradise, and Muhammad ascends from this Rock to Heaven. The stone itself also began to ascend together with Muhammad, but was stopped by the Archangel Gabriel. The inhabitants of Jerusalem used to relate that for many years the stone hovered in the air over the city, the visible traces on its western side being the fingerprints of the Archangel Gabriel and the trace of the horse-shoe of *Al Buraq*, Muhammad's horse. In the 21$^{st}$ century, the "stone in the foundation" or the "chief cornerstone" is located in Jerusalem on the Temple Mount, within the Muslim monument "Dome of the Rock", in the middle of which is this chief cornerstone, considered to be sacred.

Now is the time already to move on to the inner circle of knowledge about the "stone", starting with the *Ancient Talmud*, where it is said: *"The Holy One, blessed be He, cast a stone into the ocean, from which the World then was founded as it is said: Whereupon were the foundations thereof fastened, or who laid the Chief Cornerstone thereof?"*

According to the *Mishna*, "The world stands upon three things: on the *Torah* (the *Pentateuch*, or the *Five Books of Moses*), on the Foundation of the World (the foundation stone), and on the acts of the righteous."

Again in the *Mishna* (*Yoma* 5:2), it is written that the rock was in the place of the Holy of Holies *(Devir)* "from the times of the first prophets" (David and Solomon), about 15 cm higher than the ground, and was called *ha-Shetiyah*.

On the other hand, in one of the Kabalistic reference books, the *Zohar*, it is written:

*"When the Holy One, blessed be He, was about to create the World, He detached one precious stone from underneath His Throne of Glory and plunged it into the Abyss; one end of it remained fastened therein, while the other end stood out above. Out of the latter, the World started, spreading itself to right and left into all directions."* In Hebrew, this stone is called *Eben ha-shetiyah* and is predominantly given the meaning of the *fundamental stone*. However, some of the wise men of Israel say that *shetiyah* in Hebrew means "drinking" because beneath it is hidden the source of all the wellsprings and fountains from which the World drinks its water. Others, no less wise men, define it as the flat (regular), fundamental stone of the Universe, the seed or navel of Creation.

There is a tradition according to which Solomon, knowing that the Temple would be destroyed, prepared a secret room beneath it to hide the sacred ritual objects from the Holy of Holies. This may have been the same hall that the medieval Knights Templar later tried to find or found. There are still other legends, such as the one about the Holy Grail, according to which this stone is actually *Lapis Exillis* – the Stone that fell from Heaven.

In *Fig. 27*, we show the Sfarotic reading of the text from the *Zohar*.

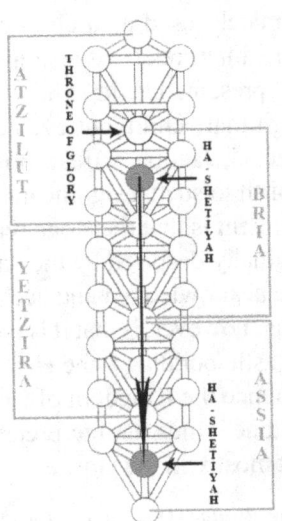

**Figure 27**

# The Psalm

*The stone which the builders rejected has become the Chief Cornerstone.*
*(Psalter Psalm 118:22[95], NKJV)*

In the Old Testament, the "stone" is mentioned only in one place in the context under consideration, namely in the *Psalter*. Here, for the purposes of the discussed question, we must note that the *Psalter* contains 151 Psalms that were not written at one and the same time and by one and the same author. In 49 of the Psalms, the author is not indicated; and the Psalm which we are interested in and which we have quoted, unfortunately, is one of them.

The text in Hebrew: אבן מאסו הבונים היתה לראש פנה, is transliterated as follows: "ehben mahahsu habonim haita lerosh pina", whereas phonetically it would sound in the following way: "eben maasu hbonim haita lerosh pinna". In order to unveil the concealed message, the meaning of each of the words used must be indicated first, because in Hebrew each hieroglyph and word has more than one meaning. In this context, we can assume that the meaning of "eben" is only *stone*, unlike the word "maasu", which has various meanings: *rejected, threw, discussed, disgust, disgusted, to refuse, to scrap, to remove, to despise, waste, remains*. The word "hbonim" means *(the) builders*, as well as *college (brotherhood) of the great Rabbis*. In the same way, "rosh" is translated as *head/ leader/ beginning*, whereas "pinna" – *peak, angle, point of contact*. In this phrase, "lerosh pinna"[96] is the *head of the nation*, the *(chief) cornerstone*.

In a literal sense, the above said means that this stone was despised by the builders, but was ultimately used as a chief cornerstone of the building. However, this phrase has its interpretations also in an Old Testament key. One of them is that the stone represents David, who was initially rejected because he was considered an illegitimate child, but eventually became king. Another interpretation refers to Rachel, Jacob's wife, who was ridiculed and mocked by all, but she later gave birth to such a significant figure in the Old Testament as Joseph. The classic comment is that the stone represents the Hebrew people themselves, who were originally despised by the nations around the world, but eventually may one day be acknowledged and accepted as God's chosen ones. The most symbolic meaning, however, is that it is the stone that will become the head of the corner of a majestic building – the Heavenly Jerusalem, which will descend on Earth and announce the Kingdom of God.

The "Old Testament stone" finds its interpretation also in the New Testament in various places, but mostly in the Gospels.

---

95  *Psalm* 117:22 in the *Vulgate; Psalm* 118:22 in the *Torah – AN*.
96  In the *Septuagint*, this phrase is written as κεφαλὴν γωνίας (kephalé/n – head + gónia/s – corner), while in the *Vulgate*, it figures as *caput anguli – AN*.

"Then He looked at them and said: What then is this that is written: 'The stone which the builders rejected has become the Chief Cornerstone'?" (*Holy Gospel of Luke* 20:17, *NKJV*)

"Jesus said to them: Have you never read in the Scriptures: 'The stone which the builders rejected has become the Chief Cornerstone. This was the Lord's doing, and it is marvelous in our eyes'?" (*Holy Gospel of Matthew* 21:42, *NKJV*)

"Have you not even read this Scripture: 'The stone which the builders rejected has become the Chief Cornerstone'?" (*Holy Gospel of Mark* 12:10, *NKJV*)

"This is the 'stone which was rejected by you builders, which has become the Chief Cornerstone'." (*Acts of the Holy Apostles* 4:11, *NKJV*)

In one of the Dead Sea Scrolls from the Qumran Caves – *Qumran Column XXII Isaiah 28:2*, we read: "For no other foundation can anyone lay than that which is laid, which is Jesus Christ." (*First Epistle of St. Paul to the Corinthians* 3:11, *NKJV*)

"Therefore it is also contained in the Scripture, 'Behold, I lay in Zion a Chief Cornerstone, elect, precious, and he who believes on Him will by no means be put to shame.' Therefore, to you who believe, He is precious; but to those who are disobedient, 'The Stone Which the builders rejected has become the Chief Cornerstone', and 'a Stone of stumbling and a Rock of offense'." (*First Epistle of Peter* 2:6 – 8, *NKJV*)

According to Christian apologists, Jesus Christ is likened in the New Testament to a Chief Cornerstone because He represents Himself the foundation of the Christian Church, and just as the chief cornerstone is most visible in the foundation of a building, the same way Christ is the most visible because He is the intercessor for the salvation of all. Also, just as the chief cornerstone rejected by the builders becomes a stone of stumbling, the same way the Gospel, the Gracious Word of Christ will increase the punishment of those who reject Him.

In this sense, we can also incorporate the views of the Qumran community, insofar as Jesus is its product. According to the Essenes, the Temple in Jerusalem was profaned, as were all the priests in it. According to them, this text in the *Psalter, Psalm* 118:22 *(ASV)*, "The stone which the builders rejected is become the head of the corner", refers to their community, which was rejected by the priesthood in Jerusalem, while for the Essenes themselves they are the true Chief Cornerstone upon which God's Kingdom and Temple will be built. This is hinted many times in the Dead Sea Scrolls, mostly in those concerning the inner rules, order, and hierarchy of the Qumran community, which was called a "fortress" and represented the Abode of God.

From what has been discussed so far, it is clear that the first reading of the "chewed phrase", already in a New Testament key, should be in the context of the personality of Jesus and His Teaching, which were rejected by Orthodox Judaism.

Undoubtedly, this phrase has also many other contexts, yet the one that is of interest for us and on which we will focus in more detail is the "construction" one – in the literal, figurative and esoteric sense. It would not be any exaggeration to assume that there is a direct reference to Freemasonry, in the symbolism of which, closely related to construction, the *stone* is present as the main building block in the form of the *"rough undressed stone"* and the *"dressed (hewn) stone"*. In support of this, we will give an example with all translations and editions of the Bible in Modern Bulgarian, in which the word *masons* is used in the quoted Psalm, as well as in the passages of the New Testament quoted by us. We have pointed out that the word *builders* is used in Hebrew and is present in translations in English, Croatian, Russian, German, French, Italian, Latin, Spanish, and Portuguese. In our comparative analysis, without being exhaustive, we have found only that the word *masons* was also used in the Romanian translation. In both cases, the more general term, *builders,* is identified with those who handle the stone, and these are precisely the *masons builders* – Freemasons. In Bulgarian, the word for *mason* is *зидар [zi'dar]*, a derivative of *зид [zid]* (i.e. "masonry wall"). Peter Deunov says that the words *зид [zid]*, and hence *зидар [zi'dar] (mason)*, derive from *Isis*, in Bulgarian: *Изида [i'zidə]* – the Goddess symbolizing Nature giving birth, which is why Masons are not ordinary builders, but agents of the fertilizing, creative power of Spirit contained in the stone.

# 16
# Undressed and Dressed Stone

## The Undressed Stone

*Do not try to shine like nephrite,
but be as simple as stone.*

**Lao Tzu**

In Ancient Judea, there was a prohibition on the erection of buildings made of hewn stone, as it was believed that the undressed stone expressed the supernatural connection with the *Living God – El Hai*. It was believed that the hewn stone was the result of human intervention, which lowered on a profane level the sacral perfection of the undressed stone, set by God Himself through Nature. According to this view, the prehistoric peoples who erected megaliths were obviously in a state of being closer to the Primordial one than those after them. The development of civilization, however, has led to successive adaptations of tradition and a change in this state of being. Thus, over time, this philosophy was abandoned, as evidenced by the Temple of Solomon, which was hardly a profane undertaking. However, there are conceptions about the processing of its building stones as not being done by human hands, with the aim to substantiate their sacral nature. The tradition of the undressed stone has been preserved in the altars, thus keeping the original symbolism; for it is clear to everyone that a magnificent building cannot be built of such stones. Confirmation of this symbolism is the *ha-Shetiyah* stone, which has already been mentioned. The question arises as to whether Freemasonry, using, in both the literal and allegorical sense, the hewn stone, does not move away from the sacral nature of the symbolism of the stone in general. It is obvious that the use of dressed stone allows for the development of the building as structure, form and aesthetics, and of architecture as a whole. In this sense, the hewn stone should be a symbol of human development and upgrading towards perfection, based on the Primordial Divine Nature of the undressed stone. Thus, the latter in Freemasonry represents the *materia prima*, containing primordial potency, which is differentiated and structured through the dressed stone. In this way, the hewn stone embodies in itself the perfection and completeness of the process of *Building the Edifice*. Thus the altar of the undressed stone symbolizes the Primordial Sacral Nature, whereas the temple of hewn stone is the Masonic process of *Building the Edifice,* which is its architectural expression. It is in this context, namely, that the symbolism of the undressed and the dressed stone in Freemasonry should be viewed. We believe that if, regarding the undressed stone, as such, things are relatively clear, then, regarding the dressed one, the case is far from being the same.

## The Dressed Stone

*A rock pile ceases to be a rock pile the moment a single person contemplates it, bearing within the image of a cathedral.*

**Antoine de Saint-Exupéry**

The *dressed stone* is a collective, general definition; nevertheless, it is liable to differentiation depending on its shape and place in the process of *Building the Edifice,* and therefore it has different symbolic contexts. Regarding this type of stone, it seems to be clear how it is used, although the problem of the place in the building of its various types turns out to be quite complex and controversial. The question arises as to whether the "first stone" is exclusively symbolic and as such it is the "undressed stone" in the literal sense, like the *ha-Shetiyah* stone (the example with the censer of the Judaic high priest), or it is a *cubic stone* placed in the corner where the building starts from and where its correct parameters are set. In a purely constructional aspect, we would say that the second option is more realistic. Let us see what Albert Mackey, a Mason and writer, considered a prominent authority, says in this context in his book *The Symbolism of Freemasonry,* commenting on the subject of the *chief cornerstone:* "The cornerstone of an edifice must be perfectly square on its surfaces, lest, by a violation of this true geometric figure, the walls to be erected upon it should deviate from the required line of perpendicularity which can alone give strength and proportion to the building."

From what has been written so far, it is clear that this chief cornerstone, which the author speaks of, is a hewn cubic stone, but it is not clear whether it is the first stone. This is specified in the following quote: "The stone, therefore, thus properly constructed, is, when it is to be deposited by the constituted authorities of our Order, carefully examined with the necessary implements of Operative Masonry – the square, the level, and the plumb – and declared to be 'well-formed, true, and trusty'."

There is no doubt that these "constituted authorities of the Order" solemnly lay a first stone, marking the beginning of the construction process, which, because of this ceremony, is called *symbolic*.

According to these quotations, in the end it is necessary to conclude that the chief cornerstone is the "first stone", symbolically placed in the corner of the foundation, and that this first stone is cubic and with ideal proportions. However, this conclusion contradicts the religious tradition that this stone is with uneven surface and in no case represents a hewn cubic stone. This contradiction deepens even more in view of the accepted position in some Rites for the situating of the newly adopted as an apprentice in the northeast, symbolically identifying him with the "first stone". To illustrate this, at the risk of repeating ourselves, we will again turn to Albert Mackey's book, pointing out a few quotations that we will put under analysis. In the chapter entitled *Symbolism of the Cornerstone,* we read the following, "... An important ceremony in the ritual of the First Degree of Masonry... In this ceremony the candidate becomes the representative of a Spiritual Cornerstone... The Cornerstone, as the foundation on which the entire building is supposed to rest, is, of course, the most important stone in the whole edifice." (Here we will only allow ourselves to add that the candidate turns out to be the most important whom the whole Lodge rests upon?!)

"The position of the stone in the north-east corner of the building is altogether symbolic... The East, then, is, in Masonry, the symbol of the Order, and the North – the symbol of the profane world. Now, the Spiritual Cornerstone is deposited in the north-east corner of the Lodge, because it is symbolic of the position of the neophyte, or candidate, who represents it in his relation to the Order and to the world. From the profane world he has just emerged. Some of its imperfections are still upon him; some of its darkness is still about him; he as yet belongs in part to the North... He is not altogether a profane, nor altogether a Mason... He is neither; he is an Apprentice, with some of the ignorance of the world cleaving to him, and some of the light of the Order beaming upon him."

According to Mackey, this duality corresponds to the "cornerstone" in the northeast. In this regard, we continue to quote in the hope that we will not be extremely boring: "One surface of the stone faces the North, and the other surface faces the East. It is neither wholly in the one part nor wholly in the other – that which is incomplete and imperfect, and is, therefore, fitly represented by the recipient of the First Degree, at the very moment of his Initiation." (Here, too, we will allow ourselves to ask: How does this imperfection correspond to what was stated at the beginning, that the candidate embodies in himself the Spiritual Cornerstone, in his capacity of that foundation which the whole building is supposed to rest upon, being for that reason the most important stone in the whole construction of the edifice?)

Further on, Mackey makes the following clarification: "In the ritual 'observed at laying the foundation stone of public structures', it is said, 'The principal architect then presents the working tools to the Grand Master, who applies the plumb, square, and level to the stone, in their proper positions, and pronounces it to be *well-formed, true, and trusty*'."

After that, he continues: "The cornerstone of an edifice must be perfectly square on its surfaces, lest, by a violation of this true geometric figure, the walls to be erected upon it should deviate from the required line of perpendicularity which can alone give strength and proportion to the building."

From the above exposition, it becomes clear that, according to Mackey, the cornerstone, or the chief cornerstone, is the foundation stone and at the same time – the first stone, the laying of which at the north-east corner is entirely symbolic. Despite this symbolism, however, the stone must "be perfectly square on its surfaces", "well-formed, true, and trusty", being "the foundation on which the entire building is supposed to rest", and therefore is "the most important stone in the whole edifice". On the other hand, the author, substantiating the symbolic nature of the cornerstone, explains that it "is incomplete and imperfect, and is, therefore, fitly represented by the recipient of the First Degree, at the very moment of his Initiation... Some of its imperfections are still upon him; some of its darkness is still about him; he as yet belongs in part to the North". To us, the confusion is great, while to the readers, if they accept things superficially and on trust – maybe not so much. Perhaps the lack of in-depth analysis and the repetition of established clichés have also played a bad joke on Mackey himself, who is a prominent Freemason and has personally admitted the even more prominent Albert Pike into the AASR (Ancient and Accepted Scottish Rite).[97]

In any case, there are deep contradictions in what is written, leading to confusion regarding the symbolic core essence of the chief cornerstone, as well as its form and function. On the one hand, it symbolizes the neophyte, and, on the other hand, it is well-shaped and with ideal proportions, which is why it represents the foundation stone which the whole edifice rests upon, and as such, is the Spiritual Chief Cornerstone. It turns out that the accepted as Masonic Apprentice, who has yet to smooth and grind and polish the "edges of his own imperfection", in a symbolic sense represents the "well-formed, true, and trusty" chief cornerstone, "perfectly square on its surfaces", which the whole edifice rests upon, in this case – the Lodge. Apart from the already indicated semantic and logic contradiction in what has been stated, it is not true in itself. On the one hand, there is no way for the apprentice to be the perfect mainstay of the Lodge; and, on the other hand, from a purely architectural point of view, there is also no way for the whole building to be supported by the stone in the north-east corner. This means that the symbolism, form, place and purpose of the chief cornerstone are not covered by what Mackey has said, mainly because of its exclusivity,[98] which in our opinion is not due to its primacy in laying. We have allowed ourselves to quote this author, because he is considered the authority setting the parameters of the meaning and essence of Masonic symbols.

---

97  Mackey raises Pike in all possible 29 Degrees of AASR in one day – on March 20, 1853 in Charleston, South Carolina. Ten days after receiving his Degrees, Pike is nominated by Mackey as Deputy Inspector General of Arkansas. Pike receives the 33rd degree on April 25, 1857, and is elected Sovereign Grand Commander of AASR on January 3, 1859, holding this position for 32 years until his death – *AN*.

98  There are three other similar stones in the rest three corners of the foundation, to which such importance is not attached – *AN*.

## The Undressed Stone and the Apprentice

> *The most important aspect of humans – these are their own aspirations, not their achievements, because it is their own egoism that demands achievements.*
>
> ***Talmud, Yevamot***

Here is what another authority has written – Jean Palou, in his book *La Franc-Maçonnerie (Freemasonry)*: "The undressed stone is one of the fundamental symbols of Freemasonry. In general, Masonic authors turn this symbol into a moral allegory, often quite utilitarian. They liken the newly admitted Mason – the apprentice, to an undressed stone which he has to tool on his own, working constantly on himself. If we stand on a metaphysical level, the undressed stone (the apprentice) is an individuality ("I") that must be hewn in order to reach the personality (his own self) so that he may be liberated from all roughness (the hewn stone) and included into the integral edifice formed by Freemasonry".

Palou's explicit standpoint is evident: that the apprentice is an undressed stone – however, when he becomes the "hewn stone", it is only then that he is included into "the integral edifice formed by Freemasonry". Nevertheless, contrary to what has been written so far, only a page further he states: "The first stone of the building is always laid at the northeast corner... Similarly, in Speculative Freemasonry, the newly initiated one – the fundamental symbolic stone of the future edifice – is positioned in the northeast corner of the Lodge." We leave to the readers to draw their own conclusions, because we did not understand when the apprentice joins "the integral edifice" – whether as a first stone, or later, as a hewn stone liberated from all imperfections.

Perhaps here is the place to quote what is written in the Catechism of the *United Grand Lodge of Bulgaria (UGLB)*, adopted from that of the Lodges Members of the *Grand Lodge of Ancient Free and Accepted Masons of Germany (GL AFAM)*: "According to the Masonic view, each member of the Union represents a rough, undressed stone. He must be constantly hewn in order to become, through self-knowledge, a rectangular, cubic stone that can be used to build the Temple of Humanity, to be useful to human society. Hence, the question: *'What are the apprentices working on?'*, as well as the answer: *'On the unhewn stone'*. The rough stone is viewed as a symbol of the imperfection of the mind and heart, which ought to be ennobled through Freemasonry. It symbolizes humans in need of improvement towards perfection, who must comply not only with the current traditions and customs of their own environment, but also with the Eternal Laws of Morality and Justice. The character of each person contains roughness, which, according to the Masonic symbolism, has to be tooled. A Freemason ought to hew the undressed stone in order to obtain from it a cubic one suitable for embedding into the common edifice."

We agree with the allegorical and symbolic meaning of the above written; however, it deepens the contradiction of the likening of the apprentice to the cornerstone, in view of the form and function of the latter. According to the above quote, the apprentice, when turning into a cubic stone, only then becomes ready for embedding. It means that he cannot be possibly symbolized by the first stone in the edifice, which is placed in the corner to set the correct parameters of the building. We do not find any smoothing of this contradiction, as well as any answer to the question of why the newly admitted apprentice symbolically stands in the northeast, where this stone is laid, also in "Approved Oration, Oration Number: OR10053, Level: Beginner" of the *United Grand Lodge of England (UGLE)* of 2012 entitled *The Foundation Stone*, addressed to the "Provincial Grand Orators". We will quote part of what is written there:

"... The newly initiated Candidate... hears these words which you are all familiar with at the start of the First Degree Charge: 'It is customary, at the erection of all stately and superb edifices, to lay the first or foundation stone at the north-east corner of the building...' In this important part of the ceremony, the candidate is in the northeast corner of the Lodge, standing as a just and upright Mason."

"We are told that the candidate is placed in the north-east corner of the Lodge, figuratively to represent the foundation stone. A possible Masonic explanation for using the particular position is that it symbolizes the Entered Apprentice beginning his Masonic life. He is turning the corner from the darkness of ignorance, and is facing the dawning light of the East. He has received some light in the East and is in search of more. Another Masonic explanation is that the 'North' refers to the outer or profane world, and the 'East' – the inner world of Masonry; and hence the north-east is symbolic of the double position of the neophyte, partly in the darkness of the former, partly in the light of the latter."

"The high symbolic importance of the foundation stone was well established by the time of the building of King Solomon's Temple. The builders of ancient times were highly skilled in constructing walls. They knew how to economise without compromising the integrity of the buildings, by constructing corners and supports of carefully dressed stone. These cornerstones which guaranteed strength and stability became a colloquial term in biblical times, and are referred to in the Old Testament to describe leaders or prominent men."

(Here, too, we cannot refrain from asking the following rhetorical question: How do these dressed cornerstones, symbolizing these leaders and prominent men, correlate to what is written above about the neophyte?)

We will continue quoting the speech:

"In order to answer the question of the Candidate's location in the northeast, perhaps we should look at building customs and traditions at the turn of the 18th Century when our original rituals were written. In particular, whether it was traditional to lay the foundation stones of stately and superb edifices at the north-east corner! Before the advent of Freemasonry, a great deal of ritual was performed at these stone layings. For example, one early English record shows this to be the case at *Vale Royal Abbey, Delamere Forest, Cheshire*, around 1338, and reads as follows: '… Edward, the most illustrious King of England, in an assembly of all the greatest people of the kingdom, with his own hands put the first stone in place where the great altar was to be built… The foundation stone (or cornerstone) is the first stone set in the construction of a new edifice, which is important since all other stones will be set in reference to this stone, thus determining the position of the entire structure. Many old records show the stone as having been laid at the north-east corner. *There is, however, no documentation to support the theory that this had any bearing on those who wrote our ritual, but it does seem likely that it was the case; it would otherwise seem to be too much of a coincidence.* Certainly once Freemasonry was established, Masons were often called upon to perform the ceremony of laying a foundation stone for important buildings; and these were invariably carried out at the north-east corner. Unfortunately, the tradition has not been so much in evidence since the First World War."

From what is written there, we have certainly learned that the foundation stone (or cornerstone) is the first stone invariably laid at the northeast corner, "since all other stones will be set in reference to this stone, thus determining the position of the entire structure". We also learned that the newly admitted apprentice was positioned in the northeast part of the Lodge so that he may metaphorically represent the foundation stone. However, we did not understand the logic of the "position of the neophyte, partly in the darkness", and how it coincides with the position of the "first stone", the perfect sides (surfaces) of which ought to determine the perfection of the process of *Building the Edifice?*

The answer to the question about the newly admitted apprentice in the quoted oration is also extremely unsatisfactory: *"Many old records show the stone as having been laid at the north-east corner. There is, however, no docu-*

mentation to support the theory that this had any bearing on those who wrote our ritual, but it does seem likely that it was the case; it would otherwise seem to be too much of a coincidence".

Again, we wonder whether it is one the same stone which is called the "first stone", the "foundation stone", the "cornerstone", the "stone laid in the north-east", the "chief cornerstone"?

Therefore, since there is no traditional view, we continue looking for other sources on this topic. Such is the dictionary of the authoritative English Freemason George Oliver, *A Dictionary of Symbolical Masonry*, quoted quite often by Albert Mackey. In it, we read the following: "The Masonic Foundation-stone is said to have been inscribed with the awful Name or Word which is confided to the Perfect Master *(Perfect Master: 5$^{th}$ Degree of the Scottish Rite – AN)* when he has arrived at the highest dignity of the science. The characters were placed within an equilateral triangle and circle, as a symbol of the Divine Being under Whose protection this consecrated stone was placed, and hence it was frequently termed the *Stone of Life*. The Rabbins believed that, from the potency of this Word, the stone was invested with oracular powers, and many other singular virtues."

We shall also quote the definition of *cornerstone* in Oliver's *Dictionary*: "The first stone in the foundation of every magnificent building is called the *cornerstone,* and is laid in the north-east, generally with solemn and appropriate ceremonies… Its position accounts in a rational manner for the general disposition of a newly initiated candidate, when enlightened, but uninstructed, he is accounted to be the most superficial part of Masonry… In Alet's Ritual *(named after the bishop of Alet – AN)*, it is directed to be 'solid, angular, of about a foot square, and laid in the north-east'."

These definitions once again confirm the exceptional importance of the first stone, which is laid in the northeast. However, in addition, for the first time, someone distinguishes it, at least verbally, from the foundation stone. We also learn that because of the protection of the Divine Inscription on the foundation stone, it is often referred to as the "Stone of Life". According to the Hebrew tradition, however, in view of this quality of this stone, it was called *ha-Shetiyah,* and according to this tradition, it is the "first stone", which is the navel of the Earth, so it cannot in any way be a cornerstone. Thus, for the first time, it can be concluded that the cornerstone and the foundation stone are not identical, and that the foundation stone is the first symbolic stone, despite what George Oliver has written – that it is the cornerstone placed in the northeast. Unfortunately, there is no explanation as to why it is laid exactly in this place. We have seen that such an explanation is not contained also in the quoted "Approved Oration".

Many researchers have sought historical confirmation of the positioning of the stone in the northeast corner. One of the most ancient is certainly the case of laying the first stone in 1114 for the construction of Crowland Abbey, Lincolnshire, where "The venerable Abbat Joffird himself laid the first cornerstone on the eastern side, facing the North." Further in the same text, however, there is a remark from the master builder, where he explains that this was done for practical reasons, i.e. the position of the Sun at sunrise in the northeast is most appropriate.

Nearly 200 years later, there is another case of the Rosslyn Chapel in Scotland. The significance of these examples is unfortunately downplayed by the fact that there are many other constructions where the first stone was laid in the other three directions. For example, the *Dumfries No. 4 Manuscript* of 1710 positions quite precisely the Master in the Lodge, as well as the cornerstone of the Temple of Solomon, to the southeast. This is also the position of the cornerstone of the White House and the Congress Building in Washington, D.C., as well as the University of North Carolina, the first state university (1798). If indeed the northeast corner is an ancient Masonic symbol, then why, in one of the oldest written catechisms, as well as in these significant buildings, is the temple stone not placed there? Here is an excerpt from this manuscript:

"Q.: Who laid the first stone in the foundation of the Temple?
A.: The above said Hiram.
Q.: What place did he lay the first stone?
A.: In the **south-east corner** of the Temple."

In the catechism published in the London newspaper *The Post Boy*, which we already quoted, we read:

"*Q.: Who are the Four Corner Stones?*
A.: Four Fellow-Craftsmen.
*Q.: Who are the four Capitals?*
A.: Four **'Prentices**.
*Q.: **Who is Cupola?***
A.: **The new Brother**."

In this text, a radically different symbolism is noticed, which likens the newly adopted Brother to the cupola – the finishing element of the building, whereas the four corners are symbolized by fellow-craftsmen. There is also no unanimity regarding the position of the Master of the Lodge. The catechism of the first known printed edition of the Masonic Rite, published in *The Flying Post* in April 1723, positions the Master and the "Mark of the Craft" at the southeast again, which confirms what was said in the previous *Dumfries No.4 Manuscript* about the significance of this position.

In still another catechism, *Institution of Free Masons* of 1725, we read the following:

"Q.: Who rules & governs the Lodge & is Master of it?
A.: *Jehovah* the Right Pillar."

In *The Grand Mystery of Free-Masons Discovered* of 1724, we find the following:

"Q.: Who rules and governs the Lodge, and is Master of it?
A.: Irah/ Iachin, or the Right Pillar."

The position of the Master in the southeast is also indicated in *A Mason's Confession, ? 1727* and published in *The Scots Magazine* in March 1755: "To be particular,... the Master Mason stands at the south-east corner of the Lodge, and the fellow-crafts next to him, and next to them the wardens, and next the entered prentices."

The question arises as to when and why in the Masonic Rite of the United Grand Lodge of England a change occurs in the positions of the Master and the first stone, and hence of the newly admitted apprentice? As we have seen, the *Mother Lodge of the World* itself does not give any answer to this question in the oration approved by itself. However, our research, without claiming to be exhaustive, has found out some facts that we need to share in order to shed light on the issue.

*Masonry Dissected* by Samuel Prichard of 1730 is one of the most influential and successful early expositions of Freemasonry. By 1760, it had been republished 14 times. Prichard presents the earliest version of the Legend of Hiram, as well as the Third Master's Degree Rite. His influence on the development of the Masonic Rites is enormous, and his practices dominate until 1769. He is the first to hint in the ceremony about the positioning of the newly initiated apprentice in the northeast, although this is done at the beginning, not at the end of the admission. Prichard firmly points out the East as the position of the Master, whereas the West – of the two Wardens.[99] He also specifies the positions of the old and the new apprentice, with only the North being mentioned regarding the latter, not the North-East as the usual position. The conclusion so far is that in 1730, in the Masonic Rites there is no ancient original tradition and symbolism associated with the cornerstone to position the newly admitted apprentice in the northeast corner.

In 1760, the Masonic Rites became more established, and changes in them can be traced in the following Masonic expositions: *Three Distinct Knocks* (1760) and *Jachin and Boaz* (1762), according to which the Master is positioned in the East, the First (Senior) Warden – in the West, and the Second

---

[99] Thirty years later, the Second (Junior) Warden is repositioned from the West to the South – *AN*.

(Junior) Warden – in the South, as it is today in England and America. The position of the newly adopted apprentice was established at the northernmost part of the Lodge, although his final position was not yet been determined.

In 1772, William Preston publishes his book *Illustrations of Masonry*, which brings a significant change into the Masonic Rite. This book creates order in the chaos of these Rites by presenting an official version of lectures, forms and ceremonies. The Lodges were no longer forced to rely on the memory of their own members, on unauthorized manuscripts, or on unreliable expositions. The quoted book was officially approved by Grand Master Lord Petre (Robert Edward Petre).

When William Preston presented the official Masonic Rite, he did not publish anything esoteric, nor the exact distribution of the speakers' sides, nor explanations regarding the movements in the temple. He does not mention any special position for the new apprentice, nor for the Master, nor the Wardens; and yet, he has described in detail the requirements for "The Ceremony Observed at Laying the Foundation Stones of Public Structures". Preston gives instructions regarding the garments, the music, the order of the procession, the hymns, the prayers and the laying of the stone, but not a word is mentioned regarding the position of its laying. In the context of so much elaborate detail, the lack of information about the precise position of the cornerstone reveals that it was not of essential significance.

*Illustrations of Masonry* provides a solid foundation on which the future Masonic Rites will be built; however, even Preston's work does not solve all ritual issues. In 1772, there are two rival Grand Lodges of England – the "modern" one, founded in 1717, and the "ancient" one, since 1753, with different ideas regarding the ceremonies, not to mention the countless separate Lodges, each with its own views on rituality. The two Grand Lodges competed for control over the craft until 1813, when they merged into the *United Grand Lodge of England (UGLE)*. After this event, the *Emulation Rite* gives definiteness to the Rite in principle, and above all, regarding the specific topic in view. It was practiced at the *Emulation Lodge of Improvement*, which first met on 2 October 1823, in *Freemasons' Hall* in London, and is held under the sanction of *Lodge of Unions No. 256* in the English Constitution. Access was restricted to Master Masons only. The purpose of the Lodge is to preserve the Masonic Rite practiced by it and officially adopted by the newly formed *United Grand Lodge of England* in 1816.

One of the main founders of this Rite is considered to be Peter William Gilkes. The Rite was published after his death in 1833, and in it, it is claimed that the very Rite is related to the most ancient Rites of Operative Freemasonry. We will quote a short excerpt from the *Emulation Rite* for admission of a Seeker:

The Worshipful Master *(addressing the newly admitted apprentice):* "It is customary, at the erection of all stately and superb edifices, to lay the first or foundation stone at the North-East corner of the building. You, being newly admitted into Masonry, are placed at the North-East part of the Lodge, to represent figuratively that stone, and from the foundation laid this evening, may you raise a superstructure – perfect in its parts and honourable to the builder."

From the exposition so far, at least to us, the conclusion is clearly outlined that the symbolic identification of the newly admitted apprentice with the first stone (cornerstone) laid in the northeast in the Rites of the *United Grand Lodge of England,* as well as other Orients, is not based on ancient, original and firm Masonic tradition. Furthermore, as it turned out, this identification leads to a contradiction between the symbolic aspect of the Northeast, corresponding to the ambivalent characteristic of the apprentice, on the one hand, and the purely constructional qualities and shape of the cornerstone, on the other.

We have penetrated into this somewhat boring specificity and detail only and solely to substantiate the essential conclusion that relating the newly admitted apprentice to the stone in the northeast corner is an innovation, moreover – not in the overall Masonic symbolism; whereas, how appropriate it is – we leave this to the judgment of the reader. We believe that we have given enough examples – and yet, at the risk of boring the reader to the extreme, we will allow ourselves to quote parts of some Masonic Minutes, which seem to deepen the ambiguity on this subject, but they still introduce a new aspect that gives us the opportunity to return again to the chief cornerstone and to what is written by Jean Palou.

## Fragments of Masonic Minutes

*From French sources:*

"The cornerstone is placed at the summit as the crowning of the building. It is one of its kind, with its unique form, and is also a symbol of the Unity that embodies everything, thus closing the cycle."

"The cornerstone at the summit is also called 'the eye of the dome', as it is reflected in each of the foundation stones at the four corners of the base. In the Masonic symbolism of the English tradition, the newly admitted Mason apprentice is considered to be the cornerstone of the Temple which is to be built, and is therefore placed in the northeast."

*From the Grand Lodge Alpina of Switzerland:*

"... In one of the Rites, the following is quoted: 'It is written in the Bible: 'Behold, I lay in Zion a stone for a foundation, a tried stone, a precious cornerstone, a sure foundation' (*Isaiah* 28:16, *NKJV – ed.*) – the stone that was worthless to the builders has become the chief cornerstone of the temple (that of the dome, of the arch). In Gothic cathedrals, the cornerstone, also called *chief cornerstone (key of the dome),* corresponds, along the vertical line, to the stone representing the altar. The cornerstone not only performs the function of connecting two structures, but also of evenly distributing their load, and therefore it represents a fundamental irreplaceable element for the harmony of the whole edifice. Symbolically, the sharp corner of the typical vaults of the Gothic style represents the synthesis of Masonic thought."

*From the Confederation of Regular Grand Lodges of the United Mexican States:*
"Therefore, the apprentice is positioned in the northeast corner at the base of the edifice, at the place of the first stone, as a symbol which means that the apprentice has to build the Temple within himself, and has already laid the first stone. That is why apprentices represent the fundamental elements of Masonic philosophy. On the other hand, the Worshipful Master is the other cornerstone, through which, the arch of knowledge and the light of the Masonic Temple are closed. The difference between the two stones consists in the fact where their purity and knowledge of Freemasonry are positioned, the first being a rough stone, and the second – a perfectly dressed one."

*From a Lodge in Argentina:*
"G.A.O.T.U. (The *Great Architect of the Universe*) is the Supreme Primordial Principle, the true Cornerstone of the Masonic Temple, represented by the stone closing the vault. Under the influence of this Principle, Freemasons hold their workshops in the Lodge, which becomes a reflection of the Universe."

The written in these Masonic Minutes sounds quite familiar, which is due to the multiplied inertness in viewing the topic, perhaps because of what has already been said by some, considered to be authorities, and mostly due to lack of understanding of the discussed symbolism. However, there is a perceptible development on the topic of the *cornerstone,* as new symbolic and constructive aspects appear in its capacity also of the *last stone, summit stone, keystone,* and ultimately, the *chief cornerstone,* which was rejected by the builders. All of them are influenced by the works of René Guénon – however, inadequate examples are given with domes and pointed arches of cathedrals. We say *inadequate* because the verse "The stone which the builders rejected is become the Head of the Corner" is in the *Psalter (118:22, ASV),* containing Psalms dating from the 15th to the 9th century BC – an epoch in which the only significant edifice built by the Hebrews, according to them, is the Temple of Solomon, the roof of which, however, was wooden. We will dwell on this question further. We will now quote also a mysterious person who has written several alchemical treatises, under the pseudonym *Fulcanelli*, who will shed light from another angle on the symbolism of the "first stone". In his book *The Mystery of the Cathedrals,* we read the following: "It is thus that the ground plan of a Christian building reveals to us the qualities of the first matter, and its preparation by the sign of the Cross, which points the way for the alchemist to obtain the First Stone – the Cornerstone of the Philosophers' Great Work. It is on this stone that Jesus built His Church; and the medieval Freemasons have symbolically followed the Divine example. But before being dressed to serve as a base for the work of gothic art, as well as for the philosophical work of art, the rough, impure, gross and unpolished stone was often given the image of the devil. Notre Dame of Paris possessed a similar hieroglyph... It was a figure of the devil, opening an enormous mouth... The common people called this image *Maistre Pierre du Coignet ('Master Peter (stone) of the Corner')*... Now, this stone, which was intended to represent the first matter of the Work, personified under the aspect of Lucifer, was the symbol of our cornerstone, the headstone of the corner."

We find the above written rather vague and contradictory. In the end, it is not completely clear whether the first stone, a symbol of the first matter, is the undressed stone from which the chief cornerstone is made, or we are talking about one and the same dressed stone. On the one hand, the first matter representing chaos is associated with the undressed stone, which is why it is associated with the Devil, respectively Lucifer, who represents a symbol of the chief cornerstone, because the latter is his emanation. On the other hand, however, it is claimed that the First Stone, namely, is the Cornerstone of the Philosophers' Great Work, and on this stone Jesus builds His Church.

In order to introduce some logic into all of this, we will say that, in our opinion, in the given quotation, Lucifer should be the undressed stone, symbolizing the first matter, while Christ should be the Chief Cornerstone obtained from it. However, we utilize what Fulcanelli has written only as a direction of thinking, leaving the readers to draw their own conclusions. For the same reason, we will quote also Moïse Amyraut, a French Protestant theologian and metaphysician, who says: "The stone which the builders rejected was the supporting cornerstone upon which the whole structure of the building rested". We hope that the author speaks in a symbolic context, because otherwise it would mean the deliberate destruction of the building.

After the English Mason George Oliver, who is considered an authority, has brought some clarity by differentiating the cornerstone from the foundation stone, we, in order to shed more light on the subject, will turn to another authority in Christian symbolism and architecture. This is Jean Hani, a French philosopher and Traditionalist author, and a professor of Greek philosophy and literature at the University of Amiens. According to the theologian Jean Borella, Hani was the first author in academia to successfully marry Guénon's insights to the contemporary study of Hellenistic religions and Christianity. In his book *Le Symbolisme du Temple Chrétien (The Symbolism of the Christian Temple)*, Jean Hani writes the following: "There have been various altars in the Temple of Jerusalem... In the Holy of Holies, there was no altar, in the true sense of this word, but a stone, particularly sacred – the *ha-Shetiyah* stone – upon which the Ark of the Covenant was placed... The rock with the great altar represents the centre of the world, whereas inside the Temple of Jerusalem, another stone represented it in an even clearer way, and that is the *ha-Shetiyah* stone, positioned in the Holy of Holies, upon which the Ark was placed. For some, this stone is none else but Jacob's stone. The *fundamental stones* are the cubic stones placed in the four corners of the building; the one placed at the northeast is usually called *fundamental stone* or *first stone*. The *foundation stone*, or *ha-Shetiyah*, is the one positioned in the centre of the foundation of the building. Finally, the cornerstone – either the 'chief cornerstone' or the 'head of the corner' – is actually the one at the other end opposite to the *ha-Shetiyah* stone on the same vertical axis, and it represents the *keystone*. However, some confusions coming from far away have downgraded these different denominations. This results in a mix-up of the *fundamental stone* with the *foundation stone* – or the *central stone* – and very often the word *keystone* is used for the first stone or for the fundamental stone in the northeast corner, and even for the *ha-Shetiyah* stone... These four stones may certainly be called 'cornerstones', because they represent exactly the corners of the foundation, so from this point of view they perform the same function as the summit stone, which has the task to join and solder two walls or the two arches of the vault. Only these stones, like the *ha-Shetiyah* stone, are cubic ones, while the cornerstone at the summit has a specific and unique shape, such that it cannot find a place during the construction process, to the point that "the builders rejected" it: its purpose is understood only by the builders who have passed "from the Square to the Compass", that is, from the square to the circle, or from Earth to Heaven – the spiritual ones. To the *ha-Shetiyah* stone (the altar) below, the cornerstone in the vault corresponds – the summit stone, the keystone."

The above written demands the conclusion that Jean Hani distinguishes three types of stones: a *fundamental stone* or *first stone*, placed in the northeast; a *foundation stone (central stone)* – *ha-Shetiyah*; a *cornerstone placed at the summit*, which is why it represents the *summit stone*, the *keystone*, and ultimately – the *chief cornerstone*. It is evident that Hani is mainly influenced by René Guénon, and therefore he defines the *ha-Shetiyah* stone as a cubic one, like those in the four corners of the foundation, with which we do not agree, as with some other formulations of his, and it is utmost time to dwell on what was written by the respected by us Guénon. Of course, what we will engage the attention of the readers with will no longer be unknown to them, in view of the authors quoted so far, and yet, we are still obliged to finally get acquainted with the original as well. We may, like the authors quoted by us, paraphrase and retell, but still, for more complete illustration, we will provide the reader with a very small part of the quite detailed elaborate work of the wordy and lengthy René Guénon in his book *Fundamental Symbols: The Universal Language of Sacred Science*.

### René Guénon

"The 'foundation stone' is the one which is positioned first, at the very outset of the construction of a building (and this is why it is also called the 'first stone'); how then could it be rejected in the course of this very same construction? For that to be so it is necessary, on the contrary, that the 'cornerstone' be such that it cannot as yet find its place; and in fact, as we will see, it cannot find it except at the moment of the completion of the entire edifice, and it is thus that it really becomes the 'head of the angle'."

"The 'foundation stone' can, in a certain sense, be called a 'cornerstone' as it usually is, for it is placed at an angle or at a corner of the edifice; but it is not unique as such, the edifice necessarily having four angles... It in no way differs from the foundation stones of the other angles except by its situation, and it is not distinguished from them either by its form or its function, being just one of four supports all equal to each other. It could be said that any other of the four 'cornerstones' 'reflects' in a sense the dominant principle of the edifice, but it could in no way be considered as being the principle itself. Moreover, if this were really all there is to it, we could not even speak logically of '*the* cornerstone', as in fact there would be four of them. Thus the cornerstone must be something essentially different from a 'cornerstone' understood in the current sense of 'foundation stone', and all they have in common is that they both pertain to the same symbolism of construction."

"The 'cornerstone'... It is because this stone has a special and unique shape which sets it apart from all the others that not only can it not find its place in the course of the construction, but even the builders cannot understand its purpose... And... they decide to 'heave it over among the rubbish', believing it to be unusable. The purpose of this stone cannot be understood except by another category of builders, who have not yet come upon the scene.

These are they who have passed 'from the try-square to the compass'... The geometric forms which these two instruments respectively serve to trace, namely, the square and the circle which are known to symbolize in a general way Earth and Heaven... The square form corresponds here to the lower part of the building, and the circular form – to the upper part which, in this case, must consist either of a dome or a vault. In fact, the 'cornerstone' is in reality a 'keystone'... Thus this stone, by its shape as well as by its position, is really unique in the entire edifice, as it must be to symbolize the principle on which all depends."

"The 'summit stone' and the "foundation stone' are on the same vertical line so that the 'foundation stone' is as the horizontal projection of the 'summit stone' on to the level of the foundation. It could be said that the 'foundation stone' synthesizes in itself, even while remaining on the same level, the partial aspects represented by the stones of the four angles."

"The *cornerstone*... represents the 'stone come down from Heaven'... This same stone is, on the other hand, identified with the one which Jacob consecrated at Bethel. Nor is that all: according to the Hebrew tradition it would also seem to have been the stone which followed the Israelites in the desert and from which flowed the water they drank of, and which according to St. Paul's interpretation was none other than Christ Himself. It is then supposed to have become the *ha-Shethiyah*, or 'foundation stone', placed in the Temple of Jerusalem beneath the Ark of the Covenant, and thus marking symbolically the 'centre of the world', likewise represented in another traditional form by the *Omphalos* of Delphi."

At the risk of boring the reader to the extreme, we will quote some more essential fragments of this book:

"The 'cornerstone', taken in its true sense of 'summit stone', is designated, in English, both as *keystone* and as *capstone* (the last term is sometimes found also written as *capestone*), and as *copestone* (or *coping-stone*)... In *capstone*, the word *cap* is obviously the Latin *caput*, 'head', which brings us back to the designation of this stone as the 'head of the angle'; this is the stone which 'achieves' or 'crowns' an edifice; and it is also a capital, which is in the same way the 'crowning' of a column."

"As for the word *copestone*, the word *cope* expresses the idea of 'to cover'. This is to be explained by the fact, not only that the upper part of the edifice is its 'cover', but also – and we would even say especially – that this stone is placed in such a way as to cover the opening of the summit, that is, the 'eye' of the dome or vault, of which we have already spoken."

"We can now return to the representation of the 'cornerstone' in the form of a diamond... Generally, the stone or the metal which was considered as the hardest and the most brilliant has been taken, in different traditions, as a symbol of 'indestructibility, of invulnerability, of stability, of light, and of immortality'; and these qualities in particular are very often attributed to the diamond."

"The 'summit stone' may not in every case be the 'key of the vault', and in fact is only so in domed structures. In every other case…, there is none the less a 'last stone' which, placed at the summit, plays the same part as the 'key of the vault' in this respect, and which consequently corresponds to it from a symbolic point of view, but without it being possible to designate it by the same name; and as much must be said of the special case of the 'pyramidion' to which we have alluded on another occasion… The 'pyramidion', that is, the stone forming the upper point of the pyramid, is in no way a 'key of the vault'; but it is, none the less, the 'crown' of the edifice… The expression 'head of the angle', in the literal sense, fits it quite well, as does also the figurative sense of the Hebrew word for 'angle' as meaning the 'chief'."

From the above excerpts, it surely becomes clear to the reader that all those who have written on this subject are more or less influenced by René Guénon, so the question arises as to why we had to quote them as well, and not only him. The answer is that we would like to prove the lack of an ancient original Masonic tradition and knowledge of such a key topic as the undressed stone and dressed stone. We believe that this is so because in his works, which are the most extensive and in-depth on this subject, Guénon does not use such a tradition but an article by Ananda Coomaraswamy in *The Indian Historical Quarterly*, which he comments on and develops further with his views and knowledge of the Hebrew, Sufi, Hindu and Islamic traditions. We also show that, in the absence of any tradition, one should not blindly repeat and multiply someone else's views, which are considered authoritative. We have seen that even prominent Christian theologians are no exception. It is no coincidence that one of the symbols in Freemasonry is the rooster, which is an indication towards vigilance. We ought to be careful regarding everything said by authorities that has not stood the test of tradition and time. After all, some of the main characteristics of Freemasonry, evincing its permanence, are formed by the circumstance that it possesses truths that are not subject to time and continuity of tradition. However, if, in the absence of any authentic tradition, without being vigilant, we repeat and disseminate in various contexts even what is said by authorities, we may turn untruths, half-truths and even truths into pseudo-truths. Therefore, in the following lines we will be vigilant also with regard to what has been written by the respected by us René Guénon, in order to winnow the grain from the chaff, if any, and thus we will show attitude also towards everyone else who have written on this subject.

From the examples given so far, it became clear that according to Guénon, "the 'cornerstone'... has a special and unique shape which sets it apart from all the others", and is not in any case the "foundation stone", also called "first stone", notwithstanding the fact that the latter may also be called *cornerstone*, as it is laid in the corner of the building. This means, however, that it does not differ from the other cornerstones in the foundation, in view of their general functional purpose: to set the right angle to the walls of the building. The definition of the "foundation stone" in the singular is due to its superiority in laying, hence its symbolism as the beginning of something new. The definition of a "cornerstone" is also in the singular – however, as we have learned, its uniqueness is due to its shape.

In his work *Black Stone and Cubic Stone*, René Guénon writes the following: "The 'cubic stone' is essentially a 'foundation stone'... but clearly, this is no reason for identifying with the 'cubic stone' a 'black stone' which was really conical. There is only one particular case in which there is a certain connection between the 'black stone' and the 'cubic stone': this is where the cubic stone is not one of the 'foundation stones' placed at the four angles of a building, but rather the *ha-Shetiyah* stone at the very centre of its base, corresponding to the point of impact of the fallen 'black stone', just as, on the same vertical axis but at its opposite extremity, the 'cornerstone' or 'summit stone' (which, on the contrary, is not of cubic shape), corresponds to the initial and final 'celestial' position of the same 'black stone'."

From this example, on the other hand, it becomes clear that the "foundation stone", along with the other cornerstones in the foundation, all have a cubic shape, which means that the chief cornerstone does not have such a shape. Its shape is determined by its purpose as a "key of the vault", as well as a summit stone that completes or crowns the building.

**Figure 28**

# Keystone

> *When the solution is simple,*
> *God is answering.*
>
> **Albert Einstein**

From an architectural and constructional point of view, a *keystone* is a wedge-shaped stone marking the summit of an arch or vault, which in architecture has the function to constructively support the element centrally in one whole so that it does not collapse. The keystone represents such a stone only in this type of constructions, and has the shape of an inverted isosceles trapezoid. In this situation, strictly speaking from a construction-architectural angle, we do not find any option in which this stone can be called a "cornerstone" or "head of the corner". There is no such a stone also in the triangular arch, as well as in the pointed arch of the Gothic vault, because such a stone is structurally absent in them. Here we recall the Masonic Minutes of the *Grand Lodge Alpina of Switzerland,* which speaks of the "keystone" ("cornerstone") of the sharp-pointed Gothic arch, which performs a balancing function, and we leave the conclusions to the reader.

This is how the outline is formed of our first disagreement with Guénon's view that the "cornerstone" is the keystone, which is essentially the "head of the angle", because the shape of the keystone does not allow it to be a stone at any corner.

Guénon says that the "summit stone" – which is the *chief cornerstone* – "may not in every case be the *key of the vault*", which means that sometimes the keystone is the last stone. These are the cases when, in its capacity of a *copestone,* it crowns the dome of a building and is placed in such a way as to close the opening at the summit, i.e. the "eye". Thus, each last stone, except in these cases, represents a *summit stone* and is essentially a *chief cornerstone*, but it cannot be called a *keystone*. This means also that the "key of the vault" does not always represent the last summit stone. In this sense, the presentation of the "chief cornerstone" may be in the form of a diamond as a symbol of indestructibility, stability and firmness, but the typical example given by Guénon is with the pyramidion at the summit of the building, which, however, from a structural point of view, is not the "key of the vault".

According to these examples, it seems that the following question arises inevitably: If, in a building, there are both a keystone (at an arch under the dome) and a summit stone (at the dome), all at the same time, which is quite possible, which one shall be called the *chief cornerstone,* since by definition it should be unique?

The question is not posed and discussed – however, its answer will clearly distinguish the two stones, because, the way they are presented, it seems to us that their border is quite in a typical "Sfumato" style. According to Guénon's views, the summit stone is the "stone come down from Heaven", and, as such, it represents the sacral principle of the building, which is the core essence of the chief cornerstone, no matter that it is laid last. Thus, the answer to the question asked in Guénon's conceptual context should be that the *capstone* is that chief cornerstone, which is the "head of the corner" and represents the stone rejected by the builders. The same, but with greater force, can be said also of the *copestone* in the shape of a truncated cone for the dome, or as a pyramidion, which descends as if from above into its corresponding nest, in order to crown the building rather as an ornament. In this sense, it has a symbolic character rather than any structural significance. This also applies to the summit stone of the dome, which, according to us, unlike Guénon, does not play the role of a keystone. Thus, the conclusion is inevitable that the *keystone* has an extremely structural significance and cannot be identified with the *capstone*, much less with the *copestone*, as Guénon does, because it represents the last one (the finishing one) only regarding the arch and the vault, but not the building itself. Confirmation of this is a building with a flat roof, where the last stone, which must be in one of the corners, cannot in any way be a keystone. This example shows, on its turn, that the chief cornerstone, as the last stone, may also be cubic, contrary to what Guénon has said. His view that it must have a unique shape is perhaps based on the explanation that the stone was thrown "among the rubbish" by the builders because they did not know its purpose, according to a legend.

## Legend of the Stone

One day the builders of the Temple of Solomon received from the quarry a stone of unusual shape and measurements. They tried to put it in different places on the construction site, but saw that it could not fit anywhere, so they decided to get rid of it, threw it by the roadside and continued working. Seven years passed and the Temple was completed, and only the last stone was left to be laid. Since the builders did not have a suitable one available, they went to the quarry to ask for it. There they were told that many years ago they had dressed it and sent it exactly according to the construction plan. The builders returned to the Temple, absorbed in thought, and then remembered of the rejected stone. They found it right where they had placed it so long ago, among the overgrown weeds, dirty but perfectly intact. They immediately knew from the shape that this was the stone they were looking for. They washed it and placed it at the summit, finishing the Temple.

This legend underlies the Mark Mason ritual, about which a high-ranking Italian Freemason writes the following: "A Master Mason joining the *Royal Arch* directly from the 'Blue Freemasonry', as many do under the English Constitution, is confronted with a sudden and confusing change of symbolism. This is so because a very important intermediate step has been skipped: that of the 'Mark', which adds a substantial background and symbolism to the construction of the Temple, the main arch and the keystone, representing a clear introduction to the *Royal Arch* ceremony".

The *Legend of the Mark Master Degree* tells of the creation, by a Fellow Craft, of the keystone, the discovery of which allowed the creation of the arch through which one walks into the most sacred part of the temple. This stone, hewn in an unusual shape, was at first thrown among the rubbish by the Wardens, and the Fellow Craft was punished; however, later on they realized that the completion of the temple depended on this stone, the mistake was corrected, and the Fellow Craft was raised to the Mark Master Degree. The keystone was searched for, found and placed at the summit of the arch, and thus the temple was completed. This event is celebrated in the beautiful ceremony of the *"Most Excellent Master"*.

We do not know whether this legend is authentic, or it is the fruit of the Mark Ritual; and still, what bewilders us most is that the stone is placed at the summit of the arch of the temple. However, we are most puzzled by some phrases from the content of the *Royal Arch Rite*, where the Brothers are *"Exalted"*, and which we will allow ourselves to quote:

"Rise, **wrench forth** the keystone, and prepare to receive the light of the Holy Word!"

"... We therefore enlarged the aperture by **removing** the keystone."

"... The secrets of the *Royal Arch* were only regained by **wrenching forth** the keystone thereof."

According to Catholic criticism, this means "removing" Jesus Christ, likened to the keystone. Further on, we will focus on the relation between Jesus Christ and the keystone, but here we cannot fail to point out that the removal of this stone is ridiculous nonsense, as this would lead, as we have already explained, to the collapse of the arch. This misconception, in our opinion, is again due to the identification of the *keystone* with the *capstone*, since we believe that the quoted phrases refer to the last stone, which represents a "stopper" of the summit aperture of the temple, without any constructive purpose. Zealous Catholics can rest easy because Masons do not "remove" Jesus Christ in His capacity of the Keystone.

Since this Rite often mentions the *Royal Arch* in Solomon's Temple, and there is no trace of this Arch in the Bible, this reawakens our vigilance and urges us to explore the Temple of Solomon from a purely constructional point of view.

**Figure 29**

# 17
# The Temple of Solomon

## Sources

*Now Solomon began to build the house of the Lord at Jerusalem on Mount Moriah, where the Lord had appeared to his father David, at the place that David had prepared on the threshing floor of Ornan the Jebusite.*

**2 Paralipomenon (Chronicles) 3:1, NKJV**

Glen Knape – a teacher, writer, editor, publisher and Master Mason, in one of his most famous works – *The Temple and The Word*, writes the following:

"… This leaves us with three, presumably allegorical temples, including:
- The Tabernacle
- King Solomon's Temple
- Ezekiel's Temple"

253

"We may safely consider them entirely allegorical, as there is no hard evidence that any of these three temples were ever physical buildings!"

"How we experience this structure depends on how we approach it:
- If we approach it as the persona (body, emotions, and mind), we see the Tabernacle. The three initiations then represent the spiritual progress of the persona.
- If we approach it as the Soul, we see the Temple of Solomon. The three initiations then represent the spiritual progress of the Soul.
- If we approach it as the Spirit, we see the Temple of Ezekiel. The three initiations then represent the progress of the Spirit."

From the quoted text, it becomes clear that this author considers the Tabernacle and the Temple of Solomon to be absolute allegories and symbols of the human being as a triune entity, not as actually existing objects. His statement that "there is no hard evidence that any of these three temples were ever physical buildings" is accepted by us in the sense of "outside the Bible", and yet, even in this context, it is not precise. We find such a statement in the book of Flavius Josephus – *Antiquities of the Jews,* from where we quote Book VIII, Chapter 3:2: "The roof that was over the house was of cedar; and truly every one of these rooms had a roof of their own, that was not connected with the other rooms; but for the other parts *(the veritable Temple – AN),* there was a covered roof common to them all, and built with very long beams, that passed through the rest, and through the whole building, that so the middle walls, being strengthened by the same beams of timber, might be thereby made firmer". Further on in the same chapter, it is written: "The whole structure of the Temple was made with great skill of polished stones, and those laid together so very harmoniously and smoothly, that there appeared to the spectators no sign of any hammer, or other instrument of architecture; but as if, without any use of them, the entire materials had naturally united themselves together, that the agreement of one part with another seemed rather to have been natural, than to have arisen from the force of tools upon them."

The main source, but not the only one, as it turned out, regarding the existence of the Tabernacle and the Temple of Solomon is, of course, the Old Testament, in which the following is written: "When David was dwelling in his house, that David said to Nathan the Prophet, 'See now, I dwell in a house of cedar, but the Ark of the Covenant of the Lord is under tent curtains'... But it happened that night that the Word of God came to Nathan, saying, 'Go and tell My servant David, 'Thus says the Lord: 'You shall not build Me a house to dwell in'." *(1 Paralipomenon/ Chronicles* 17:1 – 4, *NKJV)*

This lays the beginning of the prehistory of Solomon's Temple. King David is forbidden, by the Most High, to build the House of the Lord, because

David has shed a lot of blood, but instead he prepares everything for the future construction, and bequeaths to his son Solomon to build the Temple.

"... I had it in my heart to build a house of rest for the Ark of the Covenant of the Lord... and had made preparations to build it." (*1 Paralipomenon* 28:2, *NKJV*)

What is needed for the construction is described in great detail, but regarding this topic, we are interested in what is said in *1 Paralipomenon* 22:2 – "and he appointed masons to cut hewn stones to build the House of God" *(NKJV)*.

The information contained in *1 Paralipomenon* 28:11 is also important: "Then David gave his son Solomon the plans for the vestibule, its houses, its treasuries, its upper chambers, its inner chambers, and the place of the mercy seat" *(NKJV)*. And, most of all, that everything is indicated directly by the Lord: "... 'All this', said David, 'the Lord made me understand in writing, by His hand upon me, all the works of these plans'." (*1 Paralipomenon* 28:19, *NKJV*)

In the course of seven and a half years, Solomon keeps building the House of the Lord, described in detail in *2 Paralipomenon*. After finishing this House, he consecrated it with ceremonies and prayers, again described in great detail. However, nothing is mentioned neither of the first stone, nor the last stone, nor the fundamental stone, nor the cornerstone, nor the chief cornerstone. If we accept what Guénon has said, then, with the exception of the fundamental stones, the other stones should crown the vault, the arch or the dome of the edifice. We need to find out what the roof of Solomon's Temple was like.

**Figure 30**

In the Bulgarian Synodal edition of the Bible, or *Bulgarian Orthodox Bible (BOB)*, it seems that at first glance there is no explicit information about what material the roof was made of. This is so because the Bulgarian word for *"overlaid"* that is used here, *"обложи" [ɔb'lɔʒi]*, has a twofold meaning and is originally perceived in the meaning of *"tiled"*, *"faced"*: "Тъй съгради той храма, завърши го и го **обложи** с кедрови дъски." ("Thus he built the Temple, finished it, and **overlaid** it with cedar boards.") (*1 Kings 6:9, BOB*)

According to the *Dictionary of the Bulgarian Language*, however, the word *"обложи"* means also "(he) *covered* (it with something)". To make sure that it is used in this meaning, we have made a reference to the *New International Version (NIV)* of the Bible, where we read the following: *"So he built the temple and completed it, **roofing** it with beams and cedar planks."*

After that, we have resorted to a comparison with the Roman Catholic version of the Bible, in which the same verse is written as follows: *"Dette inizio alla costruzione del tempio e la portò a termine, e **coprì** il tempio con assi e con travatura di cedro."*

Finally, we have come also to *TANAKH* – the so-called *Hebrew Bible*, as well as its English translation:

1 *Kings*, Chapter 6:9

ויבן את־הבית ויכלהו ויספן את־הבית גבים ושדרת בארזים

*"So he built the house, and finished it; and he **covered** the house with planks of cedar over beams."*

We have found that the words used in the three quotations are ***roofing***, ***coprì*** – from ***coprire***[100], and ***covered***, all of them with the meaning of "covering".

To be absolutely sure that the point is about covering, we will quote also the following text from the *New International Version (NIV)* of the Bible:

*"He **lined** its interior walls with cedar boards, **panelling** them from the floor of the temple to the ceiling, and covered the floor of the temple with planks of juniper."* (*1 Kings* 6:15)

It is evident that other words are used to describe the panelling of the temple, different from those denoting its covering. In the Bulgarian Synodal translation, one and the same word is used in both cases – *"обложи"* ("tiled", "faced", "covered"), but in one of these cases, with the meaning of "covered".

We believe that no further evidence is needed that the roof of Solomon's Temple was covered with cedar beams and planks. However, we should ascertain also its shape, and for that purpose, the shape of the Tabernacle will help us, because it is considered to be the prototype of the Temple.

---

100 *Coprire:* "to cover", "to wrap", "to shield" – *AN*.

**Figure 31**

## The Tabernacle

*So the Holy Tent [Tabernacle] was set up on the first day of the first month during the second year after they left Egypt.*

**Second Book of Moses – Exodus 40:17, EXB**

Many scholars, with Julius Wellhausen at the head, whom we already know, fully agree that the whole story of the Tabernacle is the work of priests, and they date this narrative to the period of exile or after that. In the 20th century, there was much discussion whether the story of the Tabernacle is fabricated, or it represents a true historical fact. As a whole, however, most analysts of the *Second Book of Moses – Exodus* of the Old Testament, do not believe that this represents an authentic narrative, including with respect to the very Tabernacle in the desert. As Wellhausen comments, "It looks too heavy to be a mobile structure, with its 1.25 tons of gold, 4 tons of silver, and 3 tons of bronze used to build it. The Tabernacle is much more likely to represent the idealized tent-shrine at Shiloh or that of David than to have actually existed in the wilderness at the time of Moses".

According to Wellhausen, the Tabernacle is a fabrication of the sacerdotal scribes, who could not imagine Israel without a sanctuary in its most ancient history. Therefore, the Tabernacle is a copy of the Temple, not its prototype. It is very likely that there was a tent-shrine that was used during the exile in Babylon and which represented the destroyed temple, but not the one described in the *Second Book of Moses – Exodus*. The story of the Tabernacle legitimizes the sacerdotal authority, adding to it the ancient and Divine authority that this stratum simply did not have before. Connecting it with the Temple of Solomon and presenting it as its predecessor gives reason to think of a continuity that does not actually exist.

And, if there is any disagreement regarding the Tabernacle of Moses, whether it existed or not, then, regarding the one that was in Shiloh, no one has any doubt: "Now the whole congregation of the children of Israel assembled together at Shiloh, and set up the Tabernacle of Meeting there. And the land was subdued before them." (*Joshua* 18:1, *NKJV*)

According to John Gill, God chooses Shiloh as the first place to build His House among people. This was the place where the Tabernacle was placed for the sake of His Name and Glory. Most probably, this place was chosen because of its more neutral, independent and suitable location for positioning the central Temple. Moreover, recent archaeological research confirms its presence there.

Craig Keener – an evangelical pastor, professor, New Testament specialist, and author of many books on religious topics, writes the following: "Not surprisingly, the Tabernacle follows known Egyptian construction practices. Undoubtedly many Israelites knew what Egyptian temples looked like. The Tabernacle was a tent-shrine, and such shrines had a long history in Egypt."

According to the Hebrew tradition, the Tabernacle is an image of the Universe. Through a Divine Enlightenment, Moses was given knowledge with which he could recreate the Creation in a miniature which has certain limits. To us, there is no doubt that the Tabernacle is a specific symbol of the Kabalistic Tree, which is why we will present certain views on this symbolism associated with the *Five Gardens,* or *Five Faces.*

The First Garden is the Lower Face of *Assia,* which represents the purely physical world and the outer side of the courtyard of the Tabernacle.

The Second Garden is the Upper Face of *Assia,* which also represents the Lower Face of *Yetzira.* This corresponds to the "Upper Earth", as well as the "Lower Eden", and represents the courtyard beside the Tabernacle.

The Third Garden is the Upper Face of *Yetzira,* which is also the Lower Face of *Bria.* They are related to the "Upper Eden" and the "Lower Heaven", and represent the very Sanctuary of the Tabernacle.

The Fourth Garden is the Upper Face of *Bria* and the Lower Face of *Atzilut.* Here we have the "Upper Heaven" and the "Lower Divine" – this represents the Holy of Holies.

The Fifth Garden is the Upper Face of *Atzilut* and represents the Divine "Beyond" of the Tabernacle itself.

Thus, we return again to the construction symbolism, in order to draw a conclusion from the stated facts and hypotheses that regardless of whether the Temple is a prototype of the Tabernacle or vice versa, they are interconnected and have to be analogous in structure and form. In contrast, however, we see how they differ, especially in the area of the roof, and the Temple is depicted with a flat roof, unlike the Tabernacle. On this subject, John Gill has written in his *Exposition of the Bible* that it is true that most oriental roofs almost always have an outer flat roof, whereas the inner ceiling is vaulted, and that the Temple, as we have already seen, was built according to the model of the Tabernacle, which requires a gable roof.

Volume 16 of the *British Masonic Miscellany* – a collection of 20 volumes of Masonic works by various authors – contains, among the rest, *King Solomon's Temple* by Alex T. Brand, where we read the following: "The form of the roof of the Temple is uncertain. As is well known, all eastern houses and buildings have flat roofs, but the Temple was probably an exception... It is affirmed that the roof was composed wholly of cedar wood, which is in itself presumptive evidence of a pitched roof, since flat roofs required the use of stone or cement to form their floor. The marginal reading of "planks" is "rows". These rows were probably shingles, or wooden slates, which require to be so placed as to secure the regular overlapping of one another, to render them rain-proof. These shingles rested upon beams, or rafters of cedar, thus justifying the statement that the House "was covered with cedar". The Temple is thus to be conceived of as having a gable roof, this being the only way in which the analogy of the Tabernacle Tent could be followed".

We come to the conclusion that the roof of Solomon's Temple must have been made of cedar planks, and also gabled, to be analogous to the Tabernacle. However, what René Guénon and his followers have said about the keystone – the summit stone, in their constructive capacity of the "key" of the vault or dome, does not fit into this wooden roof, just as it does not fit into the content of the so-called *Testament of Solomon*, on which we will dwell briefly.

# The Testament of Solomon

> *"And all the workmen, and all the demons helping them came to the same place to bring up the stone and lay it on the pinnacle of the Holy Temple..."*

Some claim that this is an apocryphal book of the Old Testament, the original of which is in Hebrew or Aramaic, written in the 1st century AD. The most ancient edition of the text, preserved to this day, is written in the popular Greek form *Κοινή – Koine Greek.*[101] It contains numerous theological and magic topics, ranging from Christianity and Judaism to Greek mythology and astrology. Therefore, it is assumed that, despite the Judaic elements in its very creation and editing, it is Christian.

The text is written in the first person, with King Solomon being the author and protagonist. Nevertheless, its first publication dates to between the 1st and 5th century AD.

The *Testament of Solomon* describes how the king succeeded in building his Temple by commanding the demons through his magic ring entrusted to him by the Archangel Michael. Adarkes, the king of the Arabs, asked Solomon for help against the vicious demon of the winds, Ephippas. However, Solomon forgot about this request until he had a problem with the construction of the Temple in Jerusalem. The stone he wanted to lay as a cornerstone was so heavy that all the craftsmen and demon workers could not move it. Solomon gave his magic ring to a servant and sent him to the Arabian desert, where, using its power, the servant captured Ephippas in a flask. Solomon commanded Ephippas to move the cornerstone. The demon obeyed and inserted the heavy cornerstone at the entrance of the Temple. Solomon perceived this as an omen, according to the words of the Old Testament. We will quote part of the *Testament of Solomon.*

"Canst thou raise this stone, and lay it for the beginning of this corner which exists in the fair plan of the Temple?"

"... And the flask... I placed it under the stone, and (the spirit) girded himself up, and lifted it up top of the flask. And the flask went up the steps, carrying the stone, and laid it down at the end of the entrance of the Temple. And I Solomon, beholding the stone raised aloft and placed on a foundation, said, 'Truly the Scripture is fulfilled, which says: 'The stone which the builders rejected on trial, that same is become the head of the corner'." (*Psalms* 118:22)

---

101 The word comes from κοινός: "ordinary", "common", "public" – *AN.*

We understand from this passage that it is about a stone laid at the beginning of a corner, upon the foundation, at the end of the entrance of the Temple, which excludes the possibility of it being a keystone, summit stone, or last stone.

In this Testament, however, we read also the following: "And Jerusalem was built, and the Temple was being completed. And there was a stone, the end stone of the corner lying there, great, chosen out, one which I desired lay in the head of the corner of the completion of the Temple. And all the workmen, and all the demons helping them came to the same place to bring up the stone and lay it on the pinnacle of the Holy Temple, and were not strong enough to stir it, and lay it upon the corner allotted to it. For that stone was exceedingly great and useful for the corner of the Temple."

The word that is used, *pinnacle,* is unambiguous, with the proviso that it is still translated from the original and means *summit, apogee, peak, climax, culmination point, highest point*.

From the quoted two passages, it is seen that they are about one and the same stone, however, once laid in the corner of the foundation, and once – at the head of the corner, at the summit point of the Holy Temple. In addition, regarding the stone in the foundation, the words are used about the fulfilment of what is written in the Scriptures, which refers to the summit stone. We believe that these contradictions, as well as other alogisms, are due to the mechanical assemblage of various texts. In any case, however, there is the laying of a stone at the summit of Solomon's Temple, which convinces us more and more that it is a matter of symbolism rather than reality. As we have already mentioned, *Psalm* 118, concerning the rejected stone, is not dated; but even assuming that it dates to the time before the Temple was built, we do not think that its author would have meant foreign, non-Hebraic buildings such as the pyramids or the Babylonian ziggurats. Given that the Judaic priests did everything possible to glorify as heroic the shameful periods of slavery, they would hardly have left such a verse in the *Psalter*. If it refers to a real building, then it should only be this exceptional and great Hebraic achievement and pride – the Temple of Solomon. However, we have found that its roof is wooden and gabled, so there could be no stone on it, especially one that cannot be raised. Also, even if there were some vaults and arches under the roof, of which there is no evidence, they would have keystones, which, however, cannot in any way be the head of the corner, because, as we have already clarified, there is no corner at the summit of the arches and vaults.

The whole exposition so far about the Chief Cornerstone as the Head of the Corner, in the context of *Psalm* 118, verse 22, was to logically substantiate and deduce our thesis that this verse does not refer to a particular and really existing physical temple and its keystone, or summit stone. The whole Psalm is a praise of the Lord, and the discussed verse does not fit into it at all from the point of view of any construction process in the literal sense. Only in view of the terminology (stone, builders) can it be said that construction symbolism is used to illustrate and explain macro- and microcosmic spiritual processes and transformations. In his book, *Histoire de la Magie (The History of Magic)*, Éliphas Lévi also believes that "the Cornerstone, Cubic Stone, and Philosophers' Stone (all these symbolic names) mean one and the same thing". In another of his books, *Le Livre des Splendeurs : études sur les origines de la Kabbale (The Book of Splendours: Studies on the Origins of the Qabalah)*, he is even more explicit regarding the symbolic nature of Solomon's Temple: "The Temple of Solomon was, actually, a purely symbolic structure. The project, the buildings, the decorations, the vessels represented in it the synthesis of all sciences. It was the very Universe, it was the very philosophy, it was the very Heaven. Solomon elaborated the construction plan, Hiram carried it out with great wisdom; the construction managers possessed the science of details, the labourers worked on the design plans of the masters. Such a hierarchy, so reasonable and correct, was adopted in Freemasonry as a model of the perfect society: and so Freemasonry succeeded, in a kind of eclectic and independent Judaism. The Masonic Brothers are willing to rebuild the Temple – namely, to rebuild the primitive society on the foundations of the intelligent hierarchy and progressive initiation, without being hindered by the priests and kings: and that is why they are called *Franc-Maçons*, i.e. *Free Masons*."

In this sense, we agree with René Guénon when he speaks of the symbolic value of architecture, noting that any sacral edifice built according to strictly traditional norms has a "cosmic" meaning and correlates simultaneously to the Universe and the human being. Exactly for this reason, however, we do not agree with his interpretation of the stone thrown "among the rubbish", with regard to the word "rejected". According to Guénon, the purpose of this stone is known by another category of builders who, at this stage of work, do not yet intervene – they are those who have already passed "from the Square to the Compass". Undoubtedly, this conception is influenced, as we have said, by one of the legends about the Temple, but obviously also by the theory of the so-called "Square Masons" and "Arch Masons".

Following this line of thought, in conclusion we will describe some of the views of Neville B. Cryer on this topic – a priest and Ancient Master Mason, who has written 21 books on similar subjects – which he reveals in his book *The Arch and the Rainbow,* in the chapter entitled "Straight or Square Masons and Round or Arch Masons".

Some Masons were less skilled and therefore performed only straight work, hence the term "Straight Mason", while those who were skilled enough to produce arches and other curved masonry work became known as "Arch Masons"; the latter took higher wages because of their greater skill. In those days, when the sign of the "Square and Compass" was displayed, it meant that both types of Masons congregated. According to what type of a Mason was the Apprentice going to become, he was given the Square or the Compass. The "Straight Masons" and the "Arch Masons" could rely on parallel paths very similar to each other, their most significant difference consisting in the Rite of rising to the Fellow Craft Degree: according to the "Straight Masons", the stone is lost, being the "Cornerstone", while in the Arch Rite, it is the "Keystone". Therefore, it can be said that from the point of view of initiation, the "Cornerstone" and the "Keystone" can be considered to be of equal worth, as well as their tools, the Square and the Compass, which belong to them.

In the transition to Symbolic Freemasonry, two phenomena occurred: in the first place, part of the symbolism of the "Straight Masons" was adopted in the "Blue Masonry", whereas part of that of the "Arch Masons" – by the "Mark Masonry". The second phenomenon is the introduction of the Master's Degree through the Legend of Hiram, which contributed to the appropriation, by this new Degree, of part of the symbolic heritage, which in Operative Masonry was a prerogative of perfecting the Fellow Craft Degree.

We should not think that an Apprentice is familiar with all the properties of the Square – or, if so, then his functions would not be simply those of the rough hewing of the stone, which was the exact function in "Straight" Masonry. Working hard, Apprentices took out the stones and hewed them, the Fellow Craft smoothed them, and when he considered them ready for construction, it was his duty and responsibility to subject them to the assessment of the Wardens or the Master. From this, it becomes clear that the Fellow Craft Degree occurred and developed in the quarries. This was the classic Operative Degree, which unfortunately did not survive the changes of 1717.

## The Master's Degree

*When you aim for perfection,
you discover it is a moving target.*

**Bushido**

From the above written, it becomes clear that according to this author, the introduced Third "Master's" Degree has appropriated a large part of the function of the Fellow Craft Degree, making it senseless. When talking about the Third Master's Degree, however, we cannot fail to point out also the views of Jean-Marie Ragon, who is considered "the most erudite Mason of the 19th century", as well as one of the great thinkers of the Fraternity.

In his book *Orthodoxie maçonnique (Masonic Orthodoxy),* Ragon writes that the Third Degree was created in 1649 by Elias Ashmole, a prominent antiquary, an active monarchist, and one of the founders of the Royal Society. According to Ragon, this Degree, which is currently being performed, is not the one originally conceived by Ashmole, but a version modified by himself. It was originally purely Egyptian, and thus it fitted into and completed the first two, which were also created by Ashmole. However, after being modified by him, it is left unfinished and detached from the rest. Ragon explains the original Third Degree in the following way: "Hiram was Osiris (the Sun); Isis (his Widow), is the Lodge (the emblem of the Earth); Horus, the Widow's son, is the Free Mason, the Initiate (the child of the Widow, and of Light)".

After the Rite is modified by Ashmole, it changes from Egyptian to Biblical – or, as Ragon says, "Talmudic", completely detached from the first two. According to Ragon, the connection that is subsequently established between the first two Degrees and the Third Master's Degree represents the two pillars and their biblical names. Initially, these pillars represent Egyptian obelisks – the embodiment of the East and the West as directions, whereas in Freemasonry they become a symbol of the solstice. After the Degrees are transformed from Alchemical into Christian ones, there is fierce resistance, especially from the part of the Irish, who do not acknowledge the Third Catholic Degree, considering it a foreign body inside the Order that has to be converted. Nevertheless, in the end, precisely the biblical vision prevails, and instead of remaking the Master's Degree, the biblical names of the two pillars are added, to impart some continuity into the whole Rite. The established three Degrees are considered to be the ones that build up a Freemason as a core essence.

In the foreword to the 2005 edition of *The Aldersgate Ritual,* in the part, entitled *Aldersgate Chapter of Improvement,* it is written: "… Pure Ancient Masonry consists of three Degrees and no more, viz. those of the Entered Apprentice, the Fellow Craft, and the Master Mason, including the Supreme Order of the *Holy Royal Arch*.(…) The Supreme Order of the *Holy Royal Arch*", which is "an extension to, but neither a superior nor a subordinate part of, the Degrees which precede it".

It is no coincidence that all other Rites containing various Degrees are called "extensions" or "superstructures".

According to René Guénon, however, Ancient Operative Freemasonry consisted of seven Degrees, and since they were not known to the founders of Speculative Freemasonry in their entirety, this has led to serious gaps in the current symbolic three Degrees. An attempt has been made to remedy these shortcomings in the higher Degrees, which cannot be said to be completely successful, because the true Operative tradition has been lacking.

The Master, due to the very fact that he possessed the "fullness of Masonic rights", had access to the whole knowledge in the initiatic form to which he belonged, and precisely this is expressed in the ancient concept of "Master of all Degrees", which is completely forgotten.

In this sense, Anderson was accused of altering the Ancient Constitutions and Rites of Operative Masonry by reducing the Degrees, which had been seven before that, and also of introducing a rapid Apprentice Degree admission performed in one ritual, whereas in Operative Masonry it took seven years as a "Seeker" before the admission into the Brotherhood was performed. Another reform introduced by Anderson is that of the Master's Degree and the Rite of Hiram's death, against which many traditionalist Freemasons immediately rose, seeing in this an infiltration of *dark magic,* including *necromancy.*

According to Robert Ambelain, the great figure in Freemasonry is Jean Théophile Désaguliers, considered to be the most likely true founder of the Grand Lodge of England (not Anderson, who was "a man-of-all-work"). Undoubtedly, he opened the gates of the Lodges to representatives of the Jewish community, which, until then, had not been possible due to the purely Christian Rites of Operative Freemasons. This justifies the agnostic aspect of Anderson's Constitution regarding an indeterminate religion, concludes Robert Ambelain.

From what has been discussed so far, the conclusion is increasingly confirmed that the prenatal predisposition of Modern Freemasonry is quite confused, vague and to great extent ignoring the traditional essence of Ancient Freemasonry. Against this background, we wonder about the essential meaning of the requirement, by some Brothers, to zealously observe the currently existing Rites as the embodiment of an ancient original Masonic tradition. However, all of this is not in the focus of our book, so let us go back to the main topic of the "rejected stone". If we take it literally that a stone was delivered prematurely to the construction site, and that the "Straight" Masons, because of their ignorance, threw it among the rubbish like something useless, then we will not justify the significance of the Psalm verse through such a minor event. It is unlikely that the importance of this verse will be justified by the need to illustrate the cognitive differentiation of the "Straight" and the "Arched" Masons from both the operative and the symbolic aspect. We believe that this verse has a deep esoteric and mostly Kabalistic meaning, and that its "keystone" represents the verb *rejected.* This requires from us to clarify the etymology and meaning of this word in principle and in the context of the Kabalistic reading of the verse.

## The Meaning of "Rejected"

In order not to fragment too much with examples, we will quote the verse under consideration only from the Italian and English versions of the Bible:

Italian: *La pietra che gli edificatori avevano **rigettata** è divenuta la pietra angolare.*

English *BBE (The Bible in Basic English): The stone which the builders **put on one side** has become the chief stone of the building.*

English *KJV (King James Version): The stone which the builders **refused** is become the head stone of the corner.*

The verb form used in all the three versions means only and solely "rejected", while in these languages other words are used for the meaning of "threw away".

In the *Orthodox Jewish Bible (OJB)* in the *Psalter, Psalm* 118:22, the same word is used as in *Psalm* 89:38: "But Thou hast cast off *[mem-alef-samech, see same word Psalm 118:22]* and abhorred, Thou hast been in wrath with Thine Moshiach." ("Your Messiah")

From the quoted examples above, and especially from the latter, it becomes clear that the word "rejected" cannot in any way have the meaning of "threw away" in principle, but rather in particular of "threw into the rubbish" or "threw aside".

In Hebrew, *maasu* has the meaning of *rejected, cast away, contemned, abhorrence, being abhorred;* however, in the case in view, it is used in the context of *rejection, renouncement, disavowal, demarcation* from someone or something, which is rather within the scope of ideological and moral-ethical relations. In this sense was also the interpretation we have already pointed out of the "rejected stone" in an Old Testament key – namely, that it is King David, Rachel, and the very Hebrew people, while in a New Testament key, it is Jesus Christ. We have said, however, that at the deepest level, the whole phrase can only be understood from a Kabalistic point of view, and this is not unusual, because in principle the Old Testament has such an interpretation. For this purpose, however, the word "rejected", which we commented on as being the "keystone" of the verse, has to be used in another connotation, but it will by no means be an end in itself and far from its already mentioned meanings. We will again make use of the Mark Master Ritual, in which, as we have already described, precisely the legend is enacted of the "rejected" keystone, which was not recognized and therefore thrown among the rubbish, but after that found and used for its intended purpose. We refer to this ritual because, in it, the Sign of the Mark Master is performed, who, as stated in the ritual, hints at the main words of this Degree: *Heave-over*, which are important for our research.

In order to go further, however, we will quote part of the ritual, i.e. the following dialogue:

"A.: (...) The principal words of this Degree.
Q.: What are they?
A.: Heave-over.
Q.: To what does it further allude?
A.: To the rejection of the "Key Stone" by the Overseers."

In the answer, the word *rejection* is used, which is a derivative of *reject* (as in *Psalm* 118:22 of the American version of the Bible), which means *spurn, decline, rebuff*, but also *eject* (e.g. the disk from the disk drive).

*Heave-over* is a very rarely used archaic idiomatic expression, the meanings of which are: "uplifting", "raising"; "lifting with great effort above, beyond or through sth". We consider the meaning of the word *rejection* to be *ejection*, in the sense of lifting or pushing up.[102] Exactly such an upward movement is represented by the very Sign of the Mark Master, yet in the end, a throw over the shoulder is imitated. We do not know, and it is not clear from the ritual, why, after the stone is thrown away, it has to be done in this difficult way – by pushing up over the shoulder. However, we believe that this is not accidental, because otherwise it would be complete nonsense. There is no information on this subject, but still we have managed to find the following explanation of the Mark Degree in lectures on Ancient Masonry, held in the period 1917 – 1927: "The Mark Master Degree, represented by the Fourth Major Arcanum *(of the Tarot – AN)*, corresponds to the sign Scorpio; thus this Heave-over, alluding to the rejection of the Keystone, refers to the sign Scorpio. The ten locked fingers represent the union of man and woman, and the front of the right hip symbolizes the constructive power of Scorpio, which by most is discarded, or used negatively in Venusian pleasures as indicated by the left side of the neck *(through where the stone is being thrown away – AN)*."

As we have already mentioned, Mark Masonry claims to be a preserved authentic tradition, which is why, without agreeing with all the above, we interpret it in a general esoteric key, and its meaning is that the stone symbolizes the sign Scorpio, which, on its part, is an expression of sexual energy, rejected by some religions as demonic force of temptation, and therefore condemned as destructive. In other religions and profound esoteric traditions, however, this energy is utilized as positive and transforming power, awakening the latent energies of Kundalini and leading to Spiritual Enlightenment.

---

[102] The origin of the verbs *eject/ reject* lies in the Latin verbs *eicere/ reicere – AN*.

In this sense, we should not throw it over "the left shoulder of pleasure" but rather sublimate and elevate it to the highest spiritual centre, which in the Yoga tradition is called *Sahasrara,* whereas in the tradition of Kabala – *Keter.*

Therefore, we believe that the use of the term *Heave-over* is a reminiscence of the true meaning of the verse 22 we studied in *Psalm* 118, combined with the legend of the rejected stone. This explanation is in unison with the subsequent exposition on the subject in a Kabalistic key, the key word being the one that is translated as "rejected", in the sense of *cast aside,* but we believe that its ideological meaning is an upward movement. A confirmation, in the end, is also the verse itself, according to which the rejected stone has become a head that has a summit position and implies an upward movement, an elevation. According to René Guénon, "the crown and the horns are, in their essence, expressions of ascension", so the coronation symbolizes precisely this movement. Once it is implicitly clear that it refers to such a movement (ascension, elevation), the word "rejected" denoting it could be replaced by a term indicating the method of this ascension. Then the verse in the translation should take on the following form: "The stone which the builders *pushed up/ ejected* has become the head of the corner".

Here is the right place, as an illustration of what has been said so far, to recall the Riddle of the Sphinx: *Is the Most High Amen, with all His Omnipotence, capable of creating a stone that He Himself could not lift?*

The answer is that this stone is the Human Being who has been given free will, and no one can possibly lift it unless the very Human Being wishes that. In this sense, it becomes clear that to "lift" in the Riddle means to exalt, to elevate to His image and likeness. The same ascension is meant in the verse in view, because the "Head of the Corner" is nothing else but the Sfara *Keter,* the Crown of the Kabalistic Tree – and we have already explained that the coronation represents ascension (on the throne).

The "summit stone", as René Guénon maintains, "fully corresponds to the literal meaning of the phrase 'head of the corner', as well as the figurative meaning of the Hebrew word 'corner', denoting 'chief leader'..." – and in a Kabalistic key, this meaning indisputably refers to the Sfara *Keter.* From here we begin the veritable essential Kabalistic interpretation. Since this has to be in the context of Freemasonry, the building block of which is literally and figuratively the stone, we will list its designations as a result of our research so far: *foundation stone, fundamental stone, stone in the foundation, symbolic stone, first stone, cornerstone, chief cornerstone, keystone, "key of the vault", summit stone, stone at the summit, Heavenly stone, stone from Heaven, last stone, covering stone, head of the corner, Philosophers' Stone.* With the exception of those with one and the same meaning, all have to find their place in the process of *Building the Edifice,* and most of all – in the Kabalistic Tree. Shedding light in the spirit of Kabala will give us the opportunity to view this subject from another angle and see the Truth from that position.

## The Kabalistic Interpretation

At the beginning of the topic of the chief cornerstone, we quoted *Sefer ha-Zohar* regarding the *ha-Shetiyah* stone by means of which the Worlds were created. According to tradition, when the stone was thrown from the Upper World, it left behind itself a hole in the Tree of Life, and this hole is known as the Sfara *Daat.* Now is the moment for the promised explanation of why we think this is the Sfara *Daat* of the *Bria* Tree. For this purpose, we will quote again part of the *Zohar* text:

*"When the Holy One, blessed be He, was about to create the world, He detached one precious stone from underneath His Throne of Glory and plunged it into the Abyss."*

Knowing the meaning of the terminology used, we understand that "Glory" is an indication towards the *Atzilut* World, whereas "He" is an indication towards the Sfara *Keter* of the Tree of Life; "His Throne" is a direction that the Sfara *Tiferet* of this Tree is referred to. Therefore, the "precious stone underneath His Throne" is in the Sfara *Yesod* of the *Atzilut* World, which is *Daat* of the *Bria* World in the unfolded Kabalistic Tree. Thus, the hole left in the Abyss is the Sfara *Daat* of the *Bria* Tree, which means that the transition between the Worlds is the *Yesod – Daat* tunnel.

We have already explained that the term *ha-Shetiyah* is literally translated as *the stone (foundation) of drinking,* since it is the stone of "Living Water", which, according to all traditions, brings Life (Immortality) – an indication towards the Tree of Life, and more precisely, as we have found out, towards its Sfara *Yesod,* whose Name of God is not accidentally *Shadai El Hai* – the Great Architect of the Universe. This "stone", after creating the three lower Worlds, settles in *Assia* as the foundation-laying stone around which all materiality is organized, thus representing the navel of the physical world. This means that it should be in the Sfara *Yesod* (translated as "foundation") of the *Assia* Tree. In Papus's book *La Cabbale, Tradition secrète de l'Occident (The Kabala: Secret Tradition of the West),* the Sfara *Yesod* is defined as the "Cornerstone of Stability". We agree with this definition insofar as this Sfara represents the foundation of the Kabalistic Tree and the Worlds. That is why the cornerstone of the foundation and the *ha-Shetiyah* stone in its centre ought to symbolically represent, in a Kabalistic key, the Sfara *Yesod* in the *Assia* World.

Returning to the Operative aspect of the construction symbolism, we can already conclude that in buildings with a sacral purpose, the ceremonial laying of the first stone in the foundation should be identified with the *ha-Shetiyah* stone and represent its symbol. This means that the first stone is symbolically laid in the centre of the base, where the central altar will be, and where the projection of the summit stone falls. For this reason, it is an undressed stone, as the stone beneath the altar of Solomon's Temple is – and being symbolic, it has no structural or any constructional (building) purpose. In our opinion, René Guénon's assertion that the stone under the summit of the dome is a cubic one should apply only and solely to the altar (after the view is dropped that the altar should be of an undressed stone). We cannot say why and when, but from these examples it becomes clear that the role of this first and entirely symbolic stone is given by Freemasons to the cornerstone in the northeast, which, as we already understood, has an important constructive function – to set the parameters of the building. In our opinion, according to what has been explained so far, in Operative Masonry, two first stones should be laid, which are not mutually exclusive but complementary: one of them – symbolic, with a due ceremony, and the other – functional and positioned in working mode. In view of the importance of the cornerstone in the constructional aspect, it cannot in any way be symbolized by the seeker who has just been admitted as an apprentice, and who, according to Masonic allegory, has yet to smooth the edges of his own imperfection. Therefore, we believe that positioning the newly admitted apprentice in the northeast as a symbol of the cornerstone is not part of any authentic Masonic tradition. We are convinced that, in a Speculative aspect, the *ha-Shetiyah* stone symbolizes Freemasonry in general, together with its archetypal character, whereas, in particular, it symbolizes the sacrality of each newly formed Lodge and of the altar on which its Master performs the sacred rites. Therefore, the undressed stone symbolizing the *ha-Shetiyah* stone should be the only "first stone" to be laid ceremoniously and identified with the newly installed Lodge. In a Kabalistic key, we have understood that this stone is the Sfara *Yesod* of the *Assia* Tree, which is connected with the Sfara *Daat* of the *Bria* Tree, and thus the connection with the Spiritual World is accomplished. Continuing within this Kabalistic context, we must note that what has been explained so far, however, does not concern the fallen Sfara *Daat* from the *Yetzira* World into the Sfara *Malkut* in the *Assia* World, and its transformation into an invisible one. This is a process that is symbolically represented through the "Fall" of Adam, who, becoming consubstantial with the *Tree of Knowledge – Ets ha-Daat,* takes the principle of knowing good and evil down with him into the Kingdom of Action. This means that the involutionary Tree of Knowledge, which originally extended itself in Paradise, within the frames of the *Yetzira* Tree, after the "Fall" has grown and expanded, marking the edge of the physical world. In this way, the human being resides in the *Assia* World with the acquired divisive dualistic consciousness, not with the whole united consciousness which humans had in the Garden of Eden. As we have already mentioned, the task of human beings is to perform the Great Deed of restoring *Malkut* of the *Assia* Tree at the position of *Daat* of the *Yetzira* Tree.

If, according to Masonic symbolism, we liken each Sfara to a particular stone, then what has been stated means that the *Malkut* stone rises and stands into the place of the Sfara *Daat,* and this Sfara becomes visible. There is an upward throwing of a stone – yet is this the stone that the builders rejected? Kabalists say that the restoration of the Sfara *Malkut* onto its position in *Daat* is the goal of humankind as a whole, which shows that Masons, as an Initiated part of it, should have accomplished it on the individual plane, so the completion of their Great Deed should include another achievement, greater and more significant than that of humankind. It means that in the researched by us verse 22 of *Psalm* 118, another piece of knowledge is encoded – namely, that, after restoring *Malkut* of *Assia* into the Sfara *Daat* of the *Yetzira* World, which is a transition to the Sfara *Yesod* of the *Bria* World, the builders pushed (ejected) the foundation stone *(Yesod)* of the *Bria* Tree upwards. Here we shall remind of the elaboration works of René Guénon, who says that there is no way to reject a stone in the foundation, as the building will collapse. Everything would be so if only and solely purely building construction symbolism is used, as Guénon does. However, we believe that in the verse under consideration we are given a Kabalistic technique for the accomplishment of an inner spiritual process of Initiation, which can be very conditionally illustrated through the construction symbolism of the stone. In this sense, we can say regarding the Sfara *Yesod* that, although it is the foundation, there is nothing to prevent it from being pushed upwards, because it is a matter of raising the consciousness. The lack of Kabalistic reading and the adherence to the strict constructive functionality in the process of building an edifice have forced Guénon and his associates to throw the chief cornerstone and "heave it over among the rubbish". We also throw a stone, yet not the "chief cornerstone" and not "among the rubbish", but rather upwards, through the levels of consciousness of the Kabalistic Tree, so that this stone becomes the "Head of the Corner". In this sense, we will continue to draw a parallel with the construction symbolism as part of the Masonic one. After we have specified terminologically and positionally some of the types of stones on the Kabalistic and constructional plane, we should also move on to the emblematic keystone.

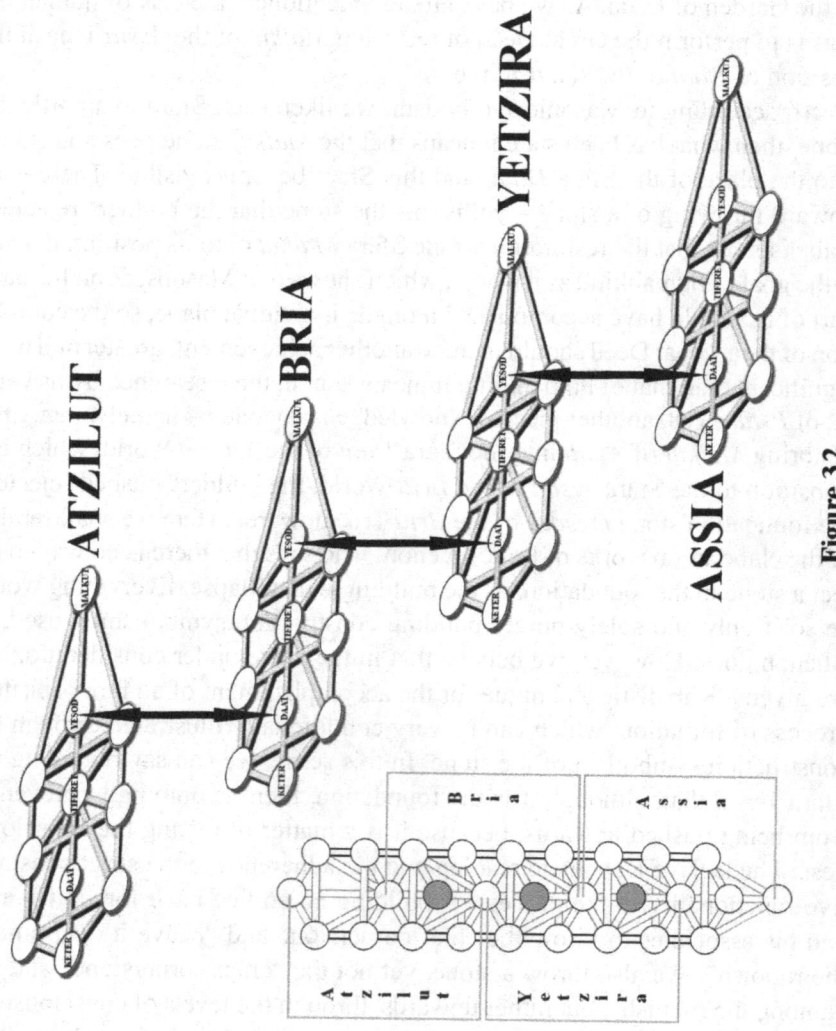

**Figure 32**

From the exposition so far, the conclusion is inevitably drawn that the keystone, in view of Kabalistic knowledge, is the key that unlocks and locks the gate to the Worlds. In the involutionary direction, this mechanism will be the Sfara *Yesod* of the previous world, which "locks the gate" after the creative force passes to the next one. However, since we are viewing an upward movement, it means that this is about an evolutionary uplift of consciousness, so the "unlocking mechanism" represents the Sfara *Daat*, which leads to the Sfara *Yesod* of the next world. *(Fig. 32)*

In the end, we can say that the evolutionary keystone, in the Kabalistic aspect, represents the Sfara *Daat*. It is no coincidence that it is symbolized in the esoteric traditions by the Sacred Mountain, on which the chosen ones climb up and receive revelations underlying the foundation of various religions. In the micro-matrix of the human body, the material equivalent of the Sfara *Daat*, as we have already explained, represents the occiput, where the spinal column is connected to the skull, the place where the most ancient brain is located – the *medulla oblongata*, which some would call the "reptilian brain". It is part of the brainstem, so it can most generally be said that it performs a conductive and reflex function, and is not engaged with the thinking processes. Essentially, we would characterize its elementary impact as follows: the more, the better; the more shiny and remarkable, the more the generating of a desire for possession; will towards power and affirmation of the conquered; rituality and worship of the traditionally ancient. From the *medulla oblongata*, the centres of emotions are subsequently formed, and after that, from the emotional brain, the thinking brain issues – the *neocortex*. The *medulla oblongata*, from a certain perspective, visually has the shape of the keystone (inverted isosceles trapezoid), which, as we have seen, is laid in the basis of the Mark Masonry Ritual, which, in turn, lays claims to authenticity of tradition. However, we will not comment on whether it is in any way connected with the reptilian race, so as not to enter the territory of speculative theories, which are extrinsic to our exposition. Still, it is not any speculation if we make a connection between the *medulla oblongata*, which is a key to the other superstructure parts of the brain and is located under the "dome" of the skull, with the keystone maintaining the vault under the dome of the edifice. Furthermore, from a Kabalistic perspective, the keystone is the Sfara *Daat*, the anatomical correspondence of which is the base of the occiput, where the *medulla oblongata* is located. It represents consciousness in another dimension, and this is so, because, as we have learned, it corresponds to the next world. We have already substantiated that the *keystone* is not the *capstone* (the stone that completes or crowns the building), nor the *copestone* (the one that closes the aperture at the summit, i.e. the "eye" of its dome). These two terms are for the stone which is also terminologically referred to as "summit stone", "stone at the summit", "Heavenly stone", "stone from Heaven", "covering stone", and "head of the corner".

# 18
# Head of the Corner

### The Kabalistic Key

This is how we came to the emblematic stone, representing the "head of the corner", about which we said that it cannot in any way be the summit stone of any dome or arch, of any spherical surfaces in general, because they have no corner, whereas in buildings where there are corners, mostly in cathedrals, the rays of the corner touch each other directly. The only significant exception is the pyramidion; however, the Hebrews hardly had the pyramids as a standard, and we have also realized that there was no way they could possibly have in mind the Temple of Solomon with its wooden roof. Therefore, the term "head of the corner" should not be literally associated with building construction. Thus, only its decoding through a Kabalistic key is left. Through it, we have understood that this phrase refers to the Sfara *Keter* of the Kabalistic Tree. From it, two paths start towards the Sfara *Hohma* and the Sfara *Bina*, which form an angle of 120 degrees, while the Sfara *Keter* represents the head of this angle. Kabalizing 120 yields the significant number 12 and the even more significant number 3. The Ancient Hebrew word for *corner (angle)* is *pinnah*, and *lerosh pinnah* is translated as "head of the corner". In addition, *pinnah*, by the root of the word, is connected to *pne*, meaning "face", and the close connection between "head" and "face" is quite obvious. In this sense, we can paraphrase the phrase "head of the corner" as "head, face, chief of the corner", and in another context – "chief of the 12 ones". *(Fig. 33)* Here we will mention that some of the titles of the Sfara *Keter* are *The Great Face, The Greater Countenance, The Vast Countenance, The White Head, The Non-Existent Head*, whereas its correspondence in the Microcosm is the skull. Achieving this Sfara is called "Completion of the Great Work". In the single Kabalistic Tree, everything seems clear at first glance, but in view of the unfolded Tree, where there are four Sfarot *Keter,* the question arises as to which one of them is referred to in the above stated? To find the answer, we will use the Kabalistic knowledge that only humans are given free will, as well as the opportunity to rise above the Angels, and even above the Archangels – the Spirits of *Bria,* because the human being is the only "image and likeness" of Elohim. It is believed that the supreme Archangel Metatron, dwelling in *Keter*

of *Bria*, the most Sublime Being ever created, was a human – "And Enoch walked with God" (*Genesis 5:24, NKJV*). *Enoch* means *Initiate* in Hebrew, and therefore we believe that the highest level of Sacred Initiation that a human can ever reach is the level of the Archangel Metatron, or the Sfara *Keter* of *Bria* – the Crown of Creation. It is affirmed that Enoch was taken by God's Chariot from the physical world directly into the Spiritual World. We consider this an indication that the human consciousness is able to ascend along the Central Pillar of the Kabalistic Tree directly to *Keter* in the *Bria* World.[103] It is clear that this ascension, according to the verse under consideration (*Psalm 118:22*), ought to be familiar to esoteric science, including within Freemasonry, all the more so as the figure of Enoch is part of its tradition and rituality. It is another question whether the 13th and the 14th Degree within the frames of the Scottish Rite, which deals mainly with the "theme of Enoch", are adequate to the highest level of Sacred Initiation, which we will provisionally call the "Enoch Level of Sacred Initiation". We leave the answer to this question to the Initiated into this Rite.

If we count the Sfarot in the *Bria* Tree, we will see that they are 12, and above them is *Keter* of *Bria*, which represents the "Head of the 12 Ones". We have already mentioned that the Hebrew word for *corner (angle)* – *pinnah*, also means *face;* and the Sublime Spirits of the *Bria* World are called "Spirits of the Face of Elohim", the highest of them being Metatron, who represents their head.

We will stop here with examples, analogies, and evidence in support of our conviction that the definition "Head of the Corner" in the verse under consideration refers to the Sfara *Keter* of the *Bria* World. In the context of all that has been said on the subject so far, the whole verse, "The stone which the builders rejected is become the Head of the Corner", is an indication towards pushing up along the Central Pillar of the unfolded Kabalistic Tree of the Sfara *Yesod* in the *Bria* World to the Sfara *Keter* of that World, which represents the "Head of the Corner", or the "Chief" of the 12 Spiritual Sfarot. *(Fig. 34 on p. 282.)* In addition to "Archangels", they are also called "Benei Elohim", translated as "Sons of Elohim" or "Sons of God". *(Fig. 33 on p. 276.)* In the New Testament, one of the Beatitudes is the following: "Blessed are the Peacemakers, for they shall be called *Sons of God*". (*Matthew 5:9, NKJV*)

---

[103] It is important to note that Enoch remained in the Heavens and never returned. Is this an indication that a consciousness like that of Enoch cannot be acquired while you are still incarnate on Earth? – *AN*.

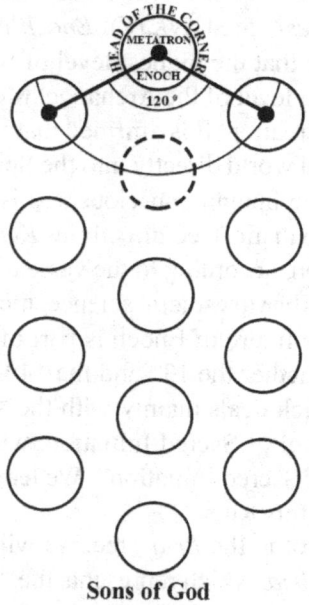

**Sons of God**

**Figure 33**

We have already mentioned that Peacemakers are the Builders of Worlds, as Freemasons should be, which is why they can be called "Sons of God", which, on its turn, means that they have the potential to reach the level of the *Bria* World. Humankind has yet to throw up the stone from *Malkut* of the *Assia* World to *Daat* of the *Yetzira* World, and the Builders of Worlds are given the opportunity to eject (push) it upwards into the Spiritual World of *Bria* so that it becomes the "Head of the Corner". Naturally, this is the symbolism and the algorithm of an inner process of Initiation, of raising or turning the sphere of consciousness to the level of the Creator, where our "I" (Self) merges with His "I" (Self), and our will obeys His Will. Thus, Jesus, one of the Sons of God, says in the Garden of Gethsemane, "Father, if it is Your Will, take this cup away from Me; nevertheless not My will, but Yours, be done." (*Luke* 22:42, *NKJV*) This is a sign that Jesus has acquired the Spiritual Consciousness of the *Bria* World, better known as the "Christ Consciousness", identical with the Yogic term "Turiya", but in the context of what we have explained, He should have received the "Enoch Sacred Initiation".

## "My God, My God, Why Have You Forsaken Me?"

Here is the right place, speaking of Jesus, to go back to His words at the cross, "Eloì, Eloì, lamà savahthanì?",[104] in order to find out whether the popular translation is accurate and adequate, and also whether this is exactly what Jesus has said. To this end, we will quote a commentary on this issue by John Gill, considered to be an authority: "As for the word *Sabachthani*, we are not sure, it appears to be from the Aramaic word *sbq* which means *to forsake or abandon for a purpose*. The Aramaic word for just simply *to abandon, to forsake because it is unwanted* is *taatani*. If Jesus had really meant that God had abandoned him or forgot him, he would have used the word *taatani* ("forsake") or *nashatani* ("forget"). However, the Jewish *Targum* (Aramaic translation of the Hebrew Bible) does use the Aramaic word *sbq* in *Psalms* 22:1, which is probably why the scribes added the footnote "which, being interpreted, means…". In other words, they were not sure they had correctly quoted Jesus so they assumed he was speaking *Psalms* 22:1 and put in a little commentary to offer their opinion as to what he really said."

Without further boring the reader with the etymological examples and references of the author, we will say that, in the end, the words *Eloi, Eloi, lama sabachthani*, according to him, mean the following: "Listen to My Heart, this is why I came to Earth in the first place, this is My purpose: to die for you".

According to another authority – Adam Clarke, Jesus's words, reconstructed by Mark and Matthew, are neither in Hebrew nor in Syriac, but are close to them and mean the following, "My God! My God! To what sort of persons hast Thou left Me?", or "To what hast Thou abandoned Me?", which, according to the author, means that these words "are rather to be referred to the wicked Jews than to our Lord".

Most analysts believe that the word *sabachthani* contains the biggest amount of "unknown quantities", one of which is whether its meaning is identical with that of *azavthani* in *Psalm* 22:1. Some maintain the standpoint that *sabachthani* is neither a Hebrew word nor an Aramaic one, and that the closest to it is *zevahtani*. According to them, it is a derivative of the root verb *zavah*, meaning *to sacrifice, to slaughter a sacrificial animal,* and thus the whole verse will be translated as "My God, My God, why have You sacrificed/slaughtered Me?" In this sense, they comment that if Jesus wanted to ask why He was abandoned, then He would use the word from the Psalm of David *azavthani*, without introducing the foreign word *shebakthani*. Thus, it is concluded that Jesus has said, "Why do You sacrifice Me?", in this way directing our attention towards the essence of the cross – the redeeming sacrifice.

---

[104] "My God, My God, why have You forsaken Me?" (*Holy Gospel of Matthew* 27:46, NKJV) – AN.

According to the *Israel Institute of Biblical Studies,* the Evangelist Mark is the only one to use transliterated words from Aramaic. The Aramaic word *shevaktani – you left me/ you abandoned me,* may refer to the Hebrew word *shvaktani – you rejected me,* but since it is in the *Gospel of Mark,* the translation should be with the Aramaic meaning. Thus, in the *Gospel of Matthew,* this word has to be interpreted in a purely Hebrew sense – *you rejected me.*

In the apocryphal *Gospel of Peter,* the words of Jesus are conveyed as follows: "... 'My power, My power, you have forsaken Me!' And when he had said it he was taken up." The word used, translated as *power,* is δύναμις *(dunamis),* which also means *might, sturdiness,* and therefore we think it refers to the life forces that had left the body of Jesus.

Some researchers maintain the version that Jesus spoke a North Aramaic dialect and that those not speaking this dialect found it difficult to understand. As proof of this, those under the cross thought that He was calling the Prophet Elijah. In this case, we wonder what Jesus said after all, since the two Evangelists were not eyewitnesses, but only recorded what was rumoured. Here we can mention also the exotic version that, still, Jesus did call Elijah, who was the reborn John the Baptist, and that, in this way, Jesus actually summoned the Spirit of John, on whose magic power he relied. This is in the context of what has been claimed by some authors: that John and Jesus practiced black magic, of which they were accused. There is a version that John's head is preserved and used by Jesus, who is surprised to find on the cross that its magical power has left him, and cries out in tears the name of Elijah, who is the titular, so to say. At a later stage, according to the Inquisition, the Templars and Cathars owned the head of John the Baptist.

## Our Version

Having quoted a small part of the different opinions and interpretations on the topic, we see no obstacle to present our version as well. If we assume that the exact words of Jesus are conveyed in the canonized verses, then we wonder: What is the point of asking the question "why"? Does He not tell His disciples that He will be betrayed by one of them, and does He not predict to Peter that the latter will deny Him three times? Along this line of thoughts, how could possibly He, the only Son of God according to the Christian doctrine, not know of the bitter cup which He had to drink according to the Will of His Father? It is hardly probable – because otherwise we would have to admit that He expected to be saved until the end, instead of being the Saviour Himself. So the option remains that His question was rhetorical – yet who under the cross would understand it as such? In this situation, what would the message be for the believers from a disbelieving "Son of God", being abandoned by his own God to die desecrated on the cross? Although we have not found any other such opinion in our research, we believe that the words of Jesus may not have contained any question but rather appealed to be "rejected", in the sense of "ejected upwards", "raised high", or the more popular word – "ascended". From the Evangelist Mark, we have learned that Jesus, like Enoch, was ascended to Heaven, but unlike the latter – through undergoing the death on the cross, in order to sit at the right hand of God, thus becoming the New Testament Enoch.[105]

"So then, after the Lord had spoken to them, He was received up into Heaven, and sat down at the right hand of God." (*Holy Gospel of Mark* 16:19, *NKJV*)

We have explained that the main method for evolutionary Initiation is prayer, and therefore Jesus may have offered such a prayer from the cross – "My God, My God, lift Me up to Yourself!", so that this prayer "ejects" Him upwards in order to receive the final Supreme Sacred Initiation: Unity in Communion with the All-Father. This is how the last words of Jesus can also be interpreted: "Father, into Your hands I commit My Spirit!" (*Luke* 23:46, *NKJV*) They are not in conflict with what is said in the *Gospel of Peter:* "My power, My power, you have forsaken Me!", because, as we have clarified, it does not refer to Divine Power, which could be a substitute word for *God*,[106] but to a word meaning *vital force*. However, if Jesus is the Saviour, He would not pray for His own salvation but for the salvation of all humans.

Since our version is related to the meaning of the word "rejected", we will continue to unlock with it the deep esoteric secrets in a Kabalistic key. In this regard, according to some Kabalists, the Messiah is to be found in *Keter* of *Yetzira;* and if we assume that Jesus is a Messiah, then He has descended from there into the *Assia* World to fulfil His mission, and after that ascended much higher than His Messianic position, if we follow what was written by Mark the Evangelist. However, he, unlike his Master, cannot be said to have been a Kabalist, or at least it is not evident from his Gospel that he was such, and we have not come across anyone claiming the opposite. Therefore, the expression "sat down at the right hand of God"[107] should not be taken as an indication towards any positioning on the Kabalistic Tree.

---

105 Some believe that Enoch is the Archangel Metatron, whose name means "next to the throne" – *AN*.
106 Meaning that the phrase "My power" may have been transformed in the canonical Gospels into the phrase "My God" – *AN*.
107 The *Septuagint* does not use various Names of God but rather a universal word – *Theos*, which on the Kabalistic plane means the Sfara *Keter*. In this sense, that phrase is an indication that Jesus ascended into the Sfara *Hohma*. Besides, the first Christians used to identify Jesus with Wisdom, i.e. with *Hohma* – *AN*.

However, if we still adapt the Gospels and Kabala, the question arises as to whether Jesus is "the stone come down from Heaven", and whether it coincides with the "head of the corner", of which René Guénon says that "this stone, precisely by reason of its origin, is as it were 'in exile' in its earthly sojourn, whence moreover it must finally reascend to the Heavens", according to the various traditions concerning this same stone or its equivalents. Since we agree that this stone is "in exile" in the physical world, and since we associate it with another similar definition – "Shekinah in exile", which refers to the Sfara *Malkut,* we come to the conclusion that "the stone come down from Heaven" refers to this Sfara, but only of the single Kabalistic Tree. Since we have agreed that it is "encoded" inside this stone that it will ascend to Heaven again, it could be likened rather to Jesus, but not, as some believe, to the Holy Grail, the purpose of which is to remain on Earth, because, as we have already mentioned, the role of this Holy Receptacle is that the energy of the Upper Worlds is retained in *Assia* – the "World of Action".

We have already explained that the "I" in the expression "I and My Father are one" (*John* 10:30, *NKJV*) refers to *Keter* of *Assia,* where Jesus fulfils His Mission.

If we revert again to the construction symbolism, and if this stone has "come down", how will it possibly have the function of a keystone in the structure of the building, since the latter would fall apart without it? This suggests that the "the stone come down from Heaven" has no structural purpose and therefore it should be a *copestone* – the one that closes the opening at the summit of the building, or also a *capstone* – the last stone, the summit stone, the chief stone symbolizing the Kabalistic "Head of the Corner". We believe that the *capstone* symbolizes the Sfara *Keter* in the Tree, and in this sense it represents the Sacral Principle of the edifice being built from down upwards, of which, however, it is the finishing stone, the "last stone", which, not in the construction sense, but on the Kabalistic plane, is the "Head of the Corner", and as such, it is established in the manifested Universe. However, the following question arises again: What is the meaning of this purpose of that stone, if it is the stone "come down", the stone "in exile", which has to return to Heaven again? After all, has it not voluntarily "come down" into the human world to save it? Naturally, the answer we will give ought to be in the context of the Kabalistic Tree, and in no case do we have any claims to establish a monopoly over the Truth. In the unfolded Kabalistic Tree, in view of the accomplishment of the Plan of the Great Architect of the Universe, the most important are the World of Formation – *Yetzira,* where the forms are generated, and the *Assia* World, where they are accomplished and materialized. This is so because the goal of any architectural project is to be accomplished in practice. In this sense, when discussing the symbolism of the "fallen stone", we must have in mind that it actually means two stones. The first one symbolizes the "falling" of the Sfara *Daat* from the *Yetzira* Tree into the *Assia* World, which has found its expression in the expulsion of Adam, or the so-called "Fall" of humans. The second one is related to the Sfara *Keter*, the "finishing stone" of the *Yetzira* Tree, which we identify with Christ, the "Heavenly" stone, having also "come down" into our *Assia* World. The described above can be interpreted as follows: the Sfara *Daat* of the *Yetzira* Tree represents the keystone in the structure of the two Worlds described. In its "falling" ("fall"), this structure is in danger of disintegration. That is why the "Heavenly" stone, Christ, in the person of Jesus, represents the Sfara *Keter* of *Yetzira*, which has no structural significance because it is a *copestone* – the one that closes the opening at the summit of the building, or also *capstone* – the last stone, the summit stone, the chief stone, goes in "exile" in the *Assia* World, the world of incarnate humans, in order to save that world. This, entirely conditionally and figuratively speaking, will happen, as the "Heavenly" stone, on its return, carries with it upwards also the human stone, which will become the keystone again. Therefore, if we accept the statement of the Christian Church that Jesus Christ is the Saviour, on the Kabalistic plane it means in principle that He, by ascending, has taken the position of the keystone – the Sfara *Daat* in the *Yetzira* World, instead of humankind as a whole, thus saving the structure from disintegration. This, however, is a whole position below the place where we said that the Messiah is positioned (the Sfara *Keter* of the *Yetzira* World), and perhaps this is the true essence of Jesus's sacrifice. *(Fig. 34 on p. 282.)* In some people's minds, probably the terrible thought will occur that, according to the version presented, the place of the Messiah remains "vacant". Let them not worry but rather be calm, because actually what is described should not be taken literally, and besides, the core essence of the Messiah is permanent, though manifesting itself in different embodiments. Everything explained so far applies above all to the Messiah in principle, and in particular – to the Messianic personality Jesus Christ proclaimed by Christians.

After all, Jesus may have offered from the cross such a prayer that would "eject" Him upwards so that He may take the position of the keystone in the Sfara *Daat* of the *Yetzira* Tree instead of humankind. Then, in the apocryphal *Gospel of Peter*, the words of Jesus would have the following meaning: "My power, My power, eject Me upwards!" However, if we assume that His words, as conveyed in the same Gospel – "My power, My power, you have forsaken Me!", are authentic, it means that His Mission is not fulfilled, so the structure of the Worlds continues to fall apart.

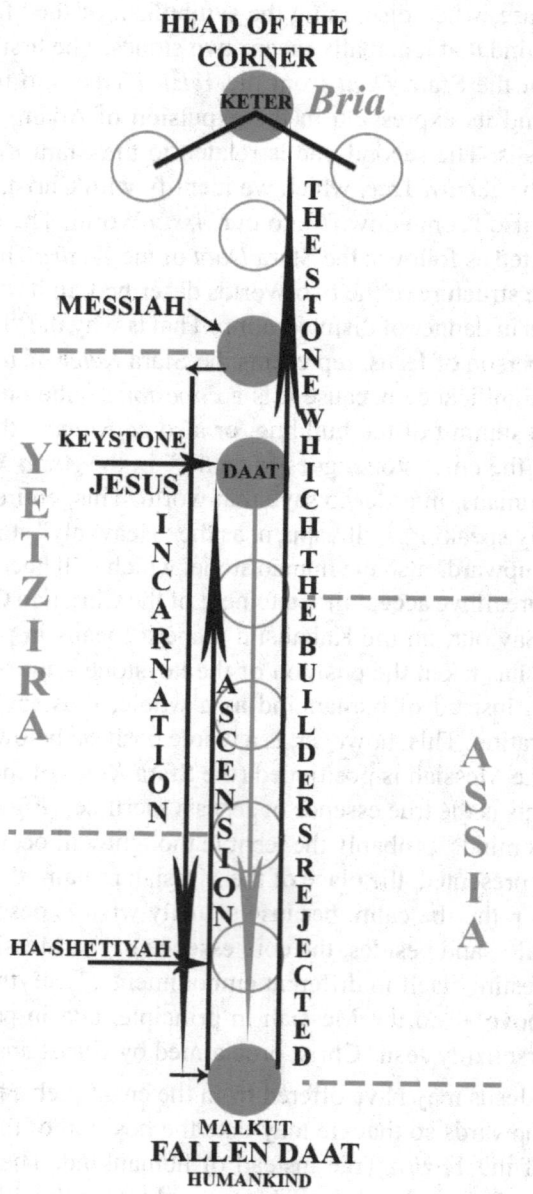

Figure 34

A confirmation of the above said is the current state of humankind, which, if it were already "saved", would not remain plunged into even greater sin – alienated from the Spiritual World and from God. More than two thousand years after Christ, humans still do not understand and still have not turned into a way of living those messages of Jesus regarding the "other cheek", the "second coat", that you should "love your fellow", and also "love your enemies". Now they have many coats but no fellow. We all know the popular wise saying that if you do not help yourself, then even God cannot help you. In this sense, we have already explained that even God cannot lift the stone-humans unless these stone-humans decide, by their own free will, to follow the "Heavenly" stone. That is why, if we still assume that Jesus is the Saviour, then He has saved Humankind as a whole by taking on the function of a key-stone in the *Assia-Yetzira* structure of the Kabalistic Tree. Humans, however, ought to themselves restore *Malkut* into the position of *Daat* (i.e. to walk the whole path from 9 to 12 o'clock) and become saviours of their own existence. This means that they have to regain their own original state of innocence and become consubstantial with God. This process is related to the energies of the soul and the body, and also their transformation, ultimately leading to the raising of consciousness to the levels of the Kabalistic Tree. Jesus has pointed out the way for everyone to accomplish this, through the words: "I am the Way, the Truth, and the Life." (*Holy Gospel of John* 14:6, *NKJV*)

Thus, through the example of Jesus Christ, humans are given the chance to restore the "fallen" Sfara on the individual plane. The algorithm of this achievement is contained in the steps of Jesus on His way to Golgotha, which we would define as the *Christian Arcana*. The Builders of Worlds, however, are given the opportunity to "eject" the stone upwards so that it becomes the "Head of the Corner". As for whether these are the Freemasons, in the form of a structured organizational form – we do not undertake to state this, taking into account the vast *eidos* of the term *masons* or *builders*,[108] especially since it refers to an individual inner Initiatic process. As Jesus Himself says to His disciples, "To you it has been given to know the Mysteries of the Kingdom of God, but to the rest it is given in parables, that 'Seeing they may not see, and hearing they may not understand'." (*Holy Gospel of Luke* 8:10, *NKJV*), and also, "He who has ears to hear, let him hear!" (*Holy Gospel of Matthew* 13:9, *NKJV*)

According to an esoteric law, "For everyone to whom much is given, from him much will be required." (*Luke* 12:48, *NKJV*) We wonder whether Freemasonry is already faced with the hard task of paying off…

We will revert again to the construction symbolism and will recall that the uniqueness of the keystone allots it the principle function and position of a structural keylock, not coinciding with the position of the last stone, the sum-

---

108  Only in the Bulgarian Bible and a few other Bibles, the word *masons* is used, while in all the others, the word *builders* is used – *AN*.

mit stone or the covering stone, and for that reason it also cannot be named "head of the corner". On the Kabalistic plane, however, we have substantiated the thesis that the Saviour, from the position of the "summit stone", may also take the place of a "keystone" in the person of its Avatar, such as Jesus is considered by Christians.

In our opinion, there exists still another case in which the function of a "keystone" is performed by a Divine Core Essence, which does not primordially have such a purpose. This is *El Shadai Hai* – the Great Architect of the Universe, Who occupies the place of the keystone in *Daat* of the *Bria* World. We have already clarified that the "precious stone underneath His Throne" which He detached and plunged it into the Abyss, left a hole in the Abyss, which represents the Sfara *Daat* of the *Bria* Tree, where the keystone should be. This is the place named *Palace of the Will,* from where the voice of the Holy Spirit echoes, constituting the creative instrument of *El Shadai Hai,* through which He operates. Thus, the function of the keystone in the *Bria – Atzilut* structure of the Kabalistic Tree, in our opinion, is performed by the Great Architect of the Universe, which is completely natural, having in mind the essence of this Name, as well as its position – in the Sfara *Yesod* of the *Atzilut* World, – coinciding with *Daat* of *Bria*. *(Fig. 23 on p. 186.)*

All that has been explained so far is an attempt, from our side, to present complex and deep macro- and microcosmic, involutionary-evolutionary processes in the language of constructional and Kabalistic symbolism as simply and schematically as possible. However, the literal and strictly formalized reading would distort the core essence of what is written and will distance the reader from the Truth.

Now, against the background of Kabalistic science, we are about to find out whether Jesus Christ is also the "Philosophers' Stone", to which many liken Him. To answer this question, we will need to ascertain whether the Summit Stone or Keystone, which we identified with the Saviour, are consubstantial with the Philosophers' Stone.

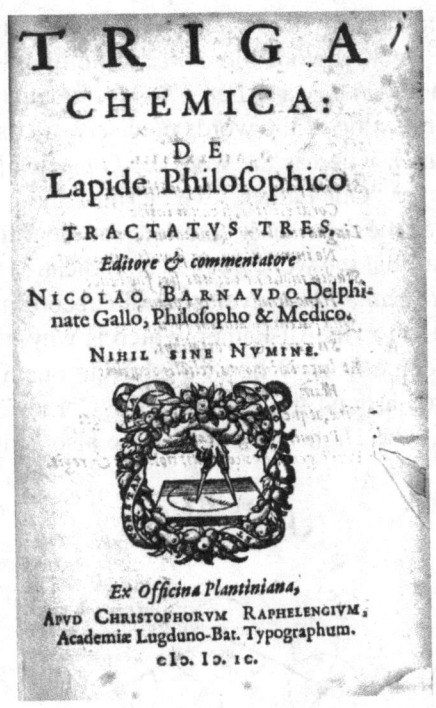

Figure 35

## The Philosophers' Stone

*Entium opus tendit ad perfectionem,*
*praeparatur que sic lapis philosophorum.*[109]
**Nicolas Barnaud**[110]

In ancient times people worshiped the Sun under the form of a black stone called *Elgabal (Elagabal), Elagabalus*[111] or *Heliogabalus*. This is the

---

109  From Latin: "Everything tends to work for perfection, being prepared just as the Philosophers' Stone" – *AN*.
110  Author of the Alchemical treatise *Triga Chemica: De Lapide Philosophico* ("Chemical Triad: Regarding the Philosophers' Stone") – *AN*.
111  *Elagabalus* or *Heliogabalus,* born Varius Avitus Bassus, is a Roman emperor of the Severan dynasty, who is identified with the eponymous Syrian or Phoenician deity Elagabalus. He rules from 218 to 222 under the official name of *Marcus Aurelius Antoninus*. Being a religious fanatic, during his reign he demonstrates disrespect for Roman traditions and sexual taboos, trying to impose the cult to Elagabalus, a Syrian deity of the Sun, in whose honour a temple was erected on the Palatine Hill. The sacred stone was also brought there – a symbol of the deity: a large black conical piece of meteorite, kept in the city of Emesa (Homs, Syria), where it was returned after the fall of Emperor Elagabalus – *AN*.

Sun Stone, called in Alchemy the *Philosophers' Stone*. In Kabala, some call it *Aben (Eben)*, the Hebrew word for *stone*, combining in itself *Ab – Father* (referring to the Sfara *Hohma*), and *Ben – Son* (referring to *Tiferet*). However, when we study the meaning of the words precisely, we assume that *Ab* rather refers to the *All-Father*, whereas the word for *father* is *aba*. When we examined the Lord's Prayer "Our Father", we clarified the meaning of the word *All-Father*, as well as the fact that it correlates to the Sfara *Keter*. In view of this, it becomes clear that the word *Aben* is an indication towards merging of the *Son* with the *All-Father*. However, the rule according to *patris potestas* is that the Son returns to His All-Father, which is why it happens in *Keter* – where the Son has come from. When we return to our All-Father, a Halo of Holiness is generated around the "Head of the Corner", and we come into possession of Zion – the Higher Might, and we also acquire "Eternal Life". (Fig. 36)

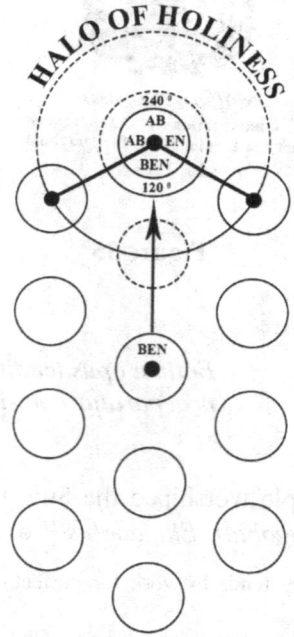

**Figure 36**

In confirmation of this, we can also say that *Ab* is a syllable that is an indication of a movement leading to the desired end or fruit. As we have learned, the ultimate goal for Freemasons is that the stone they have rejected (i.e. ejected) becomes the "Head of the Corner". However, in our opinion, this stone is not the one known by the name "Philosophers' Stone". It seems to be more characteristic with this designation in Alchemy, the purpose of which is to obtain it, which we have already essentially dwelt on. In Kabala it is called the *Sun Stone,* the *Divine Stone,* or more precisely – *Eloah Gabal,* which is an unequivocal indication towards *Tiferet,* the Sfara of *Shemesh* – the Sun. This Sfara is situated in the centre of the Tree and represents its harmonious point, from which eight channels (paths) stem, having a direct connection with the other Sfarot, with the exception of the separate *Malkut.* If we compare these channels to streams, then *Tiferet* is a "union of the streams" – which is also the most concealed meaning of the name *Michael.* The Gematria of his name is identical with the Gematria of *Aben-Gedulah (Great Stone),* and according to the Hebrew Kabala, he is the patron of the Sfara *Tiferet* in the *Bria* World, where it is overlaid by the Crown of the *Yetzira* World, in which the Universal Messianic Soul is positioned. The Spirit of this Soul, however, ought to be in the World of Pure Spirits – *Bria,* and therefore also in the Sfara *Tiferet* of that World. Thus the place of the Messiah is in *Keter* of the astral world of *Yetzira,* but at the same time also in the Sfara *Tiferet* of the *Bria* World, where His Spirit is positioned. *(Fig. 23 on p. 186.)* Since the single Kabalistic Tree does not allow for such differentiation, therefore the Western European Kabala, which is related to Christianity, places the Spirit of the Sun – Christ, as well as all the sacrificed Gods, in the Sfara *Tiferet,* which possesses the astral part of this Tree. The *Order of the Golden Dawn,* which is part of this tradition, calls this Sfara also the *King,* the *Son,* the *Human,* pointing at the Cross of Golgotha as its symbol, and at the Mysteries of the Crucifixion – as its spiritual experience. Here we are obliged to point out that Dion Fortune, a prominent representative of this Order, in her book *The Mystical Qabalah* wrote the following: "The six Sephiroth, of which *Tiphareth* is the centre, are sometimes called *Adam Kadmon,* the archetypal man". We do not agree with this statement, at least because some of these six Sfarot in the single Tree, which is actually referred to, are positioned in the *Yetzira* World of souls and cannot be part of the archetypal human. The above stated can only apply to the *Atzilut* World. In any case, we already had the opportunity to share our understanding on this topic. However, we agree with Dion Fortune when she says that "God the Father is assigned to *Keter;* but God the Son is assigned to *Tiphareth.*" *(Fig. 36 on p. 286.)*

Since we have already mentioned that the term *Philosophers' Stone* is predominantly alchemical, we will quote what Éliphas Lévi has said about the synthesis of the Philosophers' Stone: "This stone is one and multiple; it may be decomposed by analysis, and recomposed by synthesis. Analyzed, it is a powder, the so-called *powder of projection* of the alchemists. Prior to analysis, and after synthesis, it is a stone". We will now essentially recall again the process of its obtaining, which is connected with the transmutation of metals, and especially of lead into gold. For this to happen, the imperfect bond established in a metal between sulfur (the Sun) and mercury (Mercury) must be broken, the subtle must be separated from the gross, and then a new perfect bond has to be built. This means that the level of "Primordial Matter" should be reached, and after that, this perfect connection should be built, and then in the so-called *Kingdom of Apollo,* the "red stone" should be synthesized, which has plenty of synonyms but is known mostly as the *Philosophers' Stone.* Apollo is a solar deity, which is an indication that on the Kabalistic plane, the Kingdom of Apollo, where the Philosophers' Stone is synthesized, is the Sfara *Tiferet*. It is, in its essence, the universal stone by means of which, in the end, when a grain of gold is added, through its "growth" and "projection", this gold is multiplied. That is why we maintain that hence, the fundamental maxim in the Alchemical Work is derived: "In order to make gold, you must have gold". On the personality plane, this means that in order to turn the lead of egoism into the gold of Enlightenment, you must first become aware of your Primordial Divine Nature. Thus we come to the conclusion that the process of synthesizing the Philosophers' Stone should not be viewed literally but above all as an inner, energy-psychological process, bringing the body, soul and mind into perfect balance and harmony. Obtaining the Philosophers' Stone in the body means activating the "spiritual heart", the material correspondence of which is the "solar plexus", which begins to pulsate. It is behind and beyond the physical heart familiar to us, just as on the macrocosmic plane, behind and beyond the Sun familiar to us, there stands our "Spiritual Sun" – Sirius. In the Egyptian tradition, the Sun God Ra represents the material expression of the Spiritual Principle – *Amen (The Concealed One),* and together they form *Amen-Ra,* more known as *Amon-Ra.* When we become Amen-Ra – which means that the spiritual heart starts working in synchrony with the material one, and pushes energy unimpededly along the channels of the psyche between the Sfarot – we have already synthesized, in the Sfara *Tiferet,* the Sun Stone, *Eloah Gabal,* also called the *Philosophers' Stone,* and we have become "God's image and likeness". We have already mentioned that the Holy Grail is also a synonym of the Philosophers' Stone and is associated with a stone, but most often with a cup. Here is the right place to specify that the cup should be associated with the Sfara *Yesod,* whereas the "Living Water" in it – with the very Philosophers' Stone, and respectively – with the Sfara *Tiferet.* In any case, everything we have written about finding the Grail should be added to what has been exposed above regarding the Philosophers' Stone.

After all that has been explained so far, we can now examine already whether the summit stone, or the keystone, are consubstantial with the Philosophers' Stone. In view of our understanding, the keystone can in no way be identical with the Philosophers' Stone, regardless of the important function of the former, this function being rather in the sphere of practical functionality, within the framework of construction literalism, which is definitely not contained in the symbolism of the Philosophers' Stone. The latter cannot be likened to the "head of the corner" either, both from the point of view of construction symbolism and in a Kabalistic reading (according to which the Sfara *Keter* is meant, whose names do not correspond to those used for the Philosophers' Stone). Following this logic, in view of what has been said by us about the Messiah and His incarnation, Jesus (namely, that they are consubstantial with the Sfarot *Keter* and *Daat* of the *Yetzira* Tree), this *Homoousion* should not refer also to the Philosophers' Stone. Strictly speaking, however, it refers to the Messianic Soul; and yet, we have explained that the Spiritual Core Essence of this Soul is in the Sfara *Tiferet* of the *Bria* Tree – the Spiritual Sun of the unfolded Kabalistic Tree. After all, if we assume that Jesus is the incarnation of the Spirit of Christ (of the Messiah), then we can declare with confidence that He can be called the *Philosophers' Stone*. Insofar as the latter contains the Principle of a Primordial Potentiality with the possibility of unfolding and accomplishment, we believe that its archetype is positioned in the Sfara *Tiferet* of the *Bria* Tree – the World of Creation. Following the esoteric law that the subtle generates the gross, *Tiferet* of *Bria* represents the Primordial Philosophers' Stone generating the Philosophers' Stone of *Yetzira*, and finally obtains its materialization in *Assia*, the World of Action. Now it becomes clear why we maintain that, from the Sfara *Tiferet*, every next Sfarotic Tree unfolds so that the Ladder of Worlds may be constructed – the Ladder of Jacob.

It is logical to assume that the Philosophers' Stone can be likened to *Prima Materia;* and yet, from a Kabalistic point of view, we are obliged to specify that the "Prime Matter" is associated with the Sfara *Bina*, the dark womb that receives the universal vital force *Hayah* from the Sfara *Hohma*. It would also be logically grounded to form the illusory conclusion that the apprentice, symbolizing the undressed stone that can be transformed into any stone of the process of *Building the Edifice*, is close to the symbol of the "Primordial Matter". In view of the above indicated Kabalistic reading, however, the "Primordial Matter" is positioned in a very "High Place", in the "Three Heavenly Ones" (the *Supernals*) of the *Assia* Tree, and can in no way be associated with the apprentice.

## The Chief Cornerstone

> *"... Having been built on the foundation of the apostles and prophets, Jesus Christ Himself being the Chief Cornerstone."*
>
> **Epistle of St. Paul the Apostle to the Ephesians 2:20, NKJV**

Now the following question already arises with serious force: Which of all the described stones can be called the *Chief Cornerstone?* If we assume that Jesus is this stone, then, from a Kabalistic point of view, according to our understanding, it means that we are referring to the Sfara *Tiferet,* where, as we have said, the Spirit of Christ is positioned. It inevitably results from this that the Chief Cornerstone is the Philosophers' Stone. Before we further develop the topic, we will quote again part of what is written in the *Approved Oration OR10053* of the *United Grand Lodge of England:* "These cornerstones which guaranteed strength and stability became a colloquial term in biblical times, and are referred to in the Old Testament to describe leaders or prominent men".

We shall remind that this text refers to the fundamental stone placed in the northeast corner, which is also identified with the "chief cornerstone". This would mean that each and every leader and prominent man could be called a *chief cornerstone* and likened to Christ, which is unthinkable. Jesus is said to be the *Son of God,* but according to the esoteric tradition, this represents a certain Degree of Sacred Initiation, and everyone who attains it is called by this title. In one of the "Beatitudes" we quoted, the "Sons of God" are spoken of in the plural, which means that Jesus is not the only one of this kind. We can call *Sons of God* also Hermes Trismegistus, the Buddha, Moses, Abraham, Pythagoras, Muhammad, and many others. The question arises as to whether anyone who has reached the Degree of "Son of God" can be likened to a chief cornerstone? In this sense, does not Abraham, called the *Father of Nations,* or Moses, as being the leader of the Hebrews, fit into this definition? We believe that the exclusivity of Jesus Christ, Who is the only one said in plain text to be a *Chief Cornerstone,* is due to the circumstance that He was proclaimed the Messiah by Christians, unlike all the others we have given as an example, who, on the individual plane, have synthesized the Philosophers' Stone within themselves. It is precisely this Messiahship that distinguishes Jesus from the other Sons of God, who may also be Saviours for a community, a people, a nation, but not for humankind as a whole. Of course, each epoch has its own Messiah, and in this capacity, Jesus is not the only one again. Thus we come to the conclusion that the Messiah is the Chief Cornerstone of Humankind, which is the Sun Stone, the Philosophers' Stone, *Eloah Gabal,* and ultimately – the Sfara *Tiferet* of the Kabalistic Tree. Following the line of this reasoning, we agree with Dion Fortune who states the following: "The Redeemer... manifests in *Tiphareth,* and is forever striving to redeem His Kingdom by re-uniting it to the *Supernals*" (the "Three Heavenly Ones"). Such is the purpose of self-sacrifice in the name of humans, through which an emotional force is released, which balances the Kingdom and saves it. We have to note that, in the Old Testament, Abraham defeats the kings of Edom and gives tithes to Melkisedek. The six kingdoms of Edom, as we have already said, are an allegory of the unbalanced Sfarot around the Sfara *Tiferet,* symbolized by Abraham, who balances them. The universality of the symbolic message gives us reason to believe that Abraham may have been the Saviour of the Old Testament. We will immediately draw a parallel with what has been said about the process of synthesizing the Philosophers' Stone, the main characteristic of which on the human plane is the establishment of perfect equilibrium and harmony.

Here it is necessary to make the explicit clarification that everything said about the Messiah in a Kabalistic key correlates to Jesus only if we accept that He is the Saviour! However, we must note that orthodox Jews, having based their faith on the *Tanakh,* are still waiting for the *Mashiach* ("Messiah") to appear because they do not accept Jesus as such. It means that the "fallen Sfara" has yet to be restored at its original place, whereas the world is strongly disbalanced. All of this, interpreted on the individual plane, means that the sacrifice ought to be accepted so that it may have implementation power of authority. If we do not accept the self-sacrifice of Jesus, then this sacrifice has no worth or power for us. For true Christians who accept this sacrifice, Jesus is the Saviour, whereas for the rest, he is only one of the prophets or a false messiah, and they still expect the self-sacrifice of their own Saviour.

To us, there is no doubt that the *chief cornerstone,* from the point of view of the construction symbolism of sacral buildings, is not the "fundamental stone", the "cornerstone", the "keystone" or "summit stone", but rather the *altar.* It represents a projection of the *ha-Shetiyah* stone below it, and also of the "summit stone" above it, thus representing the holy harmonious point, both at the vertical and the horizontal plane. It symbolizes the Sfara *Tiferet,* which is the centre of the Kabalistic Tree, and it is no coincidence that its name means *Beauty.* We believe that the universality and uniqueness of the Chief Cornerstone are dictated by the circumstance that it forms a lot of angles, and is not the end of a single angle, just as eight channels stem from *Tiferet,* forming eight angles. Thus *Tiferet* represents the Chief Cornerstone of Wisdom and Truth, of Truth and Reason, of Reason and Severity, of Severity and Glory, of Glory and Power, of Power and Eternity, of Eternity and Mercy, and of Mercy and Wisdom. That is why the Chief Cornerstone can also be called the *Stone of Wisdom, Stone of Truth, Stone of Reason, Stone of Severity, Stone of Glory, Stone of Power, Stone of Eternity,* and *Stone of Mercy.* (Fig. 37) This is *Eloah Gabal,* this is *Helio Gabal,* this is the *Philosophers' Stone* bringing equilibrium and balance between these Sfarotic qualities so that the "Harmony of the Spheres" be achieved, and the "Masonic Regularity of the Temple" be built in order that we become the Divine Human. The methodology and the steps leading to this achievement are the subject of the *Kabala Arcanorum Re-dual* (the latter referring to the ancient authentic core essence of the word *ritual,* meaning that during a true *ritual,* a disciple ought to be transformed into a *double (dual)* of God *Re,* i.e. *Re-dual*), which is why we will only allow ourselves some essential clarifications. Before that, however, for the sake of greater clarity, we will make a final and essential retrospective of our understanding of the "stone" as a fundamental building block in the symbolism of Freemasonry.

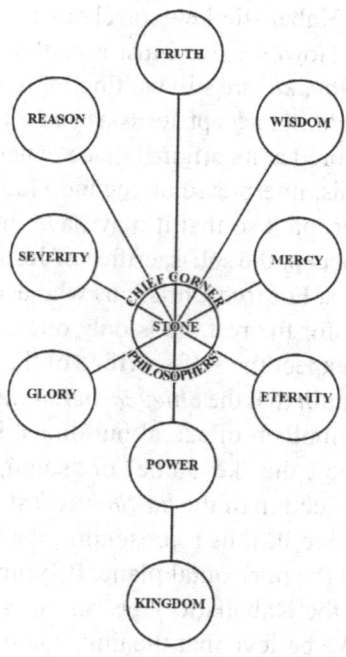

**Figure 37**

In the beginning, only unhewn stone was used for the construction of sacral buildings, because it was believed that any human intervention would desecrate the Divine Nature of the stone. Later on, this applied only to the altar, which symbolizes the connection with the sacral. There comes a moment when the Divine Nature of the undressed stone is symbolized only by the first stone laid in the foundation, which is why it is also called the *foundation stone,* the *fundamental stone,* which was the embodiment of the *ha-Shetiyah* stone. It should be placed symbolically with a certain ceremony at the very beginning of the construction process, unlike the first stone in the corner of the foundation, which has an important structural significance and sets the correct parameters of the edifice. We have traced how the cornerstone in the northeast began to be symbolically identified with the newly admitted apprentice, without this being based on any ancient original Masonic tradition. Then we concluded that this stone is not the so-called *chief cornerstone* because it does not have the characteristic of uniqueness, as there are four identical stones located in the corners of the foundation of the building. Thus we came to the thorough works of René Guénon, according to which the "chief cornerstone" is the one "rejected" by the builders, and it has become the "head of the corner", and this is also the "keystone", which is also the "summit stone" representing the principle of the building, crowning it with the crown of Divine Nature. We learned that Jesus Christ, according to the Christian doctrine, is the embodiment of the "Chief Cornerstone" and is likened by Christian alchemists to the "Philosophers' Stone". We differentiated these concepts both in a purely constructional and in a symbolic-Kabalistic aspect, and we pointed out that they should not be completely identified to each other. We concluded that the expression "head of the corner" should not be perceived in a constructional sense but in a purely Kabalistic sense, and refers to the Sfara *Keter* of the *Bria* World. We also accepted that from the viewpoint of the structure of the building, the "keystone" differs from the "summit stone", so no sign of equality should be placed between them. On the Kabalistic plane, they correlate to the Sfara *Daat* and the Sfara *Keter,* so thus the "summit stone" may be defined as the "head of the corner", but not always in the reality of the edifice as well. We also came to the conclusion that the Kabalistic correspondence of the "Chief Cornerstone" and the "Philosophers' Stone" is the Sfara *Tiferet,* and in the temple they are symbolized by the altar situated over the ritually laid "first stone", expressing the core essence of *ha-Shetiyah.* In this sense, we grounded the conclusion that if we assume that Jesus is the Messiah, then He can be called the "Chief Cornerstone" and the "Philosophers' Stone" because they are consubstantial. In the end, we realized that the emblematic psalm verse should be explored not only in a purely construction aspect, but also in a Kabalistic one, and therefore "the stone which the builders rejected" represents the symbolic "first stone" *(Yesod)* of the *Assia* Temple that becomes the "Head of the Corner" *(Keter)* of the Spiritual Temple. That is why the newly admitted apprentice, if he is to be likened to any of the "stones" referred to, that will be to the undressed "first stone" in which the Divine Core Essence of *ha-Shetiyah* is embedded, with the potential to be developed and to become the "Head of the Corner". *(See Fig. 34 on p. 282.)* This, as we have already explained, represents an inner, Initiatic Spiritual Path, which in the Masonic tradition is called "(the process of) *Building the Edifice*". This process of *Building the Edifice* should lead also to the "Masonic Regularity of the Temple".

# 19
# "Masonic Regularity of the Temple"

## The Temple

> *A Masonic carpet has the shape of an elongated rectangle... The rectangle symbolizes the construction plan of Solomon's Temple – one of the most admirable creations that ancient history tells us about.*
>
> ***Masonic Catechism***

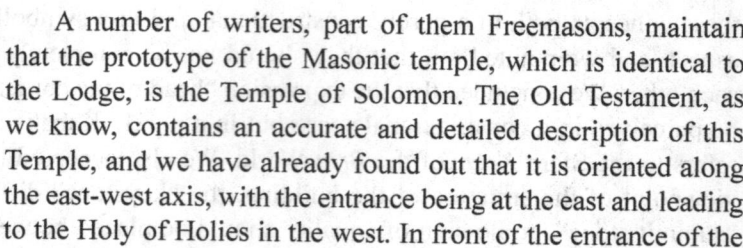

A number of writers, part of them Freemasons, maintain that the prototype of the Masonic temple, which is identical to the Lodge, is the Temple of Solomon. The Old Testament, as we know, contains an accurate and detailed description of this Temple, and we have already found out that it is oriented along the east-west axis, with the entrance being at the east and leading to the Holy of Holies in the west. In front of the entrance of the Temple on the right side facing the southeast, there was a copper sacrificial altar called "Sea". From its position (facing the east), we understand that the Temple of Solomon was entered from the east, whereas the Holy of Holies was located in the west: "He set the Sea on the right side, toward the southeast." (*Second Book of Paralipomenon/ Chronicles* 4:10, *NKJV*) The Temple was built in the western part of Mount Moriah because Shekinah rests in the west, and thus is in opposition of the ritual of the pagans who worshiped the Sun in the east. Thus it becomes clear that, according to the description, right is towards the south, while left is towards the north. However, the Masonic temples are oriented along the west-east axis, entering from the west and going eastwards, where the altar and the Worshipful Master of the Lodge are positioned. In this situation, the Masonic Lodge represents a mirror reflection of the Temple of Solomon, with the positions of the left and right being swapped.

## The Pillars in front of the Temple

> *"Then he set up the pillars before the temple, one on the right hand and the other on the left; he called the name of the one on the right hand Jachin, and the name of the one on the left Boaz."*
>
> **Second Book of Paralipomenon (Chronicles) 3:17, NKJV**

From this quote and from the previous one, it becomes clear that *Jahin* is in the south – at the right, whereas *Voaz* is in the north – at the left. This designation of the pillars as *left* and *right*, however, is according to the Temple. It means that if you are looking from the Holy of Holies towards the entrance of the Temple, then the right pillar is *Jahin*, whereas the left is *Voaz*. To the entrant, however, the pillars appear "reversed": *Jahin* on the left, and *Voaz* on the right. If we take as a point of reference the directions of Solomon's Temple, then *Voaz* should always be in the north, while *Jahin* – in the south. This explains their analogous position in the Masonic temples as well.

According to the *Schröder Rite* of Freemasonry, however, *Jahin* is positioned in the north, whereas *Voaz* – in the south. The same is observed also in the *French Rite*, in contrast to the *Scottish Rite*, in which the case is exactly the opposite.

The question arises regarding the reason for such a discrepancy between the Rites. Does it consist in the disregard that the Masonic temple is oriented along the length, as opposed to the Temple of Solomon – with the entrance from the west, and the altar being in the east, or is the idea to keep the positions of the pillars according to the entrants, as in Solomon's Temple – *Jahin* to the left, and *Voaz* to the right, not according to the world directions – *Voaz* being always in the north?

Before we continue exploring these issues, we will need to clarify the sacral nature of the Masonic temple. Each edifice with a sacral purpose, as we have already had the opportunity to explain, has a Cosmic correspondence, which is why its most widespread structure is formed along the vertical line from a square base crowned with a dome. They symbolize Earth and Heaven, respectively. The vertical structure is susceptible also to horizontal implementation, with a semicircular part being adjoined to one of the sides of the building with a square or rectangular shape. This semicircular part is the symbol of the "Heavenly" correspondence, from where light penetrates – i.e. the east. A typical example of this is also the Masonic temple.

If a cult to the Goddess is professed, then the feminine, lunar force will be operated with, and then the symbolic Heaven in the temple will be in the west, where the Sun sets and where the Moon is born. In the Temple of Solomon, as we have already noted, the Holy of Holies, symbolizing Heaven in the present context, was situated in the west.

In his book *La Franc-maçonnerie oubliée (The Forgotten Freemasonry)*, Robert Ambelain writes that one of the accusations directed against Anderson was that he disoriented the Lodge by positioning the Worshipful Master in the east, while tradition placed him in the west, and this necessitated the re-positioning of the two Wardens. According to the author, the position of the Worshipful Master of the Lodge in the west is confirmed by some old engravings from the beginning of the 18th century, where he is sitting behind the two Pillars – *Power* and *Beauty*, which have always been positioned in the west in the temple. The Pillar of Wisdom was in the east, opposite to the Worshipful Master, while the Warden was positioned behind him, armed with a sword, where he stands to this day, at the western threshold.

In the solar cults in the rituals, the masculine, solar force is operated with, so it is quite natural for the symbolic Heaven to be positioned in the East, where the Sun is born – *Ex Oriente Lux*.[112] It is indisputable that Orthodox Freemasonry uses the masculine energy and represents a specific cult to the Sun, the embodiment of which is the Worshipful Master of the Lodge, who is therefore positioned in the East. Behind him, however, in some Masonic temples and engravings, there are depictions of the Sun on the left and of the Moon on the right, while in others it is just the opposite. For those who stand against the Master, however, the Sun and the Moon represent mirror reflections. According to esoteric science, the solar force *"solve"* is positive and expanding, whereas the lunar force *"coagula"* is shrinking and formative. According to these characteristics and qualities, in view of the cardinal directions of the world, the south undoubtedly represents heat and expansion, whereas the north – cold and shrinking. Correlated to the human body facing the east, the south should correspond to the right half, while the north ought to correspond to the left half. The right side of the human being is considered to be the "solar", the masculine one, which is why the right hand is the stronger, the "giving" one. The left side, respectively, is the "lunar", feminine one, and therefore the left hand is the weaker, the "taking" one.

112  From Latin: "Out of the East, Light comes." (See *Matthew* 2:1 – 2) – *AN*.

We need to clarify that the north and the south directions, in the context of the two Pillars, should not be viewed as *north* corresponding to *negative*, and *south* – corresponding to *positive*. The north side is loaded with negativity because of what one of the Old Testament Prophets, Jeremiah, has said: "Out of the north, an evil shall break forth" (*Jeremiah* 1:14, *KJV*). From this verse, the north side, the left side, and the left path are all identified with evil and with the feminine essence as its transmitter.

With this stipulation, when we face the East, in the Masonic temple of some Orients, the Sun is depicted on the right, corresponding to the south and the right hand, while on the left is the Moon, corresponding to the north and the left hand; whereas in other Orients it is exactly the opposite. On the other hand, to the Master sitting on the Throne in the east, the position of the Sun and the Moon is the opposite in relation to those standing against him.

## About Left and Right, Masculine and Feminine

**Figure 38**

The principle point of reference for determining the left and the right should ultimately be the "Sitting on the Throne of Glory", Who, in the context of Freemasonry, is the Great Architect of the Universe, Whose symbol and embodiment is the Worshipful Master of the Lodge. He is the Will-Commander, the Giver and the Receiver, the Punisher and the All-Forgiving, He *IS*! Therefore, His right is the Right, and His left is the Left. His Right Hand is the active and creative one. If we continue with this anthropomorphic characteristic and transfer it to the Kabalistic Tree, then the Right and the Left Hand of the Creator are the two Pillars of the Tree, yet for the observer they are mirror-like reflections. Thus, conditionally, the Right Hand of the Creator, expressing and symbolizing the masculine principle, for the human standing before His Throne represents the Left, "feminine" Hand. That is why also the entirely masculine planets Saturn, Mars and Mercury, as well as their corresponding typically masculine qualities – comprehension *(Bina)*, severity *(Gebura)*, and logic *(Hod)*, are positioned in the Left Pillar of the Macrocosmic Kabalistic Tree for the observers, although for the latter these masculine qualities cannot be referred to their left, "feminine" hand.

In the same way, the Left Hand of the Creator, which is "feminine", with the sign (–), represents, to the one sitting before Him, the "masculine", right hand, with the sign (+). However, the Sfara *Hohma* (Wisdom – Sofia) and the most feminine planet Venus (the Sfara *Neza*), containing intuition, can in no way be in the "masculine" Pillar, and respectively they cannot refer to the right hand of the human being.

Thus, paradoxically for the observer of the Kabalistic Tree, traditionally the Right Pillar containing the "feminine planets" is considered to be belonging to the "Power" and is denoted as masculine (+), while the left one formed by the "masculine planets" is of the "Form" and is denoted as feminine (–). *(Fig. 39)*

| Left | Right |
|---|---|
| (–) | (+) |
| Feminine | Masculine |
| Bina | Hohma |
| Gebura | Hesed |
| Hod | Neza |

Figure 39

The real reason for the described paradigmatic configuration of the Pillars in the Kabalistic Tree is due to the mirror-like phenomena between the Worlds. This indication is given to us through the symbolism of the crossed legs of the "Goat" upon the Earth globe from the Fifteenth Arcanum. If there are discrepancies between the visions of the Prophets, they are due to the fact that some of them convey what they have seen with their "astral vision" literally, while others adapt it to the "physical view". Both are right, only the point of view is different.

Thus, the Left Pillar, to the observer, in the traditional image of the Kabalistic Tree, charged with a definite "masculine" connotation, is declared "feminine", and vice versa – the Right Pillar is declared "masculine" because of the circumstance that they are "taken down" literally from the astral world without being reversed in a mirror-like manner for the physical world. We will try to illustrate this in *Figures 40* and *41*.

**VIEW FROM ABOVE**
**ASTRAL WORLD**

| Right | Left |
|---|---|
| (−) | (+) |
| Masculine | Feminine |
| Bina | Hohma |
| Gebura | Hesed |
| Hod | Neza |

**PHYSICAL WORLD**

| (−) Left | (+) Right |
|---|---|
| Feminine | Masculine |

**VIEW FROM BELOW**
Literal shift by the observer

**Figure 40**

*Note:* In the physical world, left and right are perceived according to the existing paradigm: left − feminine, right − masculine.

**VIEW FROM ABOVE**
**ASTRAL WORLD**

| Right | Left |
|---|---|
| (−) | (+) |
| Masculine | Feminine |
| Bina | Hohma |
| Gebura | Hesed |
| Hod | Neza |

**PHYSICAL WORLD**

| (−) | (+) |
|---|---|
| Feminine | Masculine |
| Hohma | Bina |
| Hesed | Gebura |
| Neza | Hod |
| Left | Right |

**MIRROR-LIKE shift**
by the observer

**Figure 41**

*Note:* The mirror image is reversed only in relation to left − right, respectively masculine − feminine, but not in terms of polarity, because, as we have explained, in the physical world the man is the active one (+), whereas the woman is the passive one (−). That is why the plus remains to the right, whereas the minus − to the left of the observer's front.

The temple, however, is a projection of the astral world, and, respectively, of the astral Kabalistic Tree, which is why, according to the above explained, it should ultimately look as indicated in *Figure 42*.

**VIEW FROM ABOVE**
**ASTRAL WORLD**

| (–) | (+) |
|---|---|
| Right | Left |
| Bina | Hohma |
| Gebura | Hesed |
| Hod | Neza |
| Masculine | Feminine |

**TEMPLE**
**ENTRANT**

| Jachin | Boaz |
|---|---|
| (–) | (+) |
| Feminine | Masculine |
| Left | Right |

**NARTHEX**
**Physical World**
**VIEW FROM BELOW**

**Figure 42**

## The Kabalistic Tree and the Pillars in front of the Temple

The Worshipful Master of a Lodge represents a specific transmission between the Spiritual World and the astral temple and the participants in it. As we have already said, the polarity in these Worlds is different; and since they are mirror-like images of each other, therefore they swap places regarding left and right.

That is why the left and right positions should be determined by the position of the Worshipful Master. Thus, the pillars in front of the Temple of Solomon and the Masonic temple are situated in the same way in relation to the High Priest and the Worshipful Master – *Jahin* to the right and *Voaz* to the left, on the one hand, as well as, on the other hand, with respect to the entrant – *Jahin* to the left and *Voaz* to the right. *(Fig. 42)* This is yet another argument in favour of our statement that the pillars are arranged in such a configuration.

The above said is supported also by the meaning of the names of the two pillars. When translated, *Jahin* means: *"He establishes firmly"*. In this sense, it has some relation to the symbolic fundamental *ha-Shetiyah* stone.

*Voaz* literally means *"In Him is the Power"*, and also *Force, Might, Source of Strength* – and these meanings should be associated with the functional cornerstone.

The pillar called *Voaz* is named after the great-grandfather of King David, Solomon's father, which is why it symbolizes the male bloodline from David to Jesus, so we would call it the *royal* pillar. Therefore, in view of what has been said so far, it should be the masculine pillar. In this situation, *Jahin* is left to be the feminine pillar, a symbol of the female bloodline of the Levitical priests, from Aaron to John the Baptist, so we can call it the *spiritual* pillar.

The question arises as to whether the two pillars should be identified with the Kabalistic Tree. It is not argued that they were not part of the structure of the Temple and are completely independent. We have already mentioned more than once that the Temple of Solomon is the embodied Kabalistic Tree, and since the pillars are in front of the Temple, it means that they are not part of this Tree. Here, however, the knowledge of the extended Sfarotic Tree must be applied. The Temple, as a whole, is the astral projection of the *Yetzira* Tree, and therefore it is positioned in the astral world, whereas it is logical that the two pillars should be situated in the physical world, which is why they are a projection of the *Assia* Tree. According to esoteric science, in the physical world, the masculine principle is the active one with a plus sign, while the feminine principle is the passive, the accepting one, with a minus sign. In the astral world, however, things are reversed, so the feminine principle is the active one, with a plus sign. That is why also Eve in the Garden of Eden, in the astral world, is the one who takes an active position and provokes Adam. The conclusion is inevitable that the polarity of the pillars in front of Solomon's Temple should be assessed according to what has been explained above. The masculine pillar *Voaz* should be the active one with a plus sign, whereas the feminine pillar *Jahin* – the passive one, with a minus sign. Now it remains for us only to determine which pillar is on the right and which – on the left. We believe that this will not be difficult, since we know that specifically the pillars in front of Solomon's Temple reflect rather microcosmic principles related to kinship traditions and Initiatic traditions. In this case, they should be correlated to the left and the right side of the one entering the Temple.

Thus, the pillars in the Masonic temple should be situated as they were positioned in front of the Temple of Solomon for the entrants: *Jahin* – on the left, and *Voaz* – on the right.

Therefore, the "Entered Apprentice's Step" begins with the left foot, because apprentices ought to follow their own heart and trust their own intuition in their own path, marked by listening and acceptance. Apprentices symbolically cut off their own head: an indication to eliminate logic and understanding, because they do not have the necessary knowledge about them. Fellow Crafts, however, begin their step with their right foot, which is a sign that once having gained experience and knowledge, they already have to resort to logic and understanding, so they symbolically pull out their own heart. Thus the Apprentice follows the left pillar – *Jahin,* while the Fellow Craft follows the right pillar – *Voaz*. The "Master's Step" is directed to both pillars, which means that the Master has mastered both types of force, and both paths, but still starts with the left foot, which is a sign that the "spiritual" pillar has priority, or spirituality as an all-encompassing concept.

Viewing matters from the standpoint of the Macrocosmic and the Microcosmic Tree, as well as according to the extended Kabalistic Tree, represents the key to secrets leading towards the Truth. Using this Kabalistic key, we can say that *Jahin,* as a microcosmic, receiving, feminine force, receives the macrocosmic forces of the Spirit and "establishes firmly" the spiritual foundations of the Temple in the person of priesthood, whereas *Voaz,* as a microcosmic, active, masculine force, in the person of the royal dynasties, through its might, builds and fortifies this Temple, receiving the formative feminine forces of the Macrocosm. The symbolism of the two pillars is indisputable, because, as we have already said, they were not part of the structure of the Temple, and yet, since it represents the Kabalistic Tree, the pillars can in no way be not associated with the latter. Despite that, perhaps we should view them outside the context of *masculine – feminine, positive – negative.* Besides, the symbolism of the "two pillars", "two columns", "two obelisks", " two megaliths" was present still in the deep past, so it is not a Jewish "trademark", as well as the so-called "Jewish Star", "Star of David", or "Seal of Solomon". This symbolism is rather a "star symbolism", so the "twins" are probably a portal to the stars, beyond the known and beyond the profane, behind the veil of Isis.

## Movement inside the Temple

> *The Master follows the path of the Sun to reach his place in the East... The Brethren walk into the Temple, following the course of the Sun.*
> **Masonic Catechism**

The existence of north and south, of left and right is in principle the result of a conditional, conventional universal agreement. Time and space are the subjective perception of the binary world. Only the individual perception of perspective in the three-dimensional space determines where the left is and where the right is, which the image is and which its reflection is. What is important is the sacrality of the point of reference, as well as its physical manifestations. In the material world, the magnetic poles of the Earth represent such a manifestation. The very definition of *magnetic north,* however, also represents, in itself, a conditional conventional agreement. According to some, the tradition of positioning the north at the top and the south at the bottom of geographical maps dates back to Ptolemy, and in view of its conditionality, we also accept it. However, it is not at all conditional that the Earth is subjected to both terrestrial and cosmic magnetism, whereby different charges accumulate in its poles: in the North Pole – positive, whereas in the South Pole – negative. The direction of the lines of force of the magnetic field of a person, along whose spinal cord *(Sushumna),* constant current flows from top to bottom is determined by the "rule of the right hand": the thumb up indicates the direction of the current, while the folded fingers – the direction of the lines of force of the magnetic field. Or, the lines of force of a person's magnetic field are counterclockwise.

As is well known, the Earth revolves around its axis while orbiting the Sun at the same time. As a result of the Earth's rotation around its axis from west to east, the Sun seemingly rises from the east and sets to the west. It always rises at the east, but its movement for those in the northern hemisphere is clockwise, whereas, for those in the southern hemisphere – counterclockwise.

This also applies to the direction of rotation of terrestrial hurricanes, winds, waters, and all other factors. Also, as a result of the rotation of the Earth around its axis, the illusion of the rotation of the sky is obtained. The Earth's axis intersects the celestial sphere at 2 points. It is around these points, namely, that we observe the illusory rotation of the celestial sphere. They are positioned conditionally above the North Pole and below South Pole. Thus also the Sun moves in an illusory way; and the trajectory of the visible movement of the Sun, which "rotates" counterclockwise (like the Earth), is called the *Ecliptic.* Upon the celestial sphere, it forms a circle, which is inclined in relation to the plane of the celestial equator. Moving along the Ecliptic, in one year the Sun passes successively through 12 constellations that form the Zodiac. There are four cardinal points in the Ecliptic of the Sun, marking the two solstices and the two equinoxes. The real Masonic Year begins with the autumn equinox and ends at the summer solstice, ritually celebrated with the feast of John the Baptist. Thus, it includes the seasons of autumn, winter and spring, whereas summer is left for rest.

Another important clarification still needs to be made about the cardinal directions. The point of reference for their determining is the north magnetic pole; however, it should be noted that it does not coincide with the geographical North Pole. That is why the magnetic compass arrows point to the north and the south magnetic pole, but they do not coincide with the geographical ones. This difference between the two cardinal directions is called *magnetic declination*. Indisputably, all the above described factors, phenomena, processes and forces influencing humans are of significance to the Masonic temple and its rituality, and despite all conventionalities, they should be taken into account. For example, if the temple is not properly situated in space, everything explained so far loses its inner meaning. For precision, the direction of the north magnetic pole must be observed, not the geographical one, and the magnetic declination must be taken into account. This, naturally, is not necessary in practice; what is more important is that the direction of movement inside the temple coincides with the direction of rotation of the magnetic forces. This movement can be conditionally divided into *symbolic* and *operative*, such as the division of Freemasonry itself.

We will repeat again that if we were above the North Pole of the Earth, then the Earth and the Sun would look as if they were rotating counterclockwise relative to their respective axes. We have also explained that the "visible path" of the Sun along the Ecliptic is counterclockwise, contrary to its twenty-four-hour "movement" from east to west, which, as we have learned, is different in the different hemispheres. In the Masonic Rites, it is said that a Mason in the Temple "follows the path of the Sun". Naturally, this path will be the annual path along the Ecliptic, passing through the 12 constellations that form the Zodiac, which is counterclockwise. This path, however, as is well-known, is illusory because the Sun is motionless within the heliocentric system, and therefore this "movement" is "symbolic". Following this "movement" (counterclockwise), on entering the Temple from the west, a Mason has to go through the south, the east, then the north, and when leaving the Temple, he will complete this symbolic path of the Sun, ending in the west. The other illusory path is outlined, as we have said, from sunrise to sunset, but it is not constant as a direction of rotation, with regard to the two hemispheres, and therefore it cannot be unified for Freemasonry. Confirmation of this is that in some Orients, in one and the same hemisphere, a different movement is performed in the Temple, and in their Rites, it is said that "the visible path of the Sun is followed".

Furthermore, it is impossible, on entering the temple from the west, where the Sun hides, to follow its visible path, which begins with the sunrise in the east.

Here we are tempted to quote again Albert Mackey, who, in his book *The Symbolism of Freemasonry,* explains the following: "The *rite of circumambulation*... among the ancients appears to have been universal, and it originally alluded to the apparent course of the Sun in the firmament, which is from east to west by the way of the south". This is an autochthonous approach by which the Scotsman Mackey explains matters from the viewpoint of the geographical location of Scotland – in the northern hemisphere, hence the apparent path of the Sun is clockwise, or through the south. However, we have clarified that for those in the southern hemisphere, this movement is counterclockwise, or through the north. Therefore, the universality of the rotation through the south in the various traditions should not be explained through the course of the Sun, but through the symbolism of the right and left, which Mackey illustrates through the ceremony of the Greeks and Romans, called "moving from the right to the right". Its inner meaning is that the right side of those performing the rite of circumambulation should be besides the sacred centre, where the hearth, the altar or some other sacred object is situated. We believe that this rule is dictated by the "positivism" of the right, as opposed to the "negativism" of the left. According to Mackey, however, "This circuit by the right hand was done as a representation of the Sun's motion... Now, in this, the Masonic rite of circumambulation strictly agrees with the ancient one".

After this digression, we proceed to the movement called by us "operative" because it is the actual motion of the Earth, and this motion exerts its influence on everything upon the Earth. This movement, as we have learned, is counterclockwise and coincides with its direction of movement which we called "symbolic". Against the background of this "operative" movement, the direction of the motion of the electromagnetic forces in the respective hemisphere must also be taken into account. Since Bulgaria is situated in the northern hemisphere, these forces are also moving counterclockwise. Last but not least, the movement of the lines of force of the human electromagnetic field, which is also counterclockwise, should be taken into account as well. Ultimately, the "operative" movement in the Masonic temple coincides with the "symbolic" one described above.

There is no substantial ground for any movement during any ritual in any temple located in the northern hemisphere to be clockwise through the north. Even if, in view of the symbolic nature of Freemasonry, we disregard the factors determining the "operative" movement, and we position the directions, seasons and points of the solstices and equinoxes of an astrological mandala oriented to the east (in front of us), then the north on the right (for the observer on the left) will correspond to summer when the Masonic Year ends and the work on the process of *Building the Edifice* is completed. Therefore, there is no logic in any movement inside the temple that begins through the north, when the Masonic Year ends, and not through the south, when it begins. *(Fig. 43)* The only justification we can personally find for the movement adopted nowadays in the Masonic temples (from west to east through north) is the symbol of the right side, which has to be towards the centre of rotation, and yet we doubt that this is embedded as a principle in Freemasonry.

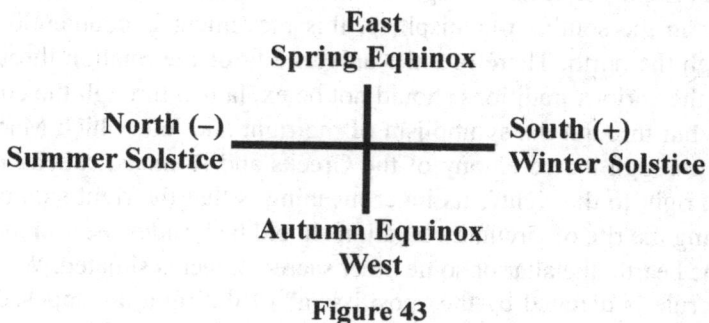

**Figure 43**

In support of our thesis, we will say also that the movement, in a purely energy aspect, is from "plus" towards "minus". Last but not least, the direction of rotation in Paneurhythmy, practiced by the White Brotherhood and given as a Revelation to Master Deunov, is also counterclockwise. Finally, the receiving force is centripetal, and it moves counterclockwise in the northern hemisphere, as we have learned. The giving, emitting force, on its part, is centrifugal, and in this case, it rotates clockwise.

In summary, we will state that Masonic Brethren should move during the Rites inside the temple, following the apparent annual course of the Sun along the Ecliptic, counterclockwise, in order to receive the transcendent force, whereas, at its ending – clockwise, in order to give off this force. During the twenty-four-hour period, they begin work at noon, when the Sun is at its zenith, with greatest might, and finish it at midnight, when the Sun is in its nadir and "exhausted", in order to give the received force out to the profane world.

Everything written on this subject, however, is in view of the contemporary orientation of the Masonic temple and of the position of the Worshipful Master, as well as with the stipulation that they are not explicitly connected with any authentic tradition. That is why it is even more important to build the Masonic Regularity of the Temple.

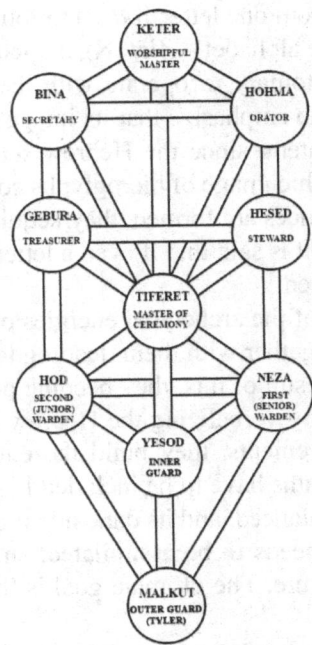

**Figure 44**

## Masonic Regularity of the Temple

> *Meditation is the only temple where, when you enter, you are truly inside a temple.*
>
> **Osho**

The Masonic temple is an etheric copy of the Kabalistic Tree; then, after its consecration, it already becomes part of the astral world.

In this Rite, the dignitaries represent an analogue of the Sfarot of the Kabalistic Tree and are transmitters of their energies. *(Fig. 44)* Each of the dignitaries has to become, at some point, as a result of the ritual work, a pure transmitter of these energies. In order for the "Masonic Regularity of the Temple" to be built, the energy entering the matrix system of the Kabalistic Tree has to be distributed between the various Sfarot through the Arcana Paths. This is how the energy model of the Sfarotic Tree is built, which in the Masonic tradition is called "Masonic Regularity of the Temple". The correct positions of the paths are established by the exact distribution of the incoming energy between the Sfarot. The measurement unit for this energy is one letter *Yod*, since it is the constructive hieroglyph of the Hebrew script, which is configured by its modifications. In this sense, we can call the letter *Yod – the "seed" hieroglyph*.

Thus the energy varies from one letter *Yod* (') to four letters *Yod,* contained in the first hieroglyph of the alphabet – *Alef* (א), depicting the *four elements.*[113]

In Hebrew, it is customary to operate with the term *letter,* but we will use the term *hieroglyph* to emphasize that its image has a primarily symbolic meaning and energy content, since the Hebrew script represents archetypal materialization. The graphic image of hieroglyphs contains magic symbolism, so when words and sentences are formed, they acquire implementation power of authority. That is why it is said that if even a letter in the Torah is changed, the world may be destroyed.

Under the influence of the archetypal energies of the Sfarot, the dignitaries begin to co-vibrate together with them, leading to transformations of their minds and bodies. As a result of this, they become pure transmitters and convey these energies, and, by verbalizing the Hebrew hieroglyphs and through corresponding body movements, they build the energy paths (connections) between the Sfarot. All paths have to be included in succession, all aspects of personality ought to be balanced, and its dark side must be mastered. The dual nature of sexuality also needs to be assimilated, since everyone has a masculine and a feminine nature. The ultimate goal is the union with the Divine Nature – the Sfara *Keter.*

Thus, the Masonic Lodge is transformed into a harmonious energy environment, which acquires the qualities of a Holy Place. In Bulgarian, the word for *holy* is свят *[svjat]* and has Aramaic origins, and means a *fulcrum* around which everything revolves and from which a harmonious circle unfolds. In this sense, the Temple represents a Holy Point spreading Light. Whoever builds the Temple becomes integrated into the Tree of Life and its energy system, the symbol of which is Adam Kadmon.

**Figure 45**

---

113  The first letter of the Hebrew alphabet, *Alef,* is composed of four letters *Yod,* opposite to each other, in pairs (Papus, *La Cabbale, Tradition secrète de l'Occident – The Kabala: Secret Tradition of the West) – AN.*

# Squaring the Circle

*Each decision ought to be taken wholeheartedly, and the result must not be sought.*

*Lao Tzu*

Building the Temple, however, both in view of the constructional and the energy aspect, cannot be accomplished unless the so-called *squaring the circle* is implemented. The latter is formed by the celestial unity of the vault and the square of the earthly elements, the transition being performed by the octagon, representing the passage from one state into another. Since the knowledge of squaring the circle is an encoded Kabalistic Secret, we will try to lift its veil a little.

*Squaring the circle,* from the geometrical point of view, means *constructing a square with the same area as the area of a given circle*. As a purely mathematical problem, finding the squaring of the circle is considered to be an intellectual activity without any practical application. However, this activity engages the minds and the attention of mathematicians, until, in the end of the 19th century, the German mathematician Lindemann proves that the number Pi ($\pi$) is not algebraic, i.e. that it is a transcendental number. In order to be able to find the squaring of the circle, it must be possible to write the number Pi by using a finite number of digits and operations, which turns out to be practically impossible. Since Lindemann proves that the number Pi is transcendental, it should follow that a square with an area equal to the area of a given circle cannot be constructed. From then on, the subject of squaring the circle ceases to excite mathematicians.

However, is this task really without any practical application? In order to answer this question, we must, only superficially, dwell on the essence of numbers. We have explained that Kabala represents calculation, and it is no coincidence that one of the designations of the Sfarot is *Numbers*. The core essence of numbers leads to the idea of infinity. The Hellenes came to this idea through the Paradoxes of Zeno of Elea, who lived in the 5th century BC. One of these Paradoxes is that the fast-footed Achilles can never outrun the tortoise if the tortoise is given an advantage before the start. Another of his Paradoxes is about Dichotomy (you can never leave the room you are in right now). The conclusion is that with infinite divisibility of time and space, motion can never start.

Algebra, mathematics and geometry are contained in Kabala, which is their original source, and the problem of finding the squaring of the circle, together with the consequences of this, have to be sought in this ancient science. Moreover, the mathematical meaning of solving this problem is only the veil hiding its true Kabalistic essence. Since this requires knowledge of the energy dynamics of the Kabalistic Tree, we will go a little further into its core essence. We have explained that the energy is distributed throughout the Sfarotic Tree, as a result of which each Sfara receives certain energy. Without going into details, we will point out that in the involution of the Creative Logos, the four primal elements are formed: *fire (Hohma* – energy of 4 letters *Yod), air (Bina* – 3 letters *Yod), water (Hesed* – 2 letters *Yod)*, and *earth (Gebura* – 1 letter *Yod)*. Summing up their energy values (4 + 3 + 2 + 1 = 10), we get the number 10, symbolizing a snake biting its tail, or a circle. The so described quaternary of 2 by 2 conjugated binaries *(air – water, fire – earth)* according to its energy essence represents also a circle. In this way, squaring the circle is obtained, since the energy of the four Sfarot forms an energy circle, and thus a specific square inscribed in a circle is built. In Masonic symbolism, it is encoded in the Square and the Compass.

We present in a quite simplified and schematic manner these multi-layered and complex spiritual-energy processes so that they may be understood within the framework of this book, the purpose of which is not to reveal them. Squaring the circle contains the doctrine of magnetism, illustrated by the ancient word *AZOT*. Besides it, the words *Tora, Taro, Orat* and *Rota* are also positioned upon the squaring – these words also contain the concept of the terrestrial magnetism. In a New Testament key, we would also point out the *INRI* tetragram, which, in addition to its traditional meaning, contains the alchemical formula *Igne Natura Renovatur Integra,* which in translation means "By fire, Nature is renewed".[114]

Through the "words of power" *(Orat),* the Master activates magnetism, whereas, through the incantation, he commands the four elements – and, acquiring implementation power of authority, he embodies the Masonic ideas. In its deepest Kabalistic core essence, squaring the circle represents practical knowledge of the mechanism of activation of *God's Chariot (Merkaba),* which is a dangerous undertaking and is not the subject of this book. Nevertheless, we will give a general exoteric description of the essence of *Merkaba.*

---

[114] According to Jean-Marie Ragon, *INRI* is composed of the first letters of the four elements in Hebrew: *Iaminim – water* (actually *Iam* means "sea"), *Nour – fire, Ruach – air, Iebschah – earth.* Another interpretation is that it refers to the Latin *In Necis Renascor Integer:* "In death, He will be reborn intact and pure" – *AN.*

**Figure 45**

## Mer-Ka-Ba

> *... Also out of the midst thereof came the likeness of four living creatures. And this was their appearance... As for the likeness of their faces, they four had the face of a man, and the face of a lion, on the right side: and they four had the face of an ox on the left side; they four also had the face of an eagle.*
>
> **Book of the Prophet Ezekiel 1:5;10, KJV**

The Chariot is a very ancient and universal symbol. It is well known that the wheel as a circle represents a general image of the Universe, as it embodies a consequence of the emanation of the centre. The two wheels connected by an axis are associated with Heaven and Earth as parts of the Cosmic Whole. This notion is associated with the symbolism of the Chariot, especially in the Hindu and Hebrew traditions. From the moment of our birth, a cocoon is built around us, separating us from the surrounding world. While we are children, this cocoon is transparent, letting God's Light through itself, and thus we are one with the Truth. As a result of upbringing and moral education, we begin to adapt, adopting the traditions of society, due to which the cocoon gradually turns into an opaque and hard shell – *qlifa*. The elastic and transparent cocoon becomes the *qlifa* of our illusory perception of the world, and on the walls of the shell we see only our reflection, which is composed of the tricks of the intellect. This is how lies and egoism are born, which turn the soul into an easy prey for evil. Hermes says that "The greatest evil for humans is ignorance regarding God". In order to get to know God's Truth, we must penetrate beyond the cocoon of lies and egoism, cut a gap in the web of words, and escape from the illusions of the intellect. This will happen when we purify our heart through the Truth, whereas our mind – through knowledge, and thus we will free ourselves from lies and egoism, and hence – from the great illusion. In addition to the described qualitative and ethical dimensions, the cocoon in which we are has also energy essence and parameters. It is a biological field of force, which is formed by the sum of the force fields of the main chakras in the body. The esoteric designation of this field of force is called *Merkaba*.

The energy might and frequency of the force field of God's creative energy, passing through the various worlds, decrease until they reach their minimum in the physical world, where they turn into unspiritualized physical energy – *matter*. Each matter is a potential source of energy, but its emission is possible only as a result of the influence of higher forms of energy. Thus, any physical energy contains the potential to be spiritualized and transformed into biological energy, which is contained in every living being. Any biological energy, on its part, builds a force field – *Merkaba*. The *Merkaba* is the receptor and re-transmitter of God's Rays containing God's Might of the Names of God. Thus we can become Co-Creators without the danger of the Might of God's energy burning us to ashes. Our vital force is the amount of energy we dispose of in order to fulfil our assigned mission. By fulfilling this mission with the help of the God-co-creative energy *Kundalini*, we activate our chakras and receive a new amount of spiritual energy in the form of *prana*, and thus, increasing our energy potential, we increase the elasticity and transparency of our *Merkaba*, up to the needed degree, to endure the expanding Universe. Thus we are transformed into more and more ethereal beings with an elastic energy shell, transmitting God's Light, and thus becoming a source of Light – Spiritual Suns.

In Ancient Egypt, from where it comes as knowledge and practical application, *Mer-Ka-Ba* can be defined as the *all-seeing eye (Mer)*,[115] the *etheric double (Ka)* and the *soul (Ba)*. This meaning gives us the knowledge that the movement is carried out by the astral body, the "astrosome" of the soul, with the sixth chakra – the all-seeing eye – already activated; or it refers to an astral journey of the soul, the all-seeing eye being its navigator.

---

115 *Mer* in Egyptian means *pyramid, light, place for ascension,* and *third eye,* and corresponds to the sixth chakra –*AN*.

# The All-Seeing Eye

> *It is a good viewpoint to see the world as a dream. When you have something like a nightmare, you will wake up and tell yourself that it was only a dream.*
> **Yamamoto Tsunetomo**

This is one of the common symbols for Christianity and Freemasonry, although it is rather a substitute for the Hebrew Tetragrammaton (and sometimes only its abbreviated expression – *Yod*), inscribed in a triangle. The triangle referred to always occupies a central position, and therefore in Freemasonry it is correctly positioned between the Sun and the Moon. Hence, the eye enclosed in this triangle should be "central", or "frontal" – that is, the "third eye" which "sees everything" in the perfect simultaneity of the eternal present. Thus, the hieroglyph *Yod* represents the "Eye of the World".

The regular upright triangle (with the apex up) corresponds to the Primordial Principle, and therefore the eye inside it looks downwards, and in addition to its general meaning of Omnipresence, it also has the meaning of Providence; whereas the inverted triangle is associated with the reflection of manifestation. However, if this reflection is viewed on the human plane, then it represents a geometric diagram of the heart. The eye representing its centre then becomes the "eye of the heart", which imparts to it the quality of an "open heart". This corresponds to the expression *El Fatah,* meaning "Be open!", used by Jesus. We also explained that *Yod* is a "seed letter", and as such can also be called a "seed in the heart", which imparts to it the meaning of the "Germ of Immortality". The hieroglyph *Yod* can be likened to a "wound" in the heart, as evidenced by Christian symbolism, according to which the "Source of Immortality" is associated with the double current of blood and water flowing from an opening in the heart of Jesus. It was precisely this "Drink of Immortality", according to the legend, that was collected into the Grail by Joseph of Arimathea. In this regard, we must point out that the cup itself is a symbolic equivalent of a heart and is traditionally depicted in the form of an inverted triangle. Thus, in the end, the All-Seeing Eye can be called the "Eye of Immortality", and it stands between the Sun and the Moon in the Masonic temple, symbolizing the Worshipful Master of the Lodge through whom Hiram receives Immortality. In this context, we can accept the widespread opinion that the Master symbolizes the Sun, only and solely in the sense of the Spiritual Sun – the Tear of Isis, or the *Yod* of the Sun.

Some believe that the *Merkaba,* in addition to the Chariot, is symbolized, in its two-dimensional image, by the six-pointed *Star of David (Shield of David),* each vertex of which corresponds to one of the chakras, and in the middle is the *Sahasrara* chakra. Others liken it, in its three-dimensional image, to two mutually penetrating tetrahedrons – the upper one with electric characteristics and masculine by its nature, whereas the lower one – magnetic and feminine. We agree with these formulations, and still we will try to develop them further from the Arcana point of view. We have already mentioned that the seven-pointed star is the pentacle of the Seventh Arcanum, and its image is the Victorious Magus, triumphing upon a Chariot drawn by two sphinxes, symbolizing the astral binary, swirling in a joint turbulence. These vortex formations drive the wheels of the chariot, nailed together so that the heads of the nails holding the rims and looking like eyes are visible. This description resembles the chariot of the Prophet Ezekiel, which in Kabala represents the *Merkaba*.

"As for their rims, they were so high they were awesome; and their rims were full of eyes, all around the four of them." (*Book of the Prophet Ezekiel* 1:18, *NKJV*)

Since the Egyptian tradition predates the Hebrew tradition, then we can say that the *Merkaba* is an analogue of the Chariot of the Seventh Arcanum, which in any case seems to be a symbol of an astral vehicle. This stellar journey, however, can in no way be accomplished without the energy of the planets with which we are in constant relation of dependency. That is why we ought to direct our look towards the astrological septagram, known as the *Star of the Magi. (Fig. 47)*

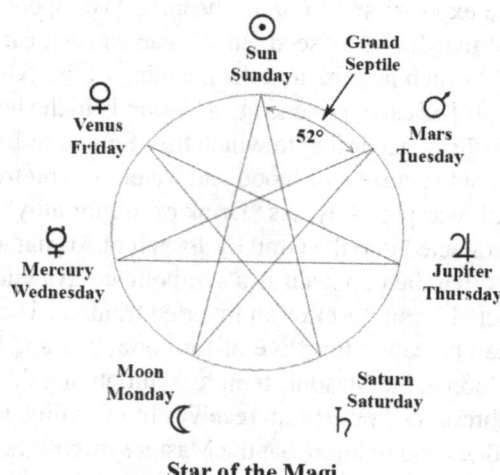

Star of the Magi

**Figure 47**

At its vertexes, the seven planets are positioned, which are known since ancient times, in the so-called *Chaldean Order* – from the fastest to the slowest planet. The distance between the vertexes is approximately 52 degrees, and this configuration is called *Grand Septile*. However, it is used only as a symbol and has no implementation power of authority.

It must be transformed into the so-called *Harmonious Sextile* (the distance between the vertexes of which is 60 degrees) – the Star of Solomon, already familiar to us, which is endowed with implementation power and is used in the operative order for magic operations. We will not explain the complex algorithm by which the way the planets are arranged on the six-pointed star is reached, but we will only point out that the purpose of their configuration is to obtain two polar triangles, conditionally called *masculine* and *feminine*. On the masculine triangle – with the apex up, the so-called "masculine planets" are positioned, and their energy flows in it clockwise. The "feminine planets" are situated on the feminine triangle (the bisexual Mercury playing the role of a feminine planet), and their energy flows counterclockwise. *(Fig. 47ª)*

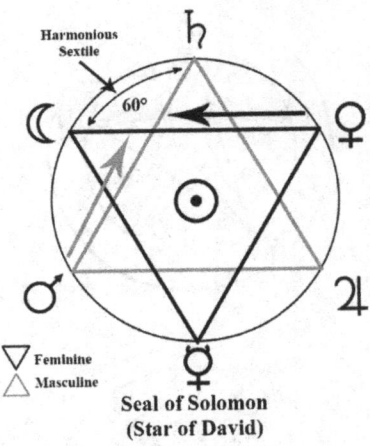

**Figure 47ª**

In view of this, we may call the feminine triangle "triangle of the heart" and "receiving triangle", whereas the masculine one – "triangle of the mind" and "giving triangle", and in the present context – "triangle initiating teleportation". This is very complex and practically involves certain experience requiring the visualization of the two triangles in the human body, as well as setting their energies into motion simultaneously, these energies being analogous to the respective planets and at the same time synchronized with the energies of the heart and the mind.

The use of an unbalanced *Merkaba* leads to destructive creativity. It means that we must, along the path of our evolution towards perfection, set the energy of the mind and the heart into perfect harmony, and then we will become true Freemasons, Builders of Worlds, and we will be called *Sons of God*.

According to some Initiates, the Archangel Lucifer once ruled the so-called *external (unbalanced) Merkaba,* and with its help, he decided to build his own world independently of God. This turned him into the "fallen" Archangel and a symbol of the universal evil – the *Devil*.

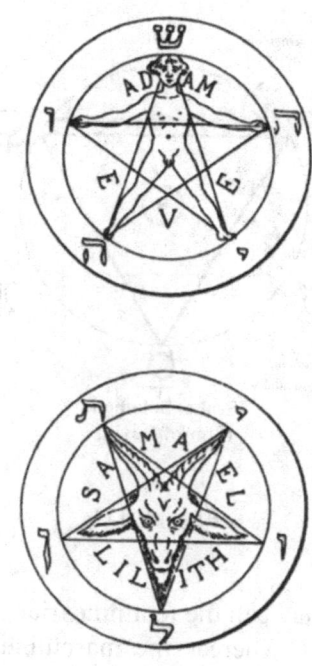

# VI
# APSE

## 20
## The Devil

### The Sin

*It makes a great deal of difference whether one wills not to sin or has not the knowledge to sin.*
**Lucius Annaeus Seneca**

The topic of the Devil is inextricably linked to sin. We have already conceptually discussed the subject of evil, sin, and the Fall, so we will now make a more in-depth comparative and esoteric analysis of their essence and origin. In a more general sense, *sin* represents a specific violation of moral and ethical norms established by society. On the religious plane, *sin* is considered to be a deed, an action transgressing the laws and rules established by God. Furthermore, the Aramaic word for *sin* means "deviation from the goal" ("missing the goal") or "error".

The topic of sin has been treated by various researchers through several basic methods. One of them is the literal method, through which they seek material evidence of the Fall in their attempts to prove that it is or it is not a real historical fact. Others, through historical interpretation, search for the exact mythological time and place, rather than specific geographical concepts and places. Proponents of the allegorical method, on their part, explore sin not as a fact that once took place in space and time, but as a metaphysical fact that is present in the activity of every human individual. In *Dictionnaire Raisonné de Bibliologie* (*Explanatory Dictionary of Bibliology*) by Gabriel Peignot, it is written that the Fall is "an event which, according to the Bible, separated the human being from God and perverted the human nature".

At the theological level, the original sin is not considered to be hereditary in the contemporary sense of this word. A person's deficiencies of the physical body and the psyche are viewed without any relation to the original sin. The full participation in Church life and, above all, the reception of the Sacraments is a guarantee of salvation. The redemption performed by Jesus Christ is done only once, and it does not by itself purify the original sin, but provides the foundation upon which, owing to one's own efforts, one can be saved. We will not do any in-depth study of this topic, so we will focus only on the views of the various religious traditions.

Adam's sin, according to the Rabbis, had some severe consequences for himself and for the Earth. In the first place, after the "Fall", *Shekinah* left the Earth and after that descended only in certain cases.[116] Adam lost his personal splendour, immortality, and giant stature. From that moment on, all humans were doomed to die, and no one, not even the most righteous, could escape this common fate. The old temptation of the Serpent was enough to bring death.

According to Christianity, the sin committed by Eve is being passed on to her descendants by inheritance, or in other words, each human is born sinful. The only thing that can free humans from sin and lead to the salvation of their soul is the faith in Jesus Christ. Jesus Christ Himself, in His words described in the New Testament, does not dwell on the sin of the forefathers. On the other hand, the subject is vividly represented in the writings of the Apostles. Thus, according to the New Testament, Jesus Christ offers His sacrifice precisely to atone for the original sin, to erase, as being the second Adam, what was done by the first one, and to restore the lost harmony between God and the human being.

According to the doctrine of the Orthodox Church, the Fall and the original sin do not substantially damage the individual human nature. The original sin is a fact, insofar as each individual suffers its consequences. Purification from this sin takes place through the righteous Christian life in the Church, especially through the participation in the Sacraments. According to the postulates of the Council of Carthage of 252 AD, "it should not be forbidden to baptize an infant who has just been born, has not sinned with anything, but only having descended from the flesh of Adam, has received the contagion of ancient death by birth", and that at the baptism of infants, not their own sins are forgiven, but the sins of others.

The Roman Catholic Church, on its part, teaches that the original sin does not change the human nature – humans are only deprived of the gifts of Grace (bodily immortality, moral purity and domination over nature), and this is in fact the punishment for Adam and Eve, which can be redeemed through the Christian Sacraments.

Unlike Catholicism and, in part, Orthodoxy, Protestantism believes that the original sin has totally perverted the human nature and the relationship between God and the human being, and that salvation itself is the result of God's Will in accordance with faith, without having a direct connection with

---

116 Many analysts consider 66 AD, during the destruction of the Second Temple, to be the moment of departure of *Shekinah – AN*.

the deeds of humans in the real world, i.e. salvation is an entirely Divine Deed that does not depend on human participation. "For by Grace you have been saved through faith, and that not of yourselves; it is the gift of God" (*Epistle of St. Apostle Paul to the Ephesians* 2:8, *NKJV*)

Islam views as sin any action that is directed against the Will of Allah, and sin itself is an action, not a state of being. The Quran teaches that humans are capable of selling their own soul to evil, and that even prophets may be sinful. According to Islam, prayer and doing good deeds are the two ways to atone for sin.

The term "original sin" is not present in the *Tanakh*. It should come as no surprise, therefore, that this doctrine was not developed in Judaic theology under that name. Rather, this concept in Judaism is called the "Serpent's Advice". The advice given by the Serpent to Eve was the one that brought death to all humankind – not any sin committed by humans themselves.

According to some Kabalists, the word for "sin" was *san*, composed of two letters – *Sameh* and *Nun*. They believe that these are the first letters of the words *sam* – "poison", and *nahash* – "serpent". Thus sin is personified by a poisonous serpent.

The image of the Serpent (Dragon) in the Old Testament symbolizes the forces of destruction and chaos. It is a creature that rebels against the Creator and that will be defeated only at the end of the ages.

## Satan

*Fear of the devil is one way of doubting God.*

**Khalīl Jubrān**

In the New Testament, the Devil is called *Satan* and is described as "a great, fiery red Dragon having seven heads and ten horns, and seven diadems on his heads" (*Revelation of St. John the Theologian* 12:3, *NKJV*) and also "the great Dragon, that Serpent of old, called the Devil and Satan, who deceives the whole world" (*Revelation* 12:9, *NKJV*). The Apostle John says that the will for evil was generated in the world of spiritual beings in the person of the Devil – "He who sins is of the Devil, for the Devil has sinned from the beginning". (*First Epistle of St. John the Theologian* 3:8, *NKJV*) He identifies the Devil with the Serpent from the *First Book of Moses – Genesis,* and also with a Dragon.

Traditionally, Orthodox, Catholic, and Protestant theology consider Satan to be the one who speaks through the Serpent and tempts Eve to transgress

God's Decrees. Christian theology views the image of Satan as identical with that of the Devil and as an Angel who rebels against God. The thesis is that Satan is an exiled Angel who only after rebelling against the Lord became a Devil, and has since begun to sin. Traditionally, the reason for his downfall is his haughty pride and envy towards the human being.

In the *Book of Enoch,* it is written that Satan is the tempter and seducer of Eve, which is the reason why he was cast out of Eden, together with other Angels, because of their evil deeds. Since then he has been called *Satan,* although until then his name was *Satanail.*

The idea of the Fall of Satan, as well as that of other Angels, has been present in the Apocrypha since the time of Babylon. Satan is at the head of a whole army of Angels who are traditionally considered to be spiritual creatures in an intermediate position between God and humans. They appear in Zoroastrianism, then in the subsequent monotheistic religions – Judaism, Christianity and Islam, according to which God does not intervene directly, but through helpers – intermediaries who do His Will. This role is performed by the Angels, who are messengers, destroyers, Guardian Angels, carriers of the soul after the death of a human, as well as helpers of humans. In the Old Testament, the Hebrew God sends His Angels to deliver messages, to protect, or to destroy. In early Judaism, there was no concept of any evil being opposed to Jehovah, and Satan is a member of the Heavenly Court. Under the influence of the dualistic doctrine of Zoroastrianism regarding the unceasing struggle between good and evil, Satan gradually turns into an enemy of God, along with his subordinate Angels. The Christian doctrine defines Satan as an enemy who hates all humankind, and whose main purpose is to turn people away from God through slander and leading into sinful transgressions. In the Gospels, the Devil represents a tempter who tries to compel Jesus Christ to abuse His Divine Power of Authority.

## Shatan

> *We are each our own devil, and we make this world our hell.*
>
> **Oscar Wilde**

The Greek word Σατανᾶς *(Satanas)* derives from the Hebrew *shatan* [ʃaʻtan] ("adversary", "opponent", "accuser") and the Arabic *sheytan,* which, in turn, derives from the Semitic root ShTN, meaning "hostile", "accusing". The most common synonym of *Satan* in most languages is *Devil* – a word that etymologically derives from the Greek διάβολος *(dyabolos),* meaning "slanderer", which has more negative connotations than the Hebrew *shatan.* Satan is often used as the name of the *Prince of Darkness, Veelzevul (Beelzebul), Velial (Belial* – "the corrupt one"), *Leviathan* ("serpent", "dragon"), *Lucifer, Azazel, Mephistopheles*. In the *Talmud* and some Kabalistic works, Satan is sometimes called *Samael*. According to Angelology and Demonology, these various names often refer to different Angels and Demons, and it is often assumed that not all of them are actually evil.

Satan is described in only a few passages in the Hebrew Scriptures. In them, he is an Angel who works for God and must ask permission from Him for everything he does. Each time this term is used in the Old Testament, it is written as *ha-Shatan,* which means *Satan.* The fact that it is preceded by a specific article *(ha)* means that no individual name is meant but rather a certain status, function, or task. That is why Satan should not be personified. However, this is exactly what Christianity does, likening him to a fallen Angel, an enemy of God and humans, an embodiment of evil, having a self-dependent status. To Judaism, however, the idea that any creature may exists that is able to oppose and counteract God, who has the power, strength, and his own will against God, means violating the fundamental biblical idea of monotheism. It is written in the Old Testament that God Himself has established the good and evil of the world. It exists so that humans may have the opportunity to exercise their own free will. In the *Torah,* it is said the following in this connection:

"See, I have set before you today life and good, death and evil". (*Fifth Book of Moses – Deuteronomy* 30:15, NKJV)

"I form the light and create darkness, I make peace and create calamity; I, the Lord, do all these things." (*Book of the Prophet Isaiah* 45:7, *NKJV*)

There is not even a single example in the Hebrew Scriptures of an Angel, including Satan, who has ever opposed God. In the *Tanakh,* Satan is an Angel used by the Lord to test the piety and devotion of humans through trials. In no part of the Bible is this so obvious as in the *Book of Job,* where the role of Satan is emblematic. He asks God's permission to test Job's virtue. The Almighty gives His permission but thoroughly outlines the parameters of the trial, whereas Satan obediently observes them. Commenting on the *Book of Job,* the Rabbis show sympathy for Satan's difficult task, which is "to break the barrel without spilling the wine".

It is obvious that one of the main functions of Satan is to test and tempt, but only with God's permission. As is well known, in the New Testament he also puts Jesus Christ to trial. This function of Satan is related to another of his roles – that of the accuser in the Divine Court of Justice.

As we have already explained, in Hebrew the word *ha-Shatan* ("Satan") also means *adversary* and is a word with a functional meaning – in that case, of *antagonist*. This function can be performed not only by an Angel but also by a human: "Now the Lord raised up an adversary against Solomon – Hadad the Edomite; he was a descendant of the king in Edom". (*1 Kings* 11:14, *NKJV*) The word used for *adversary* is *ha-Shatan*.

Not all researchers of sacred texts are unanimous regarding the supernatural character of Satan. Rabbi Saadia Gaon, an 11th century philosopher and scholar, writes in his commentary on the *Book of Job* that Satan is simply a human who questioned Job's righteousness. This thesis is based on critical interpretation of the word שטן – *adversary, enemy*, which, according to Saadia, refers only to the intentions of the personality, not to anything spiritual or supernatural. In confirmation, we will point out that there was a *functional position* of "Satan" in the Judaic religious institution, with the purpose and function to test and accuse those who had made a vow of chastity.

In summary, we will note that in Judaism the word *ha-Shatan* does not indicate any strictly determined individual but a position, a function, a task that can be performed by humans as well as by messengers of Elohim, one of whom is Satan, who has no free will nor independent existence, nor is in any way an opponent of God. In this sense, Satan can be identified with evil only insofar as the one who is subject to temptations recognizes evil in the tempter, just as perhaps students recognize evil in the teacher testing them, and even more so, the accused (defendant) – in the accuser. In no case, however, is he identified or denoted by the word *Devil*. Éliphas Lévi is of the same opinion, when in his work, *Le Livre des Splendeurs: Études sur les Origines de la Kabbale* (*The Book of Splendours: Studies on the Origins of the Qabalah*), he writes about Satan: "He does nothing which God Himself does not wish for. It is God who, using him, tempts, leads into sin and torments His weak creatures. Thus Satan is not the ruler of the realm of shadows: he is the agent of *light behind a veil*. He is of service to God, he performs God's work: God has not rejected him, for He holds him still in His Hand".

Unlike Judaism, in Islam the Devil, as already mentioned, is called *Sheytan*, or *Iblis*, and is a creation of Allah. The Devil gets too proud and decides that the Commandments of Allah do not apply to him, because he (as being Iblis) is created from smokeless fire, while the human being is made of earth, and therefore humans are inferior and of low value. As a result of the disrespect towards the human being who is the greatest among God's creatures, Iblis is cast out of the Heavens and transformed into a *genie (spirit)*. Islam is alien to the idea of Sheytan as an adversary of God, because only and uniquely Allah is Almighty, while Sheytan is only a means of testing people. However, Sheytan is dangerous to humans because he puts them under temptation, and they might deviate from the Path of Allah. From these characteristics, it becomes clear that the Islamic Sheytan has the functionality of the Judaic *ha-Shatan*, although, unlike him, contains elements of a particular personality.

Thus, also in Christianity, the *Devil, Satan,* the *Old Serpent,* and *Lucifer* are all synonyms of a particular personification, embodiment of evil. Much has been written on this subject, and the traditional statement that can be read is that the name *Lucifer* is not of Christian origin.

**Figure 48**[a]

## Lucifer

> *We can easily forgive a child who is afraid of the dark; the real tragedy of life is when men are afraid of the light.*
>
> ***Plato***

In Antiquity, *Lucifer* was the name of the planet *Venus*. In Babylon it was called *Morning Star,* as well as *Evening Star.* Ancient Roman mythology considers Lucifer to be a son of *Aurora* – the goddess of the morning dawn. In ancient Greek mythology, she is *Eos,* and her son is *Phosphoros* – "bearer of light". It is his name that corresponds to the Roman *Lucifer,* as in the *Book of the Prophet Isaiah* (14:12), in the Latin version *(Biblia Sacra Vulgata)*, it is written: "Quomodo cecidisti de caelo, Lucifer, qui mane oriebaris?" ("How have you fallen from Heaven, Lucifer, son of the dawn?"). The question arises as to whether the above said refers to Satan, since the Latin word *Lucifer* is the exact translation of the Greek word *Phosphoros* and means "bearer of light". However, how could he be any bearer of light when, in fact, "He was a murderer from the beginning, and does not stand in the Truth" (*Holy Gospel of John* 8:44, *NKJV*).

To answer this question, we will make use of what is said on the subject in the work of the biblical analyst and commentator Frank W. Nelte: "The name *Lucifer* has never belonged to Satan". According to him, when in 382 AD Pope Damasus I commissions the scholar Jerome (Hieronymus) to produce an official version of the Bible, the latter bases his translation not on the original Hebrew text but on the Greek *Septuagint* version. This is how the Latin translation of the Bible, the *Vulgate*,[117] appears, which, according to Nelte, is far from the most accurate translation of the original texts. According to the author, Jerome has understood that *Isaiah* 14:12 speaks of Satan. There the Hebrew word *Heylel* is used for *Satan,* and Jerome has translated it into Latin as *Lucifer*. This is an incorrect translation. The Latin word *Lucifer* is composed of two parts: *Lux* and *Ferous*, which literally means "light-bearer". However, this is not the meaning of the Hebrew word *Heylel*. Thus, through the *Vulgate,* the name *Lucifer* as that of Satan has been widely spread.

The conversion of the Hebrew *Heylel* into the Latin *Lucifer* is a consequence of the translation made from the Greek *Septuagint*. In it (*Book of the Prophet Isaiah* 14:12), the word *Heylel* is incorrectly translated as *Eosphoros,* an ancient way of pronouncing the word *Phosphoros*. The motive due to which Jerome translated *Heylel* as *Lucifer,* the author says, is only because in the *Septuagint, Heylel* is translated is *Eosphoros*. In both languages, the corresponding words mean "light-bearer". Thus, *Lucifer* represents the perfect translation of the word *Phosphoros* from Greek to Latin. All this is typical of the low level of the *Septuagint,* says Nelte, which is clearly seen from the translation itself, using, instead of six different words, only one Greek word – φωσφόρος *(phosphoros)*. In the same way, he continues, fifteen different Hebrew words are translated with the Greek word ὑπόστασις *(hypóstasis)*.

When the Bible was first translated into English and the translators came to the *Book of Isaiah* 14:12, they decided that instead of translating the word *Heylel,* they could replace it with the already familiar Latin word *Lucifer*.

In the Bulgarian translations of the Bible, the name *Lucifer,* with which the Prophet Isaiah addresses the fallen Angel, who envied God, is translated as *star:*[118] "Как падна ти от небето, деннице, сине на зората! Разби се о земята ти, който тъпчеше народите" (*Book of the Prophet Isaiah* 14:12,

---

117 The word *vulgata (vulgate)* derives from *vulgatus,* which means *ordinary, familiar* and *accessible to all; spreading, publication,* while the ecclesiastical Latin form *Vulgata (editio)* can be translated as "widespread edition", "edition for the people" – *AN.*
118 *Day star* is one of the names of the planet *Venus,* considered by the ancients to be a star – *AN.*

*BOB*) – "How you fell from Heaven, you *day star*, son of the dawn! You crashed down onto the Earth – you who treaded down the nations".

Without conveying the detailed philological examples and reasoning of the author, we will quote his essential conclusions. According to him, the incorrectly translated Hebrew word *Heylel*, in the context of the *Book of the Prophet Isaiah* 14:12 – 14, has a negative connotation, so the text should look as follows: "How you have fallen from Heaven, you, incredibly arrogant and mad boaster, you 'son of the dawn'!"

Thus already the above written can be referred to Satan; whereas the words of Jesus Christ in the New Testament – "I have come as a Light into the world, that whoever believes in Me should not abide in darkness" (*Holy Gospel of John* 12:46, *NKJV*), unequivocally indicate that He is a "Bearer of Light", and as such, He can be called *Lucifer*. Jerome used this word three times in his translations, and all those three times he translated it from the Greek *phosphoros*. However, the English translators translate only one of the three as *Lucifer* (*Isaiah* 14:12). They declare the second one to be a mistranslation (*Book of Job* 11:17), while deliberately translating the third one as "morning star"/ "day star": "And so we have the prophetic word confirmed, which you do well to heed as a light that shines in a dark place, until the day dawns and the morning star rises in your hearts". (*Second Epistle of St. Apostle Peter* 1:19, *NKJV*)

In this way, according to Nelte, the Apostle Peter shows us that Christ is Lucifer, but this is concealed in the translation so as not to be associated with Satan, in the context of the Christian understanding.

Nelte himself, however, says that the word *Heylel* derives from the primitive root *halal* and has two clear contradictory meanings. One of them is negative, which we have already presented, and the other is positive, concerning the brightness of light. In view of this meaning, we will dwell also on other opinions on this subject.

Some proponents of the thesis that Satan is Lucifer, in order to avoid the contradiction between the meaning of the word *Lucifer* and the evil nature of Satan, say that he was a Bearer of Light before he sinned. Other analysts, mostly Hebrew ones, ask the rhetorical question of how Christians can explain the following verse of *Revelation of St. John the Theologian* 22:16 (*NKJV*): "I, Jesus, have sent My Angel to testify to you these things in the churches. I am the Root and the Offspring of David, the Bright and Morning Star", where Jesus is called the "Morning Star", since they maintain the thesis that the "morning star" refers to Satan? Then they give also their answer: that the "morning star" mentioned by the Prophet Isaiah refers to Nebuchadnezzar, the wicked king of Babylon, and not to Satan: "You will take up this taunt against the king of Babylon: 'How the oppressor has come to an end! How his fury has ended!'." (*Book of the Prophet Isaiah* 14:4, *NIV*)

The Prophet compares King Nebuchadnezzar to the planet Venus, the light of which is still visible in the morning but disappears with the ascension of the Sun. The kingdom of Nebuchadnezzar shines brightly for a short time, just like the light of Venus, but in the end it will be overshadowed by the people of Israel, whose light endures and outlives this arrogant king who tortured and sent them into exile. Others, on their part, comment that the biblical text by Isaiah says that the king of Babylon reached greatness as a leader, but just as a shooting star, he was cast low by God because of his arrogance. Then they add that the phrase "bearer of light" is used in exactly the same way in the *Second Epistle of St. Apostle Peter* 1:19 without any relation to the Devil.

Another explanation of the "light-bearer" Satan in the context of the Christian understanding is found in the *Second Epistle of St. Apostle Paul to the Corinthians* 11:14, where the following is written, "And no wonder! For Satan himself transforms himself into an Angel of Light." *(NKJV)*

Thus, the concept is grounded that he is a false, deceitful light-bearer. The Gnostic currents, on the other hand, reverse the image of Lucifer and present him as a saviour from the Demiurge. According to this hypothesis, the *Serpent/Lucifer* from the *First Book of Moses – Genesis* incited the human being to get to know good and evil and to emancipate humans, turning them into a likeness of God.

Finally, in an objective analysis of the Old Testament, without any theological or apocryphal colourations, we can conclude that *Lucifer/Satan* is described nowhere as the prince of evil and demons, nor as the lord of Hell, where sinners will undergo eternal suffering.

However, in the much-disputed Kabalistic book *Bahir* ("Luminous"), regarding Satan, it is written: "... In God, there is a principle called 'Evil', and it dwells in the north side of the Most High, for it is written, 'Out of the north, an evil shall break forth' *[Book of the Prophet Jeremiah 1:14, KJV – ed.]*" Here, the understanding of evil as part of the core essence of God is referred to, and in this sense, it represents the necessary, functional evil.

Contrary to this understanding, in the New Testament, evil already represents a self-dependent entity: "So the great Dragon was cast out, that Serpent of old, called the Devil and Satan, who deceives the whole world; he was cast to the Earth, and his Angels were cast out with him." (*Revelation* 12:9, *NKJV*)

We see that, according to the Apostle John, the Serpent that tempted Eve is Satan, who is called the *Devil* and is definitely an embodiment of evil. Thus we return again to the ancient symbolism of the snake, which, according to Christianity, is loaded with negativity.

We have already discussed the topic of the Serpent in the Garden of Eden, and we have explained that in the original Hebrew text *(Tanakh)* of the *First Book of Moses – Genesis* 3:1, it is not written, "The Serpent was more cunning than any beast of the field which the Lord God had made", but it is rather described as "the wisest of all living beings that God had created". We have also clarified that the Ancient Hebrew word *Nahash* was used for the Serpent.

## Nahash
### *Today's Truth is yesterday's heresy!*

*Nahash* is formed by the three consonants *N-H-Sh*, having the meaning of *comprehension, penetration into things*. We will now add also other meanings that correspond to the current context: *bright, luminous, shining*, and hence – *bearer of light*. The word *NHSh* can also be related to the verb *nahash*, which means *to observe signs and omens, divination, magic*.

Thus, *nahash* represents a suitable symbol for the Ancient Sumerian God *Enki* – one of the names of the Semitic God *Dagon*, who is considered the founder of the Atlantean, Sumerian and Babylonian civilizations. *Enki* – the "Head Scientist of all the gods", the "God of magicians", had the snake as his symbol, and this is one of the reasons why it is associated with Wisdom.

As we have explained, the Devil is popularly known under the name of *Satan*, a derivative of the word *Shatan*, equivalent also to *Dragon*, and spelled also with three consonants – *Sh-T-N (Shin-Tet-Nun)*, just as *Nahash* – *N-H-Sh (Nun-Het-Shin)*. The difference is in the middle letter and in the fact that the two letters at both ends are swapped. Moreover, the Gematria of the two words is different, which, from a Kabalistic point of view, means that there is no sign of equality between them.

We will remind that *Gematria* is a Kabalistic method in which the numerical meanings of the Hebrew hieroglyphs are summed in certain words, and if they are equal, it means that there is some connection between them. In this context, it is interesting to note that *mashiach* is associated with *serpent*. The Hebrew word *mashiach* literally means *anointed*, but it also has the meaning of *saviour* (in Greek, Χριστός – Christ), which is why Jesus[119] is given this name.

Perhaps for the first time officially in the 13th century, the Judaic mystic Rabbi Isaac Alfasi associated the Messiah with the Serpent. The Messiah is the "Holy Serpent" because the Hebrew word *Mashiach* has the Gematric value of 355, equal to that of *Nahash* – the Serpent.

---

119 The very word *Jesus* in Hebrew means *Saviour*, whereas *Mashiach* literally means *Anointed – AN*.

In addition to *serpent*, *nahash* means also *bronze* or *copper*. Moreover, in Arabic, *nahas* means *trouble, distress*, while *nahaas* means *copper*. The serpent of Moses devours the serpents of the Egyptian sorcerers, which is a terrestrial model of the Kingdom of Heaven. Hence, the connection with the bronze serpent, hung on a staff and raised by Moses in the desert as a flag, in order to save everyone who looks at it. This is the prototype of the crucifixion of the "Holy Serpent", the Messiah in the New Testament: "And as Moses lifted up the serpent in the wilderness, even so must the Son of Man be lifted up, that whoever believes in Him should not perish but have Eternal Life" (*Holy Gospel of John* 3:14 – 15, *NKJV*).

Regarding the wand of Moses, there is a mysterious text in the *Zohar*, which we will only quote and leave the conclusions to the reader, in the context of what was said: "*The rod of God* is Metatron, who is life on one side and death on the other, turning from a serpent into a rod, and from a rod into a serpent".

It turns out that the *serpent power* that once tempted and caused the human Fall is the one that will save us. In other words, *Nahash* is the involutionary force that descends and draws downwards into matter, whereas *Mashiach* is the evolutionary, salvation force, ascending upwards towards the Spirit. The secret of involution is at the same time also the secret of the opposite evolutionary process. Unfortunately, the downfall is as fast as lightning, while the ascension is hard and slow along the path of the meandering serpent. *Nahash*, who in the Garden of Eden took on the role of a tempter, later called *Satan*, is also the redeemer *Mashiach*, embodied in the image of Jesus Christ. This is the snake biting its tail, a symbol of time and eternity, of light, of the beginning and the end, which can serve for both evil and good, and just like fire, it is able to burn but also to endow with life-giving Light. This is the Light of Reason, whose symbol is Lucifer. This is the Light of the Word, and its accomplishment is Jesus Christ – the Incarnate Word. As one Gnostic Gospel says, "God said, 'Let there be Light!' Then the mind was created, and the Light appeared. The mind took the form of a magnificent Angel, and Heaven greeted him with the name *Lucifer*".

The question arises as to what the role of the third force is, most emblematically associated with a Dragon – *Shatan*, which has a different Gematria, and is therefore different from the other two. Here the Kabalistic Tree will help us again. The Mashiach, the Salvation Force, blazes the safe *Path of the Middle Pillar* of this Tree. Shatan follows the so-called *Path of the Serpent of Wisdom*, which is also evolutionary, but it passes through the two side Pillars of this Tree, where the Force, unlike that of the Middle Pillar, is unbalanced. *(Fig. 50 on p. 334.)* Therefore, this path is dangerous and anathematized as satanic, so that humans may not be tempted to walk along it. This is the path of initiations, giving magic skills, independence and spiritual freedom, which is not liked by the Christian Church. The latter declares it to be the path of Satan. Satan, according to the Christian Church, has yet another hypostasis – *Lucifer*, the fallen Angel, branded as the *Devil*, because this Church is afraid of enlightened minds, putting the stigma of "denying and blaspheming God", due to not understanding the paradox that blasphemy against God praises God. *The denial of God is, in its essence, His affirmation, because it was He who has given to the mind the freedom to deny Him.*

We will remind what is written in the *Book of the Prophet Isaiah* (14:12) in the Latin version: "How have you fallen from Heaven, Lucifer, son of the dawn". If we replace the name *Lucifer* with the meaning of the very word, then the text will look as follows: "How have you fallen from Heaven, Light-Bearer, son of the dawn". The dawn, the symbol of which is the Morning Star (Venus), is a *harbinger* and *bringer* of Light, not Light itself. If dawn breaks, it means that the light of the Sun is below the horizon and it will rise at any moment. That is why Lucifer, the son of the dawn, is the Light-Bearer, the herald announcing that the rescuing light of the Sun will flood the Earth. In the context of the above said, we can draw a parallel between the Morning Star and the *heliacal rising of Sirius*, which is a sign of the annual flooding of the Nile, so dearly awaited by the ancient Egyptians. In the same way, humans await Lucifer, who will bring them the light of the Sun. Symbolically, Lucifer is the bearer of the light of progress, of renewal, of the destruction of old forms and paradigms. In this sense, we will say that Lucifer should be associated with the lucidity of consciousness,[120] yet not in the psychiatric aspect as clarity, but in the spiritual dimensions of enlightened consciousness.

There is a widespread rumour about Masons that they are followers of Lucifer – Satan, and that they perform satanic rituals. However, we have come to understand that Satan should not be associated with evil and has nothing to do with Lucifer unless we accept that his function as accuser and opponent leads to positive changes. Yes, we can say that Masons are Luciferians because they are bearers of the Light of Renewal. Was not the Masonic principle of fraternity, equality and liberty the very Light of the French Revolution? Are not the Masonic principles, as a whole, embedded in the Charter of Human Rights, which is a ray of Light in the human civilization? Are not tolerance, fraternal love, and coexistence of all religions and people in Freemasonry precisely the Light that will bring humankind out of the darkness of religious intolerance and hatred, of separation and opposition on the basis of racial and national affiliation, of property-related and social status? We might list many

---

[120] From the Latin *lucere*: "to shine" – *AN*.

more Luminous Principles and Ideas of Freemasonry but this is unnecessary because they are well-known enough, and moreover, they have become common to all humankind. Of course, we do not declare that Freemasonry is the Messianism of humans, but we do say that it is its harbinger. That is also why John the Baptist is the patron and spiritual symbol of Freemasonry. He is the Precursor of Christ, representing the Lucifer of Christ's Light – however, as being such, will anyone call him "Satan"? Does not Jesus oppose the Pharisees and the institutionalized Judaic clergy, is He not their adversary, and, in this sense, Satan? However, will anyone dare to call Jesus "Satan"? Will anyone today call Giordano Bruno or Galileo Galilei "Satan"? Freemasons have always confronted most of the dogmas of the clerical authority and its paradigms, yet treating them with the necessary tolerance and non-violence. Jesus and Freemasons are of the "opposing" ones, so that is why Jesus is crucified, whereas Freemasons are declared by the Christian Episcopal Church to be worshipers and followers of Satan as an emblem of evil. The Sons of God are crucified, burned at the stake, and thrown into dungeons by humans, because they are different from them and follow only the Truth. *Today's Truth is yesterday's heresy!*

We have already mentioned that the Messiah is compared to the Serpent. We have understood that *Nahash* means *bright* or *bright light,* but not in the aspect of our familiar physical light. In this sense, he can be associated with the Messiah, Who is the Spiritual Light for the whole humankind. We have said, however, that unlike the Messiah, Nahash is an involutionary force and is, in its essence, the all-pervading astral light, the miracle of unity – *aor.* That is why, in our opinion, Nahash is not the Messiah but rather the bearer of the bright celestial magnetism, and therefore can be associated with the light-bearer Lucifer, who, however, as it turned out, is not a Hebrew character. We have also explained that the Serpent *Nahash,* the astral realm, seeks to anchor and fix the Spirit to matter, which is why it is likened to evil, to the Devil and to Satan. We have also clarified the function of the negative coagulating pole of the astral realm, symbol of death, denoted by the word *ob,* meaning *magic.* Therefore the word *nahash* in general has acquired the meaning of *doing magic, practicing witchcraft,* and is therefore associated with something negative. And yet, it is neutral, so humans make it good or bad, just as a scalpel can save or take away life. However, Shatan is the one mostly identified with magic, having acquired the dark image of the Devil due to the New Testament.

We have clarified that Nahash and Shatan are two forces leading to the eternal cycle of circular motion, which is why their separation is conditional. If we reduce them to something that is very familiar to us – the twenty-four-hour cycle, we will say that the night figuratively descends, so it is therefore symbolized by the involutionary force Nahash, whereas the day ascends and is therefore associated with the evolutionary force Shatan. They have magical core essence, the highest manifestation of which is in the most mysterious time of the twenty-four-hour cycle – the thin light just before dawn, and the twilight after sunset.

Some may object that the meaning of *Nahash* – "bright light", can in no way be likened to the morning semi-obscurity or the evening twilight. In a literal parallel, this is so, but here we are talking about specific astral light which is not perceived by physical vision. Moreover, our idea is mostly related to the magic force of transient states of being. The pre-dawn light is the medium between night and day, just as the astral world is the medium between the physical and the spiritual world; it is the Tibetan *Bardo*, it is the *Duat* in the Egyptian tradition and the *Barzakh* in Islam. *Duat* can be translated as *lands, possessions, before dawn, morning semi-obscurity, morning twilight,* and therefore – also *the land of the morning twilight,* but perhaps most accurately – *pre-dawn light.* The hieroglyph of *Duat* is a five-pointed star: it is the symbol of Sirius, the harbinger of the rising Sun, of the nascent physical light, representing its embodiment. The words "dawn", "spell", and "praise" are formed from the same root. All these definitions contain the idea of a *transitional state* between night and day, between darkness and light, between sub-consciousness and consciousness. This borderline, however, can also be correlated to the evening twilight, as a transition between the departing day and the arriving night. In this sense, it would also fit into the concept of *Bardo,* but unlike *Duat,* we would define it rather as *Amenti* – the "hidden place" in the "west" where the Sun sets. The time of the magic operations with the greatest potential for accomplishment are these two transitional points connecting the physical phenomena and those of the psyche in the cause-effect configuration.

*Duat* represents the transition that each human has to make in order to reach Enlightenment. Therefore, the pre-dawn light is the time that brings the magic of awakening and self-renewal. In the legend of Re and Isis, when the Goddess wishes to learn the name of the Old God, he answers her: "I am *Khepri* in the morning; *Re* – at noon; and *Temu* – in the evening". The Egyptians called *Khepri* the morning Sun before sunrise. On the Masonic holiday – the Day of John the Baptist, known in Bulgaria as *Enyovden* (meaning "Enyo's Day", *Midsummer Day*), in the hour of the pre-dawn light, magic rites are performed and herbs are picked for the whole year, because at that moment they have the greatest healing properties. *Amenti,* on the other hand, is the place of twilight, containing the power of magic materialization and transition from *Temu,* the *evening Sun,* to the Full Moon, leading to transformation. The two Serpents, *Nahash* and *Shatan,* meet in the place of the pre-dawn light and the twilight, and biting each other's tails, they form the endless circular motion of Eternity. *(Fig. 49)*

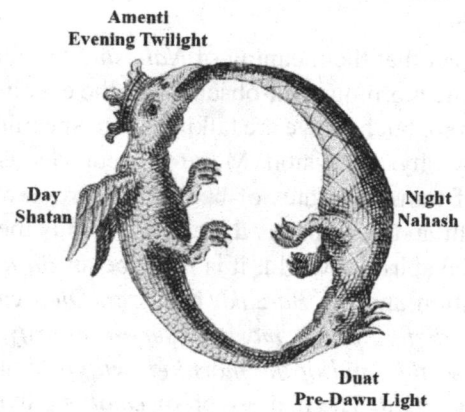

**Figure 49**

If we have to summarize, in the context of analogies with the natural phenomena of the twenty-four-hour period, we will say that Nahash is the bearer of the mystical astral light, which we associated with the pre-dawn light and with Lucifer, the bright Messianic Light-Bearer, related, in a New Testament key, to the dawn, and the harbinger of the Mashiach (Christ). The Saviour, according to Christianity, is Jesus, the only Son of God, likened to the Sun, which represents the material manifestation, or the "Son" of the Spiritual Sun – Sirius. Shatan, in his capacity of an opponent, in this case – opposing the Sun and the light of day, should be associated with the darkness of night and *Khonsu,* as the Full Moon was called in Ancient Egypt. We now consider it comprehensible that darkness and light should not be identified with evil and good, because darkness leads to light, and light – to darkness, and they are the mutually interpenetrating parts of one whole. All the entities listed above are associated, in one way or another, with the Serpent. It may now be clear already why the Serpent has always been deified in all Gnostic teachings. Outside of them, unfortunately, it is loaded primarily with negative symbolism, without taking into account its ambivalent nature. A very elementary example is that its poison, depending on the dose, can give or take away life – *Dosis sola facit venenum*[121]. Life and death, created by one and the same authoritative power, united in its essence, but dual in its manifestation. In this

---

121 From Latin: "Only the dose makes the poison" – *AN.*

sense, the Serpent represents a symbol of life and death, and above all, it may be related to the very idea of life. The Hebrew word *hayah* means both *life* and *animal, living thing,* and derives from the root *hayi,* which is also embedded in the foundation of the Arabic word *el-hayyah,* meaning *serpent,* and *el-hayah,* meaning *life.* Thus, the special connection of the Serpent with *Eve* (*Hawa* – "alive", "living") can explain the medieval images of "temptation", where the body of the Serpent is crowned with a female bust. The beneficial aspect of the Serpent, however, is most vividly found in Ancient Egypt – as the Royal Serpent, *Uraeus,* or *Basilisk.*

There is no way to exhaust the diversity of the symbolism of the Serpent, since its *eidos* is huge. Only in our exposition, it took on many and various images and essences. Before concluding the topic, however, we must make an esoteric emphasis, in a Kabalistic key, of the three most important of them, having an Initiatic meaning: *Nahash – Shatan – Mashiach.*

## Nahash – Shatan – Mashiach

> *And He said to them, "I saw Satan fall like lightning from Heaven".*
>
> **Holy Gospel of Luke 10:18, NKJV**

The descending of Nahash as involutionary force can be illustrated by the so-called *Path of the Lightning Flash.* In this sense, since Satan is also associated in the New Testament with the Serpent, for this reason, we have quoted the words of Jesus. It is no wonder if the text actually refers to Nahash, but since Satan is branded to be "fallen from Heaven", therefore his name should be present. It is interesting to mention that the Egyptian Pharaohs "descended" to Earth by means of the Serpent *Sata,* the father of lightning flashes, before ascending as the resurrected Osiris.

We have already explained, however, that the path of what we conditionally designate as the "second" Serpent – *Satan (Shatan),* is the evolutionary "Path of the Serpent of Wisdom" *(Nehushtan),* which encompasses the Sfarot not only on the left, having the characteristics of the so-called *left path,* which is traditionally considered the path of the "Dark Force", but also those on the right. As we have already said, the forces in the Left and in the Right Pillar of the Kabalistic Tree are equally unbalanced and dangerous. The path of Shatan is the gradual path of initiations, elevating us through the levels of consciousness until we achieve accomplishment of the Self. In this sense, Shatan indeed should be written as *ha-Shatan,* because, apart from everything described in an Old Testament key, he is, in the esoteric sense, a non-personalized force that is dangerous, but it is in no case evil. That is why this path ought to be walked together with a Spiritual Master, within the frames of an Initiatic community, and Freemasonry is such a community.

Finally, the Serpent indicated as the "third" one – the Mashiach, is the Path of Salvation, the Path of *Ben* (of the *Son*), which represents the Middle Pillar of the Kabalistic Tree. *(Fig. 50)* Even from the very word "salvation", it becomes clear that it refers to a one-time expansive act of "Salvation of the Self", "Salvation of the "*I*". It is a safe path because it balances the side forces in the Sfarotic Tree. Ovid says of this path: *Medio tutissimus ibis* ("In the Middle you will go most safe", or "Most trustworthily shall you tread the Middle Path"). It is also known as the "Path of the Arrow". In this Path, one is mostly alone and that is why it is also called the "Path of the Mystic". The Christian doctrine, however, has turned the non-personified "Path of the Son" into the "Way of Jesus Christ", the Son of God, through Whom only, Salvation can be achieved, and moreover – only through the intermediation of the Church. It is explainable that the Church declares as heretics and worshipers of Satan all the opponents of this dogma over the millennia, whose bright representative is, for example, Bogomilism – and why not Freemasonry as well!

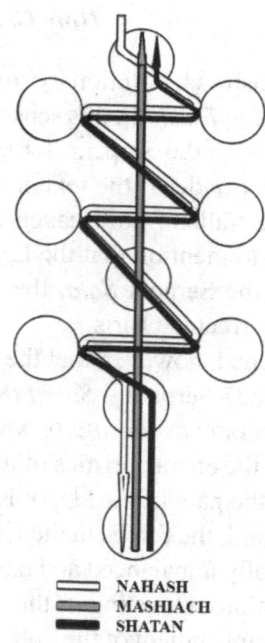

NAHASH
MASHIACH
SHATAN

**Figure 50**

These three paths can be symbolically associated with the Three Arcana Paths, corresponding to the Three Degrees of Freemasonry, but only outside the context of the Kabalistic Tree, and with the stipulation that they are not identical because they belong to different traditions. Regarding the Path of the Son – the "Path of Chorus", we believe that we do not need to make further clarifications. The Path of *Nahash,* whose name means "doing magic", should refer to the "Path of Isis" – the Goddess of Magic. Direct evidence of her magic skills is found in the *Legend of Re (Ra)*. When the Old God Re summons his child-gods to deliver him from the venom of the snake that bit him, Isis arrives as well: "And Isis came, bringing her magic words, and her mouth was filled with the breath of life, because her talismans remove the pains of any disease, and her words bring the throats of the dead to life again." This text is an illustrative testimony to the miraculous magic skills of Isis, who rules over life and death. She received them from Thoth, who embodies the Intelligence and Wisdom of the Creator, which is why their origin was Divine. Magic is the embodiment and formation of ideas, and this is an involutionary force, and we have said that the "Path of Nahash" is involutionary. In support of this, we will quote Hermes Trismegistus, who says: "The world was created through a spell" – such is also one of the meanings of the word *Nahash*. Thus, it remains that the "Path of Osiris" be likened to the "Path of Shatan", which is the evolutionary, gradual path of initiations for elevation of consciousness, but also the most dangerous one, and is therefore the path of the Master. This path leads beyond the limit we have marked with the mystical 9, the number of the Truth and the Human Being. This threshold cannot be crossed unless a return to the beginning is accomplished, numerologically denoted by the number 1, and then the number 10 will be obtained – a symbol of unity and complete wholeness. According to Egyptian Heliopolis Theology, Creation was completed with the emergence of the nine Deities from *Atum,* whose name means "complete", "perfect". With the birth of Horus, the Deities become 10, and this is his Sacred Number. Thus he represents the God, as a microcosmic reflection of Atum, or of Re, through whom a return to the Primordial Origin is performed. It is no coincidence that Jesus, Whose preceding prototype is considered to be Chorus, says that only through Him can one reach the Father: "Jesus said to him, 'I am the Way, the Truth, and the Life. No one comes to the Father except through Me." (*Holy Gospel of John* 14:6, *NKJV*)

Let us see what the Judaic analogy of the above written is. For this purpose, we must again apply the Kabalistic method of Gematria. We have already mentioned that the Gematria of *Nahash* and *Mashiach* is the number 355, which is why they are correlated, yet having no relation to the name of

Jesus – *Yeshua,* the Gematria of which is 326. If we approach in the same way and Kabalize the word *Shatan,* then we have the following: *Shin* – 300, *Tet* – 9, *Nun Final* – 700, so the value 1009 is obtained, or the number 10, which is ultimately 1 – the new beginning. We see that the number of Shatan contains the mystical 9, the initial 1, and the complete 10. As we have explained, if to the threshold 9 that ends a certain cycle, the number 1 is added as the primordial substance, as the fundamental building block, as one *"Yod"* (containing both 1 and 10), the consubstantial 10 is attained, in which there is the Primordial Origin, just like the second *He* of the Tetragrammaton, which contains the potential *"Yod"* that will give rise to the beginning of the new unfolding of God's Name, the beginning of a new cycle. The number 10 symbolizes the beginning and the end, all and nothing, the 1 from which all the numbers to 9 originate, to which this 1 is added again in order to become itself again and to set the beginning of a new unfolding.

*Ha-Shatan,* the opposing one, has the potential to cross the threshold, to break the old retrograde forms and paradigms, and to initiate the impetus of a new beginning precisely because he is an opposing force. Each unity contains everything in potentiality, yet, in order to unfold, it must be divided into its opposite, through which to give the creative beginning principle. We shall only note that the Gematria of the Supreme Name of God – *Ehyah,* which can also be represented only as *"Yod",* is also 10. For comparison, we will say that the Gematria of *Moshe* (Moses) is the number 3, of *Shlomo* (Solomon) – 6, of *Abram* (Abraham) – 7, and of *Melkitsedek* (Melhisedek) – 9. The Path of Shatan is the Path of Osiris, a symbol of wholeness (of 1), which is disintegrated and then reintegrated through magic initiation. However, he cannot carry out this initiation alone, but rather and mainly with the help of Isis and Horus, just as the number 9 is able to reproduce by itself (9 multiplied by any number always gives 9 again as a sum), but in order to change, the number 1 must be added. That is why the Path of Shatan, the Path of the "Serpent of Wisdom", encompasses also the other two Paths of the Kabalistic Tree – the Paths of Horus and Isis; whereas *Baal Havi,* in the person of the Three Wise Men (Three Magi), named *Влъхви ['vləhvi]* in Bulgarian, bow to Jesus – the Son.

If we follow the Egyptian mythology, Osiris is disintegrated through his opposing brother *Set (Seth),* who dismembers Osiris into fourteen parts, and from whose name, the designation *Satan/ Shatan* might also derive. In this context, if we are to be even more exact on the esoteric plane, and why not also on the philosophic one, we would ultimately say that Shatan is the force that initiates the disintegration changes leading to the synthesis of the Primordial Origin. And it is no coincidence that he is associated with Set, although being incorrectly considered the personified evil, so if we are to attribute such a quality to him, in view of his function of the opponent, he represents *functional evil*, in the sense of the Sfara *Gebura*, and is sometimes identified with its Archangel – *Samael*. Seth is part of the *Divine Ennead*, whereas the names of *Samael* and the personified Shatan – *Satanael*, contain the suffix *-el*, showing that they are part of the *disintegrated* God, of His essential qualities, marking His *Homoousion* with the manifested world.

We continue, on a much deeper esoteric and Kabalistic plane, in order to again direct the attention towards the fact that the words *Nahash* and *Shatan* differ mainly by the letters in the middle – *H* (the hieroglyph *Het*) and *T* (the hieroglyph *Tet*), and this is no coincidence, for in principle there is no accidental coincidence, much less in Kabala. Before that, however, we will make a vivid illustration of our already proclaimed principle not to blindly trust any authorities, according to the maxim: *Incertus animus dimidium sapientiae est.*[122] Such is considered to be the famous French occultist Alphonse-Louis Constant, writing under the pseudonym *Éliphas Lévi*, whom we have quoted several times. In his also very famous book *Dogme et Rituel de la Haute Magie (Transcendental Magic: Its Doctrine and Ritual,* Part II, p. 5*)*, he explains the meaning of the word *Nahash* by means of "the grand keys of the Kabalah" and "by the symbolical letters of the Tarot", in the following way:

"14 נ *NUN* – The power which produces combinations.

5 ה *HE* – The recipient and passive producer of forms.

21 ש *SHIN* – The natural and central fire equilibrated by double polarization.

Thus, the word employed by Moses, read Kabalistically, gives the description and definition of that magical Universal Agent, represented in all theogonies by the serpent."

We agree with the last sentence but we cannot help but object against the incorrect spelling of the word *Nahash* – with the letter *He*. Lévi himself, a few lines above those, has quoted verbatim the sentence from TANAKH, which contains the word *Nahash,* this time spelled correctly: והנחש.

This phrase is composed of the letters *Vav He Nun Het Shin,* with *Vav* meaning "AND" or "BUT", while *He* is the definite article that is placed before the word – in this case, *Nahash,* consisting of the letters *Nun Het Shin*. Therefore, in the various versions of the Bible, this phrase is translated as "And the serpent" or "But the serpent", whereas in the quoted book – "Now, the serpent". It is clear to those familiar with Hebrew hieroglyphs that *Nahash* is spelled with *Het*, not *He*. It is true that the difference between

---

122 From Latin: "Doubt is half of wisdom" (Publilius Syrus) – *AN.*

them is quite imperceptible, but once one word is put to analysis, the first condition is to establish its correct pronunciation and spelling. In this case, the wrong letter leads to a misinterpretation both regarding the correlation with the other letters and in the context of the whole word. We leave the conclusions to the reader.

After this important digression, we continue with our Kabalistic analysis. We have said that Nahash is that all-pervading creative energy consisting of the "celestial" fire (magnetism) *Shin,* balanced through the double polarization, which represents the Universal Involutionary Agent, illustrated by the Serpent called *Nahash* by Moses. The symbol of Shatan is also a serpent and is also a Universal Agent, yet evolutionary and active in the human moral world. These essential differences forming the essence and purpose in the symbolism of the two serpents are revealed through the mentioned hieroglyphs *Het* and *Tet.* Here we will have to specify that there is a difference between *Nahash* and *Shatan* also regarding the letter *Nun,* in view of the rule that when it is final in the word, it is written with the so-called *Nun Final* letter, which is different by meaning and numerical value. For this reason, the word *Shatan* ends with *Nun Final* – שטן. Not taking into account this difference, some "Kabalists" calculate that the Gematria of this word amounts to 359, using the numerical value of the letter *Nun* – 50, not the value of *Nun Final* – 700, which gives the correct Gematria – 1009. This leads also to confusion and incorrect conclusions. In addition to the Gematric difference, the shape of the letter *Nun* also exerts a differentiated idea-related and purely situational dominance over the symbolism of the two words under consideration. Since Nahash represents involutionary force, we would conditionally write it along a descending vertical, starting with *Nun* and ending with *Shin,* whereas *Shatan,* as representing evolutionary force, will be written by us from the bottom up.¹²³ *(Fig. 51)*

**Figure 51**

---

123 The arrows of the paths are straight for greater clarity, and they do not follow the actual paths of the Sfarotic Tree – *AN*.

Therefore, we will start with an analysis of the letter *Nun*, which is the 14th in *Alefbet*, and this is the number of harmony because it is identical with the Fourteenth Arcanum. According to some Kabalistic schools, the seven lower Sfarot of the single Kabalistic Tree correspond to the Seven Days of Creation, expressing seven forms of the Divine Emanation. Between the seven Sfarot, 49 possible combinations exist, creating all the properties of our reality. The numerical value of the letter *Nun*, when not being *Nun Final*, is 50, and it unites the polyphony of the world (49) in one monochord. In this context, the number 50 symbolizes the completeness containing the archetypal abstractness of forms. The way of writing the letter *Nun* by starting from the top, going down and ending with a horizontal line, marks the transition from the Spiritual World to the material one, from the abstract to the concrete, from the general to the particular. In our example, with the word *Nahash*, this transition continues in descending order through the shape of the letter *Het*, which is open only at the bottom and indicates a downward movement. The numerical value of *Het* is the number 8, symbolizing the reality of the supernatural, which in the Hebrew tradition has received the designation "World of Freedom". This reality corresponds to the ethical triangle in the Kabalistic Tree and gives the opportunity for freedom of choice, on the moral and ethical plane, between righteousness and sin. The word *sin* in Hebrew is written with the letters *Het, Tet* and *Alef*, and is pronounced in the same way as the letter *Het*. This is one of the reasons why the tempting Serpent *Nahash* (containing *Het*), which incited humans to sin, has acquired the image of Satan and the Devil. Actually, however, Adam and Eve were given a choice, so the following question arises: Was the result of this choice predetermined?

The form of the letter *Het*, unlike that of *He* (which is open at the top), does not allow any chance for exit upwards. Therefore, the only way is downwards, and for the perpetrators of sin, it is called the *Fall*, while for the rest, it is named *involution*, but for all it leads to *alienation from the Spiritual World*. However, the choice made in the Garden of Eden is the cause for the creation of the World of Action, thus leading to the completion of Creation, because the meaning and purpose of an idea is to be accomplished on the material level. If the prohibition had not been violated, the Worlds would not have expanded to the *Assia* World, and humans would not have gained the experience on the physical plane. This means that the veritable choice was between *development* and *stagnation*. The question arises as to whether the Creator has granted the human being this important existential choice, or whether it is part of a preconceived plan. Thus, the cardinal problem arises of the opposition between the freedom of choice and the Divine Design conceived. According to some Kabalists and Rabbis, the circumstance that the hieroglyph *Alef* is not pronounced at the end of the word "sin" is an indication that the Most High does not predetermine the free choice but sets only its parameters. According to others, however, it means that God is present in everything, even in sin, and that the "deviation from the goal"[124] is with His consent, and is not subject to punishment. Whether we will call the downward movement *involution,* or *sin,* and whether it is the result of the human's free choice, or of God's Providence, seems to no longer be of considerable importance, because, either way, it has already taken place, carrying out the energies of the upper Worlds into the *Assia* World, and these are the energies of Life, because the letter *Het* marks the beginning of the word *Hayim – Life.* This process is symbolized by the final letter in the word *Nahash – Shin.* Graphically, the letter *Shin* consists of the letters *Yod, Vav* and *Zayin,* with *Yod* symbolizing astral magnetism, *Vav* serving as a channel transmitting it into the *Assia* World, and *Zayin* expressing the dominance of the spiritual over materiality. Therefore, spirituality, through the celestial magnetism, descending into our world, gives it life force and *vivifies* it. In Hebrew, the word *Zayin* means *weapon* and is an indication that *Nahash* may serve for both creation and destruction, so humans have to make a choice between these two paths. The dual nature of the astral dragon is also derived from the word *sheker,* beginning with the hieroglyph *Shin* and meaning *lie, falsehood.* That is why one ought to carefully master this celestial fire and subject it to one's will, which is allegorically shown in the paintings and icons on which a Saint pierces a dragon with a spear. When this is achieved, the beginning of the evolutionary path of Shatan is set, denoted by the letter *Shin,* symbolizing the transformation of the celestial magnetism into terrestrial one *(Fig. 52 on p. 343).* With its positive power, once mastered, one ascends in order to step on the path towards Home, denoted by the letter *Tet,* which has the numerical value of 9. It first appears in the *Torah* in the word *Tov* ("good"), which is why it is assumed that it and the number 9 are expressions of good. This is so because 9 is the number of *Truth (Emet)* and of Adam, and therefore good is laid down as a principle in the human being, though the freedom of choice gives humans the opportunity to do evil as well. This conclusion is necessitated also by the ambivalence of the letter *Tet,* which in *Alefbet* takes the place between *Het* (associated with sin) and *Yod* (symbolizing Absolute Holiness), thus outlining two paths – towards good and towards evil. However, the generally accepted notion of evil as sin differs from its veritable essence, which is expressed in the domination of the ego over everything. The meaning of the word *sin* is *deviation,* which, on the moral and ethical plane, can lead us along one of the two paths indicated. In this sense, Shatan's privilege is to elevate us towards good that is symbolized by the letter *Tet* and the

---

124  The Aramaic word for "sin" – *AN.*

number 9, which represent the Ninth Path of the Kabalistic Tree, as well as the Ninth Arcanum of Sacred Magic, called the *Pilgrim*. The Ninth Arcanum is an illustration of walking along the way back towards Home. The Pilgrim walks along this path, illuminating the present with the light of esoteric teachings, leaning on experience and wisdom, and shrouded in the protectorate of the Heavenly Hierarchy. This path is within the darkness of the human moral world, full of remorse, fears and guilt, but it ultimately leads to Enlightenment. Thus, *Tet* represents a key letter in the name *Shatan*, leading to its last letter – *Nun Final*, which, with its elongated shape, symbolizes the *rectifying* of humans. That is why, in the pictorial symbolism the Saint, having attained Enlightenment and not being subject to the moral paradigm of humans, pierces the earthly magnetism in the form of a serpent. In the above described way, the astral magnetism descends through the sin (deviation) *Het* and is incarnated in *Shin*, being transformed into earthly magnetism. When mastered, it sets the beginning of the path of initiations, marked by the first letter of *Shatan* – *Shin*. From that moment on, the Adept is at the crossroads marked by the letter *Tet*, so he must choose which path to take – the path of the righteous or the path of the sinner. If he chooses the first path, he receives the Enlightenment of a Saint and acquires the moral purity of a rectified soul symbolized by the letter *Nun Final*, in order to finally be transformed into a Son of God. Thus this achievement is ultimately accomplished through Shatan, whose Gematria is 1009, leading to the number of perfection 10.

We will now dwell on another aspect of the words *Nahash* and *Shatan*. We have pointed out that they differ mainly by the letters in the middle – *Het* and *Tet*, which, on their part, are in a special relationship, illustrated in Figure 51 by a horizontal arrow. We have explained that the letter *Het* is associated with the word *sin*, meaning *deviation*, which in the diagram leads to the letter *Tet*, which is also part of the word for *sin*. We need to understand how this deviation can take place along the horizontal line, not downwards, known to us as the *Fall*. The Gematria of the two letters (*Het* – 8, and *Tet* – 9), is 17 – the sequence number of the letter *Pe* in *Alefbet*, which, translated from Hebrew, means *mouth*. The very shape of the letter *Pe* resembles an open human mouth *pronouncing a word*. In the context of our reasoning, it follows that sin is approached through the word, and therefore the Serpent in the Garden of Eden is a talking being. It is called *Nahash*, as we know, and it has affected the animal soul *Nephesh*. The difference in the spelling of the two words is the letter *Pe*. From this, we understand that, through speech, sin enters the human astral body. Through the Word, however, we are able to shift, saving ourselves from falling, and step on the Path of the Pilgrim leading back Home. Of course, this refers not to ordinary speech but to the Divine Word, because the numerical value of the letter *Pe* is 80, or 8 multiplied by

10 – the number of perfection characterizing the Divine Word. Thus, two paths are outlined, one leading to subduing the astral dragon, which is related to magic practices and magic in general, and the other endowing us with the transforming power of the Word. In Figure 51, however, the arrow between *Het* and *Tet* is two-sided, which means that by ascending along the path of Shatan, one might deviate towards sin and start going back downwards. This danger always exists, and it is part of the trials of the Spiritual Path. Besides, evil may always put on the *mask of good* if we have not penetrated into the true nature of things.

To conclude the topic, we will present the above said also according to the Sfarotic Tree, and for this purpose we will quote Éliphas Lévi again, after we have verified the truthfulness of his statement: "*Malkuth*, based upon *Geburah* and *Chesed*, is the Temple of Solomon". These words are yet another confirmation of the importance of the Ninth Path, interconnecting the Sfarot *Gebura* and *Hesed* of the Kabalistic Tree. *(Fig. 52 on p. 343.)* Depending on the location of the fulcrum of the horizontal binary *Gebura – Hesed*, the "Path of the Force" may vary. Manipulating the "Force" represents the chief cornerstone of magic practices. It is no coincidence that *ha-shem tet* ("the name *tet*"), referring to the Ninth Path, is associated with the word *shmat*, which means *pushing, displacing,* and it prompts us to make an analogy with *opposition* – the essential meaning of the word *Shatan*. This, however, is a deep Kabalistic secret, so its disclosure is not in the scope of this book. We will only specify that Shatan, as we have already clarified, is connected with magic, though rather in the realm of the moral human world as *initiation*, unlike the magic formative action of Nahash. Finally, quite essentially and schematically, we can make a summary using the Sfarotic symbolism and imagery of the unfolded Tree. The astral dragon Nahash extends into the *Yetzira* World from *Keter*, where its positive pole *aod* is positioned, to *Malkut* – its negative pole *aob*, whereas its equilibrium point is *Tiferet*; and we have said that it is called *aor* or *astral light*. The Tree of Knowledge is the Sfara *Daat* of the *Yetzira* World, which subsequently falls into *Malkut* of the *Assia* World. We assume that it had not existed, but as a result of what we called *sin*, it was created. Symbolically, speaking through images, this happened through the Tree of Knowledge, which led humans to the Fall; and, through the astral light, the Kabalistic Tree "unfolded" itself (the Tree of Knowledge sprouted) to *Malkut* in the physical world, whereas the "celestial" magnetism contained in it was transformed into earthly magnetism and its various manifestations – personal, human, animal, and others. In this way, Nahash represents the Demiurge of our world. However, whether humans, through their choice, have given a chance for this to happen, or such was God's Providence, we leave to the reader to decide. The process of creation of the binary world, as well as the formation of dual consciousness, is figuratively represented in Kabala through the "fallen" Sfara, which has to be restored by humans into its place. This can happen by mastering the earthly magnetism in *Malkut* and following the path of Shatan, which is the evolutionary path of initiations. When we reach the Sfarotic binary of good and evil, there exists a danger of going back down the sinful path of the Fall. However, if we continue along the path of Shatan, we will restore the fallen Sfara on the individual plane, and when even the last soul does so, then the Messiah will concede to the "rectified" humankind the place of the keystone in the *Yetzira* Tree. *(Fig. 52)*

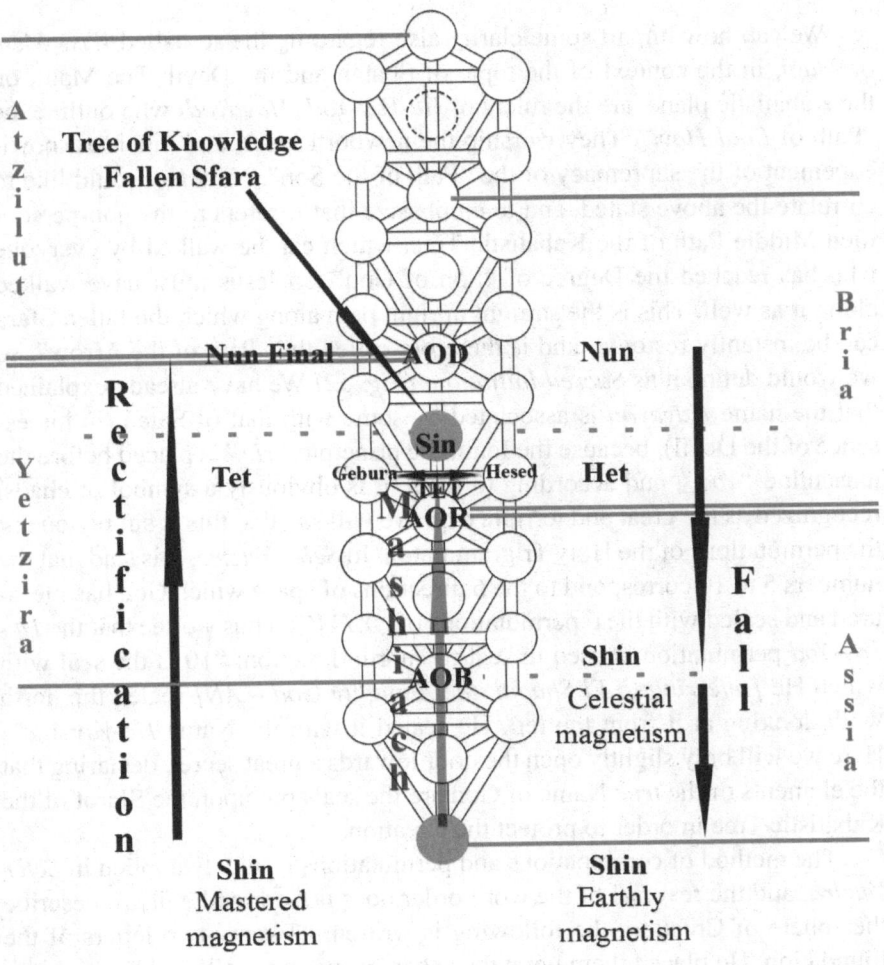

**Figure 52**

## The Three Wise Men

> *And when they had come into the house, they saw the young Child with Mary His mother, and fell down and worshiped Him. And when they had opened their treasures, they presented gifts to Him: gold, frankincense, and myrrh. Then, being divinely warned in a dream that they should not return to Herod, they departed for their own country another way.*
>
> **Holy Gospel of Matthew 2:11 – 12, NKJV**

We can now impart some clarity also regarding the so-called *Wise Men*, or *Magi*, in the context of the topic of Shatan and the Devil. The Magi, on the Kabalistic plane, are the rulers of *He-Vav-Yod (Havayod)* who outline the "Path of *Baal-Havi*". They worship the newborn Jesus, and this is acknowledgement of the supremacy of the "Path of the Son". Now we would like to correlate the above stated, and to emphasize that it refers to the non-personified Middle Path of the Kabalistic Tree, which can be walked by everyone who has reached the Degree of "Son of God", so Jesus must have walked along it as well. This is the straight upright path along which the fallen Sfara can be instantly restored, and is therefore called the "Path of the Arrow", so we would define it as *Sacred Initiation*. (Fig. 52) We have already explained that the name *Havayod* is associated by some with that of Satan (in his essence of the Devil), because the feminine principle *"He"* is placed before the masculine *"Yod"*, and according to them, it is obviously a symbol of chaos, recognized as the great and terrible evil. We will say that this is simply one of the permutations of the Holy Trigrammaton. In *Sefer Yetzira*, it is said that the numbers 5 to 10 correspond to the 6 directions of space which God has measured and sealed with the 6 permutations of *"Y H V"*. Thus we see that the *He-Vav-Yod* permutation is used to seal the north direction: "10 is the seal with which He *[referring to El Shadai, the Almighty God – AN]* sealed the north while looking at it from the left. He sealed it with the Name *He-Vav-Yod*". Here we will only slightly open the door towards a great secret, declaring that the elements of the *true* Name of God are the seals put upon the Sfarot of the Kabalistic Tree in order to protect the Creation.

The method of combinations and permutations is widely applied in *Sefer Yetzira*, and the reversal of the word order does not portend evil. To describe the sphere of Creation, the following is written: "Twenty-two letters of the foundation. He placed them upon the sphere as upon a wall, in 231 combinations…"

Further, when the 22 letters of the Hebrew alphabet are described and classified, we read the following: "Three Mothers, *Alef, Mem, Shin* – a Great Secret: wondrous, innermost, and sealed with six seals; and from them issued the Air, Water and Fire, from them issued the Fathers, and from them – the children".

Deciphering the above written, we understand that the Fathers issued from Fire, Air and Water, and these are their corresponding letters *Yod-He-Vav*, and from them, the children issued – these are their six permutations, one of which is *He-Vav-Yod*, branded as the name of the Devil – *Havayod*. Having already learned that *Havayod* is not the name of the Devil but one of God's Names, we can safely say that the Rulers of this Name follow the satanic path, as it is opposed to the Path of the Son – the Messianic Path. This is the path of Shatan, the path of formal initiations, which has gained notoriety for being the path of the Devil, called *Satan* and *Lucifer*, which is different from the Path of "Ben", declared by the Christian doctrine to be the Path of Jesus – the only Son of God. It is consciously emphasized in the Gospel that after the worship, the Three Wise Men, also not accidentally called *Magi*, go back along another way, outlining the Path of the Son which has to be walked by Jesus.

Subject to the existing paradigm, Robert Ambelain believes that the left path "... is the politicized path of Freemasonry, without soul and without light, in which the age-old and soothing voice of the ancient symbols does not sound. Then you see the Compass, a symbol of the Spirit, presented upside down, dominated by the Square, a symbol of matter, which has taken its place, or at least tries hardly to do so". We agree with the written, except for the fact that it is characterized as "left path", due to the above stated considerations.

## The Devil

***Homo solus aut deus, aut daemon.*** [125]

In conclusion, it is extremely important to point out that, as a result of this paradigm, the so-called *worshipers of the Devil* are incorrectly called "followers of Satan/ Lucifer", and this sad analogy is deeply rooted into the human consciousness – or, as one Initiate has put it, quoted by Éliphas Lévi: "The Devil – that is God, however, misunderstood". The *Baphomet* of the Templars is not properly perceived (by the Church/ Inquisition/ Christian-

---

125  From Latin: "A human alone is either a god or a demon" – *AN*.

ity), regardless of the fact that on his forehead there is an upright pentagram drawn, indicating his enlightened core essence. We can in no way ignore the negativity with which the name of the Devil and his analogues are charged, neither can we forbid devil-worshipers from being called "Satanists", which is why we use the more unencumbered name *Shatan* when denoting the "opposite path". Anton LaVey, the very founder of the *Church of Satan,* wrote in his book *The Satanic Bible* that Satan is "the spirit of progress, the inspirer of all great movements that contribute to the development of civilization and the advancement of mankind. He is the spirit of revolt that leads to freedom, the embodiment of all heresies that liberate". It sounds Luciferian; and so, what Devilish can be found in the above written, unless we assume that, for the furtherers of the status quo, the destroyer of this very status quo represents a symbol of Evil. In the same way, also Satan, as the opposing one, the one testing the willpower and faith of humans, is recognized by them in a negative way, as the bearer of obscurantism. Indeed, which humans, if not being Initiates, would liken to good that one who opposes their own will and subjects them to various trials? The natural attitude is to recognize such opponents as enemies against whom struggle must be fought for their destruction. Therefore, Satan, who tempts our ego, and Lucifer, who destroys the old forms and paradigms of our conceptual mind, both acquire the characteristics of evil in the person of the Devil. In this way, he adopts concrete forms in the astral world and is animated by the thoughts of those humans who believe in his existence, thus feeding his egregore. Therefore, to the question of whether the Devil exists as an entity generating negative energies, we will answer in the affirmative, because he is a creation of the very humans, of their fears, of their evil thoughts and feelings. The Devil is a symbol and personification of the human beings which have separated themselves from their Divine Core Essence and have deeply immersed into materiality. Dostoyevsky has also reached this conclusion, saying: "I think that if the Devil does not exist, and therefore, he was created by humans, then they have created the Devil in their own human image and likeness". We will defeat the Devil if we defeat our own selves, and thus we will become great heroes, because, as Rumi says, "Small heroes defeat their enemies. Great heroes conquer themselves". This can be done along the path of formal initiations leading to the Sacred Initiation, the analogue of which in literature is the finding of the Holy Grail.

# 21
# The "Lost Word"

## The Legend of the Temple

*One may not reach the dawn
save by the path of the night.*

**Khalīl Jubrān**

In the Masonic tradition, the search for the Grail corresponds to the search for the "Lost Word", whereas its finding symbolizes the Sacrament of True Initiation. This topic is *explicitly* related to the legend of the process of construction of Solomon's Temple, constituting the main symbolism in the Master's Degree Rite within the framework of Blue Freemasonry. According to the parable, the construction of the Temple was entrusted to Master Hiram Abiff. Three fellow crafts asked to learn the Master's Word before the expiration of the stipulated term. They decided to force Hiram to tell them this Word. They stalked him while he was alone in the Temple, and ambushed its three gates. Each of them asked for the Secret Word, and after not receiving it, struck a certain part of Hiram's body with a respective tool. The last stroke was fatal, and the Master breathed his last. The fellow crafts buried the corpse at the foot of a hill, and marked the place with a sprig of acacia. Thus, the Master's Word vanished together with Hiram. King Solomon ordered that Hiram's body be sought in order to be buried in a consecrated land, ordering the first word spoken upon its discovery to be accepted as the new Master's Word. When they found Hiram's body, they managed to remove it thanks to the power of the new Word.

This is, in its basic outlines, the parable that is performed during the Rites of the Master's Degree in different variations. Its idea, however, remains unchanged – namely, the victory over Death; for Hiram is resurrected within each and every Initiate Master.

## The Masonic Secret

*The great secret of Freemasonry
is that there is no secret at all.*

**Benjamin Franklin**

Before we continue, in order to reassure the zealous guardians of the "Masonic secrets", we will say that everything we will discuss further is present in the works of various Masonic authors, intended for a wide range of readers, as well as in the electronic space. We have explained that nowadays knowledge is protected not by secrets but by the very lack of understanding, which unfortunately applies also to Freemasons themselves. We have already commented that, in Freemasonry, not much knowledge can be obtained outside the Rites, and we have come to the conclusion that if the latter rest on a most ancient original tradition (of which we deeply doubt!), then this tradition is distorted intentionally or out of ignorance. What Benjamin Franklin has said is precisely in this sense. Diametrically, another prominent Mason, Albert Mackey, states that there is indeed a secret, but it is only symbolically represented by the "Lost Word", and that the search for it is ultimately the seeking of the Absolute Truth. In his book, *An Encyclopaedia of Freemasonry*, he writes: "The mythical history of Freemasonry informs us that there once existed a WORD of surpassing value; that this Word was known to but few; that it was at length lost; and that a temporary substitute for it was adopted. The loss of the Word must suppose its eventual recovery. The only term of the myth that is to be regarded in the study of its interpretation, is the abstract idea of a word lost and afterwards recovered".

We come to the conclusion that the *"secret"* in Freemasonry is related to the "Lost Word", which has not yet been found. In the Master's Degree Rite, this Word is not even sought, but only the ascertaining is attained of the new, *substitute word*, which has changed over the years. In this situation, the following question naturally arises: Actually, what secret or secrets has Freemasonry shrouded with its mystical veil? To find the truthful answer, we will begin with the fact that, according to the parable described, the substitute for the Lost Word must be the first word spoken. In most of the current Rites, this word is *Mahbenah*, but it is definitely not the first one pronounced. Despite this contradiction, we assume that this is the new Master's Word; yet how can one explain what was written in 1760 in the book *Three Distinct Knocks* – namely, that the Master's Word in the Ancient Freemasonry is *Mahabone*? In other editions and books before that, it was written as *Mahabyn, Matchpin, Magboe,* and after that date – in the form of *Moabon* and *Ma Habonen*. However, in the catechism of *The Post Boy*, which we have already quoted, we come across the following dialogue:

"*Q.: What is the Master's Word?*
A.: Hiram Abiff.*"

In the book *Masonry Dissected* (1730), for the first time, accessible to the general audience, the Master's Word in Modern Freemasonry appears, referred to as *Machbenah*. The same word can be seen in subsequent books and editions, written as *Macbenac, Mac-Benac, Machenac, Makbenark*. This word in today's Rites, with small deviations, is translated as *"the flesh parts from the bones"*. According to Prichard, however, it should be interpreted as *"The Builder is smitten"*. In *Thesaurus Linguae Hebraicae (Hebrew Dictionary of Synonyms)*, we find the following meanings of the word *machbenah*, which do not correspond to those already mentioned: *mantle; cloak; s.th. that envelops/ enfolds;* and also *s.th. that is concealed/ hidden under a mantle*. Close to these definitions is the opinion of Albert Pike, who believes that the word means "the place where the murdered one was hidden".

According to some researchers, the word *Mahabone* is a derivative of the Hebrew *Mah haboneh,* which is translated as "Who is the architect?", or "What? This is the architect!" According to others, the most accurate translation is "What?! Can it be the builder?"

Albert Mackey maintains that the word is *Ma-ha-bo-neh* and should be translated as "What! Is this the builder?" Albert Pike, however, objects that the correct substitute word must be of three syllables, since "the True Word was also trilateral"[126]. He believes that the word should be Mah-Ab-On, meaning "Progeny, Issue from the Potent Father". We believe that in this way it sounds much more majestic than "the flesh parts from the bones", unless in the last expression we look for alchemical symbolism in the sense of the process of decay. Something like this is hinted at in Oswald Wirth's book *La Franc-maçonnerie rendue intelligible à ses adeptes – Vol. III: Le Livre du Maître (Freemasonry, made understandable to its followers – Vol. III: The Book of the Master)* – May 1931, where it is stated that the substitute word "Macbenac" means "Son of decay" or "Son of the dead Master" (or, more precisely: "he lives in the son"). Mention is also made of "The flesh parts from the bones", which corresponds to "Moabon", another form of the Master's Word. In a footnote in the book, it is specified that "Macbenac" is a sacred word of the Masters in the French Rite, while the Scottish Rite has adopted the word "Moabon".

In *Manuel Maçonnique (Masonic Manual)* of 1820 by Claude André Vuillaume, the word *Moabon* is translated as "drenched to the bone", although it contains the root Moab, meaning "coming from the father". The same is asserted by Jean-Marie Ragon, who points out that this word literally means "from the father". He explains that "As Moab and the Moabites were eternal enemies of the people of Israel, so the Mason was given the name *Moabon,* in order to be an antagonist of the profane and of all who oppose progress". This is in line with our view of the opposing ha-Shatan.

---

126 Trigrammaton: *Yod, He* and *Vau* (יהו) – *AN*.

Regarding the word *Moabon*, in his book, *An Encyclopaedia of Freemasonry*, Albert Mackey, however, expresses the following explicit opinion: "This word is found in some of the high degrees according to the French ritual, where it is explained as expressing "the satisfaction we feel in seeing the crime and the criminal punished". There is no such word in Hebrew, and the explanation is a fanciful one. The word is undoubtedly a Gallic corruption, first in sound and then in letters, of the Master's Word".

In the final reckoning, we do not know why one Master's Word was replaced with another, and yet we do not think it makes sense to investigate this, as it is about a substitute word regarding which there is no definite information about when it appeared and what exactly it means. In this sense is also what is written in *The Book of the Words* by Albert Pike about the Fellow Craft's word *Shibboleth*: "We do not know when this word was adopted, and no one has ever been able to find any especial significance in it as a Masonic word".

Mackey, on his part, believes that the word *Shibboleth* is the link between Freemasonry and the Eleusinian Mysteries, through the Goddess Demeter. One of her symbols was indeed the *ear of corn* and agriculture as a whole, whereas the other attribute towards which Mackey turns the attention is the *lighted torch* with which she used to be represented – a symbol of Enlightenment.

According to Madame Blavatsky, "This Masonic commandment, 'mouth to ear, and the word at low breath', is an inheritance from the *Tannaim*[127] and the old Pagan Mysteries. The "word" itself is but a "substitute" for the "Lost Word", and is a comparatively modern invention. Only a limited number among the chiefs of the Templars, and some Rosicrucians of the 17th century, always in close relations with Arabian alchemists and initiates, could really boast of its possession. From the 7th to the 15th centuries, there was no one who could claim it in Europe. The real Word, now substituted by *Mac Benac* and *Mah*, was used ages before its pseudo-magical effect was tried on the 'widow's sons' of the last two centuries".

Given this lack of clarity, and since we are talking about words that have served primarily to obtain a corresponding wage – a purpose that has even dropped out in Modern Freemasonry, we do not consider it necessary to pay more attention to them. However, we are increasingly asking ourselves: What kind of tradition can we talk about in Freemasonry?

The phrase "lost word" – *verbum dimissum*, was first used by the Italian alchemist Bernardo Trevisano (the manuscript *Sloane MS 3630* is in the British Library), and some Freemasons consider the legend of the "Lost Word"

---

[127] *Tannaim* were the Rabbinic sages whose views are recorded in the *Mishna* ("repetition") in the period 10 – 220 AD. The root of the word *tanna* is Aramaic and corresponds to the Hebrew *shanah*, meaning: "to repeat (what has been learned)" – *AN*.

to take its source precisely from it. There are assumptions that this legend is structured in the familiar to us complete form by a particular person, and one of the rumours is that it is Francis Bacon.

This vagueness around the Legend of Hiram has led some to believe that the "Modern Masons" have not inherited the authentic legend. In this sense, René Guénon says that the Masters are the ones who had the seventh and last Operative Degree to which the Legend of Hiram belonged. It was therefore unknown to the "admitted Fellow Crafts" who, on their own initiative, created the Grand Lodge of England in 1717. They were unable to convey something they had not received. Oswald Wirth is of the same opinion, and according to him, the London Lodges that created the Grand Lodge of England did not know or did not include this legend in their Rites. According to him, no ancient manuscript mentions the death of the architect of the Temple of Solomon. Moreover, the first edition of the Constitution of 1723 does not even hint at the Master's Degree.

There are various claims about when and where the Legend of Hiram appeared, but we will point out several indisputable sources.

In the *Dumfries No. 4 Manuscript* (1710), which we have already quoted, Hiram is mentioned as Solomon's favourite architect, and there is a description of what he has built according to the Bible.

In the *Graham Manuscript* (1726), the legend is narrated of the Third Degree – however, it is about Noah and finding his body by his three sons, who hoped to reveal some secrets by digging up his body. Hiram is also mentioned, but only as the builder of the Temple of Solomon. It is interesting to note that the way Noah's body was taken out coincides with that of the Legend of Hiram.

We will give reference also to *The Wilkinson Manuscript* (1727), which represents a catechism containing 74 questions and answers, mentioning the mythical tomb of Hiram.

However, in the book *Masonry Dissected* (1730), for the first time, the Third Degree Rite is described, along with the Legend of Hiram, as well as the way of lifting his body with the help of the five points; the substitute Master's Word *(Machbenah)* is indicated, and it contains everything else about the Master's Degree existing in the present Rites. We have found no sources other than the Masonic legend in which it is said that Hiram was the architect or builder of the Temple.

In the Bible, the following information is given about Hiram: "So now I am sending (you) a clever man, endowed with knowledge – Hiram-Avia, the son of a woman of the daughters of Dan, and his father was a man of

Tyre; he knows how to craft with gold and silver, copper and iron, stone and wood..." (*Second Book of Paralipomenon/ Chronicles* 2:13 – 14, *BOB* [*translated from Bulgarian – ed.*])

It is clearly seen from the above quotation that Hiram "knows how to craft", which is an indication that he is a craftsman, but not a builder. The same conclusion is reached also by Umberto Porciatti from the *Grand Orient of Italy,* according to whom: "The dramatic legend cannot be said to be inspired by the Bible, because there Hiram is a brilliant artist having cast the two pillars, the Bronze Sea, and other things; and yet, nowhere is he mentioned as the architect of King Hiram himself and the leader of an endless crowd of workers, whom he divided into apprentices, journeymen, and masters. The legend is rather inspired by the initiation of Osiris, by this Third Egyptian Degree, which was called the "Gate of Death", and even re-creates it".

In his book *Orthodoxie Maçonnique (Masonic Orthodoxy),* Jean-Marie Ragon is even more extreme regarding the Legend of Hiram: "... Thus all these stories underlying the Third Degree, where the neophyte comes with all his astonishment which an old story provokes, performed unceremoniously, without any preparation or logic, can be called "rude", because lies can be found in the Bible, the stories of these lies having nothing in common with the Initiatic doctrine, neither ancient nor modern."

In this sense, Robert Ambelain, in his book *La Franc-Maçonnerie Oubliée (The Forgotten Freemasonry),* asks the following question: "Who was the one that prompted to James Anderson and Jean Théophile Désaguliers the idea to replace the dignified and simple reception ceremony, quite customary in the early 18th century, with this Rite – long and efficacious from the viewpoint of occultism, which, however, is in complete opposition to all biblical teachings, and which seems to all believers in monotheistic religions to be an absolutely dark ritual?"[128]

In *Antiquities of the Jews* by Flavius Josephus, we have found no sign of the existence of Hiram Abiff, in the sense of the written in the Bible.

According to Sergio Magaldi, Hiram is a symbol rather than the name of a real person, which represents a Hebrew word composed of four letters and two roots, and means "Life of the Spirit", or "The Spirit of Life".

The question of whether this legend existed before the creation of the Third Degree Rite in Blue Freemasonry remains still not clarified, but in any case, it is adopted as its basis.

---

128 It refers to the indwelling of another soul in a person's body, which is called *dybbuk* in the Judaic tradition – *AN.*

# The Master's Word

> *Silence is the Master of Masters
> because silence teaches us without speaking.*
> **Maurice Zundel**

At the beginning, we pointed out the essential idea in this legend: that, with Hiram's death, the "Master's Word" was lost. In one of its versions, the "Word" was in the possession of three people who had the right to pronounce it: Solomon, Hiram – the King of Tyre, and Hiram Abiff. "How is it possible that the loss of the 'Word' is presented as a consequence of Hiram's death, while, according to this legend, others know it as well?", exclaims René Guénon. In that case, "It could not have been 'lost' to the Craft by the death of but one of them!", also exclaims Dewey Buck, an American physician and psychologist, 33rd Degree of the Scottish Rite in the Northern Jurisdiction. "It would have required the death of all three to have lost such a word", he concludes. To explain this alogism, various theories are resorted to, the most widespread of which is that the word is three-syllable, so the three should pronounce it simultaneously. Albert Pike is one of the first to state that "the True Word was also trilateral", and for that reason, the "substitute word" should also be of three syllables. René Guénon reverses this correlation, saying that the pronunciation of the Hebrew Tetragrammaton as one of the Divine Names most often associated with the "Lost Word" must be three-syllable in order for the symbolism of the "Found Word" to be correct. Thus the more correct pronunciation of the Tetragrammaton is *Jehovah*, not *Yahveh*. We leave it to the reader to judge whether the pronounceable God's Name should conform to the "substitute word" or vice versa.

We are inclined, as a compromise, to agree with the concept that the "Lost Word" should have been pronounced in syllables by all three ones simultaneously, and yet, it is still not clear to us why this Word was lost with the death of only one of them. Moreover, there is no consensus on whether it was lost, after all. According to Dr. Oliver, a prominent Masonic historian, "The Word was never lost but transferred to the *Royal Arch*".

Many historians consider the York Rite to be an emanation of "original and true" Freemasonry. This is because the first certificates for the establishment of masonry guilds were issued in the city of York. Since the Mark Degrees, as well as the *Royal Arch* Degree, are part of this Rite, what has been said about it should also apply to them. We have already commented on the claims to the authenticity of Mark Masonry when we viewed the throwing of the "keystone" during the Mark Master Ritual.

In *A Comprehensive Dictionary of Freemasonry* by Ernest Beha, however, we read the following regarding the "Lost Word": "Tradition tells us that after some time the Sacred Word was found in a vault, to which access was had through nine arches, but accounts differ as by whom these arches were built, at the time the word was found, and in what manner it appeared. One tradition says the vault and arches were built by the three Grand Masters, for the purpose of concealing a copy of the most holy things belonging to the Temple, and that the vault was discovered at the erection of the Second Temple. The other tradition is that the vault was made by Patriarch Enoch, but long before the destruction of the First Temple; and that the word was found upon a golden tablet, engraven in a language more ancient than the Hebrew".

G. Gardner, on the other hand, specifies the word and its meaning, maintaining that one of the key symbolic words used in the *Royal Arch*, according to tradition, was found in a crypt under the First Temple, which emerged during the construction of the second one, and this is *Jah-Bul-On*. Found engraved upon a gold tablet, this word is composed of a combination of words meaning "I am God, the Father of all." In Freemasonry, this refers to G.A.O.T.U. According to Gardner, a more accurate and clear interpretation of the phrase is, without any doubt: "I am the Lord and Master of Light."

This brings us to the *Royal Arch* Degree, which is also controversial. Masonic authors, such as Tuckett and Count Goblet, maintain the idea of the antiquity of this Degree and its use as a completion of the Legend of Hiram, while Adolphus Woodford, Albert Mackey and George Oliver adhere to the theory that the Third Degree was "mutilated" in order to create the *Royal Arch* Degree. As for Bernard Jones, he is quite explicit: "There does not seem to be any evidence to support the statement that the *Royal Arch* was originally a part of any Craft degree".

There is no consensus observed regarding the "Rediscovered Word" in the Rite. According to Dr. Oliver, whom we have already quoted, the "True Word" has been transferred into the *Royal Arch*, while according to René Guénon, the High Degrees are primarily related to the search for the "Lost Word", so giving a "Rediscovered Word" would mean the end of this search. He thinks that "... actually, this 'rediscovered word' is nothing but another 'substitute word', and it cannot be otherwise, because the 'True Word' is absolutely unpronounceable". Nevertheless, according to him, "the *Royal Arch* is related to the Operative affiliation, so this makes it the 'most authentic' of all High Degrees".

And yet, we did not understand how far this "authenticity" goes, since in Albert Mackey's book, *An Encyclopaedia of Freemasonry,* we find the following dialogue from the old manuscript known as the *York MS*, which is now lost, but was translated by Krause, and inserted in his *Kunsturkunden:*

"*Q.: Give me the Jerusalem Word.*
*A.: Giblin.*[129]
*Q.: Give me the Universal Word.*
*A.: Boaz.*"

"It may be supposed that this "Jerusalem Word" was the word which the Masons used at Jerusalem, while the 'Universal Word' was the word common to the Craft everywhere".

On the other hand, in the already quoted book by Oswald Wirth, we come upon the following dialogue:

"*Q.: What is the name of the Master Mason?*
*A.: Gabaon.*
*Q.: What is the password?*
*A.: G.B.L.M.* (meaning *Giblim*) – This is how the stone-hewers are called in the Bible, who help together with the masons of Solomon and those of Hiram, King of Tyre, for the process of construction of the Jerusalem Temple." (*1 Kings* 5:18, *NKJV:* "Gebalites")

It is clearly seen from the examples given above that there is no unanimity regarding the "Lost Word". This is so because it may be a matter of symbolism rather than any realities. That is why we are solidary with Guénon in the opinion that the "search for the Lost Word" is a *continuous, ceaseless process* because it is a synonym of "Seeking the Lost Word" in the esoteric meaning – a symbolic phrase of the Initiates over the centuries, denoting the eternal aspiration of the human being towards the Light of Wisdom and Truth.

We sympathize with Freemasonry, and in no case are we ruthless critics of Freemasonry, but after our cursory comparative study, we begin to ask ourselves: Is not the written about Freemasons in Éliphas Lévi's book *The History of Magic* a little bit exaggerated? – "Their doctrine is that of Zoroaster and of Hermes... They are successors of the School of Alexandria, as of all antique initiations, custodians of the secrets of the *Apocalypse* and the *Zohar.*"

As a certain maxim in the sphere of jurisprudence reads, we only give the facts, while leaving to the reader the right to judge. In the same book,

---

129 *Giblim* (sometimes incorrectly written as *giblin*) is how the inhabitants of the city and district of *Gebal* were called, in Phoenicia, near Mount Lebanon, and so they were therefore vassals of the King of Tyre. The Phoenician word *gibal* (plural *giblim*) means "mason" or "hewn stone". In *1 Kings* 5:17, *KJV:* "And the king commanded, and they brought great stones, costly stones, and hewed stones, to lay the foundation of the house", the word used for "hewed stones" is *Giblim – AN.*

Éliphas Lévi has judged regarding the Freemasons of that time as follows: "At the present day, there are many who think that they are Masons and yet do not know the meaning of their Rites, having lost the Key of the Mysteries. They misconstrue even their symbolical pictures and those hieroglyphic signs which are emblazoned on the carpets of their Lodges. These pictures and signs are the pages of a book of absolute and universal science. They can be read by means of the Kabalistic keys and hold nothing in concealment for the Initiate who already possesses those of Solomon".

One of the reasons for this lack of understanding, in our opinion, is the use of the unfamiliar Judaic terminology, which enters Freemasonry after 1723 and due to its linguistic specificity leads to many inaccuracies in the pronunciation, spelling and interpretation of the etymology and meanings of words. Until then, the Christian Church and religion had a dominant role in the Lodges and their Rites. As an illustration, we will point out the Constitution of the Freemasons' *Antient Grand Lodge of England*, entitled *Ahiman Rezon*[130], in which, in the chapter about God and religion, it is written: "A MASON is obliged by his Tenure to believe firmly in the true Worship of the eternal God, as well as in all those sacred Records which the Dignitaries and Fathers of the Church have compiled and published for the Use of all good Men...".

An even clearer and more vivid testimony is contained in *The Grand Mystery of Freemasons Discovered* (1724), in which, to the question of what the Three Lights of the Lodge represent, the answer is: "Father, Son, and Holy Ghost", whereas to the question of what the two pillars *Jahin* and *Voaz* represent, the answer is: "A Strength and Stability of the Church in all Ages".

These examples again incite us to think more about the traditional roots of Freemasonry.

## The Masonic Tradition

> *The date of 1717 does not mark the origin of Freemasonry, but that of its degeneration.*
>
> *René Guénon*

The existence of tradition, and even more of science, presupposes relative constancy and continuity, which we do not seem to find in Freemasonry. In our opinion, this is due to its profanation rather than their initial absence.

---

[130] In 1756 Laurence Dermott publishes his Constitution entitled *Ahiman Rezon* (אחימן רזון), which is used by the *Antient Grand Lodge of England*, established in 1751 and lasted until the creation of the *United Grand Lodge of England* in 1813 – *AN*.

We consider the search for the "Lost Word" and its finding to be the symbolic representation of the restoration of the lost Masonic tradition and science. However, they are not distinguished for any strict specifics, which is why they include the whole tradition of the Mysteries and the esoteric science over the millennia. This is also the opinion of Denys Roman[131], a disciple of René Guénon, who says: "Freemasonry is, without any doubt, the only Initiatic organization in the world that is not connected with any specific esoterism. And, as Guénon says, this should not free Masons to be bound to any of the existing esoterisms at the moment, but should rather encourage them not to limit their own interests only within their own tradition, but, on the contrary, to keep learning owing to the 'key' of universal symbolism, for knowledge is concealed in all traditions".

Therefore, still at the very beginning of this book, we pointed out the exceptional importance of knowing and interpreting the symbols properly, especially in a Kabalistic key, as Éliphas Lévi says. That is why we will try to penetrate into the secrets of "Freemasonry under its veil" precisely through this Kabalistic key. We will begin with a dialogue from the already quoted book by Oswald Wirth:

*"Q.: Is there no trace of the True Word which they wanted to receive from Hiram?*
*A.: No, but it is considered to have been the Tetragrammaton."*

A magnificent answer – and yet, it raises again a question that seems to have no answer: Why, when it is supposed which the True Word is, a non-unified substitute word is used in the Rites, a word shrouded in much more ambiguity? We do not know the exact reason, but nevertheless, we can give some logical explanation – and it is that the Tetragrammaton is the unpronounceable Name of God according to the Hebrew Kabalistic tradition, which is why the substitute Names *Yahveh, Jehovah,* and *Adonai* are used. However, the question arises as to why, then, some of these Names, which are indisputable and unambiguous, do not represent the Master's Word? If the substitute words used were not Hebrew as well, the answer could be that the reason is the Christian orientation of the Masonic Lodges. For the sake of Truth, in some older Rites, as well as by a number of authors, the Name *Jehovah* is given as the Master's Word, but it is not imposed as the only and indisputable Name. One of the most emblematic God's Names in the Hebrew Kabala, representing the generation, maintenance and development

---

131 A pseudonym of Marcel Maugy (1901 – 1986), who spent nearly 20 years in a period of preparation (from 1926 until 1946) before being initiated as a Freemason. During this long period he had constant contact with Guénon, whom he called "the Master" – *AN..*

of the Manifested Worlds, is undoubtedly *Yod-He-Vav-He*, regarding which there are contradictory statements as well. According to some, it is the "Unpronounceable Name" of God; according to others, it is His "Great, Secret and Terrible Name"; and according to still others, it was pronounced quietly by the High Priest in the Holy of Holies once a year, at a ceremony during Yom Kippur. It turns out that it is secret, but at the same, it is known, and moreover, its meaning is explained. On the other hand, it is "Unpronounceable", and yet, the High Priest used to pronounce it. This contradiction can only be resolved if we assume that he used to say the substitute Name. This is unlikely, however, in the context of its secrecy, since *Jehovah, Yahveh*, and *Adonai* are widely used both in the Bible and outside of it. In this case, there are not many answer options. One is that the "Secret Name" is not the Tetragrammaton; another is that it is actually the Tetragrammaton, and therefore it was pronounced quietly; and the third one it is that it is the "Unpronounceable Name", in the sense of "Do not pronounce the Name of the Lord in vain!" *[Exodus 20:7, BOB, translated from Bulgarian – ed.]* – or in the literal sense of impossibility to be pronounced in a certain way by the uninitiated. To us, the latter option has the taste of Truth, which is why we adhere to it, believing that "Do not pronounce the Name of the Lord in vain!" applies only to those who are able to verbalize it correctly. This is so because God's Name can be creative but also destructive, and, as such, it is analogous to the Egyptian *"Ur Hekau"*[132] – "Words of Power", which are inextricably connected with God's Name or with the Name in principle.

---

[132] *Ur Hekau* – this is how the Sceptre of Great Magic was called, as well as the Master of the "mighty and powerful words and gestures". With his *great speech (djedet uret)*, he pronounced the Sacred Names of the Deities, and he knew the energy words needed to refer to them. The word "heka" is usually translated as "magic", but it actually means "the art of the mouth" and expresses the "magic speech" – *AN*.

# VII
# THE HOLY OF HOLIES

## 22
## The Name of God

### The Secret Name

*Name is a fence
and within it you are nameless.*
**Samuli Paronen**

The idea of the Secret Name of God, containing His Might, is present in one of the Egyptian legends which we mentioned regarding the magic abilities of Isis. It tells how Isis, taking some soil from the earth and some saliva from the God Ra, created a poisonous snake that bit Him deadly. The severe pain forced the old God to seek help from Isis, but she refused until He revealed His Secret Name to her: "Oh, tell me Your Name, Holy Father, for the one who knows Your Name shall live". He did this, as a result of which Isis gained His Might, and this forced Him to resign from the supreme power.

The Egyptians and the peoples of the East in general attached great importance to the pronouncing and applying of names with magic powers, such as those of the gods and various disincarnate beings. This was a necessity both for the living, for the fulfilment of their desires, and for the dead, in their journey and abode in the worlds beyond. Since ancient times, the *name (Ren)*[133] was for the Egyptians an integral part of the personality, equally with the *soul (Ba)*, the *etheric double (Ka)*[134] and the *body (Khat)*, whereas its defilement was equivalent to social death. E. A. Wallis Budge[135] says that ac-

---

133  *Ren* – The perpetuation of the name, according to the Egyptian proverb "Since their names are being pronounced, they live", has a very important role allowing existence after death. One of the most severe punishments for the unworthy dead was to erase their name, as with Hatshepsut and Ehnaton. Thus, the erasure of their names represents a posthumous penalty of eternal oblivion – *AN*.

134  *Ka* – the etheric double, the vital force, the life-giving spark that distinguishes the dead from the living. It resembles the Spirit in some religions. *Ka* needs a body in which to continue living even after death, so this is the reason for mummification. After the end of the Middle Kingdom, there were statues of the dead in the tombs, which represented a double wherein their *Ka* could return in the case of an accident with the mummy – *AN*.

135  Sir Ernest Alfred Thompson Wallis Budge is an English Egyptologist, with many years of service as a curator of the Department of Egyptian and Assyrian Antiquities at the British Museum – *AN*.

cording to the Egyptian tradition, one actually starts living in our world in the instant when one's name is pronounced: that is why humans could hope for some life after death only if the deities beyond had learned their names and pronounced them aloud. Also, without a name, humans could not in any way be identified in the "Law-Court of Osiris". Therefore, the texts of the pyramids of various rulers contain prayers for the preservation and "germination" or "flourishing" of the name. Also, according to Budge, all the gods of Egypt were purely and simply personifications of the Names of Re. Each of the gods is one of the organs, or limbs, of Re, whereas the Name of each god is actually God Himself. In the same way, also in Kabala, the Manifested God has emanations called *Sfarot,* which reflect His essential qualities. This is proof of the exceptional significance of the name by which an entity is identified in the various dimensions. The name given by the parents legitimizes a person in our world. However, one's *occult* (in the higher sense of *concealed* and *esoteric*) name denotes this person in all worlds. It contains the mission and destiny of the person in a given existence of this human being. It is no coincidence that the Latin expression *Nomen omen*[136] exists. However, it is not the substitute name used at some places even nowadays, as a reminiscence of the traditional belief that knowing a personal name makes it possible to influence its bearer. This occult name is given or restored after receiving a Sacred Initiation, when the transformed new personality embarks on a new path marked by a new name. Each of the Twice-Born from Above, like every one born, should receive also a spiritual name by which those Twice-Born identify themselves in the Universe.

The Name of God is undoubtedly related to the Words of Power, because it possesses the greatest Might. It is no coincidence that in the Egyptian and the Hebrew tradition, the world is created by God by uttering His Own Name. The *Words of Power* represent mostly the Names of God in the monotheistic religions or the Names of various Deities in the polytheistic ones, characterizing their vital principles and qualities. They are applied as magic formulas for the implementation of certain ideas and goals. It is believed that pronouncing them in a certain secret way leads to the desired magic effect. Some consider that this is how the stone blocks of the Egyptian pyramids were levitated. We find something more specific in this sense also in the Old Testament, where it is said that Solomon's Temple was built in complete silence, without any impact of metal objects. According to the Hebrew tradition, the hewing of stones was done by means of a special worm named *shamir,* which is an indication towards the use of magic operations. According to the ancient Kabalist Shimon Bar Yohai, it was not God who divided the Red Sea, but Moses, using the

---

[136] "The name is an omen/ destiny" – *AN.*

power of God's Name. However, in order not to misuse the Might of God's Name, a substitute one is used which does not have such power, whereas the True Name and the way it is pronounced are kept secret. This approach is permanently established in Judaism, having found expression through the latter also in Freemasonry. That is why we cannot help but dwell on some fundamental views in this sense of the Hebrew tradition, which, just like the Masonic one, turns out to be quite contradictory and inconsistent.

Some sources of the *Talmud*, the *Midrash* and *Kabala* contain knowledge of the mystical Names of God. They are usually composed of 1, 2, 3, 4, 8, 12, 42 or 72 letters, which are given special meaning and function, conditioning the essential characteristic of the Name, part of the characteristic of God Himself. The most fundamental is the already familiar to us Tetragrammaton, from which the other Names are predominantly considered to have originated, with the exception of the 72-letter Name, the way of formation of which we have already explained. Many authors consider it to be the True, Creative Name of God, which is why, in order not to be misused, it is replaced with other Names. As it is said, "Creation is contained within the frames of its limits through the Name." However, according to Gershom Scholem, a scientist who is a prominent authority, it is not certain whether the Tetragram is directly related to this Name. He believes that the 42-letter Name of God, which in the tradition of early medieval scholars was defined as an active part of Creation itself, has no visible connection to the Tetragrammaton. Ultimately, his position is that the four-letter Name is only a substitute, as other Kabalists also believe, according to whom it is *Shemamforash*. Abraham Abulafia, who lived in the second half of the 13th century, claims that "The Tetragrammaton from the *Torah* represents specific "emergency aid" behind which the True Name of God is concealed". According to Abulafia, the True Name of God is not mentioned anywhere in the *Torah*, but this opinion of his has been strongly criticized by Moses Cordovero, another great Kabalist of the 16th century.

The Hebrew tradition related to God's Name has also passed into Catholicism, as is evident by the widely used Latin phrase *"In Dei Nomine. Amen"* – "In the Name of God. Amen"[137]. We must note that such a phrase, in which there is no emphasis on the Trinity, is very rare in Catholicism ("In the Name of the Father and the Son and the Holy Spirit").

The forty-two letter Name consists of consonants and is described by Rabbi Hai Gaon (Hai ben Shrira – 11th century), though its correct pronuncia-

---

137 With this phrase, all wills, notarial acts, court trials and sentences began while Latin was the official language in jurisprudence. The Franciscan Order in the Holy Land, also called the *Custody of the Holy Land (Custodia Terræ Sanctæ)*, was founded in 1217 by Saint Francis of Assisi, and currently takes care of 74 sites, as well as of Christian pilgrims, to whom it issues a certificate, beginning exactly with this phrase – *AN*.

tion has not reached us because the vowels with which it ought to be vocalized are not known. This Name is also contained in the well-known prayer *"Ana Bekoah"*, also known as the *42 Names of Ha Shem*, created by Rabbi Nehunya ben HaKanah in the 2nd century AD. This prayer has 42 words, the first letters of each word constituting the 42-letter Name of God.

According to Jacob Leib Ha-Cohen, the core essential Names of God are two: *Yahveh* and *Ehyah*. The latter, in his view, is a permutation of the former, but the letter *Vau* is replaced with *Alef*. In Kabala, the letter *Vav* represents *exile*, or the transcendent aspect of God, just as in the Hebrew word *avdah*, meaning "lost". On the other hand, *Alef* represents the human being, or the immanent aspect of God. According to the author, *Ehyah* is the "Unique Name" of God, so thus He should be known "by all generations to come".

In *Exodus* 3:14, we do see that the Name of God given to Moses by God Himself is *AHYH (Alef He Yod He)*, pronounced as *Ehyah*.[138]

According to *Karaite Judaism*[139], the Names of God are the following: *Elohim* – the Authoritative Name of God, *YHVH (Yod He Vav He)* – the Divine Name, and *AHYH (Ehyah)*, which represents God's Sacred Essential Name.

Here is what Flavius Josephus writes in this context in his *Judean War* (5:5 – 7): "The ancient Jews used the name *Alef He Yod He (Ehyah)* instead of the Tetragrammaton. Another form used before the restrictions were imposed was *Yah-u*, which is confirmed also by Diodorus of Sicily in his work *The Library of History.*" (1:94.2) – "Whereas, among the Jews... God is called as *Iao (Ιαω)*".

Furthermore, in *Targum Jonathan*[140] we can read that the original numbers from 5 to 10 correspond to the six directions of space, measured by God and sealed by Him through the permutations of the three consonants *J, H* and *V*. These three signs in Hebrew represent also the three vowels *I, A*, and *O* that make up the magic syllable *jao*, as well as the Name *Jaho*. Both play a significant role in all magic practices influenced by Ancient Judaism.

We have already mentioned that this sealing of space through the Trigrammaton is also described in *Sefer Yetzira*, one of the preserved written Kabalistic sources, and this technique is used for protection during magic operations. There is an opinion that, until the time of Moses, the Trigrammaton had been the Name of God, and afterwards, the second *He* was added, so it became the Tetragrammaton.

---

138 In the *Bulgarian Synodal Bible* edition *(BOB)*, the Name *Ehyah* is translated as "I am the Eternally Existing One" – *AN*

139 *Karaite Judaism* is a Judaic religious movement that acknowledges only the *Tanakh* as the basis of theology and religious law, unlike Rabbinic Judaism, which acknowledges also the oral *Torah* encoded in the *Talmud* – *AN*.

140 *Targum* literally means "translation", and in this particular case it refers to a translation of the *Torah* into Aramaic. *Targum Jonathan* was written around 50 BC – *AN*.

According to Gershom Scholem, it is not written anywhere that the Tetragrammaton possesses magical and supernatural powers, but it is simply a matter of a later interpretation and exegesis. He believes that a substitute Name is meant here, and also that the use of the *Torah* for magic practices (which is actually very far from its original purpose) occurred during the Hellenistic period. This practice can be noticed also in the epoch when *Sefer Yetzira* was written, in the magic Greek papyri, which were not confined only within the *Pentateuch* of Moses, but added a *Sixth* and a *Seventh Book of Moses* as veritable manuals of magic. The mystical Hebrew literature of *Merkaba* from that epoch is full of similar mystical Names of God with unclear etymology.

The prominent Spanish Kabalist Joseph Gikatilla is of another opinion. He believes that the *Torah* is not the Divine Name but rather its explanation, whereas the Name means only what is understood in the Hebrew tradition, namely the Tetragrammaton, which is the only Name of God: "All the names in the *Torah* are contained in the four-letter Name, which is the trunk of the Tree, while the other Names are its roots and branches".

In this sense, we will say that every other Name of God that can be pronounced is related to some activity, as the etymology of those Names in the Bible shows. Only the Tetragrammaton needs no reference to any activity in retrospect. To Kabalists, this Name has no "meaning" in the traditional sense of this word, because it simply does not have a definite meaning.

The Tetragrammaton is sometimes called the "Root of all other Names" and is often described as the "Stem, Branch, and Fruit of every single thing". It can be said that, to Kabalists, the Name of God is both the shortest and the longest: the shortest – because each letter is a Name in itself; the longest – because it is expressed as the whole *Torah*.

According to Scholem, this conception about the *Torah* as only one Name of God does not mean that this Name should be pronounced as such, since it has nothing in common with the rational understanding of the social functions of a name. Declaring that the *Torah* is the Name of God means that, in the *Torah*, God has expressed His perfect Core Essence, or at least that part or aspect of His Core Essence which can be revealed during creation and through creation.

From a Kabalistic point of view, *Ehyah* is God's Name for the Sfara *Keter*, and in our view, its supremacy can be deduced from this circumstance, but obviously it is neither the Secret Name nor the Unpronounceable Name. Undoubtedly, this also applies to all known and pronounceable Names of God, including the 42-letter one and the 72-name one, although it is not clear how the former is pronounced, whereas the latter is called *Shem ha-Meforash* for unknown reasons, most often written as *Shemamforash*.

## Shem Ha-Meforash

*The hen can hatch her eggs
because her heart is always listening.*

**Book of the Elixir**[141]

We will again resort to the opinion of Gershom Scholem, according to whom no later than the 2nd century AD, the Tetragrammaton becomes unpronounceable and is described by a term that has conflicting meanings regarding its essence and function. The Name of God is called *Shem ha-Meforash* – a phrase not at all having only one meaning. On the one hand, the passive participle *meforash* can mean "conveyed", "announced", as well as "explicitly explained", and finally – simply "pronounced". On the other hand, it can mean "divided" or even "concealed"; and for all these meanings, there are countless examples in Hebrew and Aramaic from this epoch. One and the same term means "concealed" and "explicit"/ "overt". Regardless of which of the two meanings was meant in its creation, in the end, the meaning of the Secret Name prevails, avoiding any explanation. After the 3rd century, other mystical Names are added to *Shem ha-Meforash*, which are formed out of passages from the *Torah* or through obscure ways. Talmudic and Midrashic literature states that these purely mystical Names exist also in the traditional Rabbinic Judaism, not only in the writings of the magi and theurgists of that epoch. Thus, Names consisting of 12, 42 and 72 letters each are mentioned, to which meanings and specific forces are ascribed. However, it is not mentioned in what way they relate to the Tetragrammaton. When literary works mention the Powerful and Mighty Name of God, Who has conceived the beginning of creation, sealing the world and holding it in its outline, it is not clear whether it refers to the Tetragrammaton or not.

The view is widely spread that the four consonants – *Alef, He, Vav,* and *Yod,* present in the two main Names of God, *YAHVEH* and *EHYEH*, are precisely those that in Hebrew can also serve as vowels. They represent, so to speak, a link between consonants and vowels, and can be considered the most spiritual elements among consonants. This makes them especially suitable to symbolize the Divine Spirit in the body of the world and thus to compose the elements of the two Divine Names. A Kabalistic group of Rabbis forms with these four letters a certain Name of God – *EHVI,* which is considered to be the source of all other Names, the true Original Name. One of the reasons why they consider this Name to be the original one is that its Gematric value is 22. Thus *EHVI* turns into a symbol that not only represents the totality of the

---

[141] A secret book of the sect named "The Golden Pill of Life" – *AN*.

whole alphabet, but also, it is possible from it to create the two Divine Names *YAHVEH* and *EHYEH*.

The great Kabalist Abulafia goes so far as to claim that this, precisely, is the True Original Initial Name of God, which is not mentioned even in the *Torah*, so as not to become available to the masses, unprepared for the deep mystical secrets – a secret which they could abuse. Here is what he says: "If you ask me whether things are truly like that (that the letters *Alef, He, Vav* and *Yod* form the True Name of God), then why does not He manifest it as a classic Name? That would be correct indeed. However, since God wanted to conceal His Name, in order to put the hearts of the initiated to a trial, and at the same time to purify and enlighten their consciousness, it was necessary to keep this Name in secret and under cover. For this reason, it is composed of these letters, which (grammarians) call "letters of concealment". This Name remained completely concealed, so the initiated themselves could not comprehend it in any way, while the Name (in the form of the Tetragrammaton) was known to them as given by tradition, not as the fruit of intellectual knowledge. It is written: "O Lord, You preserve man and beast!" (*Psalm* 36:7, *AMP*) – which refers to the wise and the ignorant. Some have immersed in speculation about the Name *(YHVH)*, while others understand that it exists only as a tradition. The ignorant have been forbidden to pronounce it, and therefore they do not say the True Name (they only paraphrase it instead). The sages, however, were allowed to pronounce it, and they were very glad to learn the ways (methods) by which this utterance was performed. There was therefore one motive to conceal it and one motive to reveal it. However, if (in place of the Tetragram of the *Torah*) it was said that it was actually composed of the four vowels, the ignorant would have been unable to understand it".

Some Kabalists believe that the secret "Measure of the Builders of Worlds" is contained in the Name *YHVH*, written in its extended form (consisting of 10 letters), and in this way the creative force takes on shape and form.

In our opinion, *Shem ha-Meforash* is a substitute Name concealing a deep Kabalistic secret related to the way of composing the Creative Name of God. As a substitute, it is formed by the Hebrew hieroglyphs sealing the twelve Sfarot of the Kabalistic Tree, which is why it consists of twelve letters (we believe that the Sfarot are 12, but this is not the subject of the present book). By means of the *Dodecagrammaton* thus composed, following the Three Paths of the Tree of which we have already spoken, perhaps one of the Secret Names of God is synthesized, which in its entirety consists of 22 hieroglyphs, as are the letters of the Hebrew alphabet. Some will probably think that, against the background of the listed Names, there is now another one pointed out with the claim to be the Secret Name of God. On the mental level, we would say that our statement – that this Name consists of the twenty-two hieroglyphs of *Alefbet* – is not devoid of logic. Our deep conviction, however, is that each of the Names discussed can be defined as God's Name if it possesses definite/limited implementation power of authority, yet we would not call any of them "Secret", since it is present in the explanations of various authors intended for wide audience. This contradicts the principle that the True Name of God should be kept secret, because otherwise any profane, out of stupidity or ill intention, might destroy the world. We stop here because this knowledge is contained in the "Kabala Arcanorum" Re-dual and is not the subject of this book. We will only note that the Names or the Name of God are a methodology for activating the Sfarot in a certain sequence forming the so-called *Paths of the Kabalistic Tree*, rather than magic formulas in the commonly accepted sense. Therefore, outside of the above indicated Arcana algorithm, we would associate God's Name with the Divine Word.

## The Divine Speech

> *Silence is the language of God,*
> *all else is poor translation.*
>
> **Rumi**

It is said in the *Midrash* that before the Creation, God and His Name existed alone. When God uttered: "Let there be Light!", the Name became Word: it was transformed into a major part of what is contained in the Hebrew phrase *Dibbur Elohi* – "Divine Speech", the language through which God has created the whole existence and has manifested Himself in it through His creation. By turning into a particular word, the Name becomes an integral part of God's Word, through which God Himself presents Himself and communicates with His creation through speech.

According to *Deuteronomy* 4:13, "... you heard the voice of (His) words, but you saw no form; you only heard a voice" *(WEB)*.

Gershom Scholem believes that the human being, by virtue of the likeness to God, is endowed with word, and therefore the word itself is God. In support of this, he gives an example with the verse from *Genesis* 2:7, "and man became a living soul" *(KJV)*, which is translated in *Targum Onkelos*[142] as follows: "... and the human being became a Spirit endowed with speech".

---

142 *Targum Onkelos* is from the period 35 – 120 AD and is the official translation of the *Torah* into Aramaic, used in sacred services in synagogues even to this day in Yemen – *AN*.

Similar passages can be found also in other official sources. For example, the *Book of Jasher,* chapter 1, contains exactly the same verse: "... and the human being became a Spirit endowed with speech".

In many parts of the ancient *Targums,* where the *Tanakh* is translated into Aramaic, there are passages in which an Entity called "Word" (in the meaning of "a particular word" – in Aramaic: *MEMRA*) is mentioned. In many places, instead of *YHVH (Yod He Vav He),* the phrase "The (particular) Word of YHVH" is put, and in some cases, *MEMRA*[143] is mentioned in phrases where *YHVH* is not present.

In *Targum Jonathan,* for example, a distinction is clearly seen between the "(particular) Word of *YHVH*" and *YHVH* Himself: "Then the (particular) Word of God said, "Let Us create a human being in Our image, (and) according to Our likeness". According to *Targum Jonathan,* this "(particular) Word of *YHVH*" represents the Creator: "And the '(particular) Word of *YHVH*' created the human being in His own image, in the image of God *(YHVH)* He created it; *(YHVH)* created them man and woman".

Some Great Kabalists such as Cordovero and Abulafia consider the Hebrew phrase *Dibbur Elohi* – the "(particular) Word of God", to be derived from its meaning in Aramaic, "to lead", "to rule". Therefore, the "(particular) Word of God" means the "ruling of the world"; and each "Name" of God represents a specific tendency of that ruling.

From the above given examples, it becomes clear that, according to the Hebrew tradition, the "(particular) Word", which should be understood as the "Creative Word", on the one hand, is identified with God, but on the other hand, has an independent being. This view has found its reflection also in Christianity, vividly expressed by John the Theologian with the words: "In the beginning was the Word, and the Word was with God, and the Word was God". (*Holy Gospel of John* 1:1, *NKJV*)

This Word incarnated in Jesus, Who, according to the Church, is the only Son of God Who came down to Earth to save humans.

"And the Word[144] became flesh and dwelt among us, and we beheld His glory, the glory as of the Only Begotten of the Father, full of Grace and Truth." (*Holy Gospel of John* 1:14, *NKJV*)

The idea of the Incarnate Word, *Mashiach,* which we see through all of this, is that the Word Who created the human being is the One that will uplift

---

143  *MEMRA* is cited 4179 times in *Targum Onkelos,* 99 times in the *Jerusalem Targum,* and 321 times in *Targum Pseudo-Jonathan* – *AN*

144  In the *Septuagint,* for denoting the "Word", the term "Logos" (λόγος) is used, which has the following meanings: *a particular word* (as an expression of an idea), *statement, speech, Divine Word, analogy* – *AN*.

humans, so that their Divine Nature may shine forth. This, however, will take place not through the ordinary human speech acquired after the "Fall" but through God's Word granted as a gift to Adam at the moment of his creation. This Word is not a particular word, nor any magic words and formulas, nor the Names of God constituting the so-called *Words of Power ("Ur Hekau")*, but rather the *Divine Speech*, or *"Medu Neter"*[145], as the ancient Egyptians called it (whereas the Hebrews called it *Dibbur Elohi*), which transforms the human being into the "Image and Likeness of God". The idea that everything (Deities, Nature, and human beings) has occurred as a result of Divine Creative Speech is present in all theogonies, but we will use the Egyptian one again as an example, for it is embedded in the foundation of the Western esoteric tradition.

On the *Shabaka Stone*[146], the following can be read:

"Ptah is the greatest, and He gives life
to all the gods and their Ka-s.
Here, through this heart and this tongue.
Behold: each and every (particular) word of God
has occurred through the thoughts of the heart
and the command of the tongue."

This *Hieros Logos* is an expression of the idea that Creation arises as a result of the Divine Thought and the utterance of Divine Words. Each and every Law of Nature (the Deities), as well as all that these Laws do, is created in the Divine Mind and pronounced by the Divine Tongue. Nothing can ever occur in the world without the Divine "Mind" and its Speech. Everyone who has mastered the "Divine Speech" becomes consubstantial with the Egyptian Ptah, with the Hebrew "(particular) Word of YHVH", with the Aramaic "MEMRA", and with the Christian "Incarnate Word", and eventually becomes Son of God. This is so because the greatest gift given to Adam by the Gods is not the freedom to sin but rather the freedom to express oneself through speech, which makes him a likeness of them and distinguishes him

---

145  *Medu Neter* means "Words of Nature", representing the infinite forms of existence. It is very often translated by Egyptologists as "(particular) Divine Word", "Divine Scripture" and "Divine Word/ Speech". The form under which *Medu Neter* is well-known throughout the world is the word "hieroglyph", deriving from the Greek ἱερογλυφικός, composed of ἱερός – "sacred", and γλύφω – "scripture"/ "glyph" – *AN*.

146  It is named after the Pharaoh of the 25th Dynasty and contains religious texts related to the *Temple of Ptah* in Memphis from the 8th century BC, and is currently kept in the British Museum. The most remarkable part of the inscriptions on this stone is related to the creation of the world, as well as to the Gods of the Memphis Ennead, through the Word of Ptah, which possesses creative power – *AN*.

from all other beings. It becomes clear from the biblical narrative that Adam did not learn to speak by himself but was given the Divine Word, which was afterwards lost in the alienation of humankind from the Spiritual World.

According to the Hebrew tradition, the letters of the Divine Language are those which, in various combinations, underlie the foundation of the whole Creation. These are the hieroglyphs of Biblical Hebrew, considered to be the original language of the Revelation, which have the meaning of symbols with a vast *eidos* and are the expression of a universal manifestation. It can be said that the latter is formed by isolated letters corresponding to the multiplicity of its elements, and by reassembling these letters, they carry it back to the Primordial Principle and to the restoration of the Primordial Name. There is a conception that the *Pentateuch* of the Old Testament (the *Torah*) constitutes this Name, which is written with consonants, and their vocalization leads to combinations that are N in number. Therefore, it is believed that for each incarnated soul there is a personal *Torah*, with the small stipulation that this refers to the initial 600,000 people, who, of course, were Hebrew, according to the Kabalists professing this theory. The original *Torah* was written with 600,000 letters engraved on the first tablets; however, on the second ones, the *Torah* was written in its current abbreviated form of 340,000 letters. Some believe that it is given in this form for this *shemita* ("eon"), but a new *Torah* will appear for the next ones. This does not mean that it will be replaced by another one. The letters will simply be arranged in a new way according to the new time period, but no letter will be added or removed. As Aristotle says, "Tragedy and comedy are created with the same characters". There are some conceptions that the new reading and the new meaning could take place by combining the consonant letters into other words, composing new sentences, conveying other things. Although the sequence of letters is preserved in this way, their new differentiation, however, contradicts one of the fundamental dogmas of Judaism, namely: that absolutely nothing, not even an iota, should be changed in the writing of the *Torah*. In this sense, the only way, in our opinion, remains the different vowelling and vocalization of the existing letter combinations, so if the *Torah* is God's Name, it means that it is also God's Word, and that ultimately it is God Himself revealing Himself to us as Word. This Word once definitely belonged to humans, but after their "Fall", it was lost, and the human speech became articulate, fragmented by the fertilizing force, symbolized by the lost and undiscovered member of Osiris – his phallus. The articulate, fragmented speech literally means "division into members", "segmentation", which is done through vowels. Thus the vocalization makes the speech articulate, fragmented. In Hebrew, which is a reminiscence of the One and Integrate Proto-Language, before the Tower of Babel, only consonant letters are used for the writing of words, whereas the vocalization occurs when pronouncing them. This means that the monochrome Proto-Language was written only with consonants, since humans at that time were probably unable to pronounce vowel sounds, because this is how their pharynx was formed and how their larynx was situated. From this point of view, we can say that the "Unpronounceable Name" truly and literally cannot be pronounced by contemporary humans because they lack an adequate voice instrument for that. Now a logically consistent thought process containing certain information can be verbalized through articulate speech. From the Hebrew language used as an example, and the *Torah* written with it, it is clearly seen that letters turn into words and acquire inner sense and meaning through the use of vowel letters for vocalization. In this context, it is considered that the *Torah* is written through a series of consonant letters as one whole word, without spaces and punctuation marks to separate individual words and sentences. The articulation (vocalization) determines the meaning and logic of what is written. We have to specify that this concerns the so-called *"Written Torah"*, which has acquired its material form after the Fall, and is written by Moses as a "selected part" of the *"Oral Torah"* given to him as a Revelation. The *Torah* thus written was fragmented into words that are read as narratives and commandments, the meaning of which, however, again depends on the manner of vocalization. If we accept the statements that the words of the *Torah* are the words of God, it means that God's Speech is *integrate, non-fragmental* (i.e. *not dismembered*), or *inarticulate* (i.e. *not vocalized*), and in this sense, it is said to be *silence*. God's Word (Horus – Christ), however, is born in the physical world immaculately – that is, *dis-membered* (i.e. *articulate, vocalized*), in order to become knowable and pronounceable. Naturally, the above said should be understood in a symbolic sense rather than in a literal one. The examples given by us are a drop in the ocean of Hebrew literature relevant to the subject under consideration, and yet they are a sufficient illustration of the existence of various views, part of which contradictory. These contradictions have inevitably passed into Freemasonry as well, which uses Hebrew words and symbolism. The Truth, nevertheless, is one, but the angles from which it is observed and reproduced are different. Thus, everyone has their own "truth" and defends it with nails and teeth, because in most cases it is comfortable for them, and chiefly because their ego has proclaimed it authentic and authoritative. Therefore, tradition is necessary, which, having passed the tests and trials of time, should bring the differences to the unification of Truth, since *Sigillum veritatis simplicitas est*[147].

---

147 "The Seal of Truth is Simplicity" (Latin maxim) – *AN*.

We are One in the centre, where our Spirit is, and we are different in the periphery, where our numerous Egos, our Selves are – the shells of personality. Thus again we come to the figure "point in the centre of a circle". If we draw many lines from that point to the circumference, we will see that the greatest distance between them is on the surface. The closer we get to this central point, the more the distance decreases between the lines. Thus time, space, and differences are at the periphery, on the surface, whereas, in the central point, they disappear. That is why also the knowledge of those who are in the centre is difficult to convey to those at the periphery. This knowledge traverses the long way from the central point to the periphery, and there it already takes on different forms, which diverge from and sometimes contradict each other. The language of the circumference is different from the language of the centre, which is the language of Initiates. If we do not learn the language of Initiates, we will not be able to decode and read their messages. The path from the periphery to the centre represents passing through the illusion of the false Ego and all differences, in order to reach the central point where they practically cease to exist. There is the Unified One. Everyone who reaches this centre is one with the Truth and the Spirit of the Great Initiates, without the conventionalities and differences of time.

"Do not speak unless you have something better to offer than silence", says a Zen piece of wisdom. The language of the central point is the language of silence, and as Rumi says, silence is the language of God. The art of listening to silence is called *meditation* because, through it, direct contact is accomplished with the Spiritual World. Such a connection is achieved also through Divine Music, which is the silence between two notes, or, as Pythagoras calls it – the "Music of the Spheres". Contemporary music is swarming with sounds, but the truth is that in this way it is drifting away from God. All the notes are simply in order to hear the silence between them, just as the letters are only to notice the whiteness of the writing sheet, or as is the more popular saying – to "read between the lines". The Spirit is always "in between" – between the notes, between the letters, between the integers, or generally – in the intermediate space of eternity and infinity. Mona Lisa's smile has occupied the minds of people for centuries not because it expresses clarity and explicitness but because, with its mysteriousness, it slightly opens the door to the boundlessness of the Spirit.

God's Grace, however, not always can be received by everyone directly, but usually this happens through an intermediary who is able to verbalize this Grace, or the very presence of whom is a fine fragrance awakening the Spirit of "others". The closer we get to the centre, the more we immerse into keeping silent, and the purer transmitter we become for God's Grace, so that only the wordless individuality remains and merges with the central point. The language of this central point is the Divine Language, which is the Lost Word. The "Lost Word" is a symbolic phrase used by the sages of all centuries, and it means that the inexplicable cannot be explained by words. In the "Point", space and time disappear, and the word becomes non-fragmental, inarticulate – unpronounceable.

Freemasons are called "Sons of the Widow" (Isis) because they are Twice-Born during the Sacred Initiation, conceived by the "Lost Word", the symbol of which is Hiram, who begins to live within the newly initiated Master. Therefore, the particular Lost Word is not a verbal formula that disappeared with the death of Hiram but rather the inarticulate, non-fragmental (i.e. *not dis-membered*) Word of God, lost as the undiscovered member of Osiris. The world is created through Attitude, through the use of the article – for, when we say *human*, it sounds detached, but if we say *the human*, we are already showing attitude. The Creator has an attitude towards the World, and that is why He has created it with certain ideas, principles and qualities, and most of all – with Love. Thus, through our attitude, we also determine matters in one way or another. Some say, "This is the best person"; others define this person as the worst – and yet, it is one and the same person. Our attitude makes others good or bad. In this way, the World can be the best or the worst place: it depends on us, on our attitude, on our way of using the article. However, the use of this "article", this "member of speech", has disappeared together with the member of Osiris, and hence the Divine Nature of words.

## The Old Bulgarian Alphabets

*Time reveals everything that is covert,*
*and conceals everything that is evident.*

To Kabalists, the mysticism of language is also the mysticism of writing. In the Spiritual World, each speaking is also writing, and everything written represents potential word intended to be pronounced. If a language is chosen by God, as Hebrew is considered to be, it is extremely important that it is adequately reflected through the script that shapes and structures it.

However, not only Hebrew, but also other languages can be called *chosen by God,* one of which, we dare say, is Bulgarian. This is because it was formed over the centuries by two Revealed-by-God Old Bulgarian alphabets: the Glagolitic alphabet and the Cyrillic alphabet, the letters of which, as well as those of the Hebrew alphabet, can be called *Divine*.

According to Kabalists, the letter *Alef* is the voice of the larynx, which is the entrance for every vocal utterance, and from which every articulated sound originates, so for that reason, this letter is the first in the alphabetical list. The same can be said of the letter *A* in the initial Bulgarian alphabet – the Glagolitic alphabet. The letters in it have names, as it is composed of *глаголи* *['glagoli]* ("verbs", i.e. *words*)[148], and yet, this makes it no less significant than the Biblical Hebrew, which we will try to illustrate.

The name of the first letter is *Азъ ['azə]* – "I", of the second one – *Буки ['buki]*, of the third – *Веди ['vedi]*, of the fourth – *Глаголи ['glagoli]*, and so on. Just as the Old Testament begins with the second letter of the Hebrew alphabet, *Beit* ("Bereshit…"), the same way we will also first clarify something concerning the second letter of the Glagolitic alphabet – *Буки ['buki]*, meaning "scripts" or "letters". Initially, however, its name was *Бог ['bɔkə]* – "God", but in order not to pronounce God's Name in vain, according to God's Commandment, it is replaced with the name *Буки ['buki]*. Thus, the meaning of the first two letters is "I God", which is equivalent to the Hebrew *Ehyah* (*I Am*) – the Supreme Name of God.

After this clarification, we can now give precedence to the first letter. Just as *Alef* consists of three consonants – *A, L, F* (vocalized with *E*, which, however, is not written), the same way *Азъ ['azə]* also consists of three letters. In the following analysis, we will base our arguments on both the Glagolitic and the Cyrillic alphabet, using the well-known Kabalistic method of *Gematria*, which, as we shall see, is valid not only for the Hebrew alphabet.

The Glagolitic alphabet will serve us only as a foundation, in the context of what has been said about the first two letters, which mean *Аз Съм ['azə 'səmə]* – "I Am", by identifying and equating *Аз* ("I") with the Glagolitic alphabet, whereas *Съм* ("Am") – with the Cyrillic alphabet. If we unite the Glagolitic letters *Дз [dz]* and *З [z]* into the clearer sound *[z]*, we will see that the letters *А [a]* and *З [z]* are the first and the eighth in both alphabets. By Kabalizing these numerical correspondences (1 + 8 = 9), we obtain the emblematic number 9, corresponding to the next letter after *З [z]*, again in both alphabets: *И [i]*. With this letter, the name of Jesus begins in Bulgarian – *Иисус [i:'susə]*, Who, according to Christianity, is the Son of God, in the sense of the "Incarnate Word". Thus we move on to the letter *С [s]*, denoting *Слово ['slɔvɔ]* ("Word"), which is the eighteenth in the Cyrillic alphabet,

---

148 The term *Glagolitic* comes from the Old Bulgarian word *глаголъ ['glagɔlə]*, meaning "verb" in contemporary Bulgarian, but in Old Bulgarian it meant "a (particular) word". In this case, such is also the name of the Bulgarian letter *Г ([g]* as in *got)* – *глаголи ['glagoli]*, which in Old Bulgarian means *to speak, to say, to pronounce*. That is why the Glagolitic alphabet is poetically called "the signs that speak" – *AN*.

as well as in the Glagolitic alphabet, if the unnamed letters and the repeated letters with a similar meaning are ignored. The word *Аз ['azə]* – "I", also leads us to the eighteenth letter (1 placed next to 8 makes up 18), and it is *С [s] – Слово ['slɔvɔ]*, i.e. the Word that is consubstantial with *Иисус [i:'susə]* ("Jesus"): 1 + 8 = 9 – the letter *И [i]*. By Kabalizing the indicated numbers (9 + 18 = 27), the number 27 is obtained, or the letter *Ъ (Big Er [ə])* in the Cyrillic alphabet, and also in the Glagolitic alphabet, if the above described reduction is applied. In this way, we come to the conclusion that the Son and the Word, which constitute the Father, are contained in the letter *Ъ (Big Er [ə])*, which represents His symbol. Thus, only the letter *М [m]* remains, which is the thirteenth in the Cyrillic alphabet, and also in the Glagolitic alphabet, in the described reduction, with the example of the Glagolitic alphabet being a bonus, since we have explained that *Съм ['səmə]* ("Am") symbolizes the Cyrillic alphabet. In the symbolism already used, *М [m]* ought to correspond to the *Mother (Virgin Mary)*. If we Kabalize the expression "Holy Family" in Bulgarian: *Свето Семейство [sve'tɔ se'mejstvɔ]*, and also "The Word": *Словото ['slɔvɔtɔ]*, in the configuration *Аз Съм ['azə 'səmə]* ("I Am"), the following will be obtained: "А"–1; "З"–8; "С"–18; "Ъ"–27; "М"–13. The sum of the indicated numbers is 67, and its reduction (6 + 7 = 13 = 1 + 3 = 4) eventually leads to the number 4, symbolizing the materialization, and to the letter *Г ([g ]* as in *got*) in both alphabets, having in mind that its name in the Glagolitic alphabet is *глаголи ['glagɔli]*. Thus, *Аз Съм ['azə 'səmə]* ("I Am") in the context of the above exposition would mean "The Son, the Word of the Father speaks". The word *Слово ['slɔvɔ]* ("Word") begins with the letter *С [s]*, as well as the word *Съм ['səmə]* ("Am"), which means *Съществувам [səʃtest'vuvʌmə]* ("(I) Exist"), the first letter of which is also *С [s]*. In this sense, *Аз Съм ['azə 'səmə]* ("I Am") means *Аз Съществувам чрез Словото ['azə səʃtest'vuvʌmə 'tʃrezə 'slɔvɔtɔ]* ("I Exist through the Word"), or *Словото е Силата на Съществуването ['slɔvɔtɔ e 'silʌtʌ na səʃtest'vuvʌnetɔ]* ("The Word is the Power of Existence"). That is why the Divine Word is potentially contained in the Bulgarian speech, so everyone who speaks this language has the opportunity to turn this potential energy into kinetic one. This can be done by activating the fourth letter *Глаголи ['glagɔli]* ("to speak"), which expresses the aspect of the Mother, or the feminine energy. In Hebrew, this is the letter *Dalet*, meaning "door", and connecting the Sfarot *Wisdom (Hohma)* and *Understanding (Bina)*. The Divine Word is the Son, but the Divine Speech is the Mother *(Глаголи ['glagɔli])*, and the feminine principle is the Door towards Wisdom and Truth. We use words from the Hebrew and the Bulgarian alphabet because we believe that they are correlated, the latter being an expression of the former on the material plane. In this sense, we can note that in Bulgarian, the words *българин* ("Bulgarian"), *евреин* ("Hebrew"), and *юдеин* ("Jew"), all end with the suffix *–ин [in]*, which is a sign that their mission is related to the feminine principle *(Yin)*, which, unfortunately, both patriarchal nations have not fulfilled. Perhaps the Jews, who ignored the Mother and crucified the Son, are the reborn present-day Bulgarians, who in the Age of Aquarius will fulfil the mission to make the human speech consubstantial with the Divine Speech. There will probably be an objection that the above said should also apply to the Bulgarian words *арабин* ("Arab"), *англичанин* ("Englishman"), *французин* ("Frenchman"), *сърбин* ("Serb"), *хърватин* ("Croat"), *египтянин* ("Egyptian"), *турчин* ("Turk"), *славянин* ("Slav"), and others who also end with the suffix *–ин [in]*. We would say that the Arabic language is "Inspired by God", and yet we do not think that the Arabs (just like the Jews), with their dominant masculine principle, are able to fulfil such a mission in the foreseeable future, and therefore their karma will be ruthless. As for the other nations, this is not the case, because their languages are not in the category of those indicated, although at the moment some of them are more popular and widespread. Probably there will be such readers who will think that the listed terms are written and sound in this way mostly in Bulgarian, which is why it is untenable to make such parallels and such generalizing essential conclusions. We will say to those readers that this is possible precisely because these words are in the Bulgarian language, which is explicit in its script, and the Divine Inspiration of which is substantiated by St. Constantine the Philosopher at the Venetian Dispute, refuting the trilingual dogma. Against this background, we will go a little further into the *eidos* of the word *българин ['bəlgʌrin]* ("Bulgarian") in order to reveal its etymology and meaning. The chief cornerstone of this word is the letter *Ъ [ə]*. This is so because in the Cyrillic alphabet it replaces the consonant letter *Ayin*, which marks a specific pharyngeal sound characteristic of Semitic peoples. The main Semitic word formation is according to the principle of the three-letter root. From the Semitic root *B – A (Ayin) – L*, the familiar to us word *baal* is formed, which does not contain *Ayin*, because in other languages there is no letter for this specific sound, which is why it is most often denoted by the second letter *A*. We have already had the opportunity to say that the word *baal* is translated as *master/ lord*, but now we will make some clarifications. It consists of two parts: *ba* and *al*. The first one is a very ancient word meaning *might, skill*, whereas the second is the Semitic concept of *deity*. However, the key letter in the whole word formation is *Ayin*, which has various meanings, but the most important are *eye* and *eternity*, giving to the word *master/ lord* a Divine status. Thus, *Baal* means the *Almighty, All-Eternal and All-Seeing*

Lord and coincides with the *Almighty Living God*, called by the Freemasons the *Great Architect of the Universe (G.A.O.T.U.)*, because the *All-Seeing Eye* is an indication towards the essence of being alive.

Let us go back to the core essence of the name българи *['bəlgʌri]* ("Bulgarians"). It also consists of two parts: бъл *['bəl]* and гари *[gʌri]*. The first part is composed of three letters, and we have already explained that Ъ[149] is a substitute because it denotes a sound analogous to the one written through the letter *Ayin*. Thus, the word *baal* has become the first syllable бъл *['bəl]* in the name българи ("Bulgarians"). Its second part is composed of the *Tangrist (Tengrist)* sound combination ГР *[gr]*, which ever since Sumer has been related to the meaning *master/lord*, and so the whole name should be translated as *Divine Masters/ Divine Lords*. However, we would associate ГР *[gr]* with the words *Guru* and *Aryans*. Thus the word българи ("Bulgarians") represents a result of the transformation of the words *baal-garii* and *baal-guri*, and they forward us to the ancient Aryans representing a specific kind of Spiritual Guides and Masters (Teachers) of humans. That is why the name българин ("Bulgarian") – as well as евреин ("Hebrew") – has deep esoteric dimensions and does not mean only ethnic affiliation, but above all – a degree of spiritual elevation and sublimity. As a result, *Bulgaria* and *Israel* are not only the names of countries and certain geographical territories, but above all, they are sacral concepts and energy places – part of the chakra system of the whole planet. All this is stated not to raise the Bulgarians and the Jews on a divine pedestal but to substantiate our view that a *Freemason* is also a spiritual concept and should not be identified only and solely with one's affiliation to the existing formal establishments (Lodges) belonging to the so-called *Freemasonry*.

The organizational structure and the ways of conducting and regulating the inner life of Freemasonry, however, are not in our focus, which is why we return to the main topic.

Perhaps some readers are impressed by the fact that we have not Kabalized the letter Ъ within the framework of the word Азъ *['Azə]*. This is so because it was being pronounced too short and muffled, and also because at one point it even lost its sound value. However, it seems that precisely in this *non-phonia* it symbolizes the All-Father, Who is an expression of the Unpronounceable. As we have already said, God created the world, whereas we are constantly re-creating it through the Attitude. For this very reason exactly, if we say in Bulgarian Бог *['bɔkə]* ("God"), it will sound general and detached,

---

149 The Bulgarian speech before the Glagolitic alphabet obviously contained a specific sound, the correspondence of which was found by St. Constantine the Philosopher in the letter Ъ *[ə]/[ʌ]*, which is difficult to pronounce by non-speakers of Bulgarian – *AN*.

but if we say *БогЪ ['bɔgʌ]* ("The God"), we will already show Attitude. The presence of the grapheme Ъ *[ə]/[ʌ]*, although it has become unpronounceable, just as the "Unpronounceable Name", gives to the script, and hence to the speech, the characteristics of Divine Nature, because, as we have already explained, the Son and the Word, which constitute the All-Father, are contained in the letter Ъ *[ə]/[ʌ]*, which represents its symbol. We believe that the disappearance of the use of the letter Ъ *(Big Er)* as a final letter, in view of the action of the phonetic principle in the Bulgarian language, is as detrimental as the disappearance of the letter *Yat* – Ѣ *[ja]/ [e]*, which, according to Peter Deunov, is the Heavenly sign of the Cyrillic alphabet and represents the emblem of the Bulgarian Spirit.

Returning to the construction symbolism, we will liken the letter Ъ *(Big Er)* to the cornerstone in the foundation, which sets the correct parameters of the Cyrillic alphabet, whereas the letter Ѣ *(Yat)* – to the chief cornerstone, which represents the Philosophers' Stone of this alphabet. Despite the fact that these two letters are ignored, the Bulgarian language continues to be as Divine as the Hebrew one, and therefore such connections can be made between words, such as, for example, *baal shem,* which has become the Bulgarian word *вълшебник [vəl'ʃebnikə]* ("magician", "wizard"), or *baal havi,* which has been transformed into the Bulgarian word *влъхви ['vləhvi]* ("wise people", "magi").

Perhaps many will again think that, regardless of the arguments presented, the above stated is quite frivolous and does not correspond to the scientific paradigm. On the same grounds, however, this can be said also regarding everything written over the centuries about the Aramaic and the Old Hebrew language, through which the Bible was Co-created – the foundation of Western European civilization. The Word seems to always be identified with or personified by God Himself, His Son, various embodied Entities, and the Divine Logos; while the Divine Speech is a broader concept, and it can be a universal attainment, or at least the attainment of a wider circle of Initiates. So no sign of equality should be placed between the Divine Speech and the "Word", which is the particular "Word of God". The question also arises as to whether the particular "Word" is identical with the "Name", and whether they are contained in the particular "Lost Word" and the "Lost Name". From the "epidermal" comparative analysis that has been made, we have seen that there exists no unified traditional view on this issue, and almost each and every prominent Talmudist, Kabalist or Rabbi have their own vision and explanation. Then, we ask ourselves: What tradition can Freemasonry possibly claim in this sense, and what exactly are Freemasons searching for, unless we egocentrically assume that the Hebrew tradition originates from the Masonic one?! Our answer is that contemporary Freemasonry, in its predominant part, does not seek anything related to the esoteric traditions leading to spiritual transformation. In the past, Freemasons used to search for the "Lost Word", though not according to the understanding of the "Word" or the "Divine Speech", but rather a particular word denoting the Master's Degree. However, to look for a particular lost word only to get a Master's wage is quite ridiculous, especially nowadays, because the codifying of the particular Master's Word can be done through any substitute word. This is what happens in the Third Degree Rite, when the Fellow Craft receives a word denoting Mastery. As the particular "true" word continues to be sought and even found in the *Royal Arch* Rite, we think that the dispute which the "substitute Word" is and what it means is completely unnecessary. Undoubtedly, however, it refers to a particular Word with magic power, which the substitute one does not possess. The problem is that there is no unanimity also regarding the particular Rediscovered Word, and many authors believe that it is also only a substitute. René Guénon is of the same opinion as well, and, according to him, finding the particular "Lost Word" is the same as "gathering what is scattered", because this particular "Lost Word" is nothing else but the True Name of the Great Architect of the Universe.

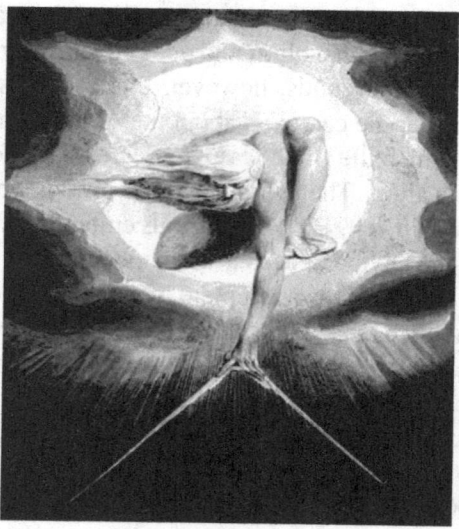

**Figure 53**

# VIII
# THRONE

## The Great Architect of the Universe

*Multi sunt vocati, pauci vero electi*[150]

We also believe that the *Great Architect of the Universe* is a substitute Name, and if any particular Name is to be sought and found, then it must be the True Name of the God of Freemasons. We will make it easier for those who have not yet "gathered what is scattered" by letting them know that this Name is *El Shadai Hai* ("The Almighty Living God"), and by trying to convince skeptics of the truthfulness of this statement, using Gematria again in relation to the Hebrew hieroglyphs with which it is written. We will start with its main characteristic – *Almighty*. The numerical value of the word *Shadai (Shin – Dalet – Yod)* is 314, corresponding to the number *Pi*, related, as we have already explained, to the squaring of the circle encoded in the Square and the Compass, but mostly containing knowledge about activating the *Merkaba,* which we defined as *All-Seeing Eye* – these are all fundamental symbols in Freemasonry. Adding to *Shadai* the Name *El (Alef – L'amed),* the numerical value of which is 31, the Gematria of the two words becomes 345. Thus, the ratio in the right-angled triangle is obtained, 3:4:5, the so-called *Pythagorean Triangle,* considered by Plutarch to be a building block of Nature, and the symbol of which in Freemasonry is the Set Square. In one of the High-Degree Rites, the Lodge can only take place if three Masters, with their rods, form a triangle with such a ratio of the sides.

If we finally add *Hai (He – Yod),* the numerical value of which is 15, in order to form the whole Name of God, then its Gematria is calculated as 360 (345 + 15), and these are the degrees marking the full circle, the essential meaning of which is brought to the Divine completeness and wholeness. The reduction of the number 360 is 9, corresponding to the Sfara *Yesod* in the Tree of Life, whose Divine Name is *El Shadai Hai,* as well as to the Gematria of the words *Emet* ("Truth") and *Adam*. The numerology of *L'amed – Vav* (36) is also the number 9, and these are the Righteous who represent themselves deputies of the Almighty God on Earth, who are the only ones to know the Veritable Name of God, and who are able to work with this Name.

---

150 From Latin: "Many are called, but few are chosen" – *AN*.

Thus we have illustrated that the most emblematic symbols of Freemasonry – the All-Seeing Eye, the Set Square, the Square and the Compass – are encoded in the Name *El Shadai Hai* and represent themselves its material substitutes, as is its substitute Name: *Great Architect of the Universe*. The Name *El Shadai Hai* characterizes one of the most important aspects of God – the Might to vivify everything, because this is the Name of the Sfara *Yesod*, positioned in the genital area of Adam Kadmon, where the fertilizing power is generated. This is the creative force, the Builder of the Worlds, gushing through *Daat* of *Bria* and vivifying the Creation. It is the God of Abraham – and this gives reason for Freemasonry to be associated with the "father of nations". He receives a blessing from Melkitsedek, whose God is *El-Elyon* – the Most High, a higher aspect of the One God, which means that Abraham is a successor of the original Initiatic tradition, which, according to the above correlation, must have passed into Freemasonry as well.

We strongly hope that this is true, although we have not found any traces left in Modern Freemasonry. This finding, however, suggests to us that the particular "Lost Word" is in fact nothing else but this tradition, namely, which was lost over the centuries and which is symbolically designated by Initiates as the *Lost Word*. Through this book, we are trying to resurrect it, just as Hiram Abiff is resurrected within every Master, so that true Spiritual Life may be revived in Freemasonry. Freemasonry is now an "esoteric corpse" whose shroud is the Veil of Isis. There are residual postmortem esoteric convulsions contained in its Rites, invented three hundred years ago, which, as we have learned, are not part of any ancient original tradition, and also there is no continuity between them. These Rites are like sewn parts of different corpses, and they turn Freemasonry into a Frankenstein devoid of Spirit. The scars on its malformed face and body cannot be completely hidden by the false lustre of its mask and precious garments, and they betray its Qlifotic nature.

Bulgarian Freemasonry is not even *non-fragmental* (i.e. *not dismembered*), because it represents itself dissociated pieces of this Frankenstein, which cannot form one whole body, even though devoid of Spirit. Unfortunately, this obsession is not only due to the communist regime, but also to its ontogenesis, marked by the peculiarities of the Bulgarian post-communist transition. It is no coincidence that we have pointed out that the Bulgarian language is "Inspired by God", and that the words of this language can be used for magic formulas and rituals with implementation power and authority. In addition, we have shown that the name българи ("Bulgarians") is a derivative of the word *Baal*, the meaning of which is *Almighty Living God*, and from the word *Guru – Spiritual Guide;* so the whole name is translated as **"Spiritual Guides, Deputies of the Almighty Living God"**. This obliges

Freemasonry in Bulgaria to be completely dominated by the esoteric tradition, moreover, since Bulgarians are successors of Orpheus and Orphism, of Boyan the Magus and Bogomilism, of Peter Deunov and the White Brotherhood, so their Mysteries and Teachings can be the Bulgarian contribution to reviving the body of Freemasonry. For the time being, we hope that this contribution will be the "Kabala Arcanorum" Re-dual created by us, which, as is clearly seen by its very title, is built upon the foundations of the Arcana and Kabalistic knowledge, which contain the characteristics of greater globality and universality, and therefore they are the chief cornerstone of Freemasonry. However, nothing can lead to transformational change unless the power of *Medu Neter, Dibbur Elohi,* or the *Divine Speech,* is used. The member of Osiris is unfortunately irretrievably lost, so for humankind the particular "Lost Word" represents the *uni-membered* Divine Speech. Even if we know the particular "Secret Word" and the "Concealed Name", there is no way they can be authentically vibrated, which is why they are Unpronounceable. Many words and names can be read and verbalized, and humans attach to them implementation power of authority, including in this book – yet will this lead to any desired result? We share the opinion of Initiates – that even if you possess Solomon's magic ring, it does not automatically turn you into a magus, and the same is valid of the "Words of Power", which will not by themselves make you a miracle-worker. As for the very magi, they perform miracles through them, but only because they have the qualities and implementation power of a magus. Their wands are magic scalpels, through which they operate proficiently; yet in someone else's hands, a magic wand is just an object, just like any scalpel, if not used by a surgeon, becomes just an ordinary knife. Magic operations, unlike surgical ones, are mental operations, and their instruments and attributes, including magic formulas, are only temporary. They are a transition towards true Magic – the Magic of Divine Speech. Through it, an inner Initiation is achieved, which is expressed in rotating the sphere of consciousness from the decade of the *Yetzira* Tree to the monad of the *Bria* Tree. The Divine Speech is beautiful – and yet, this is not because it follows the rules of human rhetoric or because it uses particularly defined magic words, but because the Spirit speaks through it. It is simple and complex, laconic and long, understandable and incomprehensible, but at the same time, it is also deeply shaking and leading to Enlightenment. It is the language of Initiates, which is the language of the central point, translated into the language of the surface. However, if we have pure thoughts, filled with Love towards everyone and everything, and if we practice *Ahimsa*[151],

---

151 A specific term in Jainism, meaning "conscious nonviolence towards all living beings" – *AN..*

then our speech will also get closer to the Divine Speech, which in Jainism is called *Satya – Truthful Divine Speech*.

In this sense precisely are also the words of Mahatma Gandhi: "It is better to have a heart without words than words without a heart". Today the Spirit has withdrawn from speech, and the latter has become Qlifotic: words are full of hatred, and they cause pain and suffering. They do not bring Truth but lies and deceit; and they do not liberate – they enslave. Their poison has permeated humans, and the only antidote is the Divine Word. Now the Divine Word no longer needs to become Incarnate into the awaited Messiah, but it ought to rather become consubstantial with the human speech. Salvation depends on ourselves, because, as Rumi says, "If you want to always shine like a day, then burn that part of you that looks like night".

The greatest art, however, is to make silence eloquent, and to transform the environment only through the fragrance of your presence. If your spiritual aura is as vast as the World, then you will change the whole World. This is the Daoist *"Wu-Wei"* – active non-action, the perfect action of the Wise. This is the core essence and meaning of the symbolism of the "Unpronounceable Name", the particular "Unpronounceable Word", the particular "Lost Word". Everything spoken by Jesus would not have this power for humans if it were not for His several words spoken on the cross, but especially if it were not for the cross itself – "wordless" but having become one of the main symbols of humankind. The "Lost Word" is a symbol of the Initiatic tradition, which will lead everyone to their own cross, in order to die, and being reborn, to fly like the bird *Benu* towards the Light, for Eternal Life.

# IX
# AMBON

**Homily**
**O human, wake up, wake up from your deep sleep!**

> *I awoke only to find*
> *that the rest of the world*
> *was still asleep.*
> **Leonardo da Vinci**

With this appeal, we will begin our speech from the *ambon*, i.e. the *pulpit* of our temple, because humankind is still asleep. This is not any allegory, but truthfulness that can only be brought to your consciousness when you wake up, because only then will you become aware that you have been asleep. We come here sleeping, and we keep dreaming our lives in this sleep, after which, if we do not wake up, we leave again from this world, still sleeping. Our familiar sleeping dream is only a dream in this existential sleeping-dream reality, in which the human being is a somnambulist, ruled by subjective unconscious and objective unconscious mechanisms. The freedom of choice and action of humans is similar to that of sleeping dreamers, who, if they do not wake up, remain captive to the sleeping-dream illusion. Thus the unawakened humans keep turning, upon this wheel of rebirths, from sleep to sleep, around the Sun and their own egocentrism, just like a butterfly around a candle. On this merry-go-round, they are riding once a horse, another time – a cart or an elephant, but due to the long ride, humans have recognized these vehicles as essential reality and have forgotten who and when mounted them there. Due to this rotation, everything around looks like some amorphous shroud in the Sfumato style, so to humans, the merry-go-round is the World. If they wish to know what there is behind that shroud, they have to jump. Then they will wake up and realize that the wheel upon which they are rotating is their own ego and is only a sleeping dream, outside of which there is another World, illuminated by another Sun. They will become aware that the Sun familiar to them is just like artificial lighting for the animals closed only between the walls of a farm, who think that this is their only luminary, giving them warmth and light. Humans, however, unlike animals, are aware that there is another, true Sun, just as Initiates also know of the existence of the "Spiritual Sun" Sirius – the "Tear of Isis", which, with its rays, determines the spiritual evolution of the Earth. It is no coincidence that from the Queen's Chamber in the Pyramid of Cheops, Sirius can be seen, which means that the ancients knew about the feminine essence and energy of this star. Ever since the masculine principle has been ruling, humankind has not been receptive to this energy, and therefore the merchants are back in the Temple. The "Heart of the Sun"[152] is wounded, and Isis sheds bloody tears for this Heart. In the Age of Aquarius, however, humans have to jump from the "merry-go-round" of their ego, and then, already awakened, they will open their eyes and hearts to the rays of the "Spiritual Sun" that will transform their souls and bodies. Then Isis will shed tears of happiness for the "rectified" humankind – the Sons of the Widow.

Some time ago, Ernest Hemingway asked the question, "For whom the bell tolls". We are now asking, "For whom the Widow weeps". Are the "Widow's Tears" due to the fact that her sons are being persecuted, insulted, desecrated and crucified by humans, or are they because of their spiritual death that will deprive them of the Immortal Golgotha? The bell tolls for each one of us, and Isis sheds a huge tear for the prodigal Freemasonry, in which the image of the Insane is seen, walking towards the abyss – the mask hiding his face from the Spiritual Light of Sirius: the true home towards which the pilgrim is heading, and in which sooner or later the prodigal son will return. Freemasonry, which is still under its veil, has to take off its false golden mask, and the "Tear of Isis" ought to wash its face. Only in this way will it be illuminated by the Light of Truth, which will decompose everything other than its Core Essence. Then, resurrected from the ashes, the revived Freemasonry will begin its work on its new process of *Building the Edifice* – in Bulgarian: *ГрадежЪ [grʌ'deʒə]*. The Path is long and difficult, full of trials, contradictions and self-sacrifice, and yet, we shall exclaim: Blessed are who have taken off their mask, because they have set foot on the *Path!* (In Bulgarian – *ПътЪ* *['pətə]*.)

---

152 The secret name of humankind, having in mind the *Spiritual Sun – AN*.

# Epiklesis

> *For now we see in a mirror, dimly, but then –*
> *face to face. Now I know in part, but then*
> *I shall know just as I also am known.*
>
> ***1 Corinthians 13:12, NKJV***

We appeal to the Holy Spirit to descend upon the word of this book and transform it into the body and blood of the Messiah Who has sacrificed Himself within everyone who receives Him. May the words and their energy be the Eucharistic bread and wine, and, as in the Great Sacrament of Communion, may they be re-accomplished inside the Spirit and Soul of the readers, so that they may be their guiding star along the Path to Wisdom and Truth. Through the power of the present words, may the bestial, just like by a sword of fire, be cut off from the human, the material – from the spiritual, the profane – from the sacral, and may the Divine "I" ascend the throne. We fervently pray that by these words we may touch the hearts and minds of those humans who are ready and willing to be awakened to the True Life, that of the Messiah, marked by the seal of Love, Forgiveness and Self-Sacrifice. We wish them to wipe the blurred glass of their consciousness, through which they see the distorted outlines of an illusory world, and to behold Reality as it is – neither better nor worse. It is possible that we might know, though without recognizing, without being familiar with; and we might be familiar with, though without being aware of, just as we might look without seeing, and listen without hearing. The disciples of Jesus saw, heard, understood and became aware only when the Holy Spirit descended upon them. Until then, they knew Jesus, watched Him and listened to Him. Therefore, when He was crucified, their faith was shaken, and Peter renounced Him three times. They were not yet ready to receive the Sacred Initiation from Above, which takes place at Pentecost. That is why, through this book, we are willing to break the paradigm of conceptual minds, to wash the souls and hearts, and turn them into empty cups, ready to be filled with the waters of the Heavenly River. We wish to attract the *Sekhem* of the word so that it may unite with its Divine Archetype and acquire the might and implementation power of authority of the Divine Speech. However, none of this will happen unless the above said is accepted by the reader. Every word is sacrificial because the ones who create it sacrifice themselves so that it may be born. This sacrifice, like any other, ought to be accepted so that it may have deep sense and result. On the microcosmic plane, Golgotha becomes devoid of deep sense for those who do not believe in Golgotha.

Therefore, we hope that our self-sacrifice will be accepted and that the souls will conceive with the word, so that they may be Twice-Born from Above and become pure as children, free as *Horus*-es, and bright as the Light of the Spiritual Sun.

# X
# ESCHATON

*When the Path comes to an end, make a change – if you do so, then you have passed.*

**Yi Jing**[153]

*"Unless you eat the flesh of the Son of Man and drink His blood, you have no Life in you. Whoever eats My flesh and drinks My blood has Eternal Life, and I will raise him up at the last day."*

**Holy Gospel of John 6:53 – 54, NKJV**

**Finis Coronat Opus**[154]

    The end has come, which crowns our deed, but our word shall not die, for it shall continue to live forever in those who recognize it as their Truth, just like those who have Eternal Life because they eat the body and drink the blood of the Son of Man. What Jesus said has a universal sound and means that words have *flesh* (informational intensity) and *blood* (energy), and when they are imbued with the Power of the Spirit, they acquire the characteristics of the Spirit, and whoever absorbs them becomes part of Eternity. Therefore, regardless of the subheading, this book is a message not only for the Freemason Brothers, but also for all who have had the will and patience to reach its end, which we hope will become for them a new spiritual beginning without end, because the Spiritual Path is endless.

    Linear temporality adds some inevitable sequence to events, which puts them into the limiting framework of past, present and future. Thus Jesus is a certain past that cannot be present in the present. Through the epiklesis nature of the Eucharist, the Church is willing to remove the limits of time and make the evangelical set of events repeatable, reviving it within everyone who has received the Holy Communion. However, we believe that it is not the personality of Jesus which is the Incarnate Word but rather His words, through which the language of the central point is conveyed. They are the

---

153  Or also *I Ching: Book of Changes – AN.*
154  From Latin: "The end crowns the deed" (Ovid) *– AN.*

eternal consecrated Bread of Communion, not made by human hand, which transforms the historical Jesus into the Eternal Christ. His Second Coming will bring the total rectification of souls and will establish the reign the eschatological Kingdom of God according to the Christian doctrine. This, however, is a future event that even the holy liturgy of the faithful cannot turn into a present one, because the absorbing of the holy gifts alone cannot establish *Ha-Shamayim Malkut*. Only God's Word is able to transform the eschatological future into an eternal present. That is why Christ is the Messianic Word, the Beginning and the End, Alpha and Omega, all and nothing, the One Who has been, Who is, and Who shall come, yet Who has already come. This is the Salvation Word of Initiates and Sons of God, which we can call the "Divine Speech", the "Name of God", the "Unpronounceable Name", the "Great, Terrible, and Secret Name of God", the "Lost Word", the particular "Lost Word" and "Master's Word", and also the "Lost Grail". All of them are part of the "Lost Tradition" of the First Times, to which the *Eschaton* will take us back, when the Ouroboros will bite his tail, and will annihilate the binary ego-consciousness, in order to establish the *Divine Homoousion of Eternity*. The tradition of the Primordial Principle could be called *esoteric*, and its universality can be associated with Freemasonry, which we have already found to be devoid of original ancient rituality. We have shown that its construction symbolism is archetypal and contains the knowledge of the various esoteric teachings. Thus, it represents itself the *mixed cup of the elements* of these teachings, just as it unites all religions and religious creeds under the aegis of the Great Architect of the Universe. In this sense, Freemasonry represents the **Philosophers' Stone** of esoterism, because through it, one can acquire knowledge about Symbols, Magic, Tarot, Kabala, Hermetism, Alchemy, and in general – about the secrets of the Macrocosm and Microcosm. Through it, the lead metal of the ego can be transformed into the gold of the True Self, the True "I", which will illuminate the human nature with its Spiritual Light, and transform it into Divine Nature. In the context of what has been said, Freemasonry represents itself the symbolic cup, whereas its esoteric content represents the Philosophers' Stone. Unfortunately, this stone is thrown away by the builders, heaved over among the rubbish, because they considered it useless. It has been standing there for centuries, kicked around from time to time, and sometimes taken out and thrown back into the mud of ignorance. The cup of Freemasonry is attractive because it is polished and expensive, but at the inside, it is in most cases full of the swampy water of the lack of Spirit. Sooner or later, those who wish to drink from it find out this fact, and are disappointed if they had intended to quench their thirst with the elixir of esoteric teachings. As for those who were attracted only by the glitter of the cup, they continue to polish it further, without caring about its contents: it does not impress them because their personal cups are filled with the same water.

Many Freemason Brothers will probably grumble, considering the above written to be quite extreme, while others will feel indignant or offended because they do not consider it true, whereas still others may agree with it in whole or in part. We will accept all opinions and judgments, for they will be within the field of Truth, because untruth is also a part of It – the Truth about untruth. By denying untruth, we will not possess the Whole Truth.

We have already qualified Freemasonry as a spiritual concept, which should not be identified and equated only with some affiliation with existing organizational structures. A Freemason is a builder-mason, yet a Builder of Worlds; and we have said that Peacemakers are Sons of God. Such are Thoth (or Hermes), Orpheus, the Buddha, Moses, Abraham, Jesus, Muhammad and many others, which is why we can also call them *Freemasons,* and still, it does not mean that they were members of any Masonic organization. Being in a Masonic Lodge, even a regular one, and even being a Master, or even a Worshipful Master, does not mean that you are a Freemason. Also, if you are a Mason of the soft stone, then even if you are expelled because you did not pay your membership fee or you violated some written rule, this cannot "expel" your Masonic nature. Just as on the Operative plane, you cannot be deprived of your skills, so on the Spiritual plane, Initiates are always Initiates. There surely are such ones in the Brotherhood who are being accused, judged, condemned, and branded as liars, deceivers, swindlers, egoists, careerists, intriguants, and various other stigmas. However, this Brotherhood should not repeat the models of the profane society, creating constitutions, statutes, internal rules, commissions, its own law court and the like, because, if Freemasons are called *free*, then only the Law will give them freedom – though not the written one, but the Law of the Spirit. It is said that where the written laws begin, there the Spirit ends. No one can be a judge of their own Spiritual Brother for having broken these Laws, because the One, in Whose Name the whole Christian world is baptized and makes the sign of the cross – that One has said: "Who am I to judge you?" If He cannot judge, then who are you to judge?!

We are not judges of Freemasonry. On the contrary: we have shown its extraordinary universality, defining it as a cup of esoteric teachings, and an open place for all people aspiring towards Wisdom and Truth, regardless of their religion, race, social status, property-related or educational qualifications. We also called it the *Philosophers' Stone,* potentially containing the deep esoteric knowledge, which, according to us, has unfortunately been rejected and thrown away. By this book, we would like to take out this Philosophers' Stone and clean it from the mud of delusions, so that whoever has eyes may see that it is a perfectly polished stone, and recognize it as the true altar in the Temple of Freemasonry. Only in this way can the particular "Lost Word" be found, which has always been before the eyes of the profane, thrown away somewhere nearby. Only in this way can that Stone be "ejected" by the Builders, in order to become the Head of the Corner. Only in this way will the esoteric corpse of Freemasonry, having crucified itself on its own Golgotha, be resurrected, because the death on the cross is an eschatological end, leading to a new beginning.

We *have faith* in the spiritual revival of Freemasonry and in its transformation back into the Initiated part of humankind, which will transform and bring it to the *Twelfth Hour*[155], in order to be resurrected on the last day, since it is said: "Blessed are those who have not seen and yet have believed"[156]. However, faith alone is not sufficient, but it must be backed up also by deeds in order to see its fruit. That is why we will allow ourselves to add: And yet, twice as blessed are those who have seen!

*May everyone make sense of their own existence, and put yet another stone in the Great Process of Building the Edifice (in Bulgarian: Великия ГрадежЪ [veˈlikija grʌˈdeʒə]) so that we can see Our Deed completed!*

**So be it!**

**Amen**

---

155  This does not refer to the "Doomsday Clock", which is symbolic and was created in 1947 by the "Bulletin of the Atomic Scientists" at the *University of Chicago*. The more the Twelfth Hour at midnight approaches, the closer the Earth is to a global catastrophe – *AN.*.
156  *Holy Gospel of John 20:29, NKJV – AN.*

The Tear of Isis
Freemasonry Under Its Veil
© Sabaor Abu Aviara 2022

Сълзата на Изида
Забуленото масонство
© Сабаор Абу Авира
София, 2017

Dolphin Marketing Press Ltd
Kemp House 160 City Road,
London, England, EC1V 2NX
Digital Marketing and
Book Publishing Agency
www.dolphinmarketingpress.com

www.ingramcontent.com/pod-product-compliance
Lightning Source LLC
Chambersburg PA
CBHW010447010526
44118CB00021B/2525